Usable Theory

Usable Theory

ANALYTIC TOOLS FOR SOCIAL
AND POLITICAL RESEARCH

Dietrich Rueschemeyer

PRINCETON UNIVERSITY PRESS
PRINCETON AND OXFORD

LIBRARY OF CONGRESS CATALOGING-IN-PUBLICATION DATA

Rueschemeyer, Dietrich.
Usable theory : analytic tools for social and
political research / Dietrich Rueschemeyer.
p.   cm.
Includes bibliographical references and index.
ISBN 978-0-691-12958-7 (hardcover : alk. paper) —
ISBN 978-0-691-12959-4 (pbk.) 1. Political science—
Research—Methodology. 2. Political science—
Philosophy. 3. Social sciences—Research—Methodology.
4. Social sciences—Philosophy. I. Title.
JA86.R84 2009
320.072—dc22   2009000514

British Library Cataloging-in-Publication Data is available

This book has been composed in Sabon

Printed on acid-free paper. ∞

press.princeton.edu

Printed in the United States of America

1   3   5   7   9   10   8   6   4   2

To those from whom I learned

_____

CONTENTS

Preface   ix

CHAPTER I   Analytic Tools for Social and Political Research   1

CHAPTER II   A General Frame: Social Action   27

CHAPTER III   Knowledge   40

CHAPTER IV   Norms   64

CHAPTER V   Preferences   87

CHAPTER VI   Emotions   107

CHAPTER VII   "The Human Group" Revisited   123

CHAPTER VIII   Midpoint   135

CHAPTER IX   Aggregations   152

CHAPTER X   Collective Action   168

CHAPTER XI   Power and Cooperation   183

CHAPTER XII   Institutions   204

CHAPTER XIII   Social Identities   228

CHAPTER XIV   Macrocontexts   243

CHAPTER XV   Cultural Explanations   265

CHAPTER XVI   Conclusion: Usable Theory?   286

References   301

Index   325

PREFACE

This book grew out of courses on social theory at Brown University. For many years, my teaching was guided by a strong conviction: that all students would benefit in their work from learning a repertoire of analytic tools that is to a large extent independent of—and shared across—the different major positions of "grand theory." I gave this kind of "usable theory" a strong emphasis even when I was expected to cover classic social theory or to give an overview of contemporary theoretical positions. This conviction was reinforced by the fact that many students, undergraduates as well as doctoral candidates, were eager to engage as soon as possible in empirical research. In addition, some worked in fields with fairly specific and settled theory frames, such as population studies.

It is hard to give credit and thanks when what is at issue are ideas learned and accumulated over half a lifetime. If I dedicate this book "to those from whom I learned," I think first of my teachers and major authors who introduced me to social and political analysis—Walter Dirks, René Koenig, Peter Heintz, Hans Albert, George Homans, William Goode, Robert Merton, and Talcott Parsons. But I owe as much to colleagues and friends who were often younger than I. Over the years, the most important were my wife, Marilyn Schattner Rueschemeyer, Fritz Sack, Wolfgang Vogt, Marty Martel, Peter Evans, John Stephens, Evelyne Huber, Shmuel Eisenstadt, and more recently James Mahoney. I have also profited greatly from more students than I can name here, as they responded to my teaching.

Finally, there are those whose influence and advice were important specifically for this book. I learned much from a yearlong seminar on research design I cotaught for three years with Dennis Hogan. During many and long conversations I became friends with Jim Mahoney, who combines profound concerns for method and theory with productive interests in empirical comparative historical research. Before I began to write in earnest, I had a semester-long inverted tutorial with my student and research assistant Matthias vom Hau, in which I presented each week the outline of a chapter and was rewarded with questions, commentaries, research help, and encouragement. I owe him immense gratitude. We wrote the chapter on Social Identities together. The colleagues who read and commented on the whole manuscript, large parts of it, or single chapters as they were written are Jim Mahoney, Matthias vom Hau, Peter Evans, John Stephens, Rich Snyder, Chuck Myers, Susan Short, Art Landy, and

Nitsan Chorev. I am profoundly grateful to them. At Princeton University Press, I am thankful to Chuck Myers for his early encouragement and patient guidance throughout, and to Lauren Lepow who turned the manuscript into printable shape with intelligence and empathy. I also wish to thank Brown's Watson Institute for International Studies for an office, support services, and intellectual company.

Usable Theory

Chapter I

ANALYTIC TOOLS FOR SOCIAL

AND POLITICAL RESEARCH

This book is an essay in empirical social theory. It will present tools for theory construction in the course of empirical research. I will describe established theoretical ideas and suggest new ones—pieces of theory that seem useful for formulating research questions, for identifying key factors important for the issues at hand, for devising explanations of puzzling and remarkable outcomes, and for exploring possible future developments.

Fully developed theories—by this I mean integrated sets of empirical hypotheses that hold under specified conditions—are fairly rare in social and political analysis; rarer than many find it comfortable to recognize. Full-fledged theories do exist in social and political analysis. The body of propositions about interaction, emergent norms, and social control generated by small group research is a well-known example. However, on most issues and problems there simply do not exist theories of this kind that can be "taken off the shelf" and applied "as is" to a given problem. At the same time, different elements of theory in a broader sense—ranging from initial conceptualizations to freestanding causal hypotheses—remain indispensable for making sense of social life. Almost inevitably, then, meaningful social and political research will involve theory construction. It is for this theory work within the process of empirical research that I wish to offer analytic tools as well as encouragement.

Foremost among these analytic tools are focused *theory frames* that guide hypothesis formation but do not themselves contain or logically entail a body of testable hypotheses. They identify the *kinds* of causal conditions and process patterns that seem relevant for a given range of issues, they offer concepts that correspond to these identifications, and they give reasons for the choices made. Though occasionally also including empirical theoretical claims, they are primarily helpful in developing testable hypotheses. We ask about theory frames how fruitful they are in suggesting empirical propositions rather than judging them as empirically true or not. Yet the utility criterion represents an indirect link to empirical reality. For instance, the study of social movements has been greatly advanced since the 1970s when structural, cultural, and rational action ideas that had been separately developed in research on movements were integrated with each other, linking a focus on political opportunities with emphases on resource mobilization and organizational capacity, as well as on social constructions of meaning through "cognitive framing" (McAdam, McCarthy, and Zald 1988; Tarrow 1994; McAdam, Tarrow, and Tilly 1997; Goodwin and Jasper 2004).

Theory frames are often underestimated; this is due partly to the fact that they fall short of the ideal of a full-fledged theory. Yet, to venture a strong claim, it is such theory frames rather than fully developed empirical theories that represent the strongest advances in the social sciences over the last 150 years. Among the many instances that come to mind are the claims of Durkheim (1893/1964) and Simmel (1908/1955) on the nexus between modern social structures and a person's individuality, the sequence of Marxian analyses of class formation, game theoretical explorations of interaction under simple motivational assumptions, Olson's *Logic of Collective Action* (1965) and the discussion that followed it, or Steven Lukes's consequential reflections on a series of community power studies in his *Power: A Radical View* (1974).

Theory frames give the context within which the more detailed theoretical work is to be done—developing fresh hypotheses, adjusting concept formation and hypothesis development to each other, complementing and elaborating hypotheses that hold promise but fail to sufficiently specify their domain or the conditions activating the hypothesized mechanisms, and the like. Throughout, I will concentrate on ideas that are portable across different substantive areas rather than on insights that are confined to specific domains such as family and kinship, work in offices and factories, or the dynamics of electoral choice in politics.

What this volume offers, then, differs from most treatments of theory in the social sciences. Some of these present mostly normative theory. Though normative theory is shot through with assumptions about how social and political life actually works, its main thrust is to state what should be, not what is. In political science, normative conceptions and their history constitute the bulk of what is commonly understood as political theory—the rich heritage of views ranging from Aristotle to Thomas Aquinas, from Hobbes and Locke to Bentham and John Stuart Mill, and today from Robert Nozick to John Rawls, Martha Nussbaum, and Amartya Sen.

In sociology, the teaching of theory typically presents surveys centered on Marx, Durkheim, and Weber in the nineteenth century and the work of such thinkers as Mead, Parsons, Habermas, Foucault, Bourdieu, and Coleman in the twentieth. Bracketing their normative orientations, it focuses on the broad theoretical orientations and grand designs of analysis the different theorists advocate—on structural functionalism, power and conflict theory, symbolic interactionism, poststructuralism, or rational action theory—rather than on empirical propositions. Such comprehensive "metatheories" may give broad context and direction to more focused theory frames and specific hypothesis formation, but they often have another, more hidden side as well. They frequently also serve as elements of comprehensive worldviews, linking theory to broad ideological and philosophical orientations. This, more than their utility as tools for theory formation, explains the intensity with which views about system integration and social conflict, the role of culture in sociological explanations, or the explanatory power of rational choice models are advanced, attacked, and defended.

These broad conceptions of theory have their place—as inventories of past social thought and as background to more specific social and political analysis. Many empirically oriented scholars treat them as not directly relevant excursions into the humanities, good for a liberal education but not very important for their own research. Arthur Stinchcombe has made this point in a memorable way about historical sociology: "When it comes down to analysis of specific cases, I would argue that when they do a good job of historical interpretation, Marx and Weber and Parsons and Trotsky and Smelser all operate the same way" (1978, 2). The construction of hypotheses, research design, and the logic of analysis in empirical research may indeed be quite similar across different traditions of metatheory.

It is for the empirical theory required in social and political research that this book will present building blocks. I will offer theory instead of surveys of theory, presenting analytic tools I consider useful rather than commenting comparatively on a range of past and current ideas and conceptions. Focusing on tools for the theory work in empirical analysis, I will deliberately leave aside the dialogue and the contention among grand theoretical conceptions.

The title *Usable Theory* may be read as both invidious and ambitious. It is not meant to be either. I have no intention to denigrate metatheoretical discussions or to dismiss normative theory, which has seen in recent decades a welcome revival. Nor do I claim that what I can present amounts to integrated empirical theories of immediate applicability. This is most of the time simply not possible.[1] My goal is a distinctly modest one: to

---

[1] This volume also does not aim to be a compendium of whatever is considered settled theoretical knowledge in the social sciences. This complex and difficult task has been tackled by others. Randall Collins's *Theoretical Sociology* (1988) made a comprehensive attempt. For earlier, more pedestrian versions that focus on presumed or established empirical generalizations, see Gilbert Kushner et al., *What Accounts for Sociocultural Change? A Propositional Inventory* (1962), and Bernard Berelson and Gary A. Steiner, *Human Behavior: An Inventory of Scientific Findings* (1964). There are of course also many reviews of particular subfields that contain important summaries of theories and findings. Regular publications of this kind are found in the *Annual Review of Sociology* series. *Current Sociology*, pub-

present some established theoretical ideas and to complement them with further suggestions that I deem useful in the interplay of research design, theory formation, and data analysis, analytic tools helpful in the do-it-yourself enterprises most social researchers have to engage in when it comes to formulating significant problems, explaining findings, and venturing estimates of future outcomes. Many of these ideas are less than comprehensive and even fragmentary. Furthermore, they are often only suggestive. Yet I firmly believe that even fragmentary ideas that stay close to the problems of empirical investigation will set theoretical imagination free and stimulate theory building in the process of research.

THE ROLE OF THEORY

Theory in its various forms is of vital importance for social and political research. While everyone is aware of its complex role, it may be useful to rehearse here a few major points. First, theoretical ideas shape the questions we ask. Thus power theory frames direct examination to power resources and conflict relations in the study of material inequality. Furthermore, the very concepts we use in the formulation of research problems are shaped by our ideas about the factors and conditions that make a difference in outcomes of interest. Jean-Jacques Rousseau noted ages ago, "Before observing, one must establish rules for one's observations."[2]

Second, theory is critical for the task of anticipating answers, once the problems are sharply formulated. The development of hypotheses to be tested—often a set of competing hypotheses—quite clearly gains from a knowledge of how comparable hypotheses fared in the work on similar problems. In the absence of specific hypotheses on related problems, there may be useful precedent in the way similar research identified the main relevant factors and conditions. More comprehensive theoretical conceptions put an inquiry into a broader perspective. In this way they can help to avoid simplistic closure in the analysis of specific questions about, say, families, work organization, or community governance, preventing a one-sided focus on domination or shared values, on harmony or conflict, on destructiveness or functionality.

The third point corresponds to the second; it is in fact the other side of the same coin: theory serves as the repository of previous research results. And it is the more useful in this function, the more systematic it is. It is

lished by the International Sociological Association, has long offered specialized literature reviews. Earlier theoretical summaries of special fields of inquiry that deserve particular mention are Donald Black's *The Behavior of Law* (1976) and Gerhard Lenski's *Power and Privilege: A Theory of Social Stratification* (1966).

[2] *Emile, ou de l'éducation*, bk. 5, in a section titled "Des Voyages." Cited after Starobinski (2002, n. 7).

difficult to know all the studies that are relevant to a given new project. Even roughly systematically ordered theory helps to give access to the theoretical gist of previous work. Without it, research produces a sea of fragmented results. This was well known to the ancient Greeks, who distinguished between well-ordered knowledge (*episteme*) and mere information about many facts (*polymathia*).

DESCRIPTION AND THEORY

To be sure, studies that content themselves with description often arouse great interest. And they are significant products of social and political analysis. But even these studies need theory. Sheer description does not ever exist.

Much of survey research fascinates because it informs about patterns in the wider society that transcend our immediate experience. How many people of different descriptions voted Republican? Who opposed the decision to go to war in Iraq? Yet the categories used for informative breakdowns of survey results imply at least a rudimentary theory of the behavior in question, of political choice for example. Theory points to social groupings with similar interests, shared experience, values, and outlooks that seem crucial for political choice.

One might claim that on many issues we can predict the future quite well by extrapolating from descriptions of the present or the past. We can estimate the need for schoolrooms and teachers in a community reasonably well after looking at the current cohort of one-year-olds. Such extrapolations form the basis of much social planning. But predictions that extrapolate from time series data in the past benefit from adjustments based on theoretical ideas, however simple and commonsensical. Pure extrapolation is rarely sufficient, especially over long periods of time. Pitirim Sorokin (1956) put uncontrolled extrapolation on his list of "fads and foibles in sociology."

Similarly, once the biology of transmission of AIDS was understood, one could derive conclusions about the likely paths of HIV infection if the established patterns of sexual behavior were known. This knowledge was generated by a research project that superseded the nonrepresentative information of the Kinsey reports (Laumann et al. 1994). Yet, though largely descriptive in character, that study required a conceptual sophistication uncommon in run-of-the-mill survey research.

All descriptive work, then, involves some theory. The most narrative of historical accounts entail decisions about what is important and why, and their storytelling is interwoven with causal interpretations that require the use of theoretical ideas, no matter how much these remain implicit. The same is true of social case studies that appeal by their vivid detail and interesting subject matter, and that might resemble novels more than other social research. Theory figures in formulating the questions asked, in conceptualizing the important phenomena, in making connections between different aspects of the things examined, in suggesting—however crudely and perhaps tentatively—cause-effect relations, and so on. These theoretical ingredients may not go much beyond informed common sense, but they are present. In the best work of this kind such elements of theory rise well above ordinary understandings. How else to explain the sense of insight created by books like Whyte's *Street Corner Society* (1943) or Hannerz's *Soulside: Inquiries into Ghetto Culture and Community* (1969)?

Varieties of Analytic Tools and Troubled Theoretical Ambitions

What is it exactly, then, that we mean by theory? It is time to take a closer look and to distinguish the variety of analytic tools covered by that label. As we disentangle and define different meanings and components of theory, we will learn more about where things stand, what is possible, what seems beyond reach, and what is to be done.

In the conventional ideal, which holds to a narrow concept of theory, a theory consists of interrelated propositions that say something general about relations and processes in social reality. A theoretical proposition is "general" in the sense that it transcends description of particular facts; it claims to hold universally, but only under specified conditions.

Some assert that such propositions are altogether beyond the reach of social and political analysis. Human behavior, this argument runs, is too variegated. Embedded in ever-changing institutional and cultural configurations, it is shaped by too many factors. And the effects of these factors vary over time, not least because individuals, groups, and organizations learn from experience. Throw in the sense that the future is open as well as common assumptions about human freedom, and the conclusion seems clear: social and political analysis cannot aspire to theoretical understanding in this demanding sense of theory. That skepticism, however, seems to go too far. A more moderate view upholds the ideal of building theoretical knowledge but finds the results often thin, perhaps embarrassingly thin.[3] Giving close attention to a few examples may be instructive.

---

[3] Eckstein (1975, 99) addressed these issues a generation ago in the context of political case studies and spoke about an "*embarras de pauvreté*." The theoretical nihilism that underlies the more extreme versions of postmodern relativism is perhaps a reaction to disappointing results in the search for scientific theory.

A broad theoretical proposition, taken from the sociology of law, differentiates between societies: "The more stratification a society has, the more law it has." This claim has been backed up with a great variety of research results. Furthermore, stratification has been shown to be related to several specific aspects of the law in systematic ways (Black 1976, 13 and chap. 2).

Another hypothesis in the area of law concerns the effectiveness of legal sanctions. Legal sanctions, it suggests, are most effective in shaping rational instrumental behavior, characteristic of commercial market transactions and relations in formal organizations, while "expressive" behavior—valued in itself, grounded in emotion, often deeply rooted in personality, and supported by close groups—is least responsive to legal sanctions (Dror 1959). This hypothesis has strong and interesting implications. It helps explain why Soviet legal policy failed for decades to transform family relations in central Asia, where traditional gender relations proved resistant to massive interventions by Communist modernizers (Massell 1974). The same proposition also throws light on the successes and failures of racial integration in Southern schools. Popular racial views and attitudes were virtually immune to legal sanctions; but the head of Alabama's National Guard obeyed instructions by President Kennedy as national commander in chief and confronted a defiant Governor Wallace, removing him from the schoolhouse door and admitting the first black student. Acting as a military officer, he responded to the formal lines of command and control. Similarly, school administrators later complied with the federal government's directives and incentives aimed at school integration. They, too, acted within the context of legal authority and more or less independent of their private attitudes. Yet after public schools were integrated, white parents and politicians often created—in line with their persistent racial positions—racially separate private schools. Here, then, are two theoretical propositions of considerable reach.

A full-fledged theory consists of several logically interrelated theoretical propositions. Black offers a number of more specific propositions about stratification and the law. Thus within a society "law varies directly with rank"; law is more often directed downward than upward in the structure of inequality; and downward law varies directly, upward law inversely with vertical distance (1976, chap. 2). As his master proposition of "the more stratification, the more law," these hypotheses state regular associations and are suggestive of causation, but they do not explicitly offer causal explanations. Yet higher-order propositions explaining lower-order ones is the principal form of logical integration of a theory. The following assertions of Adam Smith (1776/1937, 670) could serve as an at least partial explanation for Black's master theorem:

> Wherever there is great property there is great inequality. . . . The
> affluence of the rich excites the indignation of the poor. . . . The ac-
> quisition of valuable and extensive property, therefore, necessarily
> requires the establishment of civil government. Where there is no
> property, . . . civil government is not so necessary.

There may be other factors explaining the link between stratification and
law that would have to complement the interest of the rich in the protection of property; but in principle it seems possible to construct a causal
theory explaining the complex of associations asserted by Donald Black.

An example of a well-integrated theory with wide applicability is the
series of interrelated propositions about interaction, sentiments, norms,
ranking, deviance, and social control that form the core of Homans's
treatise *The Human Group* (1950). Homans's hypotheses were formalized in a remarkable review essay by Herbert Simon, later a Nobel Prize–
winner, who showed that some of Homans's propositions lacked independent standing and were logically entailed by others, while new hypotheses
could be derived from those stated (Simon 1952). I will return to that
book in a separate chapter.

These examples may suffice to show that meaningful theoretical propositions as well as logically interrelated sets of such hypotheses are not
completely out of reach. At the same time the examples also illustrate
persistent difficulties and problems.

To begin with, the concepts used to construct hypotheses often are not
clearly defined. What, for instance, is meant exactly by "more law" and
"more stratification"? Both stratification and law plainly consist of
more than one dimension. Both take many disparate forms. How to add
up pieces of legislation, implementing ordinances, judicial decisions, and
enforcement actions by police or administrative agencies? Black offers
suggestive illustrations but no clear-cut metric by which an ordering of
more or less law can be accomplished. Similarly, the distinction between
instrumental and expressive behavior is intuitively meaningful but it is
also fuzzy and complex; it, too, almost certainly involves more than a
single dimension.

If it often seems that we are faced with a trade-off between meaning
and precision—sometimes described as the trap of knowing more and
more about less and less—this may be due to the fact that what is studied
is actually shaped by several different, yet subtly intertwined factors. Initial broad hypotheses may be more open to intuitive understanding
than to controlled research. Thus the instrumental-expressive distinction
may work in the examples given because it points to behavior grounded
in well-functioning complex institutions—family and kinship roles in
contrast to bureaucratic relations and governmental authority—rather

than because it identifies two abstractable characteristics of behavior that have consequences independent of the institutional contexts in which they are embedded. If that conjecture proves right, the proposition needs extensive reformulation and elaboration. This points to the important connection between conceptual work and hypothesis development that I will discuss below.

Many hypotheses we encounter in the literature fall short in a variety of ways. They frequently do not adequately specify the conditions under which they hold. This may concern the general scope of their applicability; for example, there may be social and cultural formations in which distinctions between instrumental and expressive have a different meaning and weight than they do in others. Or a proposition may misspecify the causally relevant conditions, pointing perhaps mistakenly to the instrumental character of individual behavior rather than its embeddedness in well-functioning institutions such as a bureaucratic organization. Or a hypothesis may identify just a few specific conditions relevant for the outcome in question while leaving open that others may be equally pertinent. In the extreme, this can lead to pairs of propositions that—much like many proverbs—assert opposite outcomes. Elster (1989a, 9) offers the example of two common lines of thought: "If others cooperate, I too should do my share, but if they don't I have no obligation to do so." This may seem as plausible a psychological causal mechanism as its opposite: "If most others cooperate, there is no need for me to do so. If few cooperate, my obligation to do so will be the stronger."

A common shortcoming of a different kind underlies much of the skepticism about theoretical analysis of social and political life. Even a properly specified hypothesis may lack the detail that would make it more interesting. For instance, does the claim of "the more stratification, the more law" hold just roughly across societies of broadly different kinds, or does it also apply to differences between countries of similar wealth and complexity? If it were confined to the former, it would have a far more "academic" flavor than if it also claimed to explain differences between, say, Sweden and the United States. Similarly, if we learn from small group research that group-specific norms emerge universally with sustained interaction and that the frequency of interaction is related to agreement on norms, we may be far less interested in that formal claim than in the *content* of such emerging norms, say the specific norms held in a threatening neighborhood gang; and that is a subject on which the tradition of small group research is more or less silent. The theoretical conclusions social and political research has to offer frequently fall short in answering questions a broader audience considers important and perhaps urgent.

The difficulties of hypothesis formation just indicated are linked to a yet more important problem. A given hypothesis may correctly identify the effect of one factor on an outcome of interest and specify the conditions under which that relation holds. But the outcome—the density of legal regulation or the effectiveness of legal sanctions—may also be subject to other influences, possibly counteracting the causal effects analyzed initially. Legal sanctions may be more or less effective depending on the determination of enforcement agencies and the resources available to them, on how laws relate to moral and religious beliefs, on the ease with which behavior can be observed, and on many other factors. Unless a theory is reasonably complete in covering the often bewilderingly complex cause-effect relations, explanations have to rely on the clause of "other things being equal" without being able to point out which these other relevant things are. Predicting outcomes on the basis of such an incomplete theory is even more problematic. If social life is shaped by complex interdependencies, adequate theories have to reflect these interdependent structural patterns and cause-effect relations; all of them, in principle.[4]

More than half a century ago, at the meetings of the American Sociological Society in 1947, Talcott Parsons and Robert Merton engaged in a debate on the best strategy for theoretical advance in the social sciences. It was a momentous deliberation on the future of social science. Parsons argued for a comprehensive theoretical framework, one that would combine his own integration of certain fundamental ideas about social action in the work of Alfred Marshall, Vilfredo Pareto, Emile Durkheim, and Max Weber with an early program of systems analysis. He pointed precisely to the argument just stated, that an adequate theory must reflect the complex interdependencies characteristic of social life, and claimed that a "structural functionalism" offered an opportunity to develop an approximation to such a theory, because it made it possible to treat relatively stable patterns as (reasonably unproblematic) "structures" and to focus on the effects of processes within a social system, the "functions" of structural functionalism, contributing to or detracting from its maintenance and development. Merton held that such an all-inclusive approach was premature. Instead, he argued for "theories of the middle range." Dealing with delimited, partial explanations of such pervasive phenom-

---

[4] The preceding paragraph states the problem in the language of correlational analysis and of corresponding nonquantitative modes of work where changes in the value of several "independent" variables are related to the outcome in question. The problem remains in principle the same if we look at other approaches to causal assessment, such as the search for necessary and sufficient conditions by way of categorical comparisons of outcomes and potential causes. See Mahoney (2003) for a comparative evaluation of different modes of causal assessment.

ena as norm compliance and deviance or the conditions of efficient administrative organization, these less comprehensive sets of theoretical propositions had a better chance to create testable and tested theoretical knowledge, and could bridge the gap between all-embracing theories and empirical description (Parsons 1945, 1948, and 1950; Merton 1945, 1948, and 1968a).

Both Parsons and Merton proceeded along the lines they proposed. And both had a profound impact on the social sciences in the second half of the last century. Theoretically oriented but empirically grounded work inspired by structural functionalist ideas became dominant in the 1940s and 1950s. Parsons himself developed an ever more comprehensive conceptual framework that pointed at an extremely abstract level to functional problems and their solutions. In the wider discussion, it came to be seen as one of several alternative theoretical frameworks, with conflict theory and social ecology theory as its major competitors. Merton acknowledged the importance of such comprehensive frameworks but insisted that only theories of the middle range could forge the critical links between comprehensive theory frames and empirical research.

Merton clearly defined the nature of comprehensive theory frames, which he called "general sociological orientations" and which later came to be known as "metatheories." They represent, he said, "broad postulates which indicate *types* of variables which are somehow to be taken into account rather than specifying determinate relationships between particular variables. Indispensable though these orientations are, they provide only the broadest framework for empirical inquiry" (1968b, 142).

It is fair to say that Merton's program, focusing on empirical theory though acknowledging the role of broader theoretical orientations, won the allegiance of the vast majority of theoretically oriented researchers in the field. In fact, the influence of his overall strategy is still visible in the current thrusts to concentrate on developing "causal mechanism" hypotheses.[5] And the present project follows lines broadly similar to Merton's proposals of how to advance empirically oriented social theory.

Yet if we examine closely one famous example of middle range theory, reference group theory, we make an interesting discovery. Reference group theory held that people's judgments about reality, both their assessments of what is the case and judgments about right and wrong, are shaped by what they see as the experiences and the views of others—that is, by their "referring" to one or another group that seems relevant to them. Both in its version that deals with cognitive estimates, explaining,

---

[5] For the recent revival of interest in causal mechanisms, see Elster (1989a), Stinchcombe (1991), and Hedström and Swedberg (1998).

for instance, the views of promotion chances in different branches of the military, and in its application to normative orientations, pointing, for instance, to the role of "anticipatory socialization" in the course of career advancement, reference theory instills a good sense of explanation; but— it is not able to predict. The reason, on reflection, is clear. It makes a strong case that expectations and views derived from the experiences of others matter decisively, but it does not tell us *under which conditions* in any particular case *who looks to whom* with an impact on *which standards of judgment*. Still, it is hard to deny that reference group theory constitutes a real advance in understanding. Arguing that cognitive assessments tend to be informed by references to the experience of relevant others, it prevents the naive substitution of the observer's estimate of the "objective" situation for the understandings of the people observed; and it offers initial suggestions of where one might look when studying the origins of people's views of reality and their normative commitments.[6]

Ironically, then, the most prominent of the theories of the middle range, on which Merton placed his bets for the future of social analysis, seems to share the core characteristic of "general sociological orientations." It, too, "indicate[s] *types* of variables which are somehow to be taken into account rather than specifying determinate relationships between particular variables." However, it would be a mistake to see it as just another version of metatheory and set it and other theories of the middle range aside as similarly far removed from empirical analysis. It provides much more than "only the broadest framework for empirical inquiry."

THEORY FRAMES

Reference group theory must be understood as a highly focused *theory frame*. If one wants to understand how people's views of their world or their normative orientations come about, reference group theory offers important specific leads for developing more detailed and delimited hypotheses about who looks to which groups in setting standards for judgments.

Focused theory frames, though commonly used with considerable success, are often not recognized as important analytic tools. Virtually invisible in most discussions of theory as well as method,[7] they are in fact critical instruments of theory development. As noted earlier, much of the

[6] Merton's statements of reference group theory are found in Merton and Rossi (1968) and Merton (1968b).

[7] A recent exception is their recognition by an otherwise formally oriented theorist, Guillermina Jasso (2004).

progress of social and political analysis found expression in theory frames rather than in clusters of tested hypotheses specific enough to yield effective explanations and to make specific predictions.

Theory frames may be formally similar to comprehensive metatheories in that they largely stop short of empirically testable hypotheses; but they formulate more precise problems and point to far more specific factors and processes of relevance. Theory frames often build on past research and the puzzles created by varied results. The analysis aims frequently at substantively defined subject matter, such as revolutions, democratization, the development of welfare states, or levels of juvenile criminality and changes in fertility. But even when the inquiry cuts across different areas of substantive interests—as in the case of reference group theory, the dynamics and effectiveness of norms, or the social determinants of knowledge—theory frames have a sharper focus than do comprehensive metatheories. They are more closely attuned to social reality as it presents itself in research. Again, a few examples deserve closer attention.

Barrington Moore's *Social Origins of Dictatorship and Democracy* (1966) represents a good example of a theory frame that remained largely implicit.[8] In a complex and sometimes meandering account of several countries he arrived at three models of political routes to modernity. Throughout, he consistently deployed a conceptual grid concentrating on economic change, the state, and social classes (with a distinctive focus on rural classes). He persistently looked for long-term consequences of past conflicts and developments; and in all his case analyses he inquired about the relative strength of the major collective actors as well as their relations of alliance and conflict. This theory frame was mingled with more specific theoretical propositions that proved of repeated utility, for instance about the conditions leading to revolutionary collective action among peasants.

Theda Skocpol opens her *States and Social Revolutions* with an explicitly developed theory frame; she calls it a set of theoretical principles. Having given social revolutions a careful definition—"rapid, basic transformations of a society's state and class structures, accompanied and in part carried through by class-based revolts from below"—she concludes her review of earlier attempts to explain revolutions:

> Three principles of analysis shared by existing theories of revolution have been critically discussed. And alternative theoretical principles have been proposed in their stead. In fact, all of the shared tendencies for which existing theories have been taken to task are closely interrelated: A purposive image of the causes of social revolution comple-

---

[8] Theda Skocpol made the intellectual structure of this seminal work explicit in a searching critical assessment (Skocpol 1973).

ments an intranational perspective on modernization. And each is most readily consistent with a socioeconomically reductionist understanding of the state.

Her own theory frame stresses three opposite principles:

> We shall analyze causes and processes of social revolutions from a nonvoluntaristic, structural perspective, attending to international and world-historical, as well as intranational, structures and processes. And an important theoretical concomitant will be to move states—understood as potentially autonomous organizations located at the interface of class structures and international situations—to the very center of attention. (1979, 32–33)

These principles informed her analysis as she compared the trajectories, as well as the prehistories and the aftermaths, of the French, the Russian, and the Chinese revolutions and contrasted them with three negative cases—England, Prussia/Germany, and Japan—where revolutions did not occur, even though conditions in these countries were similar in some important ways to those in the cases of social revolution. In explanation she developed two master hypotheses—that a breakdown of state control and peasant uprising are each necessary conditions for social revolutions, and that together the two developments are sufficient to bring about a social revolution. These master propositions were then supplemented by further hypotheses that similarly followed the guidelines of the initial theory frame.[9]

Successful theory frames often have implications for research in different substantive areas. When John Stephens, Evelyne Huber Stephens, and I began to work on our *Capitalist Development and Democracy* (1992), not only were we inspired by Skocpol's *States and Social Revolutions* to develop an explicit theory frame, but we borrowed for our frame, which took off from Moore's work, some important theoretical principles from Skocpol's analysis. Other elements came from research on welfare state development, where a power resources frame had been extremely fruitful in advancing the understanding of social welfare policies (Stephens 1979b; Korpi 1983). Considering that democracy is inherently a matter of power, we turned three clusters of power relations into the core of our theory frame—the balance of power within society, the power relations between state and society, and the impact of international power relations.

---

[9] This eminently successful work has provoked much discussion. Among the best analytic and methodological commentaries are Mahoney (1999), Mahoney and Goertz (2004), and Goertz and Mahoney (2005).

This frame was further developed on the basis of past research dealing with democracy, taking account of work on states and the formation of public policy as well. Yet even though it included a number of specific hypotheses, it remained a theory frame. For explaining the emergence of democracy—or for that matter its lack, incompleteness, or breakdown— in different European, Latin American, and Caribbean countries, it was necessary to develop more specific explanatory hypotheses. This was, then, not a case of applying a single explanatory theory, understood in the strict and narrow sense, to a set of countries. Rather, we ended up explaining forty-odd cases within a consistent theory frame that focused on the relation between capitalist development and democracy.

These examples illustrate several important features of theory frames that I want to highlight. First, *theory frames build on past research*. They absorb earlier research results,[10] and they often rest on a critique of earlier frames, replacing them by analysis sketches that are more empirically adequate as well as—often—more comprehensive. They thus can be, and often are, a major form of knowledge cumulation. At the same time, the best formulate questions and anticipate answers that significantly reach beyond the work on which they build.

Second, *theory frames often come in clusters, sometimes following a common overarching frame*. They borrow from other frames that deal with similar problems, gain strength from overarching similarities, and jointly may shape broader research programs. This has been recognized in the literature by labels characterizing such patterns of commonality. Examples in the field of comparative politics include "the new institutionalism" (March and Olsen 1984), "the new comparative political economy" (Evans and Stephens 1988), "historical institutionalism" (Steinmo, Thelen, and Longstreth 1992), or most broadly "power theories" (Mahoney 2004). One can imagine a nesting of frames that leads from comprehensive orientations to ever more specific and efficient frames for the analysis of particular problems.

Third, *theory frames ensure that context is taken into account in hypothesis formation*. They help to prevent major causal factors from being omitted, guard against premature generalization of the hypotheses developed, and make it easier to identify the scope conditions of these hypotheses.

Fourth, *theory frames shed a new light on the old problem of induction*. The intuitively plausible view that theoretical insights emerge from the

---

[10] This is of great importance in areas of research where—as for instance in comparative historical analysis—the number of cases that can be studied in any one project tends to be severely limited. Using a theory frame grounded in previous research indirectly enlarges the number of cases taken into account.

study of empirical facts is clearly problematic. Sheer induction is inherently inconclusive, since empirical study is always guided by questions, and, furthermore, any set of empirical observations can support many different theoretical conclusions. A theory frame formulates precise research problems and directs the empirical analysis to a series of relevant factors and conditions. Though further hypotheses do not follow logically from theory frames, they link up to the problems and relevant factors identified in the frame used. Broadening a concept earlier developed by Znaniecki (1934), this interplay of theory frame, empirical research, and specific hypothesis formation may be called "analytic induction" (Evans, Rueschemeyer, and Skocpol 1985, 348–50; Rueschemeyer, Stephens, and Stephens 1992, 36–38).

Fifth, *theory frames are open to revision.* Theory frames are not protective fortifications shielding the analysis from critiques that proceed from different premises. This is important to stress precisely because frames do define problem formulations and guide the construction of specific hypotheses. Revisions may be based on the research and theory building engendered by a given frame, or they may respond to persuasive "outside" objections. That empirical findings suggest revisions of a frame shows that theory frames respond to social reality although they are not themselves directly testable.[11] Discussions of Skocpol's theory of social revolutions have questioned her strong version of structuralism, insisted on a greater role of culture, and emphasized more strongly the limited domain to which her theory frame applies—states with international ambitions in a phase of transition out of agrarian socioeconomic structures. Similarly, *Capitalist Development and Democracy* (Rueschemeyer, Stephens, and Stephens 1992, 281– 91) concludes with revisions of the initial theory frame that resulted from its own case analyses: "The middle classes turned out to be more central to the political developments in South America than they were in the advanced capitalist societies; working-class strength and ideology showed more complex effects on democracy than originally conceptualized; and the concept of labor repressive agriculture required modification. Yet the theoretically most far-reaching finding concerned political parties. Their role . . . emerged as a crucial determinant of democratic consolidation" (281–82).

Finally, in light of what this volume seeks to offer, it bears repeating that *theory frames are openings for do-it-yourself theorizing.* This must

---

[11] Since theory frames, unlike textbook theories, do not entail but only suggest testable hypotheses, they are not subject to textbooklike confirmation and falsification via the empirical examination of derived propositions. However, their utility is put into question when using them leads to less successful hypotheses than does drawing on alternative frames. Similarly, plausible explanations building on factors and processes not included in a theory

not be obscured by the confidence that derives from working in a research tradition defined by a nesting of theory frames that have proved fruitful. Theory frames suggest where to look, pointing to the *kinds* of hypotheses that have a chance to be valid rather than entailing more specific hypotheses by simple deduction. They need to be "filled in" with the hypotheses that allow us to arrive at a causal understanding of the phenomena we wish to explain, and that may be successful even in predictions. It is by the success of this empirical theory work that frames prove themselves.

HYPOTHESIS DEVELOPMENT

Our earlier discussion of the difficulties and common shortcomings in the construction of theoretical propositions suggests that many hypotheses we encounter in the literature are underspecified as to the conditions under which a certain outcome obtains. They are, as Arthur Stinchcombe has put it with some irony, "bits of sometimes true theory."[12]

But incomplete propositions with some apparent validity are important springboards for hypothesis elaboration, for developing more completely specified hypotheses about causal and structural relations. If we return to Elster's example of two contradictory reactions to the participation of others in a matter of common interest (the cooperation of others could plausibly diminish one's sense of obligation to participate, but it also could conceivably increase it), we might explore whether the two reactions can be set apart by the strength of preexisting commitments to the common concern and by preoccupations with other material or immaterial interests that also make demands on one's time and resources. If the two contradictory reactions are both intuitively plausible, it is intuitively plausible as well that hypotheses which take strength of commitment and the weight of competing concerns into account would not end up in a stalemate that is mocked by the German proverb "If the rooster crows on the dung heap, the weather will change or it will stay the same."[13]

Using intuitive plausibility as a first "smell test" for theoretical ideas points to an important resource for theory construction. We navigate everyday life with a good deal of theoretical knowledge. We live by predictive theories. This is apparent if we reflect on any significant episode of our own decision making or on occasions when we critically assessed

---

frame may reveal it as misleading, incomplete, or one-sided. A frame may of course also fail because it is too vague and unspecific to encourage successful hypothesis development.

[12] Stinchcombe (1998, 267).

[13] Wenn der Hahn kräht auf dem Mist,
   ändert sich das Wetter oder es bleibt, wie's ist.

the narrative accounts of important political developments. Much of the theory we use in everyday life remains implicit. We could not easily formulate it as a set of theoretical propositions, but it is still available to us as we make decisions and act. A good analogy for this phenomenon—indeed a well-known instance of it—is the fact that we "know" the grammar of our language well enough to speak and write correctly, but we don't know it so thoroughly and explicitly that we could write out the grammatical rules. Yet on reflection we can recover a good deal of the implicit theory by which we live. This resource is not available to everybody in equal measure. We say of a person who stands out among others that she has exceptionally "good judgment." Among the most important wells of good judgment seem to be varied experience and an understanding that makes the most of that experience. The counterparts to these sources in formal social and political analysis are, of course, knowledge of multiple empirical investigations and theoretical reflection. If social scientists occasionally refer to the outcome as analytical or sociological "sense," this indicates that even among professionals engaged in social and political analysis some of the theoretical "knowledge" remains implicit, submerged in the knowledge of many things, but perhaps more easily recoverable through reflection.

A good starting point for hypothesis formation is explanations of processes that we understand very well in commonsense terms. Such explanations nearly inevitably imply theoretical propositions. These can be extracted and refined on reflection. How far can they be generalized beyond the immediate context of which they gave a convincing account? Which limiting conditions suggest themselves when such generalization seems inappropriate? Are there cognate hypotheses that seem to fit situations and processes at odds with the initial causal account? Further hypotheses are likely to emerge if we ask *why* a certain causal nexus seems to hold.

Identifying the specific conditions under which a given causal or structural relationship holds amounts to defining the domain of a given set of hypotheses. Often, however, it will be more feasible and sufficient to indicate such a domain in a summary fashion, without detailing all specific limiting conditions. An example would be Theda Skocpol's (1979) statement that her account of social revolutions is confined to agrarian bureaucratic states.

Quite obviously, ideas found in the literature that are appealing and yet not fully worked out are another springboard for hypothesis development. Weber's treatment of bureaucracy (1922/1978) offers an interesting example.

Most sociologists and political scientists are familiar with Max Weber's concept of an ideal type. In the first place, it is presented as a complex concept—say, of charismatic authority or of bureaucracy—in which certain features and tendencies observed in reality are combined in stylized and exaggerated form into a pure model. In this conception, it serves as a structuring and ordering device for realistic observations of social realities that can be described as different "deviations" from the pure type.

Weber's use also implies, however, another conception, in which an ideal type contains elements of embryonic theory or theory frame (cf. Kalberg 1994). Thus Weber claims that close approximations to the pure type of bureaucracy are the most effective means of large-scale administration; and it is possible to interpret the insertion of different features into his construct of bureaucracy as implicit hypotheses about efficiency (for instance, hiring and promotion by merit), while others point to the explanation of coordination and cohesion in the organization (for instance, hierarchy of offices; action according to rules; full-time employment; tenure in, but not ownership of, office). Clearly these hypotheses that are implied in the construction of the pure type of bureaucracy need further elaboration and specification, especially if a researcher tries to use them for the explanation of the workings of really existing organizations that differ in various degrees from the pure construct.

Here it may be useful to reflect briefly on the interrelations between concept formation and hypothesis development.[14] In the first place, it is critically important to be clear about the kinds of concepts we use. Thus Weber's conception of an ideal type might be called a relational concept, used for ordering empirical observations by the degree to which they approximate or deviate from the pure model. Relational concepts are often not sufficiently distinguished from classificatory concepts, which allow us to sort descriptions of social reality into different categories. Even more important is the distinction between concepts that seek to define the essence of a phenomenon—the law, for example, or the family—and concepts that simply aim to identify certain phenomena distinctively. An essentialist view of the law may well quarrel with definitions that neglect voluntary compliance and focus on an organization ready to implement norms by coercion, while this focus may prove very powerful when one wants to investigate the effects and interrelations of legal and nonlegal norms. Essentialist concepts have their place in social philosophy. In empirical research they may serve to keep the conceptual core of a theory frame balanced, attentive to all relevant causal conditions; but they can also unduly limit the flexible adaptation of concepts to the repeated reformulation of hypotheses, and they often result in interminable squabbles about the "right" definition.

A peculiar form of inept concept formation—sometimes but not only or necessarily associated with essentialist concepts—defines causal factors in such a way that they logically entail all or part of the anticipated outcomes. This results in claims that are true by definition, that is, tautolo-

---

[14] For an important extended discussion see Goertz (2006).

gies, which often remain unrecognized as such. Examples are definitions of civil society that include among its characteristics tendencies favorable for democracy. Even if the tautological character of this often celebrated idea is recognized, as it often is not, the procedure is inept because it wastes the opportunity of stating and examining important empirical hypotheses about links between a more austere concept of civil society and democratic governance.

Flexibly changeable concepts are crucial for theory frames when the issue is to adjust conceptualization to the questions asked and to the expected findings. Thus Weber discarded Marx's conception of class as based in the ownership of the means of production or the lack of it; he substituted a market-based conception of economic class and supplemented it with conceptualizations of status and domination. Another example, also drawn from Weber's work, is his claim that a threefold distinction of systems of domination based on traditional, rational-legal, and charismatic legitimation and the corresponding organizational forms of rule would lead to more profound and adequate insights into the dynamic of rule than does the time-honored distinction of rule by the one, the few, and the many.

We find the same processes of reconceptualization when we examine the construction of specific hypotheses. What is at stake here is more than the familiar need for constructing precise "operational" measures that correspond closely to the theoretically intended meaning. Defining concepts that pin down those aspects of the phenomena under investigation which appear to stand in a regular relation to each other is an important and difficult phase of theory construction, one that involves going back and forth between the formulation of concepts and hypotheses and the gathering of empirical information. An ingenious seminar assignment of the late William J. Goode illustrates the point. Goode asked his students to read closely a theoretically relevant piece of research, identify the central concepts, look for subtle—often just implied—variations in the definition of these concepts throughout the text, and explore how these variations were associated with changing interpretations and hypotheses. The second, creative part of the assignment invited the students to come up with their own reconceptualizations and hypotheses made possible by this conceptual work.

CAUSAL MECHANISMS

Causal mechanisms hypotheses are an important variety of empirical hypotheses. As theoretical propositions of a special kind, they have recently received much-deserved attention. Grounded in realist philosophy of science, the renewed focus on causal mechanisms seeks to go beyond correlational indications of causation. Furthermore, its proponents claim that searching for causal mechanisms is an important way of linking empirical research and theoretical analysis. A causal mechanism is a condition, relation, or process that brings about certain events and states. Strongly conceived, it is a sufficient condition of specified outcomes.[15] Causal mechanisms are often—and in some conceptions they are inherently—unobserved; but they can reasonably be inferred from observations. Power in its different incarnations (Lukes 1967) represents an important set of examples of causal mechanisms.

The Humean theory of causation focuses exclusively on regularities among observable variables. However, as is well known, correlational analysis does not unambiguously identify causation. Some of the reasons are obvious. A correlation between A and B (for example, the correlation, allegedly found in nineteenth-century surveys of rural villages, between the number of storks on the roofs of houses and the number of children within them) may be "spurious" because a third condition C (for instance, the agricultural mode of production) is involved in bringing about both A and B. Less obviously, some causal relations may not reveal themselves through available frequency associations, be it because several alternative causal mechanisms are at play that can substitute for one another or counterbalance each other, or because the indicators available for quantitative analysis do not tap the mechanisms at work, however indirectly. Finally, correlations may establish stable relations that plausibly, though vaguely, point to underlying causal patterns, but they do not reveal through which processes the statistical relationship comes about; the actual causal mechanisms remain in what has been called a "black box." For certain broad policy purposes, it may be sufficient to establish that women's education is associated with declines in fertility and to leave out of consideration the causal paths in which education of women brings about differences in fertility behavior. Yet when it comes to understanding variations and exceptions in the fertility outcomes, knowing more about the specific

[15] The metaphor of "mechanism"—using, say, the clockwork behind the movements of the hour and minute hands as a simile for the hidden systems of the body—is old indeed. According to the *Oxford English Dictionary* it was "in early use chiefly with reference to natural objects"; but the dictionary also cites a formulation of Harriett Martineau in 1833: "The mechanism of society thus resembles the mechanism of man's art."

For current research on social mechanisms, see, in addition to the works cited earlier in n. 5, for instance the recent work of Tilly (1995, 1997, 1998, and McAdam, Tarrow, and Tilly 2001). On the philosophical grounding of causal mechanism analysis, see Archer et al. (1998), Wendt (1999), and Gorski (2004 and 2007). Mahoney (2001b) was useful for the comments that follow. Also enlightening is the brief discussion in the entry "Causal Mechanisms" in *The Sage Encyclopedia of Social Science Research Methods* (Lewis-Beck, Bryman, and Liao 2003).

causal paths becomes important. The effects of different kinds of education on prevailing fertility norms, the role of sheer knowledge about conception and contraception, the status and power effects of education on gender relations, and the complicated interactions among education, income, and fertility preferences are only some of the factors that may make a decisive difference.

The claim of the realist theory of causation that the identification of causal mechanisms is fundamental to causal understanding is persuasive. Frequency associations can only give indications about the underlying mechanisms. Yet for our purposes in this book little is gained by taking a strong position on the philosophical understanding of causation. Statistical association remains a major tool of research and constitutes one important link between evidence and theoretical understanding. At the same time, assertions about causal mechanisms have to be supported by empirical evidence regarding the presence of a mechanism that is not directly observed, regarding its causal nature, and regarding its relevance for the phenomena to be explained.

An instructive set of overarching causal claims and empirical findings developed around the explanation of the rise and spread of modern democracy. In a now classic paper, Seymour Martin Lipset (1959/1963) established a strong correlation between indicators of economic development and assessments of democratic constitutionalism. This was contradicted by skeptical judgments about any direct causal connection between the two phenomena of broad social change, which such analysts as Max Weber (1906), Karl de Schweinitz (1964), Barrington Moore (1966), and Guillermo O'Donnell (1973) derived from their exploration of particular cases. But the correlation was repeatedly confirmed by cross-national studies that employed a variety of sample compositions and measurement techniques. The views on the underlying causal processes varied. Lipset did not take up the tenet of Marxian theory that the interests of bourgeois capital owners were the main driving force behind democratization. He pointed to advances in education, communication, and equality that accompany economic development, and he saw the middle classes as the main prodemocratic force. Phillips Cutright (1963), who refined Lipset's statistical analysis, emphasized the features of modernization theory included in Lipset's account and offered an explanation in terms of system theory: a democratic regime form reflects the greater complexity of modern society, and only democracy can cope with this greater complexity in the long run. Our own work in *Capitalist Development and Democracy* took off from the contradictory results of two modes of empirical research (Rueschemeyer 1991). We considered the cross-national correlations as an established empirical generalization any causal account would have to explain. At the same time we were impressed with the greater theoretical sophistication of the historical case comparisons. That inspired the construction of the theoretical frame briefly sketched above. After the examination of forty-odd cases we saw the central causal mechanism linking capitalist development and democracy in the changes of the balance of power within society that were induced by capitalist development—a decline in the power of large landlords and an increase in the power and autonomy of classes previously excluded from participation, especially but not only the working class. The newly dominant bourgeois capital owners did not systematically advance democracy with full participation, while the middle classes and small farmers supported democracy unequivocally only if they were free from hegemonic influences of anti-democratic forces. These changes in society were modified and varied in their political effects by the power relations between state and society and by the impact of the international power balance on a given country. The point of this lengthy excursion is not to claim that these problems have now a settled solution but rather to illustrate the useful interplay among empirical findings, claims about underlying causal mechanisms, and renewed empirical investigation.

Focusing on causal mechanisms does more than deepen the knowledge that can be gleaned from correlational analysis. It holds the promise of invigorating the interaction between theory and research, both within and across different modes of research. If quantitative research can demonstrate that the interpretation of one or a few cases may mistakenly identify causal patterns, looking for social processes that generate statistical regularities challenges the prevailing mode of quantitative research in which variable characteristics of units, rather than social action and social processes taking place under different structural conditions, are the elements of causal assessments. Seeking out and testing underlying processes that, driven by identifiable actors and processes, can explain the correlations between variables will not only invigorate the theory component of quantitative research, its design and interpretation, but will also establish closer links with theoretical ideas that inform other modes of research.[16]

On closer inspection, we find several different conceptions of what causal mechanism hypotheses will accomplish as well as of what constitutes the exact nature of causal mechanisms. Many theorists try to go back to the level of individual action in their causal arguments, combining the causal mechanism program with the position of methodological indi-

---

[16] If the illustration given above comes from the particular area of research with which I am familiar, it is easy to point to examples from different corners of the variegated landscape of social and political research. For example, the late Aage B. Sørensen (1998), a major quantitative social scientist, developed similar ideas forcefully in the field of social mobility and labor market studies. See also Mahoney (2001b).

vidualism. The strong version of this combination, which accepts *only* explanations that rest on theorems about individual behavior, faces obvious obstacles in the real world of social analysis. Hedström and Swedberg (1998, 12) quote the philosopher David Lewis:

> Any event that we might wish to explain stands at the end of a long and complicated history. We might imagine a world where causal histories are short and simple; but in the world as we know it, the only question is whether they are infinite or merely enormous. (1986, 214)

In the present state of our knowledge, it would obviously be wasteful to insist that social institutions, structural conditions, and the relations between collective actors can play a role in causal accounts only if they are in turn explained by the multiplicity of individual actions that constituted them.

There are major differences among the various conceptions of "causal mechanism." Mahoney (2001b, 579–80) lists twenty-four different definitions (and adds another of his own). Much of this must not detain us here, but it is useful to highlight a few points. Some programs of mechanism research remain closely related to correlation analysis, seeking to throw light into the "black box." Others aim to offer a foundation for causal theory independent of the covariation of variables. In addition to differences arising from divergent positions on methodological individualism, it is clear that causal mechanisms specific enough to fully explain events of interest differ significantly from such overarching causal claims as we just encountered in the studies and arguments about development and democracy. Jon Elster (1998) advances a conception that combines the ambition of explaining particular events with a fairly strong version of methodological individualism. In addition, he is skeptical of the explanatory use of probabilistic hypotheses. As a result, his plea for mechanisms offers only limited hopes for analytic advance. Concentrating on psychological and social psychological mechanisms, he stresses that typically both the conditions that activate a given mechanism and the outcomes generated are indeterminate, as illustrated in the example of cooperative and uncooperative responses to the participation of others. This skepticism is not shared by all or even most analysts pursuing causal mechanism. McAdam, Tarrow, and Tilly (2001) are far more optimistic. They see in the search for causal mechanism a fundamental shift in comparative historical work away from a focus on complex events such as revolutions and toward identifying "mechanisms and processes [that] play significant parts in quite disparate episodes, but produce varying overall outcomes depending on their sequence, combination, and context."

Causal mechanism hypotheses, then, have a special character, explaining why things happen by showing how outcomes are produced. In developing hypotheses against the background of theory frames, they take their place alongside other hypotheses identifying noncausal linkages between structural elements—say, between marriage, descent relations, and family ties—as well as causal hypotheses taking off from statistical covariation. Causal mechanism hypotheses are likely to play a special role because they may link up more easily with the exploratory work on causal relations and their conceptualization that is at the core of theory frames.

We have encountered different kinds of analytic tools ranging from comprehensive orienting frameworks à la Parsons to focused theoretical frames for studying more specific, often particular substantive problems, to causal mechanisms and other hypotheses, whether or not these are fully specified as to their conditions. We also found occasional sets of interrelated hypotheses that may be called theory in the narrow sense. The relative sparsity of fully developed theoretical propositions and their concentrations into theories leads us back to the repetitive refrain in this sketch of some problems of social theory construction: a researcher has to provide in the course of virtually any project theoretical frames and propositions on her own, even though previous research and the theoretical tradition offer tools for this work.

WHAT LIES AHEAD?

In the following chapters, I intend to offer analytic tools for theory construction in a very broad sense. I do not rule out the established ideal of theory construction, to build complex theories with full-fledged theoretical propositions as their components; but I will concentrate attention on the more modest intermediate goals along the road, on formulating questions, conceptualizing relevant factors and conditions, developing hypotheses as well as complementing and elaborating existing ones, creating and revising focused theory frames, and putting research results into a broader framework. Almost all social and political studies require theory building in the process of research that can work with these tools. What I offer will not be lists of "how-to" recipes. I will rather focus on analytic questions and arguments that can improve the theoretical imagination.

The next chapter sets out a conception of social action as a broad framework and baseline. It is followed by four discussions of knowledge, norms, preferences, and emotions as analytic components of social action. These chapters complement and develop the rational calculus core of rational action theory and provide wide-ranging material for hypothesis development. A revisiting of Homans's *The Human Group* and the small group research it epitomized not only presents a fully developed theory but also integrates the preceding cluster of four chapters and shows the broad relevance of small group processes. A chapter of midpoint reflections concludes the first section of the book and opens the view to more comprehensive social and cultural structures.

These more comprehensive patterns figure prominently already in this first section's consideration of the analytic components of elementary action and interaction, but they receive sustained attention in the second half of the book. This begins with an examination of the aggregation of individual actions into larger phenomena. That is followed by discussions of collective action, power and cooperation, institutions, and collective identities. This series of chapters ends with a discussion of large social structures as consequential locations for individuals, groups, and organizations and a consideration of the role of culture and ideas. A brief conclusion takes stock and rounds out the volume.

Chapter II

A GENERAL FRAME: SOCIAL ACTION

The first proposition of our inquiry into usable theory may come as a surprise: *A comprehensive theoretical framework is of great utility for social research and analysis.* This despite the fact that general theoretical orientations are far more removed from social reality than are focused theory frames, as is evident if we compare the core ideas of functionalist systems theory or materialist conceptions of history with theory frames that deal with the role of reference groups in the formation of attitudes or with the origins and consequences of revolutions.[1]

There are three main reasons why a general framework has significant utility. First, comprehensive theoretical frameworks can be the springboard for more focused analyses. For example, the general paradigm of "economic man," applied beyond the specifically economic sphere of social life, has given rise to focused theory frames such as the models of sophisticated game theory or Mancur Olson's (1965) formulation of the collective action problem and the subsequent discussion. Second, comprehensive frameworks offer a view of the broader landscape in which more specific inquiries are located. Thus general theoretical orientations that insist on tension and conflict as endemic in large social formations— one might think of the dialectic views of history advanced by Hegel and Marx—raise questions about the long-term prospects of any particular dominant development. Finally, perhaps most important, general theory frameworks offer a better chance to relate diverse research findings to each other. "If only I could dig canals in my mind that would increase the internal trade among the stocks of my ideas," mused the eighteenth-century German philosopher Georg Christoph Lichtenberg; "but there they lie around by the hundreds without being useful to each other."

---

[1] To recapitulate briefly, in the preceding chapter I have distinguished comprehensive frameworks of concepts and broad orientations from focused theory frames. The latter give more specific guidance to hypothesis formation but still fall short of presenting (or implying logically) a full range of testable empirical propositions. Both comprehensive theoretical orientations and focused theory frames differ from full-fledged theories—logically integrated sets of hypotheses with definite empirical implications—that are commonly described in textbooks but found in really existing social science less frequently than one might expect.

SOCIAL ACTION AS AN ANALYTIC FOUNDATION

This chapter will argue for adopting a comprehensive theoretical frame centered on social action. The basic building blocks for such a framework are found in two major traditions of social theory. Rational action theory, which takes off from elementary economic theory, has its roots in the utilitarianism of the nineteenth century. The classics of modern sociological theory—Vilfredo Pareto, Emile Durkheim, Max Weber, and, in America, George Herbert Mead—initiated the second tradition, which emphasizes more complex aspects of human action. These two lines of thought are frequently viewed as hostile to each other; but they are not as mutually incompatible as they are often seen to be. Rational action theory applies a core model revolving around the choice of means for given ends to issues and puzzles ranging from the interrelations between economic exchange and the social division of labor to the difficulties of generating collective action out of common interests. The conception of action offered by Pareto, Durkheim, Weber, and later Mead raised significant questions about the social constitution of human actors, about the role of rationality, and about changing needs and wants. These ideas can be seen either as a challenge to the framework of rational action theory—this is how Durkheim thought of his critique of utilitarian individualism—or as openings for giving it greater explanatory power, which was the thrust of the arguments of Pareto and Weber. Taken together, these two traditions—bound to each other by controversy as well as important commonalities—have been the most influential theoretical perspectives since the end of the nineteenth century.

Adopting a social action framework as a tool of orientation and rough integration is a pragmatic choice, not a dogmatic commitment. The primacy we give to the usefulness of analytic tools requires tentativeness. It leaves open the possibility that alternative views are supported for good reasons. In fact, it is quite likely that any comprehensive theoretical framework plays down some important features of social life, even to the point of virtually excluding them from view. Therefore we may well suspend our option for action theory in the study of certain problems.[2]

Equally important, I have no intention of embracing ideological affinities that have been associated with a paradigm of intentional individual action. The action frame does not commit its users to a philosophy of individualism and a libertarian view of individual freedom, which some rational action theorists espouse. Nor does its adoption entail a distancing

---

[2] Occasionally employing alternative broad orientations may be as worthwhile as seeking to integrate contrasting emphases in a hybrid. Reinhard Bendix and Bennett Berger (1959) suggested such alternation as a strategy for gaining broad theoretical orientations.

from the ideas of solidarity and equity grounded in ontological views of social reality such as those of Emile Durkheim. Yet there are good reasons for choosing action theory as a comprehensive theory frame. In both of its traditions, it has proven itself fruitful—a source of more focused theoretical investigation and a powerful tool of integrating a variety of particular inquiries.

Both approaches begin with the model of a goal-oriented actor who finds herself in a physical and social environment relevant for the attainment of her goals. They differ in their conception of this actor. Weber (1922/1978) held that "meaningful action"—in contrast to sheer "behavior," conceived as devoid of subjective meaning—must be the elementary building block of social and political analysis. That means in the first place that social action must be explored from the point of view of the actor. And it entails also that action is embedded in social relations, large and small. Social action may take different forms depending on the role of intentions, of rational calculation, of normative orientations, and of emotions, as his four types of action—instrumentally rational, value-rational, emotional, and traditional action—make clear. The sociological perspective of George Herbert Mead (1934) conceived of human actors as socially constructed and emphasized the symbolic mediation of all interaction. Parsons (1937) insisted with Weber that human action cannot be understood without reference to the actor's point of view. The subjective or internal dimension of action that then comes into view includes the perception and interpretation of the actor's environment, normative orientations, and changing tastes and preferences; it is permeated by emotions that respond to experience and link cognition, valuation, and preferences together.[3]

Opening the Internal Space of Action

Human behavior is not as much determined by the joint effect of inborn tendencies and the physical environment as is that of animals. In the less complex animals, behavior can be rather well explained and predicted once their biology and the environment are known. The open space created by the relative indeterminacy of human motivation and action is "filled" by norms and values; by varying levels of information, interpreta-

---

[3] While this view of the internal dimension of social action builds in particular on Pareto, Weber, and Mead, Parsons (1937) has given it the most extended and systematic formulation. The distinctive emphasis that I give to the dynamics of preferences, of knowledge and ignorance, of norms and values, and of emotions is indebted to this early work, though for Parsons highlighting the role of normative orientations had a singular priority.

tion, and analysis; and by changing preference structures. These are given energy, coherence, and direction by emotions and complex codes of symbolic communication. All of these involve human creations, though they build on innate foundations such as elementary needs or the capacities for language and empathy.

This more complex conception differs from the strongest and the most simple version of rational choice theory. "Thick" rational action theory (as distinguished from more open-ended "thin" versions that just presuppose intentionality) does acknowledge the importance of the subjective dimension of action as it focuses on the rational means-end calculus of actors; but it does so only to immediately close that open space again, attending solely to the rational pursuit of the goals specified and assuming a well-understood environment. Behavior is then shaped by rational and therefore predictable responses to a given environment.

Even a simple model of rational action has considerable heuristic value, provided that the actors and the situations in which they find themselves are well understood. When we know fairly well what others know and understand, which norms they are likely to obey (and which to elude or break), and what their relevant concerns are, we often use a rational calculus of the other's costs and benefits to predict with some confidence what his or her actions will be—whether a colleague will accept an appointment offer, whether a contract has a chance to succeed, or even whether it makes sense to respond with talk or sanction to unacceptable adolescent behavior.[4]

However, a more comprehensive approach suitable to a broader variety of actors and situations needs to answer—or make reasonable assumptions about—the questions that were raised about the subjective or internal dimension of action: How are preferences constituted? How are goals chosen? How are means evaluated? Which understandings of the situation inform the choices? How do norms and values influence the adoption of goals and means? And how do normative orientations themselves come about and change? A fully developed rational choice theory, then, must surround its core of a rational calculus model with a belt of subsidiary theoretical ideas. These have to deal with needs and wants, cognitive understandings, normative orientations, as well as emotions, inquiring

[4] A former graduate student, who was about to return to India to direct a demographic research institute, once asked me what theoretical advice I could give him for his new work. My answer came as a surprise to him: since he knew rather well the people whose migration and fertility choices he was to study and was thoroughly familiar with their social locations and cultural orientations, rational action theory would go quite a long way in illuminating things. This suggests that if the most general and formal core of rational action theory is given narrow *scope conditions*, within which the subjective aspects of action are known or can be reasonably estimated, the comprehensive general framework is transformed into a highly focused theory frame.

about their causal determinants, the dynamics of their change, and their impact on action. Without a set of such subsidiary theoretical ideas, the rational action paradigm will remain weak in substantive content.[5]

If we can advance our understanding of the dynamics of preference formation; of knowledge and ignorance; of norms and values; and of emotions that link preferences, cognition, and normative orientations to each other, we will make major strides toward reconciling the two social action frameworks. The next four chapters will deal with these four dimensions of the subjective or internal side of social action. This quartet of chapters is critical for the project as a whole. These chapters will specify the questions that have to be asked about meaningful social action and explore the dimensions of its subjective space. They will suggest insights that help in devising particular hypotheses. Aiming for focused theory frames, they will provide baselines for realistic theoretical argument about the dynamics of preferences, knowledge, norms, and emotions.

Their utility, then, goes beyond the elementary level of analyzing action and interaction. Taking off from the internal dimensions of individual acts, these chapters will have to explore how larger social and cultural contexts shape these elements of social action and interaction. The templates and paradigms of norms, knowledge, preferences, and emotions are, after all, largely collective human creations. At the same time, beliefs, complexes of norms, patterns of preference, and paradigms of emotional responses are *constitutive elements* of the meso- and macrostructures that emerge from, but then surround and influence individual action and elementary interaction. These chapters will therefore be of great importance when, in the second part of the book, we turn to an analysis of larger processes and structures—of aggregation, collective action, varied forms of organization, institutions, social identities, and broad structural contexts. In the next-to-last chapter we return to them specifically as we conceive of culture as the collective creations grounded in the internal dimensions of action.

---

[5] Rational action theory did generate a variety of specific rational models. Well-known examples are analyses of supply and demand under perfect and oligopolistic competition or the repeatedly mentioned models of collective action and nonaction. These rational models—often varied in their assumptions about preferences, the situation faced, or limitations of knowledge, which determine the outcomes—can be seen as theory frames of a special kind. They fail, as Moe (1979) has shown, to meet the positivist, "covering law" criteria of theory; but they "operate as intermediate heuristic mechanisms that aid in conceptualization, facilitate analysis through their simplicity and deductive power, point to relevant relationships, and thereby contribute to the development of empirical laws." As they "cannot explain empirical phenomena, but may point the way to theories that do" (237), they are in effect theory frames of a special kind. I have no wish to devalue such rational modeling; but more substantive explorations of the internal dimension of action hold the promise of introducing greater realism into the premises of these models.

The subsidiary theories I advocate remain at present incomplete and fragmentary. I will present analytic ideas about the dynamics of cognition; the genesis, transformation, and effects of norms; the foundations of preferences, their change, and their impact on behavior; and the role of emotions in linking valuation, cognition, and preferences and in forging human attachments. Each of these discussions will take rational action theory as a point of departure and reference. What can be offered will not overcome the limitations of our current theoretical knowledge, and it will not turn action theory into a full-fledged theory capable of specific prediction and explanation across a wide range of situations. But it will contribute to an expanded social action framework that retains a strong focus on intention and rationality. At the same time, these discussions will seek to offer focused theory frames, reasoned conceptualizations as well as specific hypotheses about knowledge, norms, preferences, and emotions that by themselves are analytic tools and springboards for further theory building.

Critical Questions about the Action Frame

If we insist that the internal dimensions of action point to important and unavoidable questions and indeterminacies, one may well ask: why not join the linguistic and cultural "turns" that in the 1980s and 1990s swept from literary theory and anthropology into historical and social analysis, and that took off from similar considerations? These movements claimed that language with its variable interpretability is at the heart of any social relation, and that—beyond the literal role of language in communication—all social relations and their developments are constructed through "semiotic" actions with multiple meanings. Some concluded that social structures and processes are themselves in effect "texts" that must be read by the observer/interpreter, and that are inherently readable in different ways. These claims were often associated with ontological and epistemological premises—premises about the primacy of cultural construction over material and structural conditions and, in extreme formulations, about the impossibility of causal analysis. These premises were held to separate human studies radically from the natural sciences. Interpretive "paradigmatic explanation," which focuses on codes that make language performance and its understanding possible and extends this "grammatical" analysis as well as ideas of literary assessment to all "semiotic" action, would replace "positivistic" causal explanation.

It is true that the cultural studies movements responded to the same open questions to which Weber pointed with his claim that meaningful actions rather than behaviors devoid of interpretable meaning are the "material" out of which social relations and structures are built. It is also true that the cultural movements offer one explanation as to why social and political analysis cannot point to a rich body of covering laws that emerged from persistent research into the consequences of different causal constellations under specified circumstances. Why, then, not accept their rejection of positivist social science?

I will not engage in extended philosophical discussion here, but merely state three simple arguments. First, I am not willing to give up on the quest to explain important social processes and structures even if those explanations may remain—possibly forever—partial and incomplete, and thus will not be of much help to people looking for predictions about specific outcomes of interest. I might note that most texts of the new movements are in fact full of causal arguments, albeit often implicit ones.

Second, the ontological premise that the human world is so radically different from physical and somatic realities that there must be a complete discontinuity in intellectual approaches seems fundamentally counterintuitive. We do, after all, conduct our lives on the basis of understandings and goals that imply causation and presuppose the possibility of empirically checking relevant facts. What people know and believe does make a difference in their actions, and so do changing interests and their priority ordering. To identify these beliefs and preferences within a reasonable margin of error may be difficult but is not impossible.

Third, whatever the ultimate validity of the inherently contestable metatheoretical premises of the interpretivist positions as well as our own, they can be seen simply as guesses about research strategies. They are then to be judged by their fruits, that is, by the results of research conducted on one set of premises rather than another. I am betting that theoretical and empirical explorations of the components of the internal dimensions of action will be a more useful strategy than a focus on semiotic construction of all things social that leaves the indeterminacies of the internal dimension of action essentially untouched.[6]

---

[6] For the preceding paragraphs, I took my cues from William Sewell's impressive "Interpretivist Manifesto" (Sewell 2005). I should note that our disagreements are not absolute. First, focusing on ideas about reality, on normative orientations, and on desires and preferences clearly raises questions of interpretation and hermeneutics for the strategy I advocate as well, even though on a most elementary level I would insist that language and observable actions frequently allow quite clear and unambiguous inferences, at least within tolerable margins of error. Any advances in hermeneutic understanding of more complex meanings will be welcome far beyond the confines of cultural studies. Second, Sewell not only concedes but insists that phenomena other than mutual understanding (and misunderstandings) are of critical importance for adequate description and explanation of social patterns and developments. (I am not sure whether this qualification gives a new meaning to Sewell's formulation of "paradigmatic explanation" or whether I misinterpreted this mode of explanation in the first place when I read it as an alternative to causal explanation.) Third, Sewell

The social action paradigm is not without other rivals and critics than those associated with the linguistic and cultural turns. And their objections take specific aim at certain features of the social action framework that also deserve brief discussion. Some social theorists—very prominently, for instance, Anthony Giddens (1979, 1984)—find fault with the centrality of intentions in both traditions of social action theory. Giddens and Bourdieu (1977, 1990) emphasize the lack of reflective consideration and the taken-for-granted character of much routine action. Emile Durkheim and more recently Stephan Fuchs (2001) refuse to take individual action as the starting point of analysis, because they claim that the fundamental causal direction runs from society to the individual and not vice versa. This critique sees individuality as a variable function of social structure.

Following my resolve to keep things simple, I will again not engage in a metatheoretical discussion of these claims. Both of the views just cited prove useful when one approaches certain problems. This is most obviously true for the views of Giddens and Bourdieu on unreflective routine action. Unreflective routine action is frequent in the everyday life of the most "modern" social formations; but for many important decisions—even on many issues regulated by tradition—some conscious review of relevant facts, priorities, and normative constraints is common, even in societies considered "traditional."

The causal impact of inclusive social patterns on individual behavior and elementary interaction, on which Durkheim and Fuchs insist, raises bigger questions. This leads into important questions of how to approach larger social structures and processes, and how to relate micro– and macro–social phenomena to each other. To anticipate, I prefer to leave these matters open rather than looking for a single general framework on macro–social structures and on macro-micro relations in social life.

At present, it does not seem possible to explain all more comprehensive social and cultural phenomena by recourse to individual action and elementary interaction. Therefore I have no intention of endorsing the claim that all group and collective phenomena can be reduced to individual action. At the same time, speculations about social phenomena as a reality of a different kind, defined by emergent properties that are *in principle* immune to psychological and social psychological explanation, are similarly inconclusive.[7]

---

not only concedes but insists that there are limits to treating all social relations and processes as "text," that is, constituted out of explicit speech and its wider semiotic analogues. He points among other things to the unanticipated consequences of much interaction. For extreme, though not necessarily rare outcomes, he might have invoked Shakespeare's formulation of "sound and fury signifying nothing."

[7] Relating the problems of emergence and reduction in social analysis to work on the brain-mind nexus, Sawyer (2001, 580) comes to a similarly open-ended conclusion:

This said, it is important to recognize that—whether a detailed demonstrable reduction is possible or not—elementary social actions can help constitute complex social phenomena such as groups or states. And as emergent patterns these have causal consequences distinct from their constitutive components, much as the effect of water on fire is very different from the effects that oxygen and hydrogen would have by themselves (Gorski 2007).

In the treatment of the relation between elementary social action and meso– or macro–social structures one is perhaps entitled to follow Max Weber's pragmatic example. Weber opens the conceptual framework of *Economy and Society* (1922/1978) by distinguishing four types of social action. Yet instead of trying to derive social structures from this baseline, he simply moves "up" to complex social relations—to an administrative organization, for example—and then asks what role different forms of individual motivation and action are likely to play within this setting.[8]

I follow Weber's precedent also in a broader sense. I am skeptical about analytic models that assume strong equilibrium tendencies in comprehensive social systems. Twentieth-century functionalism in sociology was the most influential attempt to provide such a framework for meso– and macro–social systems; it built more on Durkheim than on Weber. Marxian social analysis, with its base-superstructure model and its dialectical conception of historical development, also had strong functionalist elements, both of a change-maintaining and a steady-state-maintaining kind (see Elster 1982 and the ensuing discussion in *Theory and Society*).

That social patterns and processes are interrelated in complex ways is one of the abiding insights that have emerged from a century and a half of social policy interventions in industrial societies. Universal schooling and the public provision of support in old age and illness are programs with multiple consequences, foreseen as well as unanticipated ones. Pro-

---

"Whether or not a social property is reducible to individual properties or a social law reducible to individual laws, is an empirical question that can only be resolved through empirical study."

[8] Here is a passage assessing why officials in systems of domination comply with orders and regulations: they may be bound to obedience "by custom, by affectual ties, by a purely material complex of interests, or by ideal (*wertrationale*) motives. The quality of these motives largely determines the type of domination. *Purely* material interests and calculations of advantages as the basis of solidarity between the chief and his administrative staff result, in this as in other connexions, in a relatively unstable situation. Normally other elements, affectual and ideal, supplement such interests. In certain exceptional cases the former alone may be decisive. In everyday life these relationships, like others, are governed by custom and material calculation of advantage. But custom, personal advantage, purely affectual or ideal motives of solidarity, do not form a sufficiently reliable basis for a given domination. In addition there is normally a further element, the belief in legitimacy" (Weber 1922/1978, 212–13). For a good discussion of Weber's analytic procedure see Kalberg (1994).

found changes in productivity, in social mobility, and in family and kin relations are only some of these outcomes. There is no doubt, then, about the presence of powerful systemic interdependencies in social life.

It is these insights that led sociological functionalists to borrow ideas from the anthropology of nonliterate societies and to claim that the most complex as well as the simplest societies could best be understood as functioning wholes in which different parts contribute to the maintenance of the overall system. Parsons, the most important figure in sociological functionalism, joined the framework of social action to a social systems analysis that took values as its central analytic reference point. His program began with a relatively sparse frame of questions, when he urged social theory to analyze how social processes contribute to—or detract from—the stability of the relatively persistent structures of the whole (1945). As the program developed, it proved fertile, both instigating a rich variety of research projects and integrating different lines of research, as, for instance, linking family and kinship patterns to the division of occupational labor and structures of social inequality. Indirectly, it generated a revival of conflict theory among its critics. As a broad metatheoretical frame, then, structural functionalism was a success: it was fruitful.

Yet as the framework later developed into ever more complex abstractions, it met with growing critique as well as a studied avoidance. These responses virtually eliminated it from the concerns of social and political theory. However, it is worthwhile to note that the basic conception of functionalism continues to be a valuable guide if policy studies ask what it takes to attain certain goals, be it to deepen democracy through increased political equality, to make public schools a success even in deprived communities, or to create effective states in developing countries. Here the logic of inquiry leads to the same kinds of questions as those posed by functionalism: in what ways do certain conditions contribute to the goal of changing the larger system? But that logic is so obviously suggested by common sense that the kinship with functionalism is easily overlooked.

At the same time, there is now common agreement on the fundamental fallacy of a functionalism that claims that a process which has functional consequences for an important feature of social life exists because of this contribution; that, for instance, the incest taboo exists because it protects family solidarity and the authority of parents. Such a claim can be maintained only if it can be shown that strong mechanisms link the outcome back to its functional support. Such "feedback" mechanisms might simply rely on unintentional "Darwinian" selection, the failure and elimination of social patterns that are not supported efficiently. They may involve intentional combinations of learning, insight, and power. Or they could depend on a variety of other social processes.[9] For many persistent patterns or stable processes of change—be it the successful upbringing of the young, the continued expansion of market processes, or the steady growth of state expenditures as a proportion of overall resources in a country—there exist several alternative supportive mechanisms that may substitute for each other or just multiply the support for the outcome in question. In fact, it is perhaps a useful hunch that many or even most patterns and processes that serve important purposes of powerful interests, be they based widely or held by dominant minorities, are "overdetermined," resting on multiple sets of sufficient conditions.

When the paradigm of society as an integrated whole with strong equilibrium tendencies is taken as a blueprint of the actual functioning of social life rather than as a model to which really existing societies can be compared (and found to differ in various degrees), the objections become overwhelming. Yes, interdependencies are important, but they constitute typically varied patterns of a historic character, and the interconnections are often rather loose. It is also true that social life is full of equilibrium tendencies; but what tends to be maintained may be poverty and destitution, rampant corruption, or electoral apathy as well as sustained economic growth, a valuation of compassion, or increasing regard for human dignity. Everybody knows of the multiple and often decidedly suboptimal equilibria that obtain in families, offices, and communities as well as in economic and political "systems." There exist clearly varied "goal states," maintained by different forces. And social formations of significant complexity are unlikely to see unitary "goals" pursued. Assuming a single unitary goal state of societies almost inevitably becomes a veiled way of stating the analyst's own values.[10]

When we proceed beyond the fundamental framing of individual action and elementary interaction, then, I aim for relatively specific theory frames, say about institutions or different forms of organization. I do not think that we are able to devise realistic focused theory frames about macrostructures in general.

[9] On "path-dependent" continuities that rely on positive feedback mechanisms, see Pierson (2004, esp. chap. 1).

[10] The sketch of some of the problems related to functionalist analysis given above is just that, a sketch; and it is a brief and incomplete one. I should emphasize, however, that while all issues mentioned have fairly wide incidence, not all can be laid at the doorstep of the major protagonists of twentieth-century functionalism in sociology, Talcott Parsons and Robert K. Merton. Parsons, for instance, always recognized a tension among different "system needs" and made this a central tenet of his models, thus implicitly leaving the overall goal state of a societal system indeterminate as well as subject to contest. And Merton's essay "Manifest and Latent Functions" (1968c, first written in 1948) presented most of the critical arguments mentioned, even though Merton maintained a delicate "loyalty at a

A Tentative General Theory Frame

What is the upshot of these reflections? I propose a social action framework that seeks to expand the hard core of rational action theory but remains sparse in its broader ramifications. As such it serves to outline diverse problem formulations and to interrelate and integrate them. At the same time, this framework is wide open to the impact of more comprehensive structures and processes on individual action and elementary interaction. It also recognizes the complex interdependencies and equilibrium tendencies ubiquitous in social life, but approaches the overall systemic character of social life as extremely variable. It does not rule out tight integration in some societies, especially in simple ones, but anticipates comprehensive social systems to be often quite loose, full of contradictions, and rife with destructive tendencies. Really existing social formations are more open-ended and flexible than commonly used analogies suggest, whether these employ the body or computer systems as metaphoric models.

The general frame I propose makes for three continuities I deem important. First, it links up with common sense. There are those who treat common sense with contempt.[11] Relying on common sense can indeed distort our understanding of things social. Focusing on our experience of everyday life, it privileges psychological and social psychological interpretations and brings institutions and larger social structures only with difficulty into view. "Society cannot be seen," was a recurrent bon mot of my teacher René Koenig. However, continuity between a theory frame and common sense offers a critical advantage: it allows us to mobilize our implicit knowledge. As noted earlier, we live our lives on the basis of far more theoretical insight than we realize. For those who regularly digest intelligent news, this extends even to complex larger structures and processes.[12] Here is indeed a great resource for social analysis that we will have occasion to invoke again and again.

A second continuity that characterizes the framework proposed is that it fits with much of actually existing empirical research, including survey work and demographic analysis as well as participant observation and

---

distance" to the work of his former mentor Parsons. On the critical role of feedback mechanisms in legitimate functional analysis, see Stinchcombe (1968).

[11] While spelling out his very different theoretical project, Fuchs says: "An obstacle to sociological advances, it seems to me, is obsession with persons and personhood, with beliefs, plans, goals, and intentions. With some materialists I share the suspicion that common sense is not a decent scientific theory, and cannot be so, since it is not a scientific theory to begin with" (2001, 5).

[12] Talcott Parsons once entertained the naive question of a visiting college graduate: "From where do you get your ideas?" His answer: "I regularly read the *New York Times*."

large-scale comparative work. Most empirical research proceeds with a common sense–based methodological individualism that does not, however, feel obliged to trace every complex social formation or development to its individual action components.

Third, a social action framework offers continuity with past theorizing, both grand and middle range, provided that the action frame is open to the "emergence" of social and cultural structures, large and small, and to their impact on individual action and elementary interaction. The vast bulk of past social theory is built on the premise that individual agency is ultimately central to the understanding of the social world.

We now move to explore the theoretical problems related to cognition, norms, preferences, and emotions. These four chapters seek to complement the core of rational choice theory with wide-ranging explorations of the subjective dimensions of action. They aim to develop broad substantive theory frames as well as to offer more specific ideas and building blocks for hypothesis formation in the course of research. These chapters also lay a foundation on which later discussions of selected features and issues of macrostructures can build. Yet as we explore knowledge, norms, preferences, and emotions, the required openness to the impact of comprehensive social and cultural patterns means that we will repeatedly have to refer to relevant factors that are located "above" the level of individual action before we later focus specifically on these meso- and macrofeatures of social life—on aggregation and collective action, on institutions and organizations, as well as on comprehensive social structures and cultural formations. Ironically, this messiness is a consequence of even a limited acknowledgment of the systemic features of social life.

Chapter III

KNOWLEDGE

A Utilitarian Starting Point

Questions about the information and the understandings that underpin people's actions are often ignored or treated rather casually in social science. Thus many economic models make the radically simplifying assumption of full transparence of the relevant facts. Simplistic presuppositions about what people know also prevail in most social research. Typically, issues of understanding and analysis—the background knowledge that enables people to make sense of particular facts and guesses—are even more neglected than are questions of information. Often the use of crude indicators such as years of education is the only way in which this level of analytic knowledge is "measured." Beyond that, we typically overestimate how predictable the outcomes of alternative courses of action are, even if people are well informed and possess good analytic knowledge.[1] Yet on reflection it is obvious that different levels of information and understanding as well as illusions and distortions are as important determinants of action as is the rational pursuit of given goals.

Perhaps surprisingly, rational action theory is less cavalier in dealing with these questions than are many other research traditions. Therefore a bundle of propositions underlying the model of rational action offer a convenient starting point for exploring the dynamics of social knowledge. Successful action requires realistic analysis of the situation. Ignorance, misunderstandings, and illusions have punishing consequences, while realism contributes to success or at least helps fend off undesirable outcomes. These consequences can be understood as powerful "feedback mechanisms" reinforcing realistic analysis. To the extent that people are interested in the outcomes of their actions, they will search for the necessary information and understanding, and seek to correct erroneous presuppositions and interpretations.

This set of simple—and, as we will see, actually too simple—propositions has a number of interesting implications, which contradict the com-

[1] Max Weber's famous argument for an "ethics of responsibility" is a good example. In contrast to the "ethics of conscience," which extols absolute standards and forbids particular behaviors, it presumes knowledge of how alternative courses of action will turn out (Weber 1946).

mon assumption that people have most of the time a realistic understanding of their situation. People will seek adequate information and analysis only if they are interested in outcomes for which that knowledge is relevant. Exploiting the fact that this interest is a matter of degree, rational action theory sees the search for information as subject to cost-benefit analysis. The higher the cost of information and the lower the interest, the less likely a realistic understanding of the situation. Even in the case of intensely pursued interests, better knowledge may be so costly as to be unattainable. For issues of low concern, even quite accessible information may be neglected.

The "costs" may not just take the form of money and effort; and at issue is not simply finding information but accepting it as persuasive. Therefore available information that is at odds with cherished beliefs and expectations (say, about the achievements of one's fellow nationals or the human rights record of "our" troops) but is not very relevant for meeting one's own actively pursued interests will not easily be absorbed. Embracing it would not enhance but would actually reduce the actor's "utility."

 While information may be available at less than prohibitive costs, the analytic knowledge needed for understanding, explanation, and prediction may not be.[2] Furthermore, the analytic knowledge and understanding of people may be so undeveloped that they cannot reasonably assess the need for further information or evaluate the implications of information they did obtain. Analytic knowledge—the commonsense equivalent of developed theory frames, predictive hypotheses, and theories—depends to a large extent on the knowledge horizon in a given time and place. In addition, there is the question of how much access different actors have to the knowledge that is in principle available in their culture.[3]

Actors may conclude—for reasons of insufficient information, insufficient analytic understanding, and/or the inherent nature of the situation—that issues which are of critical importance to them are *uncertain* and therefore unpredictable. Uncertain outcomes must be distinguished from risks and gains that can be anticipated with a certain probability. Often, but by no means regularly, it is possible to establish such probabilities at least in a rough way. Probabilistic risk assessment weights the likely loss or gain with its estimated probability. This is of great value to actors

[2] To take a dramatic example, absent the later understanding of recession and deflation, the last pre-Nazi government of Germany responded to the Great Depression with budget cuts and reduction of public salaries rather than deficit spending, thus reinforcing the downturn. See James (1989) on this historic failure.

[3] It bears noting that limited access to "high" culture may also result in cognitive advantages. The question of access pertains to all more or less exclusive spheres of culture, and these may include obstacles to knowledge as well as avenues of learning. Some "common people" may be free from high-culture idealizations, illusions, and cognitive inhibitions.

who are engaged in large sets of repeated actions. For others, however, who face decisions about a singular outcome—say, about surviving a dangerous surgical intervention—probabilities are difficult to make meaningful. Very low and very high ones tend to be taken as quasi certainties, while the wide range in the middle approximates uncertainty in the technical sense.

Inquiring how economic firms deal with uncertainty, some economists—most notably Herbert Simon (e.g., 1955, 1957)—have developed a model of economic action guided by "satisficing" rather than maximizing gains. Simply put, if a past course of action yields satisfactory results and if attempts to increase returns further run into the problem of uncertainty, the response is likely to be "Leave good enough alone." Satisficing is a rational response to uncertainty that does not have further negative consequences for realism.

Since uncertainty is common in various spheres of social life, and since many actors are not much helped by probabilistic information about gains and losses, we should expect to find many other coping mechanisms, some quite similar to satisficing, some strikingly different. A number of them can be identified easily; and many of them do have cognitive consequences.

Magic is perhaps the most famous. Malinowski (1948) showed that uncertainty about outcomes of great concern, say in fishing or gardening, may be answered by rituals that seek to activate supernatural forces. He distinguished magical beliefs both from empirical knowledge about crops and fishing and from religious beliefs not concerned with pragmatic contingencies. Magical practices and beliefs may have lost legitimacy in modern societies but are widespread nevertheless.

Clinging to established ideas in the face of social change that is ill understood and uncertain in duration is another response to uncertainty. For instance, in the United States many hold on to a sense of discrimination against their ethnic group in the face of declines in interethnic hostility, changes that are not easily pinned down with certainty and even more difficult to assess when it comes to confident prediction.

Relying on precedent and established rules of thumb—in other words, relying on tradition—often responds to a particular and particularly important uncertainty: the unpredictability that emerges when complex social arrangements that have served interrelated ends come under pressure for change or—more simply—are just questioned. The prime example is established family and kinship roles, but the logic holds for many similar complexes of interwoven interests, norms, and understandings. Traditionalization, relying on how things have been done before rather than on rationally persuasive argument, is closely analogous to satisficing. However, in contrast to satisficing behavior in modern economies, traditional precepts often have a normative character. At the same time, they have profound cognitive consequences: embedded in language and proverbs if not simply in silent practice, they tend to remove the patterns of behavior in question from reflective inspection.

Another, related reaction to uncertainty is embracing the views of others. James Madison has put the point eloquently: "The reason of man, like man himself, is timid and cautious when left alone, and acquires firmness and confidence in proportion to the number with which it is associated" (Madison, *The Federalist*, No. 49). Put more positively, dialogue with others can help deliberate reasoning, an element of decisions strangely absent from simplistic rational choice models. In the case of collective decisions, some deliberation is unavoidable (Wendt 1999, 125–30).

Relying on what others think may or may not have damaging consequences for realism. Others may be better informed, and the views of many observers, if somehow aggregated, tend to be more accurate than a single person's guesses; but relying on the opinion of others can also be thoroughly misleading. In either case, this response to uncertainty represents an opening for social influences on ideas about reality that we will discuss further below.

Substantial complications are introduced once we move beyond a single actor and consider the interaction of different parties. This is of paramount importance because the better part of people's knowledge is derived not from the actors' direct observations and their own analysis but from the information and the understandings conveyed by others. Information as well as keys to understanding may have been brought to the actor's attention in connection with current problems; or they may have been—especially in the case of tools for understanding—learned in the past, perhaps inherited from previous generations. This distinction is important because cognitive schemata acquired in the process of socialization often have an opaque character that inhibits rational examination (Berger and Luckmann 1967). Some of these schemata are embodied in the very language and commonplace formulations people use, sediments of past experience and interpretation. Francis Bacon made this fundamental point more than four hundred years ago.[4] This historicity of ideas about reality is a feature they share with social norms and other fundamental features of social action, a feature that will concern us repeatedly.

[4] Bacon (1620) developed a theory of four distorting mechanisms, which he labeled "idols." One group is the *idola fori*, or distortions of the forum, built into the very mode of communication (43, 59). An example is the common way of talking about revolutions, which embodies the voluntarism Skocpol (1979) rejected in her theoretical frame for explaining revolutions (as in "if reforms do not come about, people will go on the barricades and make a revolution").

The actors who communicate or receive information and analysis may have divergent interests. Therefore the flow of knowledge depends on trust. This gives personal communication a distinct advantage. People may also trust impersonal modes of communication (by mass media, governments, corporations, religious organizations) in varying degrees; but it has been shown that a good deal of impersonal communication is filtered through personal interaction contexts (see the early formulation of a "two-step flow of communication hypothesis" by Katz and Lazarsfeld 1955). Personal networks and relations of trust to others strongly affect which claims and interpretations are accepted as reliable.

Divergent interests may lead some actors to keep others uninformed and/or to prevent them from drawing certain conclusions. Consider: Why do parents as well as states keep secrets and even lie about a good many things? Or: Why do advertisers hide their interest in profit behind professions of caring? Many actors—individuals and representatives of organizations and institutions—derive significant advantages (not necessarily just of a plainly selfish kind) from establishing and maintaining such "knowledge asymmetries."

There is more to the interest-knowledge nexus than distortions in the flow of information. Interests drive the search for knowledge, for information as well as for analytic knowledge. This has far-reaching implications since the questions that are of interest, and therefore the insights and understandings relevant for people's concerns, vary across actors and categories of actors. The information and understanding sponsored by influential actors, be they individuals or various organizations and institutions, is in effect partial. It is misleading for those on the receiving end whose interests did not inform the search for that information and analysis. This insight is at the core of the idea of "cultural hegemony" (Gramsci 1928–37/1975). It is of tremendous importance for fairly obvious reasons. To illustrate with regard to social inequality, trustworthiness tends to be associated with one's place in the structure of inequality even as different locations in that structure engender different interests. At the same time, the well-off—those with more education, greater wealth, and more power—have a better chance to gain and to spread information, analysis, and interpretation. Note that in this general formulation the idea of cultural hegemony follows simply from the assumptions of divergent interests, their differential influence on the knowledge search, and the nature of human inquiry. It does not depend on intentional withholding of information, intentional misleading of the audience, or outright lying.[5]

So far we have only spelled out a number of implications and corollaries of the initial bundle of propositions underlying the utilitarian model of

[5] Nor does it imply that the analyst has privileged insight into the "objective interests" of people, whose "false consciousness" she can then denounce on the basis of these insights.

rational action. Far from leading to the conclusion that most people will most of the time have a realistic understanding of their situation, these propositions indicate a variety of sources of ignorance, lack of understanding, illusion, distortion, and deception. However, the propositions about information and analysis implied in the utilitarian model do point to powerful factors increasing the likelihood of a realistic understanding of the actor's situation. The qualifications just discussed can be understood as specifying conditions under which this effect does not come about.

 It is noteworthy that the implications of the utilitarian action model cover a good deal of the classic enlightened search for the limits of realistic knowledge. "Hobbes . . . ," Hannah Arendt (1967, 106) tells us, "held that only 'such truth as opposes no man's profit, nor pleasure, is to all men welcome'—an obvious statement which, however, he thought important enough to end his *Leviathan* with." Once multiple actors are taken into account, the corollaries of the utilitarian model also cover much of the thinking about ideology and ideational domination that such thinkers of the Enlightenment as Destutt de Tracy and Helvetius and later Marx and Engels developed in the eighteenth and nineteenth centuries.

Is the utilitarian model sufficient to illuminate the multiple influences shaping social knowledge? I will sketch below a more comprehensive theory frame. Before we turn to that alternative model, however, it seems useful to consider some distinctions among different forms of "knowledge." Different types of ideas about reality seem to stand in distinctive relations to social structures and processes. Therefore, even a cursory examination of various kinds of knowledge and their social dynamics will give us a richer sense of how perceptions, understandings, opinions, memories, and explanatory ideas are shaped by social factors.

Kinds of Knowledge, Types of Social Influence

Knowledge, beliefs, ideas about reality—this covers a broad territory. But we will not try to develop a detailed and inclusive typology of knowledge. The conceptual distinctions that I will offer serve just one purpose—to identify forms of knowledge that seem to follow different dynamics in their interaction with social conditions or that constitute links between social conditions and other forms of knowledge. These distinctions, then, are based on orienting ideas that can become elements of more focused theory frames. At the same time, I will present just a set of more or less aphoristic observations rather than give these ideas a systematic ordering. A loose assembly may be as effective in mobilizing the reader's memory and imagination, or even more so.

Some important distinctions we have already encountered. Thus I pointed to the difference between sheer *information and analytic tools*, arguing that the latter usually receive less attention. The use of analytic tools (as well as relevant background information about past events) varies more with upbringing and social condition, and it is also more subject to social influence than is sheer information. On many topics, the ease of using analytic tools is confined to a small and privileged segment of the public. This is likely to be a major factor explaining the finding of Philip Converse (1964) that large majorities of American citizens hold inconsistent and contradictory political beliefs.[6]

The degree to which relevant *empirical evidence* is available separates different kinds of knowledge from each other. It is, of course, one criterion that sets science apart, but it makes a critical difference in everyday experience as well. Where clear-cut empirical evidence supports a belief about matters of real concern, the impact of *social influences on beliefs* declines dramatically. In turn, we saw that people look to and defer to the views of others when they face uncertainty. Given insufficient information and understanding, one respects—quite rationally—the views of others presumed to be "in the know"; but there is also a tendency to go along with the opinions of those one likes and trusts, to defer to assertions of prestigious figures and organizations, and to believe frequently repeated assessments. Generally, the greater the deficiencies in information and understanding and the less urgent the interest in accurate information, the more important are these social influences based on numbers, trust, status, and reputation for knowledge. In the extreme, social influences can become so strong that social psychologists have spoken of the creation of a "social reality," supported by common opinion but quite possibly at variance with the facts (Festinger 1950, 1954).

In the two introductory chapters, I argued that *implicit analytic knowledge* is a potential resource for theory building, though one to be used with circumspection. Implicit knowledge is also of tremendous importance in the social life that we study. For most people it is closely related to and shaped by the routines and practices of everyday life. While it can be changed by experience, it is not easily exposed to critical reflection and remedial education. Implicit background knowledge plays a significant role because it "frames" the ways experience and information are interpreted.

---

[6] The findings of Converse and similar later research notwithstanding, ordinary citizens often are able to make political choices that are roughly reasonable in light of their social position and their material and immaterial interests. They take important cues from people, organizations, and institutions whom they trust (of the extended literature, see Sniderman, Brody, and Tetlock 1991; Zaller 1992; Pierson 2001; and Brooks and Manza 2007, chap. 5).

A long tradition that goes back to the ancient Greeks holds that *social experience and understanding* have priority over other forms of knowledge. Max Scheler (1926/1980) formulated this as a general claim: In most cultures and in everyday life, people's social experience and understanding shape the understanding of other phenomena.[7] Emile Durkheim and Marcel Mauss (1903) had used the same principle to explain crosscultural differences in fundamental categories of thought. A more prosaic corollary has important implications for social views and outlooks: people's immediate experience tends to be generalized to less well-understood phenomena. This means that we can expect similar locations in the wider social structure to engender similar outlooks and cognitive frames.[8] It also means that people's perceptions of wider social conditions—say, of the distribution of income and wealth in a country—will often be shaped by their immediate social environment.

This idea links up with theoretical arguments and research showing that different social milieus create a distinctive *habitus* (Bourdieu 1977) or *mentality* (Geiger 1932; Rueschemeyer 1958b). These studies emphasize the role of implicit knowledge, and they see common assumptions, cognitive frames, and even factual beliefs as closely intertwined with valuation, emotion, and propensities toward particular behavior patterns.

People's *conceptions of wider social contexts* and their attitudes toward broader collectivities such as social class, status groups, as well as ethnic and national identities can probably be best understood if we explore how these outlooks grounded in similar primary experiences interact with the attempts by various elites to influence and control people and to shape their outlook (Rueschemeyer 1976). If elite understandings and values are at odds with popular mentalities, these varied outlooks will prove quite resilient. If elite appeals articulate well with them, there may emerge powerful synergies. Much like mentalities, the elite views also tend to fuse cognitive and evaluative elements. But they are usually more self-consciously thought out and explicitly articulated. They thus represent the paradigm of an ideology.

---

[7] "Because explanation is always something relatively novel reduced to something known, and because society is . . . always 'more known' than anything else, we can expect to be true what a large number of sociological investigations have already shown: the subjective form of thinking and intuition, as well as the classification of the world into categories, i.e. the classification of knowable things in general, are co-conditioned by the division and classification of the groups . . . of which a society consists" (Scheler 1926/1980, 73).

[8] This is a recurrent theme in the work of Karl Mannheim as well. See, for instance, his papers "Conservative Thought" and "Competition as a Cultural Phenomenon"(Wolff 1971, 152–222, 223–61) and on the problem of generations (Mannheim 1928/1952). Rueschemeyer (1958a) identified this as a major contribution in his critical evaluation of the work of Scheler and Mannheim.

The idea of *ideology* has a long and complex history. In contrast to the views of the Enlightenment and Marx and Engels, which centered on interested distortions of reality, later conceptualizations see ideology as a common element of culture, in which knowledge and analysis are joined to value commitments (Parsons 1951, 1967). Geertz (1973) embraces the interest theory but sees the antagonistic advancing of collective interests as only one of the ideological responses to unsettled times full of social conflicts and structural inconsistencies. The other responds to social "strains," focusing on the reconstitution of social order and solidarity in line with dominant values. Speaking of interest theory and strain theory as the two main approaches to the genesis of ideologies, Geertz formulates succinctly, "For the first, ideology is a mask and a weapon; for the second, a symptom and a remedy" (201). Yet in their purpose and result, the two types are not altogether different. Both "render otherwise incomprehensible social situations meaningful [and] . . . so construe them as to make it possible to act purposefully within them." "Whatever else ideologies may be—projections of unacknowledged fears, disguises of ulterior motives, phatic expressions of group solidarity—they are, most distinctively, maps of problematic social reality and matrices for the creation of collective conscience" (220).[9]

This cursory overview of different types of cognitive beliefs has given us a richer sense of the multiple interactions between ideas and social dynamics. We now turn to questions that lead beyond the utilitarian model in the search for a promising theoretical frame to guide analysis of the social dynamics of belief formation.

A MORE COMPREHENSIVE MODEL: DOUBLY ENGAGED IDEAS

The rational action model provides important clues about social determinants of "knowledge"; but it also tends to block out some of these factors, and others come only incompletely into view. An alternative,

---

[9] The sociology of knowledge grew out of the critique of ideology in the eighteenth and nineteenth centuries and reached a first culmination in the work of Karl Mannheim (1936). As it became primarily concerned with ultimate questions of epistemology and the philosophy of history, the sociology of knowledge lost its promise both as a field of empirical inquiry and as an element of a comprehensive theoretical framework for empirical social science (Rueschemeyer 1958a), though Parsons gave knowledge a central place in his move toward systems analysis (1951, chap. 8). The attempts of Robert K. Merton (1941/1968d and 1945/1968e) and others to harness it to the exploration of empirical problems failed to take hold. Merton retreated from the broader sociology of knowledge and focused on the sociology of science, where he had begun his intellectual journey (Merton 1936/1968f, 1938/1968g).

more comprehensive approach starts from the view that ideas about reality—as an element of all human action and forms of social life—are bound up in complex interactions and interdependencies with other aspects of action as well as with broader social processes and structures. This is true as much about cognition as it is about the other elementary components of social action—norms, preferences, and emotions. The interdependence model embraces the view that knowledge serves the pragmatic purposes of individuals, groups, and organizations, and that it is shaped by the feedback mechanisms that derive from pragmatic success and failure, anticipated or real. But it goes beyond this insight by viewing ideas about reality at the same time as interrelated with the other analytic aspects of social action and as constitutive elements of social structures and cultural patterns.

Building on ideas of Pareto and social psychological theories about "social reality," Parsons speaks in his discussion of belief systems of a pervasive duality of relevance, which can be seen even in the elementary interaction between two persons, ego and alter: "That there should be a common belief system shared by ego and alter is in certain respects as important as that the beliefs should be adequate to reality outside the particular interaction system" (1951, 328).[10] This claim immediately raises obvious questions, the questions provoked by any argument about functional relevance: For whom and for what is a given set of shared beliefs important? And through which mechanisms is that commonality secured? But it is clear that only by developing hypotheses about the full range of these interdependencies is it possible to gain a grasp of the social conditions affecting ideas about reality and the role ideas play in turn in emergent social structures and processes. Ideas about reality, then, are shaped by two broad sets of determinants: by the varying interests in knowledge, ignorance, and illusion as portrayed by the utilitarian model and by the forces that build up social action, interaction as well as small and large social structures, out of constitutive elements, of which cognition is one.

---

[10] Of all the classics of modern sociology, Pareto was most concerned with "nonlogical" (unverifiable or mistaken) beliefs. He considered most of people's ideas to be rationalizations or *derivata*. Underlying these, however, he identified several broad classes of recurrent behavior tendencies, roots of belief, preference, and action that he called *residues*. Among these are inclinations toward innovation as well as toward stability and, most directly relevant here, the "residues of sociality" in counterpoint to "residues concerned with the integrity of the individual." S. E. Finer (1966) offers an excellent analysis of these ideas, which Pareto developed in his *Treatise on General Sociology* (1916).

Ideas shaped by their interdependence with social structures and processes have a parallel in cognitions shaped by their interdependence with personality structures and processes. The psychology of knowledge has important implications for the sociology of knowledge; but, following the example of Pareto, we will not be concerned here with such psychological propositions, except as not further examined givens.

The interdependence model claims that knowledge is closely intertwined with different patterns and levels of social integration, but also
with varied forms of social antagonism. If ideas about social reality are
shaped by mechanisms that protect the cohesion of groups and broader
collectivities, defining their boundaries and difference from others, reinforcing distinctive value orientations, and maintaining shared as well as
antagonistic interests, it follows that the determinants and consequences
of ideas about reality are profoundly involved in one of the central problems of social theory—the question of how social order is constituted or—
to use a formulation that accommodates conflict as well as cohesion—
how *social structuration* is accomplished. Often this problem is too narrowly focused on society-wide orders of great stability. It is equally pertinent when we are faced with smaller-scale and possibly quite fragmented
and delicate forms of commonality or antagonism. In fact, some of the
mechanisms involved may be more clearly visible in smaller social configurations and in fragile patterns.

BELIEFS AND SOCIAL STRUCTURATION

It may be useful to step back a little and take at least a cursory look at
how the problem of social order has been treated. Different theoretical
frames have pointed to quite different answers. These are sometimes presented as standing in sharp conflict with each other; but they may also be
seen as partial approaches that can usefully be combined. Parsons (1937,
1951) gave in his own theoretical strategy priority to values and norms,
a gentler alternative to Hobbes's view that authoritarian rule represents
the antidote to a chaotic war of all against all. Parsons criticized the utilitarian forerunners of today's individualist rational action theory as incapable of dealing with the problem of social order. By contrast, Michael
Hechter, one of the main advocates of rational action theory in sociology
today, has advanced a pluralist view of the current state of the discussion
(Hechter and Horne 2003). Here explanations focusing on values and
norms stand side by side with others emphasizing cognitive ideas, ranging
from religion to prevailing opinions and science. Other partial explanations derive from power and authority, spontaneous cooperation of individuals, and the impact of interacting groups and networks. One might
well add two more clusters of relevant factors: the dynamics of the formation of preferences and their crystallization into actively pursued interests,
as well as the social generation and the control of emotions. In other
words, knowledge and the three other dimensions of action we are now
subjecting to an analysis—norms, preferences, and emotions—are critical

ingredients in the creation and maintenance of ordered social patterns. They help constitute different forms of structuration and are in turn shaped by them. I will first look at some contributions of cognitive beliefs to the creation of social order and then turn to what this suggests about the dynamics of belief formation.

Certain cognitive ideas represent—and help constitute—the very center of social life. Durkheim thought of beliefs about the power and the benevolence of divinity as symbolic recognitions of the power of society, at once constraining and enabling. Consequently they demand and are accorded awe and respect, and contradicting them provokes anathema. Religion and its secular equivalents contain the most comprehensive if often implicit cognitive premises: while they are quite removed from immediate pragmatic concerns and thus less subject to the discipline of experience and reality testing, they typically build on past beliefs and myths. This makes for long-lasting historical continuities (even if these engender incongruities with current conditions, as, for instance, when the images of shepherd or lord remain central in nonagricultural societies), and it accounts for the diversity of religious ideas across cultures.

The constitutive role of cognitive beliefs is evident in virtually all social formations. Many social norms, their legitimacy as well as people's compliance with them, rest on beliefs about their wisdom. These beliefs may invoke the insight of wise elders or of an anonymous tradition, or they may rationally explicate the purpose of the rule in question. They may just point to the alternative of chaos, or they may describe specific advantages secured by the norm, pointing, for example, to the protection of innovation by patent rights.

Social roles such as those of mother, manager, or college student rest on complex cognitive premises that give them meaning, spell out an orientation in time, articulate them vis-à-vis others, and stabilize them. For important social patterns we can expect a nesting of meaning structures. Different levels of social formation and the corresponding ideas then are interlinked; for instance, the ideas undergirding parental roles link up with the premises of community life, with beliefs about how society at large works, and with religion or its equivalents.

Wendt (1999, 122–35) argues persuasively not only that views and interpretations of changing situations causally affect the pursuit of established interests but that the very construction of interests depends on cognitive premises. This applies even to the definitions of national interest that are at the center of "realist" conceptions of international relations. Different assessments of the risks from interstate anarchy underpin, on the one hand, a defensive emphasis on security and, on the other, a definition that aims for expansion and dominance. Thus Wendt points out that

Stephen Walt, who takes a defensive position, is more sanguine than others about the risks of controlled nuclear proliferation.[11]

Cognitive premises also enter into negative definitions of situations and social patterns. To consider a social relationship exploitative involves much more than merely confronting it with a normative standard of fairness. It presupposes an understanding of how the relationship in question comes about and works; it entails a realistic view of how it *could* work; and it often results in projects of action, which in turn raise complex questions of what is possible.

In the study of the active pursuit of change we encounter another example of general significance: belief in the chances of a social movement's success—or that of a scientific team—energizes and binds the movement or group together. Raising doubts about it can put their cohesion into question and debilitate their efforts.

COGNITIONS ARE LINKED TO OTHER COMPONENTS OF SOCIAL ACTION

Cognitive beliefs, then, play an important role in the constitution of social phenomena, large and small, harmonious and antagonistic. They share this role with the other elementary components of social action—normative orientations, preferences, and emotions. Looking briefly at some interconnections among these analytic components of action gives some further insight into the dynamics of beliefs.

Ideas about reality are often closely intertwined with values, and this *value-cognition nexus* is of great consequence for beliefs. Strong valuations infuse beliefs with emotional energy, often rendering cognitive ideas less open to change and revision. At the same time, values and norms may specifically protect beliefs from distorting influence and urge searching for cognitive adequacy. Here are some specific examples and hypotheses about the cognition-value nexus:

[11] Importantly, Wendt distinguishes between constitutive and causal relations. Applied to cognition, different ideas about the situation may, in conjunction with given interests, *cause* adoption of one or another strategy. By contrast, cognitive premises may have played a *constitutive* role in the formation of these causally relevant interests; their causal effect is then indirect, embodied in the interests that are being pursued. This distinction is critical if causal mechanisms are seen as the main tool for explanation: the causal effect of mechanisms is different from their constitution. The distinction will be useful when we later (in chapters 7 and 8) review how different kinds of social action and interaction are constituted by the four components of the internal dimension of action—knowledge, norms, preferences, and emotions.

- It seems that in the early phases of individual development, information and understanding are linked without mediation to prohibitions and ideas of good and bad. Growing up requires greater tolerance for the tension between recognition of what is and ideas of what is desirable and objectionable, a special case of "cognitive dissonance." Yet the early fusion often continues unless recurrent situations and social influences force a differentiation. Here is probably a chief reason why the informal mentalities characteristic of different social milieus as well as the understanding of important roles and other social patterns in which people are involved combine cognitive and normative ideas with little differentiation.

- The assumption that good things go together and reinforce each other is a major feature of untutored ideas about social life. The insight that this is often not true is one of the first fruits of realistic social analysis.

- Ideas that undermine or put into question cherished values and value-infused ideas face more difficulties in every phase of knowledge creation—from conception to general acceptance—than cognitive ideas that are in harmony with accepted values.

- Formal ideologies derive much of their persuasive appeal and their capacity to explain people's experience and to guide their attitudes and actions from the way in which they closely join values and emotions to description and analysis.

- When we later examine the impact of organizations and institutions, we will encounter norms and practices that protect scientific inquiry against interference.

Values, norms, and cognitive ideas about reality are often associated with another element of pervasive relevance, *social attachments*. These, too, are emotionally charged and receive strength from their grounding in emotions. Such bonds of solidarity shape how a social relationship and its place in the world are seen. Again, a few examples may be useful:

- The power of social attachments is expressed in the classic outcry of national loyalty: "My country, right or wrong!" But the raw chauvinism of this formula must not lead us to think of the underlying mechanism as rare. What is rare is merely its explicit formulation.

- Knowledge claims that one's in-group or praised models fall short of ideals—"befouling one's nest," "washing the family's dirty linen in public"—are treated with special skepticism; they may be shunned completely, played down as shameful, or treated

    as privileged information, relegated to the poison cabinet of in-
side knowledge.

- Correspondingly, an in-group's opponents are often seen as
  mean, misguided, dumb, conformist, envious, cowardly, and
  unfair—stereotypes that mirror inversely the in-group's proclaimed values.
- About families, villages, and other collectivities it is often asserted
  that the interests of all members are in harmony with each other.
  It's outsiders who create problems. This, of course, is frequently
  at odds with the facts, but it supports group cohesion, and it
  often serves the interests of the members who are better off.[12]

That preferences shape cognition is clearly recognized in the rational action tradition. And this is acknowledged in the interdependence model as
well. On the one hand, people and organizations are most likely to make
every effort to gather relevant information and understanding if high-
priority preferences are at stake. On the other, questions that are unrelated
to preferences or affect only matters of low priority may well be answered
by what is commonly recognized as "wishful thinking."

SOCIAL INFLUENCES ON BELIEFS

The constitutive role of beliefs in the creation of social order instigates
social influences that shape cognitive ideas in multiple ways. This is especially true if these ideas are positively or negatively related to important
interests, strongly held values, and intense social attachments and aversions. At the simplest level, much depends on *perceptions of agreement
and dissent* by others. A given view is supported and strengthened if relevant others hold the same belief. It is challenged by a sense of being isolated from opinion prevailing among people and groups that matter.

    References to the beliefs of others shape ideas in a complex manner.
The most important variations seem to derive from how different views
are distributed across people's immediate and more distant group affilia-

---

[12] Max Weber, perhaps inspired by personal experience, noted this in the very introduction of the concept of a communal relationship (*Gemeinschaft*): "There is, for instance, a
wide variation in the extent to which members of a family group feel a genuine community
of interests or, on the other hand, exploit the relationship for their own ends" (Weber 1922/
1978, 41–42)

    If the belief in the harmony of interests favors the better-off members, its existence may
not be due to the interested manipulation of those who are disadvantaged; it could be an
unmediated expression of the sense of belonging; or the sense of belonging may instigate
the belief, which then is further nurtured by those who gain from it. The causal mechanisms
by which such beliefs come about, then, can be quite complex.

tions and from the way people and their relationships are embedded in the larger social structure. Aside from individual factors such as a person's past experience, the most important social causes of a person's ability to hold her own in a field of varied opinion are the support of close associates and the confidence and credibility that derive from what we might call "social certification." The latter includes not just formal certifications of competence but also informal attributions of ability and cognitive authority as well as the more diffuse validations that go with different positions in the structures of social inequality, especially in the hierarchies of social status.

Given a modicum of social support and social certification as well as an interest in holding on to one's views, the effect of the views of others may be quite modest. But the divergence may not be without consequence. Georg Simmel (1908/1955) advanced the ingenious idea that a person's position in a set of concentric social circles will engender solid and relatively simple ideas, both normative and cognitive, while a person who participates in very different milieus will display much more differentiated and individualized views. Elizabeth Bott (1957) found empirical confirmation of this hypothesis in her study of how opinions were related to contrasting configurations of social networks. Confronted with divergent opinions and not simply yielding to them, people often develop a much more thought-out repertoire of arguments than do those who never found their ideas challenged.[13]

The overall pattern of support and challenge by the views of others has an interesting implication: the more the actual diversity of opinion is transparent in a given social location, the more this diversity is encouraged and maintained. Conversely, if "deviant" ideas are not gaining publicity, are perhaps shamefully kept silent, or are driven underground by prevailing ideas, diversity is diminished if not necessarily extinguished. Strong thrusts of common opinion, such as the ideas that swept the United States after the Al-Qaeda attacks on New York and Washington, tend to diminish diversity of opinion, and this effect may extend well beyond the immediate focus of the new and newly empowered ideas. In the time after the 9/11 attacks it was not just the discussion of how to prevent or prepare for renewed terrorism that was constrained; greater conformity prevailed throughout political opinion.

The linkage of beliefs with values and norms has a consequence that goes beyond this dynamic of mutual validation and challenge in a given

---

[13] If hunkering down to a stubborn adherence to one's earlier views is a possibility as well, this reminds us of the need to spell out in great detail the conditions that separate alternative outcomes of similar causal mechanisms. My hunch is that in this case the strength/weakness of social support and the perceived chances of convincing significant others may be the most important factors differentiating the two hypotheses.

social sphere. It brings forth responses of *social control*. One may be
tempted to think of "thought control" as an extreme and rare phenomenon, but in fact it is the bread and butter of social life. It is clear on
reflection that social control is rarely content with shaping overt behavior.
Rather, overt behavior is often monitored not so much for its own sake
as with an eye to what it reveals about a person's "real" beliefs and commitments. This kind of subtle and deep-reaching social control is a critical
ingredient in most central processes of social life. Socialization—of children and of adults—is but one example. Social control is, of course, most
effective if it can count on some subjective receptiveness. Much social
control does not just come from the outside but can count on a readiness
to respond and comply.

A quite common, though extreme response to "deviant" ideas is to view
them as more or less pathological. Again, examples abound. Some beliefs
are simply seen as "crazy."[14] A penchant for optimistic assessments may
be denounced more mildly as wishful thinking, while an inclination toward pessimistic views may provoke—jokingly or not so jokingly—the
diagnosis of paranoia.

It seems useful to distinguish two forms of social control, one that is
intentional and self-consciously deployed, the other simply flowing from
the dynamics of social perception and interaction. In the first case, an
actor—perhaps occupying a position that requires such behavior—may
monitor the behavior of others for indications of beliefs and respond to
unwanted ideas with sanctions, ranging from "a good talking-to" to rede-
fining the relationship and possibly to exclusion and ostracism. The reactions are intended to change the beliefs and to keep others from being
influenced by them.

The second form of social control is a result of unself-conscious changes
in perception and behavior that are not inspired by any intent of correc-
tion. The holders of deviant beliefs just lose respect as well as affection,
which isolates them and lowers their influence. While it is less recognized,
this second form of social control is often more effective than the first. As
an analogous maxim has it: kids often learn more from what parents do
than from what they say.

Some ideas are more likely than others to be subjected to control attempts. The control of social knowledge will be the stronger, the more

[14] In 1954 McGeorge Bundy, then Harvard's dean of the Faculty of Arts and Sciences,
asked Robert N. Bellah, then a graduate student working with Talcott Parsons, to have his
mental health examined because, he explained, some members of Harvard's governing body,
the Corporation, thought that people who had been Communists must be crazy. Bellah
had been a member of the Communist Party in 1947 through 1949 and was, during his
undergraduate years, a leader of the university-recognized John Reed Club devoted to the
discussion of Marxism at Harvard (Bellah 2005).

important the ideas in question—important, for instance, in terms of shared values and of common enemies; more generally, important in the eyes of those with more influence, authority, and power.

The "social realities" created by social influence and social control often have, once established, their own momentum. Not only are they often associated with a lack or weakening of reality testing; but, as noted, they also tend to constitute unexamined frames, in which new information is ordered and interpreted. This is a major mechanism that stabilizes beliefs. It gives the dynamics of cognitive ideas an interesting historical dimension. Once formed in a certain constellation of concerns, interests, influences, and pressures, beliefs often remain stable despite changing circumstances, reflecting past rather than present conditions. This persistence is an instance of a quite pervasive feature of social life that technically has come to be known as "path dependence" (Mahoney 2000; Pierson 2000).

Such mechanisms engendering continuities over time are, however, counterbalanced by others that increase openness toward change. One of the major factors introducing greater openness is generational turnover, especially if it goes along with intergenerational differences in education. Another source of support for openness is the knowledge institutions we will examine below. They are characteristic of modern societies and have collectively been diagnosed as an "institutionalization of change."

It is clear that the impact of social factors on ideas about reality may well induce distortion and illusion, though this is not necessarily the case. We have noted the obvious fact that looking to the opinion of others may be realistically enlightening. Similarly, schooling in physics, geography, and biology involves the social control of ideas as much as does indoctrination in a beautified version of national history. But quite clearly social pressures are often motivated by concerns other than the truth. And they may be powerful indeed even if they advance distortion and illusion.

We also must not overlook that in quite a few instances beliefs that are false or exaggerated have results that many find desirable. Unrealistic confidence in the success of a common undertaking may contribute to that success. A sense of futility, which often inhibits the initiation of collective action owing to the uncertainty of spontaneous cooperation, may not arise if many potential participants falsely believe that cooperation is no problem. Norms, as we will see later, are more easily maintained if the extent of actual deviance is not known.

But if on the one hand realism may potentially be overwhelmed by noncognitive concerns and pressures, it may also be effectively protected by norms about personal integrity and the respect for truth. The strength of these opposing forces varies considerably across different situations, milieus, and cultures. We may gain some insights into how the potentially conflicting factors shaping belief formation can be reconciled if we now turn in the final section of this chapter to a brief consideration of the role of institutions and organizations in the dynamics of cognition. Both formal organizations and institutional structures may be seen as sorting devices that can limit the contradictions arising from different mechanisms determining the formation of beliefs. Beyond that, they are important in the creation, storage, and diffusion of knowledge.

INSTITUTIONS AND ORGANIZATIONS OF KNOWLEDGE

Complex organizations, when compared to individuals and small groups, have critical advantages in the gathering and processing of information. This has well-known conditions that are well understood even if not always fully realized: adequately trained specialists give full-time attention to their pursuits; their efforts are systematically coordinated with each other; and they respond to well-tailored incentive systems. Specialization and a universalist outlook are key here, and their implications are perhaps not altogether obvious. Specialization allows for a sharp focus on one or a few matters of concern, shutting out others, including personal preferences and attachments.[15] It therefore can separate cognitive pursuits from value concerns and material interests, set aside some of the motives underlying wishful thinking, and protect against outside efforts of social control. A universalist orientation, one which concentrates only on features of a situation that are germane to the goals pursued, and which abstracts from the particulars that are not relevant, is shared by officials of formal organizations as well as scientific observers. This analytic disposition is built into the very structure of formal organizations. For these reasons, all formal organizations—not only those primarily concerned with the creation and dissemination of ideas and knowledge—can be powerful mechanisms of information gathering and processing. This is why Max Weber could claim that "bureaucratic administration means fundamentally domination through knowledge" (1922/1978, 225).

The advantages of complex organizations over individuals and small groups are not, however, without limits. These advantages are greatest in

---

[15] Generally, focusing on one or a few matters of concern facilitates rationality as it permits the neglect of broader consequences of the means chosen to reach a given goal. This is the precise obverse of the major condition of traditionalization that we discussed briefly above. Traditional action is reasonable if several different persistent issues—each with its own optimal solution that may well be inconsistent with those of other matters of concern—have to be dealt with within a single social arrangement, such as family and kin groups in agrarian societies.

systematic information gathering for given purposes and in generating theoretical knowledge. They are weakened if the purposes at hand are contested. And they diminish radically when it comes to information about diverse local conditions and to the understanding of complex interdependencies that vary from place to place. Thus Friedrich von Hayek (1939, 1945) has argued that competitive markets provide information about the local incidence of scarcity, demand, and supply in a way that cannot be replicated in centrally planned economies. And in *Seeing Like a State* James Scott (1998) contrasts the complexity and accuracy of local understandings underlying practical knowledge to the simplifying "commercial and fiscal logic" that disregards the local constellations of particular phenomena.

Highlighting the advantages of complex organizations also does not deny the importance of singular individual achievements, such as those of Albert Einstein, whose innovations revolutionized physics, or of Max Weber, who offered new comprehensive social science perspectives building on a unique synthesis of the historical and comparative historical research that had accumulated during the nineteenth century. Yet limited as they may be, the potential cognitive advantages of formal organizations are significant. This is especially true if we allow for important variations in the structure and the functioning of organizations rather than stick to a caricature of Prussian or French bureaucracy as the only form available.[16]

Many organizations are specifically concerned with knowledge; they are devoted to its creation as well as to its diffusion in educational systems and in the mass media. Some of these organizations embody a sharp concentration on cognitive exploration and the transmission of knowledge. Others give equal or greater emphasis to the cultivation and inculcation of values, even as they also are concerned with social and political analysis and/or the transmission of knowledge; these include general schools as well as think tanks of various kinds and organizations concerned with promoting one or another ideology. Still others, such as religious organizations, are more concerned with norms, values, and nonempirical ideas, though they, too, may include a concern for social knowledge as well. The superior capacity in knowledge creation, the cultivation of ideas and their transmission, which these normatively oriented organizations share with

---

[16] To recognize the diversity of organizational forms is a central accomplishment of twentieth-century research on formal organizations in American sociology and economics. Arthur Stinchcombe (1990) has made a most original contribution to the understanding of organizations as information processing systems, in which he argues and demonstrates that different problems of information and uncertainty give rise to different features of economic and other organizations.

other formal organizations, adds an important dimension to the issues of cultural hegemony.

A significant feature of modern societies is the institutionalization of knowledge creation. This means that knowledge creation, regulated by its own norms and values, is set off from other activities and concerns, protected against interference, and supported with endorsements of its legitimacy as well as substantial resources. If the implication that science needs protection sounds strange, this only underlines the effectiveness of the institutionalization of knowledge creation: its protection is taken for granted. On reflection it should be clear that any innovation disturbs the status quo and that, more specifically, advances in applied science and technology inevitably upset established work practices, change the value of skills and investments, and create winners and losers.[17]

Among the crucial features of the institutionalization of knowledge creation are the ways in which it is linked to education. The details vary across modern societies, but in all of them the creation of knowledge is closely associated with higher education for the elite. And lower levels of education are also, if less directly, informed by the advances made in systematic research. Both linkages create loyalties that are important for the protection of knowledge development. At the same time, it is clear that the inculcation of values has an important place in general education. This may lead to conflicts, and has done so repeatedly. For instance, conflicts about relative influence of religion and secular knowledge—of church and state—on education are found in many different countries.

Another social arrangement that indirectly adds to the legitimacy of unencumbered knowledge creation comprises the different institutional forms of structuring the delivery of expert services. Inherently, there is a *knowledge asymmetry* between experts and those whom they serve. At the same time, the matters experts have knowledge about are of great concern, both to their clients and to society at large. This means that experts are potentially dangerous. Arrangements that we label professions and professionalism deal with these dangers. These arrangements include not only the collective self-control claimed by the associations of market-oriented expert occupations but also the controls that private and public formal organizations exert over employed experts. There is some dispute about the extent to which these controls actually provide effective protection for clients and the related public concern, but that is a discussion that would lead us too far afield.[18] Both effective institutional forms of

---

[17] This was from the outset a major theme of the sociology of science; see Parsons (1951, chap. 5), Ben-David (1971), and Merton (1938/1968g, 1973).

[18] See Freidson (1970, 1988) and Rueschemeyer (1973, 1986), building on and responding to earlier work of William J. Goode and Robert K. Merton. For the purposes we

using expertise and exploitative evasions of real control build on the tendency to accord knowledge-based occupational pursuits respect and high standing, a tendency that seems to be a near-universal feature of prestige rankings across societies (Treiman 1977).

The creation of *social* knowledge represents a special case. On the one hand, it partakes in the broader institutionalization and protection of knowledge creation. On the other, it clearly does not enjoy the same degree of autonomy and freedom from "outside" influence and control. This is partly due to the fact that systematic social analysis is not radically separated from the common discourse on social, economic, and political problems. In contrast to the natural sciences, the questions informing social research problems are far less determined by the internal development of the discipline in question and instead are often shaped by political, economic, and social concerns in society. Furthermore, as noted earlier, comprehensive theory frames are often linked to ideological and philosophical components of worldviews. This, too, opens social and political analysis to "external" influence and control. An antidote of great importance is a sharp differentiation between the inevitably present elements of valuation and the more strictly cognitive concerns. Such differentiation does not eliminate the problem, but it allows for critical reflection and examination.

The importance of coming to terms with the value implications of social research is underlined by the fact that in all modern societies, ideologies are also institutionalized in various forms. This includes not only partisan ideological institutions but also those that are designed to cultivate, maintain, and replicate commonly accepted social values. Public discourse in the United States often sees the competition between different views and outlooks as a replication of economic markets, as is illustrated in the phrase "the marketplace of ideas." The implied optimism about the outcomes of such competition—the best idea, much like the best gadget, wins out—overlooks that the marketplace of ideas is radically different from the market for carrots and mousetraps. It is plagued by market failures that are above all rooted in pervasive knowledge asymmetries and in dif-

---

pursue in this volume, approaching issues in the manner indicated suggests an observation about theory construction. Absent a theory of the professions in the narrow and demanding sense of theory, identifying common problems and alternative solutions represents a significant intermediate step. The basic *generative problem* indicated above is this: how does one design institutional arrangements for the use of expertise, a matter fraught with some dangers? The different views of the professions—emphasizing individual and collective self-control or controls by private and public "third parties"—point to different and differently effective responses to the same problem. The primary question, then, generates further, more specific and detailed problems, corresponding to the particular interests that are deemed worthy of protection and to the vulnerability of different kinds of clients.

ferential influence. Those with disproportionate resources and influence will support certain ideas and help them win acceptance, while neglecting or denigrating others.

The ensemble of all the organizations of learning, including those primarily concerned with the cultivation of social values, define the knowledge horizon of a social formation. Inevitably, the knowledge that is in principle available is accessible to different groups and categories of people only in highly variable fashion. At the same time, individuals, small groups, local milieus, and larger segments of society, which are characterized by mutual loyalties, often insulate themselves—defensively, as it were—against a good deal of the thinking that is on offer.

CONCLUSION

Jointly, two central ideas about the dynamics of belief formation give us a theory frame for understanding people's ideas about social reality. Cognitive beliefs are critical for attaining individual and collective goals. And they are elements in the constitution of social order with its multifarious components—roles, collectivities, institutions, and definitions of difference and antagonism. These outcomes can be considered "functional contributions." What brings such contributions about? A combination of interest and reality testing is at the heart of the generation of realistic knowledge, though that process is fraught with difficulties and with gaps that allow for distortion and illusion. The more comprehensive interdependence model, with its dual reference to realism as well as to the role of beliefs in constituting social structures and processes, adds social influence and social control as major factors. The broader model sees potentially conflicting factors as central to belief formation: interests in realism as well as deception interact with people's reference to the beliefs of others, with the social control of ideas, and ultimately with the support ideas receive because of their constitutive roles in accepted social patterns and processes.

The impact of the opinions of others and of their efforts to bring beliefs into line with strongly held views and values can be crude and very effective. Yet all societies have some arrangements that modulate these pressures. All have different role expectations—from age roles to experts—that encourage realism, independence, and innovation. Since the high cultures of antiquity powerful institutions have enabled and honored the cultivation of knowledge in the more complex societies. Modern societies have built on these traditions and created institutions for empirical inquiry that are protected against social interference, though the effectiveness of these protections varies across political-economic systems, over time, and according to the sources of outside pressures. They are not fool-proof anywhere; but they do make a critical difference.

I am convinced that the comprehensive model combining pragmatic utility and the congruence of ideas with the dynamics of social cohesion and antagonism is a strong and fruitful framing template for empirical consideration of the knowledge of actors. The model of doubly engaged cognition—together with some of its specific implications spelled out above—can improve our ability to develop hypotheses, devise appropriate measures, and interpret results in a way that gives full due to the variability in the perception and understanding of relevant situations, and that goes beyond such tropes in common use as "wishful thinking," "group think," or "emotional illusions."[19]

Yet while we identified a number of specific mechanisms accounting for realism, distortion, and ignorance, the picture will become more detailed, more complex, but also clearer once we have considered norms, preferences, and emotions in the chapters that follow. All four dimensions of social action are interrelated with each other, all jointly shape the actions to be explained, and all are needed for the understanding of social order or structuration—order in the comprehensive as well as in the small-scale and fragmented sense, order in the sense of social cohesion as well as of persistent conflict, and order as states of equilibrium or as persistent patterns of change.

[19] The theory frame outlined may well need another qualification. The utilitarian character of the rational action model overlooks something that ought to be obvious to academics, and the interdependence model does not remedy this omission—the search for knowledge for its own sake. This search costs time and effort, but these costs are often not justified by pragmatic urgency. More generally, the premises of rational action theory omit two important features of human nature—the significance of curiosity and play (e.g., Johan Huizinga's *Homo Ludens*, 1944/1970). Idle curiosity and play seem to be built into the human gene equipment. This points to questions that go beyond pragmatic utility and the cognition–social structuration nexus. One could extend the theory frame by building more on recent advances in neurology and evolutionary biology.

Chapter IV

NORMS

Norms are pervasive in human social life. Any behavior that is relevant to others tends to be covered by norms. There is no organized social life of any kind without norms. This is true in respectable society as well as outside it: There is honor among thieves; there are norms regulating gang life in city slums.

In particular, norms regulate behavior people consider important; but norms are by no means confined to morally significant matters. Norms may stand against cruel treatment of the elderly, rule out cheating in business transactions, urge people not to be free riders in common undertakings great or small, obligate family members to seek revenge for offenses against kin, regulate the appropriate dress and behavior at social gatherings, or define a smirk during a friendly conversation as obnoxious.

Norms are—in a common understanding of the concept—expectations about how people *ought* to behave in defined situations; when not met, they elicit disapproval and some form of sanction even from "third parties," from people who do not have a direct interest in the behavior. It is the "ought"-character of norms that makes them part of the internal dimension of action. Even though its intensity varies greatly across different kinds of norms, "oughtness" implies the suggestion—and often creates the presumption—that actors accept the norm subjectively.

While norms are defined by reference to behavior, it is in fact not uncommon that people care about behavior primarily because it indicates a state of mind. What norms then intend to influence are attitudes and beliefs, for instance how serious a person is about the values related to a set of norms. Insulting words often matter most because they are taken to reveal an underlying hostility or lack of respect.

Norms are central to social and political analysis, first, because—and to the extent that—they influence behavior. At the same time, norms are of particular interest to the present inquiry because they interact with beliefs, preferences, and emotions, the other components of the internal dimension of action. Norms are also critical for an understanding of wider social structures and large-scale social change. Specifically, they are a crucial ingredient of social institutions. Institutions such as marriage, the economic complex of property, contract, and incorporation, or the institutional template of scientific inquiry are sets of rules that regulate significant areas of life and create a measure of predictability in them.[1]

If norms are important, one must not assume that they fully determine what they seek to regulate. People are not puppets in the hands of a player named normative culture. A famous essay by Dennis Wrong attacked that "oversocialized conception of man," and others followed him in this criticism (Wrong 1961; Blake and Davis 1964; Granovetter 1985). Renewed questioning about the sources of nonconforming behavior and closer attention to activities, which do not much respond to normative expectations aside from taken-for-granted background norms, are certainly welcome. Yet it has always been recognized that norm-conforming behavior must not be taken for granted. In fact, norms would hardly exist if the behavior they prescribe were not in question.

I will seek to answer questions that arise from these preliminary considerations: Where do norms come from? What makes them stable and what undermines them? And what makes them effective?

Two critical questions suggest themselves when norm-based approaches to social analysis are seen in tension with rational action theory: How do norms and their influence on behavior relate to the effects of incentives and disincentives appealing to the actors' interests? Can norms be explained because they are instrumental for collective goals? Twenty years ago, Jon Elster posed a strong challenge: rational choice theory as defined by neoclassical economics, he claimed, will be "dethroned" only if alternative theories are effective enough to replace it. Specifically, he questioned whether "sociological theory comes up with a simple and robust theory of the relations between social norms and instrumental rationality. . . . one can't beat something with nothing"(1986, 27). I hope to show that it is possible to formulate a reasonably simple and coherent theory frame about the origins and the strength of norms. At the same time, major questions about the relation between norms and instrumental rationality remain open.[2]

---

[1] In this chapter, norms as a major component of the internal dimension of action stand in the foreground; but even though macroanalysis is the main subject of the second part of the book, this chapter will also prepare the understanding of norms as a critical factor in social structure and social change.

[2] Elster specified the desiderata further: The explanatory propositions should be neither ad hoc nor persuasive only ex post. The propositions should specify the conditions and the limits of norms overriding rationality. They should spell out the conditions for strong and stable norms as well as the conditions under which norms yield to the pressure of self-interest. And they should identify the processes that undermine the operation of norms so much that they can be violated without psychic costs (Elster 1986, 24–25). It must be noted that a corresponding set of desiderata for rational action theory would demand more than that body of ideas has delivered so far.

Before we turn to questions about the effectiveness of norms and their creation, it seems useful to consider a feature that is characteristic of many norms. This is the strong and ubiquitous tendency for different norms to form patterns or clusters. As we will see, such clustering has noteworthy consequences for the stability and effectiveness of norms.

Another preliminary consideration might be the distinction between different types of norms, such as between conventions and moral norms or between legal and nonlegal norms. However, since a full-scale typology of norms would lead us very far afield, I will try to introduce certain critical distinctions only as they become important for specific arguments.

Clusters of Norms

A first form of clustering is critical for enforcement. Norms that are considered important are typically backed up by norms urging sanctions. "Don't do x!" is supported by "Criticize people who do x!" Often the second injunction is directed to specific kinds of people, parents for instance. And this specificity adds to the effectiveness of both norms.

This linkage is of some theoretical consequence because norm enforcement often seems to lack the rewards that would make it worthwhile for bystanders to get involved. There may be psychological answers to that puzzle. Following Nietzsche, one may see resentment of deviant behavior as a powerful motivator for enforcing norms, and recent experimental research dealing with the particular issues of cooperation and free riding suggests that free riding provokes strong emotions, which make sanctioning intrinsically rewarding. In fact, these reactions may have an evolutionary base.[3] On the social level, however, norms urging sanctions seem an important part of the answer, especially if they clearly allocate responsibility for monitoring and sanctions.

A second clustering of norms comprises sets of rules in which some are specifications of others. For instance, the injunction that heads of households should be prudent with the household's economic resources entails a number of specifics—they should not gamble, should not drink, and the like. A master rule behind the norm to be a prudent householder might be "Be rational, especially with things that matter and that are amenable to rational ordering." Often, specific injunctions follow from several more general norms at once. Thus the specific injunctions to be a prudent householder derive from norms against wasteful nonrational

---

[3] On the problems of sanctioning free riding, see Heckathorn (1989); on the recent experiments see Fehr and Gächter (2002), Fehr and Fischbacher (2002 and 2004), and DeQuervain et al. (2004). Hedström (2005, 151–52) offers an instructive discussion.

behavior; against addictive behavior, however delectable, and against taking unreasonable risks, however enticing.

A similar relationship often obtains between norms and values. If values—conceptions of what is good and desirable—are consonant with norms, they turn norms into obligations with a moral character. Values legitimate norms, while norms spell out what a value entails specifically. Values often urge norm-conforming behavior independent of considerations of advantage. It is the link between norms and values that gives substance to the "internalization" of norms, their subjective acceptance as binding. And it is this acceptance that makes norms an important component of the internal dimension of action.

The role of values in social life has been a major theme in twentieth-century sociology. And it has been a bone of contention. Shared values were the major point of reference for Parsons's theoretical strategy, while conflict theory claimed that this strategy neglected discord over values and played down the motivating power of material interests. We can here leave this divergence of metatheories aside and acknowledge

- that societies often are deeply divided over values and their relative importance;
- that material interests have great motivating power, in many constellations surpassing the effect of value commitments;
- but also that values may be shared across deep divisions of interest;
- that the concordance of norms with values—or their disjunction from them—makes a profound difference for the subjective acceptance and internalization of norms; and
- that this concordance or disjunction also affects their effectiveness and stability on the social level.

A closely related linkage raises similar, but analytically different issues. Certain norms serve to mark and substantiate social identity and belonging. One may be tempted to treat this link between norms and attachments simply as another instance of the norm-value linkage. Similar to values, attachments induce personal acceptance of norms and thus anchor norms in the internal dimension of action. But aside from the value given to identity and social belonging as such, issues of attachments may not involve other values, or such values may be invoked only in a peripheral way. Consider why middle-class parents may fight with their children over tattoos or rings pierced into lips and eyebrows. Adopting these bodily ornaments is in itself of little moral consequence. If it arouses powerful emotions, it is not because profound values are at stake, but—so a reasonable interpretation holds—because the conflict over rejection or acceptance is a struggle over symbolic redefinitions of social attachments—

between parents and their children and between adolescents and their nonkin peers who may represent otherness to the parents.[4]

Attachments may be at odds with values, for instance with ideals of objectivity in viewing "one's own," as we have seen in the discussion of knowledge, or with values urging fairness to strangers. In turn, attachments and value commitments may be mutually reinforcing; and this is often the case. Yet distinguishing the norm-attachment linkage from the norm-value nexus is not a matter of analytic pedantry. It enables us to appreciate better the very powerful effect attachments can have on norms as well as on the other components of the internal dimension of action.

All of these interrelations—interrelations among norms as well as linkages between norms and values and between norms and attachments—are greatly relevant for the stability and effectiveness of norms. When we want to understand conforming and nonconforming behavior as well as suspensions of norms, allowable exceptions, and, more broadly, change in norms, we cannot just confine our attention to a particular norm of interest but must also take account of its interrelations with other norms as well as with values and attachments. The overall pattern may reinforce the norm in question strongly, may add only minimally to the persuasiveness of the rule at issue, or, if it is internally inconsistent or in a state of dilapidation, may even detract from that persuasiveness.

A third clustering of norms has gained particular prominence in sociology: the configurations of rules that define social roles and role sequences. These identify the most prominent intersections between wider social structures and individual lives. Roles have, of course, significant nonnormative components. The roles of foreman, teacher, or parent and the role sequences represented by socialization in the family, in school, and in later life involve common practices, accepted understandings, as well as shared concerns and emotional commitments, even if there is also dispute and conflict about these constitutive elements of roles. In varying measure, different roles also leave room for individual variation and creativity. But the norms defining the limits of acceptable variation in fulfilling a role are an important—and for many purposes the decisive—part of the concept.

Roles articulate major relations among a defined set of actors. They circumscribe how their practices and interests as well as their rights and obligations fit together. They typically make the immediate interaction partners or specific others responsible for monitoring and sanctioning. And they represent widely understood, if also possibly contested ideas

---

[4] I will return to the intertwining of identity and attachments in chapter 13, which treats social identities as structural patterns, patterns of socially recognized membership.

about the importance of the goals and practices involved—of educating children, of getting production jobs done, of maintaining law and order, or of administering a large organization.

At the same time, the clustering of norms around a role insulates the responsibilities of that role from other obligations. For example, in the American South during the twentieth century it separated what one had to do as school superintendent or as general of the National Guard from one's inclinations and obligations as a member of the white majority, when federal authorities pressed for school integration. That these official organizational roles were shielded from regionally prevailing sentiments was critical for effective school desegregation.

Socialization as a *sequence* of roles is an even more complex clustering of norms. It has consequences broadly similar to those just noted for roles—fostering internal consistency of component norms, mutual articulation of norms among role partners, allocation of responsibility for monitoring and sanctions, and avoidance of norm contradiction by insulation.

Insulating the process of socialization often takes the form of physical isolation from others. This limits the disturbing influence of others who are not under the same regimen of socialization. A specific hypothesis holds that the more important the goal of a socialization process is considered by its designers and supporters and the more it differs from the possibly contaminating behavior of others, the more often this mechanism is used. Examples are the induction into a religious order, military boot camp, the old college in the woods, and residential colleges in general, but also the insulation from "bad influences" respectable parents provide for their children.

Finally, there are the norm complexes we call "institutions." These will be the subject of a separate chapter. Suffice it to note here that since institutions control, regulate, and sustain major spheres of social life, they often have broad constituencies that consider their integrity important and support strong enforcement.

Common to all of these clusterings is that the component norms, values, and attachments may—and often tend to—give each other mutual support. Turned around, this conclusion points to the destabilizing effects that result from contradictions among norms, values, and attachments. Avoidance of such inconsistencies and shielding against contrary influences is often supplemented by allocation of responsibility for monitoring and sanctions. In other words, the frequently recurrent clustering of norms entails a number of causal mechanisms that give norms stability and help secure compliance or, alternatively, foster change and facilitate structured deviance in the face of norms.

EFFECTIVENESS OF NORMS

Any discussion of the effectiveness of norms has to take off from a clear recognition that norm violations are pervasive. Emile Durkheim made it an axiom that crimes and other behavior violating norms exist in any society, that violations of norms are "normal." They are normal both in the empirical sense that they are found in all known societies and in the theoretical sense that a society without crime and other violations of norms is inconceivable. A society without deviant behavior would require complete consensus on norms, equal commitment to these norms among all its members, and an absolute uniformity of individual conscience and consciousness. These conditions are at odds with the necessary conditions of social life, even in the simplest and normatively most homogeneous societies (Durkheim 1895/1950; see also Phillipson 1971).

Robert K. Merton built on this Durkheimian theorem, restating it in the language of functionalism: "Strict and unquestioned adherence to all prevailing norms would be functional only in a group that never was: a group which is completely static and unchanging in a social and cultural environment which is static and unchanging. Some (unknown) degree of deviation from current norms is probably functional for the basic goals of all groups" (1968h, 236).

More specifically, Merton developed the concept of "institutionalized evasion" of norms. This coexistence of norms and tolerance for deviation is likely to emerge, he argued, where "practical exigencies" (a notion presumably including accepted considerations of utilitarian advantage and disadvantage) make strict conformity with norms difficult, especially where new norms stand against "deep-rooted norms, sentiments and practices," and where individual differences in capacity and training require exemptions. Some measure of such permissiveness "enabl[es] the social structure to function without undue strain" (1968i, 372, 397, 398).

What, then, can be said more systematically about the forces that shape norm-conforming and nonconforming behavior? We know quite a bit about which major factors affect compliance and noncompliance; we know less about how they interact with each other; and we know least about threshold points beyond which the effect of a relevant condition increases or decreases significantly.[5]

---

[5] A good deal of work on compliance and noncompliance with norms was done by law scholars and criminologists. (see, e.g., the compilations of Friedman and Macaulay [1969, 1977]; or the more recent essay by Posner and Rasmussen [1999]). Despite its obvious importance for central claims of their discipline, this work has long been neglected by sociologists; but there were important exceptions (e.g., Geiger 1947/1964; Chambliss 1966, 1967; Opp 1973; Black 1976).

It's useful to begin with a simple utility calculus. Here an actor compares her gains from deviance with the expected negative sanctions and the forgone rewards of conformity and opts for the behavior that is on balance most "profitable." An example might be parking in a no-parking zone if the expected fines do not exceed the price of legal parking. The utility calculus gains broader applicability if not only material gains and losses are considered but other interests as well, such as a concern for one's reputation. Both come together, for instance, if companies, tempted by the gains of unlawful behavior, also consider the effects on their brand reputation. In this broadened form, the model of a utility calculus roughly fits a wide variety of practices, especially "instrumental" activities that seek to attain given goals by rationally examining the situation and choosing the least "expensive" means.

Yeheskel Dror (1959) has suggested that instrumental actions such as commercial activities conducted in an emotionally neutral way are more amenable to alteration by legal rules and sanctions than are "expressive" actions that are grounded in established traditions and strongly held values.[6] The closer the practices targeted by legal norms approach the pure type of rational action, the more they will respond to legal sanctions, provided that the sanctions are predictable and strong enough. This has the remarkable consequence that specifically modern spheres of social life—above all, market behavior and acting in formal organizations—are most open to legal regulation. True, powerful actors in these areas may successfully fend off legal regulation and its enforcement; but such preventive action becomes important to them precisely because instrumental action is specifically "vulnerable" to control by means of the law and its sanctions. Conversely, "expressive" behavior patterns such as gender and family roles that are valued in themselves, supported by strong emotions, and secured by effective nonlegal norms will be far more resistant to legally induced change.

This distinction of two polar types of target behavior helps explain, as noted before in chapter 1, why Soviet policies of "modernizing" gender roles in central Asia for long did not succeed, even though the Soviet authorities had a huge advantage in political power (Massell 1974); they

[6] Talcott Parsons (1951) made the distinction between "instrumental" and "expressive action-orientations" central to his outline of social system analysis. The definitions are in complex ways related to his "pattern variables," whose conceptual development took off from Weber's model of bureaucratic organization as contrasted with kin and family roles. He defined "instrumental" and "expressive" action in a highly abstract way—by the different relations between cognition of the situation and the goals of the actions in question: instrumental actions pursue set goals and give primacy to knowing how to reach them, while expressive activities take the cognitive definition of the situation as given and give primacy to concerns of evaluation and gratification.

directly confronted established forms of expressive behavior. By contrast, federal desegregation policies in the American South were at least initially successful because they concentrated on the instrumental behavior of public officials as leverage points.

Yet though it is widely applicable, the model of a simple utility calculus leaves out a set of interconnected factors that seem to have a decisive impact on compliance and noncompliance when we consider a wider range of target activities and situations. Specifically, this model neglects, first, in regard to norms, the dimension of "oughtness" that characterizes norms with variable intensity. It neglects, second, in regard to sanctions, the internal reactions of guilt and shame that become critical if norms are internalized. It neglects, third, with regard to the subjective calculus itself, that norms may well affect, once subjectively accepted, the very assessment of costs and benefits, enlarging the benefits of conformity and diminishing its costs. And in regard to different target behaviors it neglects, fourth, as already indicated, the wide range of "expressive" activities that are not easily amenable to a utility calculus. In each of these four issues what is neglected involves commitments to ideas about what is good and desirable, to values.

The "oughtness" of norms, their obligatory character, is by definition present in all norms, but it varies in intensity. It is minimally present in norms regulating parking, but it is intense in rules against child abuse or killing. The strength of the implied moral imperative affects the zeal with which violations are uncovered and sanctioned. And it is only when norms with an intense "ought"-character are violated that the moral order seems upset and that sanctions become symbolic actions which make the community whole again, as Durkheim famously noted (1903/1961; see also Phillipson 1971).[7]

The morally obligatory character of norms is closely related to their internalization. Once norms are subjectively accepted as more or less binding, the internal sanctions of guilt and shame enter the picture. Guilt and shame turn the actor into prosecutor and judge of her own actions as it were. And guilt and shame are highly emotionally charged and thus less amenable to a smooth cost-benefit calculus than are many external sanctions. As a consequence, their effects are harder to anticipate.

One may well be skeptical of how effective guilt feelings are by themselves, if they are not supplemented by the external monitoring and sanc-

---

[7] A sheer utility calculus, which blends out the "ought"-character of norms and its appeal to subjectively held values, is perhaps more common among actors in corporate roles, both private and public, than among people who act on their own account. Hannah Arendt has raised the possibility of a morally anaesthetizing effect of bureaucratic contexts in her account of the Eichmann trial (Arendt 1963; see also Baum 1981).

tioning of people who stand in meaningful primary and secondary relations to the actor. If attracted by substantial gains from deviant behavior,
many may be quite willing and able to set guilt feelings aside if they expect
their behavior to go unnoticed by others.

If this hypothesis can be sustained for a range of norm violations, it
underlines the special role of shame. Shame is an internal sanction as well,
but it is touched off by the actor's awareness that a deviating behavior
was noted by others. This may also bring about external sanctions, in
addition to the mere taking notice. Shame, then, combines external and
internal sanctioning. Here may be the explanation for what seems to be
its particularly strong influence on behavior.

It is noteworthy that shame reactions cover a wide range of behavior
and are not necessarily limited to morally important matters, as can easily
be illustrated by simple examples—from being observed while picking
one's nose to opting for a decoration of one's living room that friends
and acquaintances find ridiculous. The disapproval of meaningful others
is a strong component of the shame reaction. Possibly this, its attachment
dimension, is the reason why a strongly moral character of the norm is
less of a necessary condition for shame than for guilt.

If shame and guilt compromise the model of a simple utility calculus
because they do not fit easily into the additions and subtractions of cost-
benefit reckoning, it is also worth observing that the weight given an item
in this calculus is not independent of norms once they are subjectively
accepted. Illicit gains, if they are seen by the actors themselves as illicit,
may well decline in their utility. The effects of individual action that is
environmentally beneficent are often exaggerated. Thus the very cost-
benefit calculus is not independent of the norms about which it is sup-
posed to facilitate estimates of compliance.

And finally there are the varieties of "expressive" activities that are less
easily influenced by external sanctions. Gender relations, many tastes and
preferences (and not only addictive tastes), and dealings with others in
terms of the in-group–out-group dynamic, to offer a number of examples,
are not easily reordered by normative injunctions because they are themselves supported by norms, buttressed by emotion, grounded in multiple
social supports, and often rooted in the very personality of the actors.

The contrast between a utility calculation model and arguments that
detail the complications connected with value orientations of the actors
can be played down. Both can be joined together, if we are content with
identifying separately the rough effects of discrete factors in statements
of the "the more x, the more y" kind. One can even label guilt and shame
as "costs," though that does not make them any more easily comparable
to the material advantage and disadvantage derived from an action.
Whether such efforts at integration are denounced as "fudging" or ac-

cepted as the counsel of wisdom, the loss of clarity or the gain in complexity points to lacunae in our understanding.

Consider two sets of simple, "the more x, the more y" propositions. The first focuses on external sanctions, the second on the subjectively binding character of internalized norms.

For any norm, compliance is the more likely

- the stronger the expected negative sanctions for deviance,
- the greater the rewards of conformity,
- the lower the gains from deviance, and
- the less the norm is at odds with other norms and the positive and negative sanctions associated with them.

If it is reasonable to assume that the actors in certain circumstances can and will aggregate these different dimensions into a net judgment, these four propositions can be turned into one:

- compliance is the more likely the greater the net gain from conforming behavior.

Such aggregation, however, is the less feasible and the less helpful for prediction, the stronger the morally obligatory character of the norms in question, the greater the role of emotion in the assessment of partial utilities, and the more prominent the internal sanctions of shame and guilt. The reason is that it is more difficult—for actors as well as observers— to find a metric that permits comparing moral obligation and guilt with external gains and losses. This brings us to the second set of propositions, which takes off from the morally obligatory character of certain norms. Juxtaposed with the first set, it adds to it but also competes with it.

Compliance with a norm is the more likely

- the more the norm is internalized,
- the more external and internal reactions to deviant behavior push in the same direction (for this proposition, shame reactions seem a particularly important special case),
- the less the norm is contradicted by other norms of a more or less subjectively obligatory character, and, finally,
- the more the norm is compatible with—or even reinforced by— "expressive" behavior patterns that are grounded in strongly held values, buttressed by emotion, supported by strong social attachments, and well established over time.

It is hard to come up with generalizations about the interaction of these two sets of factors, even though it seems possible to develop plausible hypotheses for particular circumstances. One might, for instance, speculate that the CEO of General Motors was "shamed" into cutting his own compensation in half after he announced in the winter of 2006 the dismissal of tens of thousands of workers and prepared to ask the unions for large concessions. This happened against the background of a drumbeat of exposures concerning corporate wrongdoing as well as growing unease about decades of extreme increases in the compensation of the business elite, which was often unrelated to performance. Yet most such assessments of a particular event, even if they can be confirmed by closer examination, remain ex post explanations, and the scope of the underlying hypotheses—the range of their applicability to similar issues and thus their utility for prediction—typically remains uncertain.[8]

Still, it makes sense to examine specific circumscribed social patterns and issues in order to learn more about the interrelations between different motivations for norm conformity. We might do worse than taking another look at a passage from Max Weber's discussion of why staff members in systems of domination comply with the expectations they face, a passage already familiar from an argument in chapter 1:

> *Purely* material interests and calculations of advantages as the basis of solidarity between the chief and his administrative staff result, in this as in other connexions, in a relatively unstable situation. Normally other elements, affectual and ideal, supplement such interests. In certain exceptional cases the former alone may be decisive. In everyday life these relationships, like others, are governed by custom and material calculation of advantage. But custom, personal advantage, purely affectual or ideal motives of solidarity, do not form a sufficiently reliable basis for a given domination. In addition there is normally a further element, the belief in legitimacy. (1922/1978, 212–13)

Weber makes here a number of rough claims about the dynamics and interaction of different motivations for compliance. They indirectly illuminate issues of the effectiveness of different kinds of sanctions; and they may be applicable beyond the internal workings of systems of domina-

---

[8] This conclusion applies also to such ingenious and suggestive studies as Schwartz and Orleans (1967). Their project compared the views of taxpayers after one set was exposed to normative arguments about tax obligations, while another was made to consider the risks of tax evasion. Schwartz and Orleans compared the average tax returns in the years before and after the different exposures. Conscience appeals were followed by greater changes in declared income than were sanction threats. Interviews yielded interesting, though not conclusive results about attitudes, suggesting that there are complex interactions between the perceived risk of external sanctions and subjective normative reactions. Thus exposure to sanction threats was in some subgroups associated with *increased* normative attitudes about tax obligations, leading Schwartz and Orleans to develop the intriguing notion of *"inducing morality" through sanction threats.*

tion. First, purely material interests tend to be an unstable source of compliance in the face of changing satisfaction of these interests and varying challenges to norm conformity. Second, by themselves, ideal and emotional motivations, such as charismatic commitments, can be dominant in special situations. But they, too, are unstable though for different reasons—because they push aside and shortchange everyday interests that tend to reassert themselves. In routine situations, material interests combined with habituation and custom are dominant, though normally they are also supplemented by value-oriented and emotional dispositions. The background of both routine and exceptional situations includes in systems of domination coercive sanctions, such as jail or death for treason and even perhaps for lesser disloyalties, sanctions that Weber does not mention but takes for granted. Finally, Weber's argument culminates in insisting that reliable compliance of staff members with their role obligations in systems of domination requires also beliefs in legitimacy—a concordance of the organization and practice of rule with established values and their justification.

This last claim deserves further comment, since legitimation is easily misunderstood. Too often it is simply subsumed under ideal motives for compliance. Legitimacy beliefs, even if they remain to some extent official doctrine and are not generally embraced wholeheartedly, have a very peculiar effect. They seal and protect the other motivations. Without them, prudent avoidance of negative sanctions would look like cowardice; the pursuit of positive rewards would be hard to distinguish from greed and opportunism; idealistic commitment might be seen as emotional foolishness, and acting out of habit and custom as moral insensitivity. How profound these protective effects of legitimacy beliefs are, one could see in recent history, when political regimes and their ideological foundations collapsed and were replaced by a different order. Most discussions of these transitions focus on how the new institutions deal with the misdemeanors and crimes of the previous regime. Yet the moral reorientation of ordinary actors involved in that political system, a personal reckoning they have to accomplish in the continuing social ambience of their lives, is a matter of great difficulty and complexity. In many cases, only generational turnover can reconstitute a sense of moral normalcy.

Even with such insights from analyses of authority systems about some interrelations between different sources of norm compliance, it remains true that the two bundles of core propositions—set apart by the relative role of values, be it direct or indirect—are not supplemented by a systematic third set of hypotheses that would indicate how the different factors interact with each other, limit each other's effects, reinforce them, or just function in parallel juxtaposition. In the end, we are at a loss to pin down the conditions under which morally obligatory norms override the rational calculus of advantage or when, in turn, those norms yield to the pursuit of self-interest. Neither rational choice theory nor what one might call norm theory (though both are better understood as theory frames) is able to answer these questions with any precision.

It is possible, however, to augment the initial double set of core propositions with a number of fairly plain hypotheses, which do not overcome this duality but which importantly specify "secondary" mechanisms that strengthen or weaken the primary relations indicated.[9] I list only a sample of the many that have been advanced and are plausible:

- Sanctions are the more effective the greater the probability that they come about. As with the way people treat probabilities in everyday life, if the probability is very low, the sanctions are often disregarded; if it is very high, sanctions tend to be viewed as certain.
- Rewards have a stronger motivating effect than punishments, especially if the probability of the latter is not very high.
- The probability of sanctions, both positive and negative, is the greater the more visible the behavior in question.
- The probability of sanctions is the greater, the more responsibility for monitoring and sanctioning is allocated to particular roles.[10]

ORIGINS AND DESIGNS

Where do norms come from? As a rough approximation, we can distinguish three ways in which norms come into being. Norms can be imposed by a norm-giving authority or powerful people and groups. Norms can be created by cooperation. And norms can arise from the acknowledg-

[9] I borrow this format of primary and secondary hypotheses about norm compliance from early work of Karl-Dieter Opp on conditions for compliance with laws (Opp 1973). Opp, however, differs from the overall views on norm compliance expressed above (see also Opp 2001 and Hechter and Opp 2001).

[10] This constitutes, of course, one of the advantages of the criminal law. In fact, formal law is typically defined, following Weber, by its institutions in charge of monitoring and sanctioning. But anthropologists and students of law in simple societies have long pointed out that in some cultures, where those institutions are absent, certain figures may assume, with the consent of the wider community, an ad hoc enforcement role. Adamson Hoebel (1940) called these "champions-at-law." We have seen above that for nonlegal social norms there are often clear-cut allocations of responsibility for monitoring and sanctioning to specific roles, for instance to parents, teachers, and others in charge of socialization. In addition, community sentiment may make room for nonlegal equivalents of Hoebel's "champions-at law."

ment and normative "elevation" of a spontaneously emerging order of activities. If we simplify even further, we can distinguish norm creation from above and norm creation from below.

Imposition by a norm-giver is, of course, celebrated in many myths and quasi-historical accounts, such as those of Moses, Muhammad, and Solon. Yet imposition is also the normal mode of legislative norm creation in historical monarchies, modern authoritarian and totalitarian states, and—not least—in modern democratic polities. Majority rule, after all, imposes its will on the whole society, even though constitutional rights may protect smaller constituencies.[11]

Elementary reflection makes clear that nonlegal norms are often imposed as well, though in modern societies legal rules frequently form part of the background that makes the impositions possible. Families and other sites of socialization are obviously places where norms are routinely imposed on the young and untutored. Another large area where we encounter norms that are imposed by private actors on their subordinates is in employed work. Employers routinely stipulate a whole range of norms and standards.

Imposed norms can easily serve the interests of those who advance the rules at the expense of those who have to obey them.[12] This is, of course, not necessarily the case. Parents often care genuinely and effectively for the welfare of their children. And modern legal systems seek to limit discrimination and exploitation by insisting on the universalist application of legal rules to all people who find themselves in relevant circumstances—"nobody is above the law"—and by stressing the universalist principle also for the construction of laws and their interpretation. Nevertheless, wherever large power differences enter into the construction, interpretation, and application of norms, legal as well as nonlegal, there are significant opportunities for exploitation.

And exploitative norms stabilize what otherwise might remain an episodic form of taking advantage:

---

[11] Furthermore, well-placed activist minorities can succeed in swaying a majority of legislators, while a majority of those affected by the new norms pay no attention. And in countries with a constitution, the tiny minority of judges transform their reading of the constitution into rulings binding the society in important matters—rulings on abortion and rights to privacy, as for instance in the United States and in Germany (though with opposite results); on same-sex marriage, as in some U.S. states; and on limits to taxation of the poor, as in Germany.

[12] Imposed norms often do not apply—or do not apply in equal measure—to their sponsors. Coleman (1990) distinguished "disjoint" from "conjoint" norms: disjoint norms apply to actors other than their sponsors, while in conjoint norms the sponsors are affected by the rules as well.

Exploitative norms are far more than mere directives of the powerful. What is interesting about them is that once institutionalized, they become largely self-enforcing. Members of the weaker group ... tend to impose these obligations on themselves so as to reap maximum individual benefit in their social system. Because Chinese women with unbound feet were regarded as unmarriageable, foot binding was acceded to as the lesser of two evils. (Hechter and Borland 2001, 205)

Norms can also arise from spontaneously emerging patterns of action and interaction, patterns that over time come to be seen as a matter of rights and obligations. Repeated seating in a seminar room may lead to notions of "my seat" and "yours." More important, established usages of land often become recognized rights. And what a reasonable person would do in certain circumstances is used as a standard in much legal reasoning, a standard that clearly derives in part from the observation of common factual patterns.

Sugden (1986, 1989) has argued that *conventions*—established patterns of behavior without normative character—regulate people's actions not on the basis of collective choice and reasoned design; rather, they arise from conveniently adopted rules of thumb, such as the queuing principle of "first come, first served." These rules build on shared experience in the past as well as on analogies that ease the transfer of such pragmatic decision rules from one context to another. In many North American localities, an extension of the "first come, first served" decision rule has supplanted at four-way stop signs the official regulation, which gives the right of way to the car coming from the right. Once followed by more people than other conventions, these behavior patterns become a predictable guide to future behavior. If that predictability is frustrated, the convention may acquire a normative character—or else it may decay as a guide to behavior. Abstractly described, conventions understood as spontaneous order may seem a rather esoteric subject. But as Sugden, a British economist, points out, "the market itself is in many respects a spontaneous order" (1989, 86).

Cooperative agreement is a third mode of norm creation. This is most common in dense interaction patterns, as we will see in the chapter revisiting Homans's *The Human Group*. Every observer of a lively playground knows how kids improvise games with often complicated and continuously adjusted rules. Perhaps most famous in sociological research are the norms against overproduction that work groups in industry occasionally devise as a defense against employment rules they see as unfair or threatening.

None of the three forms is typically realized in pure form, though it is possible to find examples. Conventional decision patterns easily spawn normative expectations. Both cooperation and imposition often build on established practices and conventions and turn them into norms. Impositions frequently take their cues from cooperatively shaped norms and in a sense just firm them up; thus work rules often rely on older standards of craftsmanship that had a strong cooperative component. Cooperative agreement nearly always contains elements of imposition as it comes about with the help of subtle or not so subtle differences in power and influence. It rarely meets the standards of Habermas's uncoerced communication (1984).

If the myths of the past favor stories of imposition, softened by claims of divine sponsorship, modern models of norm creation typically build on cooperative agreement or at least a readiness to respond positively to norm proposals that solve a problem felt by all or most members in a group. The transition is perhaps marked by the story Hobbes invoked in his solution to the problem of order: an authoritarian order is accepted by people as the alternative to a life that otherwise would be nasty, brutish, and short. Latter-day rationalist accounts allow for more options than Hobbes's story does, but they often hold on to the notion that norms emerge—indirectly if not directly—with the consent of the governed and serve the interests of all or most.[13] Yet the ideas of consent of the governed and contribution to the common good derive their persuasive appeal from arguments as to what ideally should be the case; they do not necessarily throw a light on factual processes of norm creation and their explanation.

In the matter of consent, we may well agree that the extremes—imposition of norms by a few in their own interest and fully informed consent by all those subject to a norm—are virtually impossible. That leaves a wide range of realistic possibilities, which seem above all shaped by differences in power and influence as well as in information and insight.

The main problem plaguing the idea of norms enhancing the common good is that judgments of collective welfare are inherently nonempirical value judgments. No matter how advances in the common good are defined—as an increase in the satisfaction of some or many, while nobody else's utility is diminished (Pareto efficiency); as the greater satisfaction of the largest possible number of people (utilitarianism's criterion); as an improvement in the lot of those worst off (the principle of Rawls's *Theory*

---

[13] This is not true of all rational choice theorists. In a discussion of disjoint and conjoint norms, Hechter and Borland observe critically: "The individualist literature on the emergence of norms typically paints a rosy portrait. Time and again, it tells how previously unrelated individuals facing common problems or opportunities (or both) converge—under specific conditions, to be sure—to create norms that facilitate cooperative behavior" (Hechter and Borland 2001, 204).

of Justice, 1971)—there remain unresolved problems of measurement as well as underlying differences of judgment that reveal collective welfare as an "essentially contested concept" (Gallie 1955–56; Lukes 1974). Even if we could settle the question of what would enhance the common good, it seems clear that many norms are not at all oriented toward that goal. Norms, after all, can be and often have been used to protect raw privilege and to advance one-sided interests. The normative templates of slavery, many rules subordinating women, or norms regulating the involuntary service of soldiers in battles far removed from any conception of just warfare come to mind as obvious candidates for consideration.

Karl-Dieter Opp claims that "there is one basic idea that underlies all or at least most explanations of norms. This is the *instrumentality proposition* . . . norms emerge if their emergence is in the interest of a collective of people. Norms are thus instrumental" (2001, 10716). This is a broadly encompassing proposition. It can include—though this is not stated explicitly—one-sided imposition as well as cooperative agreement. It even claims as an instance of instrumentality, of a means-end relationship, the case of a norm that just expresses a strongly held value.

Insisting on the instrumental character of many processes of norm creation and norm maintenance points to an important causal mechanism. Many norms come into being and are accepted because they are *designed* to accomplish a purpose—to avoid problems and to advance toward goals. But this causal mechanism has complex conditions that are ill understood. The instrumentality proposition relies on people's having an accurate understanding of problems and solutions, which only rarely can be taken for granted. In fact, manipulating ideas about the roots of problems and the effects of proposed solutions seems a particularly promising way of winning *un*informed consent or at least acceptance. The proposition neglects, even if it does not deny, that different people and groups of people have different preferences and therefore are differently affected by the norms proposed. It also neglects that norms stand in complex relations to other norms, values, and attachments, and that these complexities put into question the usefulness of a rationalist model that concerns a single normative solution to specific shared problems. The instrumentality proposition does not come close to explaining norm creation in a general and valid way. It is one mechanism among several. Conventions, which are often turned into enforced norms, are instrumental only in a loose sense. As Sugden notes in concluding his argument: "These rules are not the result of any process of collective choice" (1989, 97).

Rationalist explanations—whether or not they are adequate to explain the emergence of norms—often fail to explain why norms persist beyond the initial conditions of their appeal. To explain, for instance, consumption rules and food taboos with hygienic considerations may or may not

make sense to those who sponsored the norms, but often does not elucidate why people hold on to them later. In turn, explanations that often
account for persistence of norms—appeals to ritual purity and pollution,
the will of god, the ways of our fathers, collective identity—are hard to
accommodate in rationalist accounts, because these explanations are
grounded in emotions and commitments that do not lend themselves to
assimilation into a cost-benefit calculus.

Given the fact that no organized social life exists without norms and
that norms tend to cluster, the emergence of many norms can be understood as a modification, an extension, or a delimitation of existing norms.
If one accepts this view, that norm creation is mostly a phase in a long
series of norm change, the question "Where do norms come from?" ultimately leads to speculations about the evolutionary origin of norms. It
seems indeed very likely that the human readiness to espouse norms and
to respond to them is interlinked with the evolutionary processes which
made for an exceptional flexibility of preferences and behavior, and which
at the same time created somatic bases for advanced cognition, reflection,
communication, language, and the development of fundamental norms
such as reciprocity.

If much norm creation in reality constitutes a modification of existing
patterns of norms, it seems appropriate now to turn to the question of
how norms change, and how specific norms decline and disappear. Quite
clearly, this is a wide-open field of issues, as norms stand in interaction
with the major factors that shape social life, ranging from changes in
environment and technology, through transformations in economic resources, structures of inequality, political organization, and the smaller-
scale life worlds, to cultural change in knowledge and values. A few highlights must suffice.

How Do Norms Change?

All norms need interpretation. This is as true of the commandment "Thou
shall not kill" (which may or may not forbid capital punishment or lethal
warfare) as it is of the constitutional rule against cruel and unusual
punishment or the injunction to honor and obey one's parents. Any glance
at the operation of the law, which more than nonlegal norms aims at
explicit and precise formulations, shows that continuous interpretation is
a major source of legal change, notwithstanding persistent admon-
ishments and protestations that the judiciary should "just apply the law."
Judicial transformations of existing law are especially noticeable in the
Anglo-American common-law tradition, where, for instance, a single
decision by Judge Benjamin N. Cardozo (*McPherson v. Buick*, 1916)

transformed product liability law as it expanded obligations beyond the immediately contracting parties of dealer and buyer and put the burden for injuries due to a faulty car on the manufacturer.[14] But lawmaking by judicial interpretation is inevitable in any legal system. And it has its analogues in nonlegal norms.

In an important sense, any enforcement of a norm, be it through praise and reward or through critique and punishment, implies an interpretation of the rule. The everyday equivalents of prosecutor, judge, and jury continuously interpret social norms. They define a norm's importance, give weight to degrees of conformity and deviance, disregard minor infractions or highlight them as part of a "slippery slope." In addition, sanctioning is often the occasion for explicitly stating the rule in a detailed and situationally specific way. Both of these quasi-judicial actions create the opportunity for norm change. Both are mechanisms that allow for smooth transformations of what the norm exactly mandates, and both can do so the more easily the more the change remains implicit and unannounced.

Whether such changes stay within a small social circle or reverberate more broadly depends on the visibility of the enforcement process in question and on the authority the sanctioning person commands by virtue of her role and status. The innovation may stay within the family or other particular social location; it may have influence beyond it because it appeals to others who confront a similar situation; it may be critiqued by disapproving third parties or accepted because of the moral capital of the innovator. Clearly, the allocation of monitoring and sanctioning obligations to particular roles, which we discussed earlier, can make a critical difference in the containment or broader spread of a given innovation.

A more explicit form of norm change often derives from conflict over rules. Changes in how the interests of different parties are affected by the norm and changes in their relative power may put the basic rationales of the norm as well as its specification and application into question. If norm change comes about as the result of conflict, it is likely to be clearly recognized and perhaps even fixed in writing. Changes in student power within the university as well as changes in the job market in the early 1970s induced such conflicts in Brown's Department of Sociology and led to a proliferation of written regulations for graduate study. Yet even written rules can lapse from institutional memory and be supplanted by practices at odds with them, unless there is a constant stream of cases to be decided.

---

[14] Among the many treatments of legal change by judicial interpretation, two books stand out in my view: Morton Horwitz (1977) analyzed how in the three generations before the Civil War judges fashioned out of earlier English traditions a law suitable for rapid development in a competitive capitalist economy. In a complementary analysis, Horwitz (1992) traced similarly dramatic judicial transformations of legal norms from the late nineteenth century onward.

At several points, we have encountered the impact social inequality has on the normative structure. This can hardly be overestimated in processes of norm change as well. True, the maxim "might makes right" is realistic only under exceptional circumstances. But the relative power of the parties is reflected in every shift of a norm's interpretation. Both the power differences and the interpretive changes may be small at any one point; yet they can amount to large effects if repeated often enough over time. As the old Latin proverb has it, *gutta cavat lapidem*—a steady drop carves the stone.

Why assume that norm change is pervasive and, in fact, inevitable? The reality of norm change is unquestionable. In any field of social life—be it family life, gender relations, interaction between different status groups, the obligations of employers and employees, or forms of dress—one has only to look back one or two generations (not to mention three or four) to see significant transformations of norms. Norm change is inevitable for complex and interdependent reasons. Thus changes in technology and in the material conditions of social life can transform the meaning of given norms and force a change in rules. With the advent of electricity, orthodox rabbis *had* to decide whether turning electricity on is the same as—or different from—making fire, and thus whether it should be forbidden or allowed on the Sabbath. Changes in the conditions of social life and related transformations in the understanding and the meaning of different social patterns put the rationales of many norms up for reconsideration. At the same time, these changes affect the ways in which different interests are impinged upon by various norms as well as the relative power with which these interests are pursued.

The clustering of norms, values, and attachments with which we began our discussion of norms makes a critical difference in the change of norms. One major effect of these complex interrelationships is to reduce the pace of norm change. The transformation or persistence of a given norm must not be analyzed in isolation. Attachments, in particular, seem to give norms robustness and stability.

At the same time, these interrelations make a substantive difference as higher-order principles give guidance and legitimation to the process of norm change. Thus higher-level norms or values may be retained when more specific norms are dropped. For instance, many liberal arts colleges retained in the 1970s a diffuse holistic responsibility for their students, while they relaxed specific norms about dormitory life that derived from older versions of this in loco parentis obligation and that now clashed with the insistence on gender equality. In different constellations, alternative higher-level norms may be summoned to ease the norm change. Thus ideals of responsible parenthood were invoked to justify birth control and abortion. Such reformulated or new patterns of legitimation not only are potentially decisive for the acceptance of norm change; they also may avoid or contain what might be the consequence of more abrupt norm change—damage to the wider moral order and to people's confidence in that order.

Concluding this discussion of norm change, we turn to a question that brings us back to the issues of the effectiveness of norms as well as their origin and design: under which conditions do norms decline and fail? Answering this question will largely detail points already made.

Norms will decay when lots of people find it difficult to meet their demands. At the same time, norms may be reinforced by the strong feelings of those who have sacrificed to be true to them. Still, norms begin to be questioned when many have trouble living up to them, especially when well-intentioned and "good people" have trouble living up to them. Who are "good people"? Those who have a reputation of strong moral character, a reputation that is often reinforced by—and perhaps even a mere reflection of—a respected status in the community. If people's difficulties with the norm in question are minor, and if the infractions can be concealed, norms may be adjusted along the lines of Merton's notion of "institutionalized evasion." This points to the social advantages of hypocrisy: the norm or value in question is upheld, while violations are to some extent tolerated.

By the same token, a norm is decisively undermined if "good people" break it publicly and get away with it. This quickly leads to the perception that "everybody does it," unless sharp status distinctions legitimate a double morality, as has long characterized gender relations or caste-like status differences.

The decay of a norm will be accelerated the more it is at odds with other norms and the less it draws strength from related norms, values, and attachments. Similarly, the decay will be hastened if those "in charge"—be it people in particular roles, such as parents or community leaders, or organizations with a normative mission, such as churches—withdraw their support, neglect to monitor and sanction violations, avoid public criticism, or, in the case of the state, remove criminalization (as, e.g., in regard to abortion or drugs).

Frequently, the tension between the demands of a norm and growing problems of compliance take a long while to build up. The decline and failure of the norm may in those cases constitute the rapid conclusion of a much longer process. This seems to be the explanation of the fairly sudden decline of birthrates in countries like Ireland.

CONCLUSION

Norms and values are a critical component of the internal dimension of action, together with knowledge, preferences, and emotions. As we proceed with this quartet of chapters exploring the internal dimension of action, we will learn more about the interrelations linking cognition, normative orientation, needs and wants, as well as emotions. In this chapter, I have also tried to go beyond the baseline of social action to lay the foundation for a better understanding of the role of norms in the formation and change of social structures.

Where does this discussion leave us? Norms often have a strong effect on how people behave. And this effect often goes beyond—and even against—the gains and losses anticipated from positive and negative sanctions associated with norms. What I could offer were more often useful orienting ideas and causal mechanism hypotheses with uncertain conditions than hypothetical propositions that were specific and definite enough to allow explanation and prediction. Rather, what emerged are, as in the case of knowledge, the elements of a theory frame, a frame that identifies central questions and that offers robust ideas about the origins and dynamics of social norms as well as about their effectiveness. The clustering of norms, values, and attachments and the links between norms and structured social inequality turned out to be of particular importance.

I have sought to bring together—both to confront and to integrate—a norm-oriented theory frame in the tradition of sociology with the theory frame of instrumental rationality emerging from elementary economics. Neither one nor the other can overcome the lack of definitiveness that is inherent in their frame character; but as theory frames they are in principle compatible with each other, formulating precise and important questions and jointly pointing to the most important factors relevant for answering them, even if these ideas are not specific enough to allow for explanation and prediction without further investigation of supplementary hypotheses. If our focus on the subjective dimension of action gives special emphasis to normative orientations that the rationalist frame has trouble accommodating, it does not at present seem feasible to integrate both approaches into a single frame or to replace one with the other.

Chapter V

PREFERENCES

Much less is known about preference formation than about the dynamics of norms and social knowledge. This, even though the subject has been of concern since the earliest reflections on human nature. It has been discussed under many different headings: instincts and other motives, needs and wants, interests, utility functions, desires, and tastes. Preferences tell us what people are after. They represent the relative value of different activities and outcomes to the actor—the value of goods and services available on the market, of achievements and outcomes without a market price, of material and immaterial satisfactions, as well as of gains forgone when a choice is made between alternatives. We have reason to think that preferences and their rank order are more variable than is implied by models of the rational pursuit of given ends. The actions we want to explain may be profoundly shaped by differences and changes in the ends people pursue.

Preferences can be inferred from observed choices. Samuelson (1938) argued for a "revealed preferences" approach. But such inferences are not without ambiguity. And, of course, they are pointless in the explanation of behavior since they were reconstructed from behavior. Social scientists can also study preferences by asking people to reflect on their choices and hypothetical alternatives.

Though difficult to ascertain, preferences are critical for understanding behavior. They define the costs and benefits of action that are at the core of a rational choice calculus. More generally, preferences drive behavior. They are not, however, the same as behavior (Sen 1973): Behavior and preferences are not subject to the same kinds of influence. Different combinations of preferences can result in the same choices. And preferences always face constraints in the situation the actors find themselves in.

The fact that solid knowledge about the formation of preferences is sparse has encouraged—especially in the field of economics—radically simplifying assumptions and strategies of analysis. Many economists treat preferences as given, leaving the study of their genesis to other fields.[1]

---

[1] Gary Becker went further and made the assumption that the basic preferences are universal across subgroups and societies, and that they are stable over time: "Since economists generally have had little to contribute ... to the understanding of how preferences are formed, preferences are assumed not to change substantially over time, nor to be very differ-

Furthermore, economic analysis commonly focuses exclusively on self-regarding preferences, treating the concern for the welfare of others as well as normative commitments—other-regarding and process-regarding preferences—as negligible factors.

While many may be willing to discount altruism in rough assessments of economic behavior, treating the regard for norms as negligible is surely less plausible. Without normative regulation neither production nor market exchange can function effectively. Economic competition would truly deteriorate into cutthroat struggle (Bowles and Gintis 1993). Whether strong profits are the result of cheating and stealing or of law-observing business transactions makes a difference even to the most passionate advocates of free markets.

Reasonable theory-strategic arguments have been advanced for each of the conventional assumptions of economics. And economics has achieved—partly owing to those assumptions—an analytic rigor unparalleled in the other disciplines of social knowledge. Yet each of these assumptions must be suspended and examined (though not in every case abandoned) if we want to develop a more realistic picture of social action across a wide range of situations and structural contexts.[2] This is especially urgent if economic analysis, understood broadly as the study of choice under conditions of scarcity, is extended beyond the realm of market exchange to virtually all areas of social life. But even in economics more narrowly conceived, major efforts have been made to revise the premise of self-centered preferences as exogenous givens. Recently, Ben-Ner and Putterman (1998) assembled an impressive array of economists and other social scientists seeking to broaden the consideration of motivations while retaining the analytic discipline that has been achieved with an exclusive focus on self-interest.

There is little doubt that human preference structures vary substantially. They are not stable across cultures and periods of history. They

---

ent between wealthy and poor persons, or even between persons in different societies and cultures. . . . The preferences that are assumed to be stable . . . are defined over fundamental aspects of life, such as health, prestige, sensual pleasure, benevolence or envy, that do not always bear a stable relation to market goods and services" (Becker 1976/1986, 110).

[2] "Economists have followed Hume, rather than Aristotle, in positing a given and self-regarding individual as the appropriate behavioral foundation for considerations of governance and policy. . . . the premise provides a common if minimal analytical framework applicable to a wide range of issues of public concern, it expresses a prudent antipathy toward paternalistic attempts at social engineering of the psyche, it modestly acknowledges how little we know about the effects of economic structure and policy on preferences, and it erects a barrier both to ad hoc explanation and to the utopian thinking of those who invoke the mutability of human dispositions in order to sidestep difficult questions of scarcity and social choice. Realism, however, cannot be among the virtues invoked on behalf of the exogenous preferences premise" (Bowles 1998, 102).

vary within a society across classes and other social categories. They vary individually by upbringing and life experience. And this variation pertains to the comparative valuation of different material goods, of material and immaterial interests, and—not least—of self-regarding, other-regarding, and process- or norm-regarding concerns.

Authors such as Rousseau, Marx, and Durkheim have made historical transformations in the needs and wants of people central to their theories. Durkheim insisted that individual and social consciousness is shaped by the structure of society and that preferences—or, in the old terminology, needs and wants—are not a suitable reference point for explaining social change since they themselves change with the changing social order. Marxist thought similarly emphasized that needs and wants differ across different modes of production, and that within a given society they are shaped by people's position in the class structure.

Scholarship documenting different preference patterns across societies that are associated with differences in social structure includes a study of "individual change in six developing countries" by Inkeles and Smith (1974), Inglehart's work on "cultural, economic and political change in 43 societies" (1997), an important recent literature analysis by Bowles (1998), as well as Cantril's earlier study of "human concerns" in twelve countries (1965).

Equally, and perhaps more important for much social research, there is also strong support for the view that preferences and ordered preference structures vary across different subgroups within the same society. Different consumption preferences of blue-collar and white-collar workers, pointing to a greater concern for status among the latter, have long been documented. Similar evidence emerges clearly in more recent studies (Bowles 1998). Among these, the long-term research project of Melvin Kohn and his associates stands out. It describes and explains differences in values and preferences associated with different occupational positions in the United States as well as other countries (Kohn 1969; Kohn and Schooler 1983; Kohn et al. 1990).

That the preferences and interests of people vary within the same society and that they vary not just at random from person to person but in systematic relation to people's position in society may seem a rather formal and fairly innocuous claim. But in fact it has far-reaching consequences. These findings put into question notions of consensus and social harmony we all too easily adopt. They question whether invocations of "the common good" have a solid foundation. They question the idea that a shared culture will successfully harmonize preferences. And they question claims that market exchange aggregates the variety of preferences in a noncoercive way (Rueschemeyer 1986, 44–46).

Nevertheless, critically assessing the prevailing simplifying assumptions does not yield much by way of theoretical guidance for dealing with preferences. I now turn to ideas that can become building blocks of a theory frame for the study of preferences.

If we ask what shapes preferences, there is no doubt that we first have to look at behavior dispositions grounded in the body. The needs for nourishment, for protection against the elements, and for the maintenance of health, as well as the desires for sensual pleasure and for sexual satisfaction clearly are rooted in the biological nature of human beings, even though these needs and desires not only have to contend with varying constraints of scarcity but are given a variety of shapes in different cultures and are subject to social regulation. Less obvious, but by now well established is another claim about the grounding of preferences in our biological nature—that *social* behavior dispositions are built into the shared gene equipment of human beings as well.

Richerson and Boyd (2005, 195) observe: "Human societies are a spectacular anomaly in the animal world. They are based on cooperation of large, symbolically marked in-groups." This anomaly cannot be explained, they contend, unless we assume that prosocial drives are part of the biological base of human nature. Such behavior dispositions are just that, dispositions; there is nothing deterministically automatic about them. But they create the potential for other-regarding and norm-regarding preferences.

There is a range of speculative reconstructions of the evolutionary developments that took place many millennia ago and that predate, at least in part, the emergence of *Homo sapiens*. Jonathan Turner (2002) offers in an intriguing conjecture that evolutionary changes in the neural endowment of savannah apes, which were not very sociable animals, gave rise to a configuration in human brains that dramatically increased the inclination toward interaction. This created a potential for cooperation and solidarity that—unique among the immediate evolutionary neighbors of the human species—gave *Homo sapiens* a critical advantage for survival and adaptation in varied environments.

Richerson and Boyd advance the appealing hypothesis of cultural and biological coevolution, in which social and cultural developments encouraged and reinforced biological change: "People are endowed with two sets of innate predispositions or 'social instincts'. The first is a set of ancient instincts that we share with our primate ancestors . . . enabling humans to have a complex family life and frequently form strong bonds of friendship with others. The second is a set of 'tribal' instincts that allow us to interact cooperatively with a larger, symbolically marked set of people, or tribe. The tribal social instincts result from the gene-culture co-evolution of tribal-scale societies" (Richerson and Boyd 2005, 196–97; see also Boyd and Richerson 1985). It is of critical importance that this postulated "tribal instinct" responds to symbolic markers, as that makes it capable of sustaining solidarity beyond small groups and kin relations.

We need not go into further detail on such explorations of the evolution of human nature to come to an important conclusion: a number of major kinds of preferences have a biological base. This includes undoubtedly self-regarding preferences; but other- and norm-regarding ones are almost certainly also grounded in biological evolution. And the same goes for two correlates of the inclination to respond to norms and to care for others—the concerns for status and respect, and for social bonding.

Certain social bonds stand out for their stability and powerful consequences; earlier I have called them attachments. The potential for such bonding seems to have an innate basis, even though it takes different forms across different cultures and subcultures. Some broad types are common despite such variation, if not necessarily universal: family and kin ties, love and strong friendship bonds, charismatic leader-follower relations, group relations of a specially intense solidarity (often, but not only found in groups that dissent or deviate from prevailing norms and understandings), many religious affiliations, and in modern societies the commitment many feel toward an ethnic group or nation of which they are a part.

The potential for certain preferences, then, is grounded in somatic behavior dispositions, in innate human nature. However, the actual preferences we encounter in different people, subgroups, and cultures are socially shaped. Complex social mechanisms are involved in this molding. The dynamics of preference formation cannot be understood through the consideration of individuals in isolation (Sen 1973).

Norms Shape Preferences

Normative regulation of preferences is pervasive. Consumption norms common in our own society illustrate this. First, there are legal and social prohibitions—don't consume illegal drugs; don't spend a sparse family budget on alcohol, gambling, or luxuries. Perhaps more important, there are also positive injunctions—give your children the best education you can afford; honor expectations of gift giving; generously celebrate weddings and other life events. For many, such obligations dictate major expenditures in their lifetime. Aside from specific dos and don'ts, there are standards about what should rank high or low in one's priorities, standards that legitimate some and delegitimate other preferences.

Norms about preferences vary a great deal across cultures. The factors underlying this variation are not well understood. They are likely to include different levels of wealth and its distribution, the scale of a society, the forms of division of labor and solidarity, and the diverse paths of long-term social and cultural development. But there are important constants in the regulation of preferences as well. The regulation of elementary drives—concerning sexual behavior, clothing, eating, housing—is universal across cultures and societies even though the particular forms of these rules vary greatly.

Many of the norms regulating preferences may be less sharp-edged in modern societies than in more traditional societies. The prescriptions and proscriptions may be less strictly enforced, and they vary across status groups that are more loosely defined. Yet they are powerful nevertheless. Where these norms are thoroughly institutionalized—broadly supported, backed by sanctions, and widely accepted by individuals—they themselves virtually become preferences. Paradoxically, they may then be less visible, as they are taken for granted and largely removed from conscious attention.

Does it make sense, one might object, to speak of normative regulation of inner states, of preferences and desires? Isn't the idea of normative regulation best confined to behavior? In the biblical Decalogue, the injunctions about life in society—honor your father and your mother; you shall not murder; you shall not commit adultery; you shall not steal; and you shall not bear false witness—are followed by the demand *not to covet* "your fellow man's wife, or his male slave, or his slavegirl, or his ox, or his donkey, or anything that your fellow man has."[3] Attempts to regulate desire are indeed common in all known societies. As noted in the discussion of norms, the point of close monitoring and vigorous sanctioning is often not primarily to control external behavior but to ensure inner acceptance of a norm and its underlying values. This is especially evident in the case of socialization, in the upbringing of children as well as in the processes that are to turn adults into reliable performers in new roles, as members of a work group, as doctors, or as soldiers.

Socialization, both early in life and in adulthood, is probably the most important site where people's preferences are exposed to normative social control. And not only is this normative shaping given a good deal of attention and care; it is often successful. This is true, even if failures

---

[3] Robert Alter, whose translation is used here, adds in a note, "The attempted legislation of desire is problematic enough for Abraham ibn Ezra to devote what is almost a miniature essay to the subject in his commentary" (Alter 2004, 432).

may be particularly visible, standing out precisely because the norms are considered important.

Different patterns of socialization correspond in complex ways to different stations in life. In this way, normative regulation of preferences is one of the most powerful of the mechanisms that account for variation in preferences across gender lines, classes, ethnic groups, and more narrowly defined status groups.

Normative regulation plays a role—directly or indirectly—in all other social mechanisms that shape preferences as well. But these other factors deserve consideration in their own right. Possibly the most important factor derives from structural differences in available resources, most evident in differences between rich and poor countries and differences between economic classes. I will, however, first turn to some aspects of the very nature of preferences and then focus on social mechanisms of a smaller scale before discussing the impact of structural resource constraints on preferences, as opposed to their role in constraining behavior.

LINKAGES AND SEGMENTATION IN PREFERENCE STRUCTURES

Needs and wants cannot be understood in isolation from each other. They must be studied as preference *structures*. This is, first of all, because it makes a difference how different needs and desires are ranked in relation to each other. But a second feature is equally important: they are not independent of each other. Opting for a given interest often follows from other needs and wants, and pursuing that interest in turn generates others. This is the case not only, but perhaps most prominently, because one preference may be a means toward meeting another.

The importance of the means-ends nexus in linking them points to the role of beliefs and knowledge in the dynamics of preference formation. Beliefs and knowledge about causal connections will be important determinants of preferences, and so will arguments and attempts at persuasion based on knowledge and beliefs. Wendt (1999) offers an instructive discussion of the role of knowledge in the constitution of the national interest in international relations.[4] Cognitive factors—information and ignorance, persuasion and shielding from information—may reinforce normative influences or they may counterbalance them. But their impact on preferences follows a different logic.

[4] See also chapter 3 above, where I recognize Wendt's distinction of the role of knowledge in the constitution of preferences as causal mechanisms (e.g., fundamental assumptions about international relations shaping the conception of the national interest) and its role as a separate factor of direct causal relevance (e.g., information about the link between Al-Qaeda and Afghanistan's Taliban regime)

All the components of the internal dimension of action as well as structural factors shaping the situation in which actors find themselves must be understood when preference change is studied. Fertility decisions are a case in point. Driven by production considerations, concern for old age security, a desire for human closeness, responsiveness to normative expectations, or some combination of these and other motives, they involve social obligations and attachments as well as many specific needs and wants. In complex interaction they reshape the parents' lives for the rest of their years.[5]

Family ties engender a wider range of interests and more urgent needs than do many other social relations; but other intense attachments have similar effects. At the same time, attachments may realign preferences so as to reduce radically the urgency of other concerns. Thus charismatic commitments may devalue, at least for a time, many of the preoccupations of everyday life. This is, of course, the reason why charisma is peculiarly vulnerable to routinization, that is, to the reassertion of common and structurally grounded needs and wants.

A third reason to treat needs and wants as preference *structures* derives from a certain desire, found among many and varied by social position, for an overarching coherence of their preferences. I do not mean an abstract interest in consistency, as would be expected of scholars. But many people seem to look for some consonance among their interests and concerns, be it because of a desire "to be oneself" or because they wish to present a certain image of themselves to others, an oblique response to prevailing norms. We might speak here of "first-order" preferences shaping the ensemble of other needs and wants. Examples of such overarching or regulative desires might be the wish to be a man not to be fooled with, a warm and generous person, a person with gravitas, or a reasonable one.

If preferences are better understood when they are seen as part of preference structures, it is equally important to be aware of *preference segmentation*. There are—especially in complex societies—different social realms, in which people live by relatively segmented preference structures, and these differ in particular in the role played by self-interest and regard for others. The paradigmatic example is the contrast between impersonal market exchange and long-term communal relations such as family and neighborhood. This is, of course, not to suggest that the latter are always

---

[5] A systematic comparative analysis of the many historical developments of fertility decline could yield powerful insights into preference changes in a major central life interest of people. There are dozens of detailed descriptions of these transitions, most resulting in similar outcomes, but with quite divergent pathways before that endpoint is reached. A meta-analysis of these existing studies could make a major contribution to both the theory of action and demography.

harmonious; but the frequently nasty character of trouble in neighborhood and family gives an indication of how strong the inducements are for a moderation of self-oriented preferences in these relations.

In simpler societies, where market exchange has a much more marginal place, this contrast is often particularly lopsided. Commercial relations then fall frequently altogether outside the rules of the moral community. Max Weber observed about feudal groups: "The specific ethics of the market place is alien to them. Once and for all they conceive of commerce, as does any rural community of neighbors, as an activity in which the sole question is: who will cheat whom" (Rheinstein 1954, 194).

That self-interest prevails in preference structures related to economic transactions with strangers (even though we find important differences across social and cultural formations) is, of course, the reason why economics has come to settle on the assumption of self-interest in most of its analyses. Another arena in which self-interest commonly prevails is the pursuit of political power, especially if power yields disproportionate privileges. However, both economic and political analysis cannot lose sight of the facts that self-interest is rarely free of all restraints, and that other areas of life, in which self-interest is not similarly predominant, have a strong and pervasive impact on political as well as economic life. These other, more solidary areas of life, such as households, fuel certain economic and political demands, and they critically influence the competence and outlook of workers, managers, and entrepreneurs as well as of voters, professional politicians, and political leaders.

PAST CHOICES SHAPE PREFERENCES

We learn from experience, and many tastes are acquired. The actual satisfactions from a choice made may not turn out as expected. As a consequence, disappointment may well devalue the interest pursued, while a better-than-expected experience is likely to give the underlying preferences a boost.

Adjusting preferences according to experience is one form of opting for informed choice. Learning from the choices of others can be another. Much of what looks like imitation and copying is actually just taking account of the experiences of others and adjusting one's preferences according to the insights gained.

Learning from past experience as well as from the experience of others must not be conceived as a purely individual matter. The interpretation of experience is subject to conversation, discussion, persuasion, and indoctrination.

Not all disappointments lead to a readjustment of preferences. There seems to be a strong tendency to see choices, once made, in the best light possible. "It takes Cartesian clarity of mind to follow an arbitrarily chosen course without coming to believe that it is in fact superior to the alternatives" (Elster 1983, 120). Closely related is the psychological effect of considerable sacrifices made for a course of action that turns out to be less than satisfactory. Even though these "sunk costs" cannot be recovered, they tend to encourage people to stay the chosen course: "We have given so much for this; how can we just turn away from it?"[6]

Still, rational learning from past experience plays a major role in preference formation. To gain a full appreciation of the social ramifications of this mechanism, we must realize that the availability of informed choice— of opportunities for trying things out and for assessing the experience of others and of arriving at different kinds of interpretation—varies by different locations in the system of inequality and in the range of subcultures. This contributes to systematic variation of preference structures by people's location in society.

Frequent Interaction, Mutual Dependence, and Attachments Shape Preferences

Uncoerced frequent interaction with others makes for similarity in behavior, outlook, attitudes, and preferences. Joint undertakings—eating out, having a drink together, watching games, attending concerts, going to the theater—shape tastes and interests, tastes and interests that require expenditures.[7]

Close interaction with trusted others is also one of the major sources— in many cases the major source—of interpretation and evaluation of past experience and the experience of others.

If individuals' frequent interaction is combined with significant dependence on each other for important life interests, as it is in families but also in work groups, business firms, and many other collectives, people will

---

[6] Economists often regard the consideration of sunk costs as both irrational and unlikely; but that may not be very realistic advice for understanding behavior. Irreversible sacrifices are an important element in the formation of commitment if they are not viewed as made under resented coercion or for an altogether lost cause. Personal conviction, social affirmation, and symbolic honor can make the difference between pointless loss and meaningful sacrifice. Treating the influence of "sunk costs" on future behavior as irrational may be correct in many instances, but it can be fundamentally mistaken if the analyst takes too narrow a view of the costs and benefits involved for the actors.

[7] This, in turn, is the reason why the social meaning of poverty lies in the fact that it deprives people of even modestly expensive forms of reciprocal participation. Poverty means exclusion, even without active discrimination.

to some extent take the preferences of others into account. Their own preferences then will represent compromises of potentially quite divergent needs and wants.

Stable social bonds, attachments, have an effect on preferences and their ordering that is similar in power to their impact on cognition. As they give priority to advancing and defending the interests shared with others in the same social relation—the same family, the same group of soldiers, the same nationality—attachments reinforce certain preferences, defend their place against the urgency of other wants, and potentially realign the ordering of needs and wants.

The strength of attachments—especially if supported by normative and cognitive frames—provides the main explanation for the sometimes extreme sacrifices in the name of kin, religion, or nation that otherwise would remain enigmatic. Such sacrifices in turn—if recognized and honored—reinforce the bonds and their underlying rationales; they become symbols of their value. Without belief in the importance of the bonds, the sacrifices would become meaningless; they would be nothing but pointless losses.

AWARENESS OF RELEVANT OTHERS SHAPES PREFERENCES

The behavior of relevant others may influence preference formation even if it represents the choices of people outside of face-to-face groups and communities with strong social bonds. Reference group theory may be of some help here, even though it is not able to pinpoint precisely which groups and categories of people will be chosen for "reference." One relevant idea is the "anticipatory socialization" mechanism: people adopt the preferences they see prevailing among the people whose station in life they expect to join.

Another idea—that relative deprivation creates dissatisfaction—fits into the same context. It has a venerable pedigree, as is evident from this formulation of Karl Marx: "A house may be large or small; as long as the surrounding houses are equally small it satisfies all social demands for a dwelling. But if a palace rises beside the little house, the little house shrinks into a hut."[8] Yet while any such invidious comparison may create dissatisfaction, the implications for preference change seem more complicated. There is first the fact that many, if not most, normative orders seek to constrain envy. Second, inequalities and differences in lifestyle may be normatively sanctioned and so well established that they are taken for granted and do not induce an attempt to emulate. As the Roman proverb

[8] From "Wage-Labor and Capital" as quoted by Easterlin (1974, 111–12) and Lipset (1963, 48).

puts it, "Quod licet Jovi non licet bovi"—what is granted to Jupiter is not granted to the ox. Third, if the palace is out of the reach of one's resources, it quite possibly provokes a denigrating reaction—"who needs a palace?"—a reaction familiar from the fable of the fox who declares ripe grapes to be too sour when he cannot reach them.[9]

If differences between levels of living are less well established and normatively secured, and if the choices of others do not seem out of reach, recognition, assessment, and possibly emulation of their choices becomes an important cause of preference change. As just noted, this often leads to better-informed preferences. Such comparative awareness often focuses on one's peers, people similarly situated in regard to matters of concern. But where status lines are more fluid, one factor that seems to engender copying of desires is precisely a higher status of those observed and emulated. Such trickle-down effects have been described, for instance, in the spread of fashion. Cross-status influences in the opposite direction are not unknown either. Thus choices perceived as more common in lower classes or lower status groups may be adopted by middle-class individuals as symbolic expressions of independence or of protest.

It is likely that much more specific criteria than class and status differences define for people which of the choices of others are worth adopting. But while it is easy to think of concrete examples of what some people think of "as suitable for us," the search for reasonable generalizations has been elusive. One exception is that once a choice has spread in a given milieu beyond a certain point, many additional people will take it up. In the formula of "keeping up with the Joneses," this became for a while an icon of cultural criticism, bemoaning the conformism in America or in "mass society." In reality, this conception—vague as it is about the character and boundaries of different milieus and the degree of adoption needed for the "tipping point" to be reached—simply highlights a peculiar acceleration of preference change in a succession of subcultures, something we all are familiar with from the spread of computer use, the growth of concern for the environment, or the insistence on new opportunities for women.

Collective Organization Shapes Preferences

The fact that people similarly situated in the society share a variety of interests does not automatically yield a coordination of their preferences and actions, even in matters of great concern. This is the "collective action

---

[9] This mechanism of adjustment and resignation, of which more below, obviously has far-reaching implications for social and political analysis as well as for normative social philosophy; see Elster (1983).

problem" (Olson 1965), to which I will devote a later chapter. Once some readiness for joint action is present, it is necessary to identify the interests to be taken up and to order them in terms of priorities. This social construction of actually pursued collective interests is achieved in processes of collective organization. And these processes are often dominated by oligarchic minorities.

These organizational preferences will, if membership is meaningful, shape to some extent the preferences of the organization's members. Here is a wide field of study concerning the impact of common causes in voluntary organizations, corporations as well as states. Unions, parties, ethnic leagues, and national governments can affect preferences in the same way as families and work organizations affect their members. The impact of political, class, or ethnic organizations may be more diluted than the most immediate social surroundings. If strong emotions get involved, however, as is often the case in social movements, even such secondary affiliations can change the substance as well as the priority of the things people consider important goals.

An interesting dual case study of two labor unions focuses on "inducing preferences within organizations" (Levi 2005). While operating in similar industrial environments, the International Longshore and Warehouse Union under Harry R. Bridges and the International Brotherhood of Teamsters under James R. Hoffa differed sharply in their goals and outlook, with one advancing explicitly progressive political activism and the other representing a model of American business unionism. Following analytic ideas about corporate culture (Kreps 1990), Levi offers a theory frame for analyzing the impact of organizations on their members' preferences as she details the mechanisms involved: clear and consistent communication of goals, institutions representing and enforcing the principles, and—particularly interesting—leaders who pursue the goals even at the expense of their (short-term) interests, thereby building trustworthiness and persuasiveness.

PREFERENCES AND RESOURCE CONSTRAINTS

I finally turn to the question of how preferences are influenced by structural resource constraints. We have at a number of points encountered mechanisms that make for differences in preference formation across gender roles, class positions, and subcultural milieus: relatively stable norms about preferences may grow up around different levels of economic resources; the chance of developing informed preferences by learning from past experience seems closely related to one's location in society; similarities and differences in social status codetermine from whose behavior a

person takes her cues for considering and reconsidering her own preferences. However, the view that preferences themselves—and not just the
behavior seeking to realize them—are dependent on the options and the
constraints presented by the situation is by no means generally accepted.

If one thinks of behavior as satisfying given preference structures within
the constraints of what is feasible, it is tempting to conclude that as resources rise or decline, needs and wants will be met simply in increasing or
decreasing measure according to a preexisting ordering. This is a common
premise, but it seems a misleading idea. Exploring it offers particular insights into the dynamics of preferences. I advance here the opposite view:
it is not just behavior—mediating between preferences and the situation
of action—that responds to changes in what is possible or impossible,
available with great difficulty or within easy reach. The very ordering of
preferences can and often does change, too, as the resource situation of
action changes.

Current preferences exist within a fairly close horizon that is largely
determined by currently available resources. The observation that cutting
back expenditures is often fraught with great difficulty is hardly consistent
with notions of a smooth cost-benefit calculus that simply implements
preexisting rank orders and trade-offs between different needs and wants.
Current preferences and their interrelations are more "sticky" than the
image of such a well-oiled calculating mental engine suggests.

What accounts for this? One partial explanation derives from the fact
that current preferences often represent compromises between different
individual inclinations in a group or organization, compromises that have
to be renegotiated. As noted above, this is often the case in family and
household decisions, but it is relevant as well for business firms, academic
departments, groups of political activists, or juvenile gangs. This partial
explanation is complemented by another, also discussed earlier: changing
the weight of one interest in a cluster of preferences may have complex
implications for the satisfaction of other wants. This suggests that even a
purely individual cost-benefit calculus would not easily come to unambiguous conclusions when faced with a new resource situation.

Beyond that, one might invoke habituation as a general feature of
human psychology. But this leaves wide open the question of when habit
prevails and when, alternatively, decisive innovation takes place. More
generally, Durkheim's assertion comes to mind that happiness and con-
tentment require constraints, and that both sudden reductions and sudden
increases in options lead to anomie and even to anomic suicide. While
taking off from his intriguing empirical finding that economic booms as
well as depressions were associated with higher suicide rates (1897/1951),

his broader claims about anomie lead into inherently contestable notic
of philosophical anthropology.[10]

The fable of sour grapes points to a mechanism of adjustment when
resources are insufficient to satisfy a desire. In contrast to a simple resignation to what is not possible, this is a case of preference change. Elster
(1983) calls it "adaptive preference formation" and contrasts it to other
related adaptations, including preference change through learning, dissonance reduction through rationalization and wishful thinking, and the
manipulation of preferences by others.[11]

Rejecting ambitions that are out of reach and realigning one's preferences to constraints one is unable to change represents a mechanism of
tremendous social structural significance. It is one major answer to the
puzzle of how it is possible that the few can rule the many, and how great
wealth can be enjoyed securely in the midst of austerity and poverty.

Unfortunately, the sour-grapes hypothesis shares a flaw common to
many mechanism hypotheses: it states an important outcome but is indeterminate as to the conditions required for the mechanism to "kick in."
As noted earlier (in chapter 1), incomplete propositions of this kind may
be turned into springboards for hypothesis elaboration if we consider
jointly plausible mechanisms that lead to opposite outcomes and then ask
which conditions favor one or the other. Contrary counterparts to the
sour-grapes reaction are represented by two common sayings: "The grass
is greener on the other side of the fence" and "Forbidden fruit tastes
sweet." While some reconciling hypotheses suggest themselves,[12] I will
leave the puzzle without offering here a definite suggestion.

[10] It is interesting to note how close such "essentially contested concepts" (Gallie 1955–
56) are to common issues of social and political analysis. Steven Lukes has shown this
for power (1974). Earlier, he made the same point when he contrasted Durkheim's thoughts
about anomie and the implied conception of human fulfillment with the diametrically
opposed ideas of Marx's about alienation and the corresponding vision of the good life
(Lukes 1967).

[11] I have learned a great deal from Elster's essay. For the sake of simplicity I will present
a less complex argument here, partly because this book—in contrast to Elster's paper—does
not deal with normative arguments about social welfare and justice.

[12] Under which conditions are aspirations and wants *not* likely to be adjusted to what is
possible and reachable? Some hypothetical answers are the following:

- wherever the obstacles seem merely temporary.
- wherever the desire receives strong social support

A variant of special intensity obtains if the desire becomes a symbol of collective identity.
The desire may even be preserved in ritualized form until it can reemerge more realistically;
the Jewish Passover resolution "Next year in Jerusalem" is an example.

- wherever the obstacles seem unfair, that is, where they are set up and/or function
  against strongly held norms. Travel restrictions in the former Communist Eastern
  European countries can serve as an example.

Responses to increasing resources raise similar open questions. There is the famous "law" of Ernst Engel, a nineteenth-century German statistician. Based on Belgian and Saxonian family budgets, it states that the higher a family's income, the smaller the proportion spent on food. This clearly does not get us very far. Though still accepted, it might even serve as a reminder of how little we know. And Durkheim's views about anomie may just highlight the disturbing consequences of sudden change and help to explain sticky linkages of preferences to situations one has become accustomed to; but they give little guidance as to what to expect when people respond to more steadily expanding resources.

Human desires seem in principle unlimited, expanding—individually and in the aggregate—as more options and resources become available. But the direction of such expansions is far from clear. This is not only because it depends in part on the unpredictable course of technological innovation. More fundamental questions are what kinds of new wants may emerge aside from new technological options, which often go hand in hand with economic growth, and whether the balance between self-regarding, other-regarding, and norm- or process-regarding preferences is likely to change.

Many economists are likely to point to common shifts in consumption as the wealth of nations increases. And this is paralleled by diagnoses of value shifts in a postmaterialist direction in the wealthier countries (Inglehart 1997). From such claims about overall trends one might conclude that I exaggerate the complexities involved in the relation between preference formation and the availability of resources.

Some of these similarities in trends across countries are real. But to dismiss the puzzles just indicated overlooks two qualifications. First, these are rough, aggregate similarities that conceal many more specific processes and mechanisms, which are of interest in various kinds of social and political investigations. Second, the claims of modernization theory, which envisioned a future of ever-increasing convergence for all rich countries, have fallen into well-justified oblivion.

A conversation I had some years ago with a Swedish economic historian may illustrate the second point. He claimed to have established that the consumption choices Swedes made in the latter half of the twentieth century were fundamentally similar to those of Americans, pointing, for instance, to the vast increases in the demand for higher education. That these demands were satisfied in starkly different ways in the two societies,

---

A variant of special intensity obtains if these obstacles become symbols of what is wrong with a broad situation for which specific actors can be blamed. Again, international travel restrictions in Eastern Europe before the fall of Communism are an example.

through universal state funding in one case and a substantially higher measure of private funding in the other, did not seem to him important. This overlooks, however, that the different ways of funding these and other similar developments—such as the dramatic increase of paid-for services that were previously provided within households—had drastic consequences: "From a point of rough equivalence in 1960, the Swedish state grew to nearly twice the size of that in the United States by 1995, in terms of both spending as a share of income and public employment as a share of population." (World Bank 1997, 22). The public choices involved in these divergent developments impinge strongly on individuals and families. Their budgets of disposable income are far smaller in Sweden. The trade-offs these two societies have accepted—between individual economic autonomy and social solidarity or, in the formulation of John Kenneth Galbraith (1958/1998), between an option for public austerity and private wealth and an option for public affluence and private austerity—enjoy majority support in both countries and are not likely to be overturned in the near future. They represent a dramatic contrast in the public institutionalization of other-regarding preferences.

There are many other counterindications of the convergence thesis. Among the less noted are the striking differences in preferences expressed in conservative politics in the United Kingdom and the United States. Conservative politics in Britain is virtually free of the moral and social issues that are so prominent in the United States—abortion, gay rights, the role of religion in politics, standards of modesty in the media, and so on. The point here is not that conservative politics has a different base in the two countries, but that this indicates dramatic differences in the prevailing preferences about public life in these two countries, countries that are in their overall public policies more similar than most.

Underlying the view of common and predictable responses of public and private choice as the wealth of nations increases is the idea that there is a universal or near-universal hierarchy of preferences that is revealed by changing resource constraints. This is crudely expressed in notions such as that the "finer things" in life become a concern only after more elementary physical and material needs are satisfied or, in the words of Bertolt Brecht, "Erst kommt das Fressen, dann die Moral"—feeding takes precedence over morals. It is often overlooked that situations of drastic deprivation, which seem to give support to these ideas, are at the same time typically characterized by a breakdown of institutions and civilizing norms. Examination of more stable cross-cultural differences hardly supports these ideas. For one, they are given the lie by the powerful role of religious and moral codes in very poor societies.

INNATE DISPOSITIONS ARE SOCIALLY MALLEABLE—WITHIN LIMITS

I began with innate dispositions, and it seems reasonable to return to them in closing this chapter. That the needs and inclinations which are grounded in human biological nature are socially and culturally malleable to an astounding degree can be made clear with a quite simple consideration. While the gene endowment of humans has not changed much in the last few centuries, this limited historical time span has seen a tremendous change in the character of societies and cultures. Sometimes it took only a generation or two to transform an extremely localized life, bound up largely in family and kin relations, into a cosmopolitan existence lived in divided worlds of family, work, acquaintances, far-flung interdependencies, and knowledge-based references. Not long ago, informed observers expressed doubts about the stable viability of the latter,[13] doubts that are still shared by a few but otherwise are forgotten. Old genes and new arrangements indeed!

Whether and to what extent the genetic endowment of humans shapes the organization of social life is a matter of intense controversy, with many sociobiologists going very far in one direction and many sociologists arguing as if the gene equipment simply did not matter. While I do think that the variability of human social arrangements—across cultures and across developments during the past few centuries—precludes a view that explains most organizational forms or most failures of social control by innate dispositions, some common features of social life do seem to be grounded in such genetically based behavior tendencies. Richerson and Boyd make the point eloquently: "If we assume that the social instincts have changed little if any since the beginning of the Holocene, then the evolutionary job of creating complex societies will have to have been done entirely by institutional 'work-arounds' that have alternately taken advantage of and finessed our social instincts" (2005, 230–31).

[13] Thus Parsons commented in his introduction to a translation of parts of Max Weber's *Economy and Society*: "The institutional features which preoccupied him are the ones which to a peculiar degree have made possible the distinctive achievements of Western history. . . . But at the same time they are far more vulnerable to disruptive influences than alternative forms. They themselves generate crucial strains which make a transition to different situations likely" (Parsons 1947, 84). A more radical thought along the same lines was expressed a few years earlier by Horkheimer and Adorno in their *Dialectic of Enlightenment*: "We are wholly convinced . . . that social freedom is inseparable from enlightened thought. Nevertheless . . . we believe that we have just as clearly recognized that . . . this very way of thinking, no less than the actual historic forms—the social institutions—with which it is interwoven, already contains the seed of the reversal universally apparent today" (Horkheimer and Adorno 1944/1972, xiii). I might note that both essays were written in a world shaken by the rise of Fascism and National Socialism, a fact that does not necessarily invalidate them.

Social life anywhere takes for granted that individuals look—at least to a minimal extent—after their own interests. This enters the calculations of slave holders and camp guards as well as the expectations of family members and close friends, and it underlies the widespread institutionalized expectation that individuals and households are responsible for their own affairs. There are, of course, massive cultural differences in these assumptions and expectations, differences that nearly obliterate the common denominator of a "minimal individualism."

A similar phenomenon may be even more pronounced. Prosocial preferences can be most easily instilled, maintained, and activated when the objects of other-regarding preferences are close associates. Despite some important exceptions—such as strong identifications with whole countries, even if large—the scale of membership groups and social categories seems to be associated with a declining weight of prosocial preferences. We will discuss in a later chapter the particular role of small groups in socialization, work organization in factories, and armies. In addition, large formal organizations have generally a nested hierarchy of offices. "A leader at any level interacts mainly with a few near-equals at the next level down in the system and collaborates with peers across the hierarchy." And "bonds of individual reciprocity and small group esprit leaven tendencies to arbitrary authority deriving from status in the larger hierarchy" (Richerson and Boyd 2005, 232).

A third example is found in the segmented cluster of motivations driving economic activities in modern societies, which I discussed above as an instance of the segmentation of preferences. There is little doubt that the establishment of market exchange as a differentiated institutional pattern that gives free, albeit contained, range to self-interested preferences has led to a revolutionary upgrading of economic productivity.

CONCLUSION

At the opening of this chapter, I noted that despite a long history of reflection, less is known about preferences than about cognition and norms. In the preceding pages, I have put forth hypotheses about mechanisms, tendencies, and frequently observable patterns—about the effects of innate behavior dispositions, of norms, of knowledge, of learning from past choices, of intensive interaction and mutual dependence, of attachments and communities with strong bonds, of the awareness of the choices of others in more distant social locations, of collective action, and of structured resource constraints. Though taking primarily the point of view of the individual actor, these ideas also offered some insight into the impact of broader social structures on preference formation.[14]

Taken together, the ideas presented give some indications about the relation between preferences and behavior, about the origins and the formation of preferences, about mechanisms of maintenance and resistance to change, and about causes of transformation. There is no doubt that the variation in preference structures I have sought to demonstrate and to make intelligible has major consequences for how people act. Simplistic assumptions seem unreasonable unless they apply to particular spheres of life with well-established common preference patterns that are—at least partially and for a given historical situation—stable over time.

Yet the insights that are available to us at present do not quite amount to a coherent and powerful theory frame for the study of preferences, though they may eventually become building blocks of an effective theoretical framework. In the meantime, it is hoped that they help our understanding and, perhaps in their very diversity, stimulate the formulation of more specific hypotheses in the course of research.

---

[14] This is consonant with important developments of convergence in rational choice studies and in comparative historical analysis. From very different starting points, research in both of these traditions has focused on institutions as shaping preferences, albeit also shaped by them (Katznelson and Weingast, 2005).

Chapter VI

EMOTIONS

Emotions of very different kinds—anger and fear, sadness and happiness, pride and envy, shame and contempt—pervade all social life. Neither dramatic upheavals such as war and revolution nor the more serene flows of everyday life can be fully understood unless we pay attention to emotions. The structures of status and power generate emotions that often sustain them but can also lead to strain and conflict. Individually, our very experience of living is shaped by emotions. "Emotions matter because if we did not have them nothing else would matter. Creatures without emotions would have no reason for living nor, for that matter, for committing suicide" (Elster 1999, 403)

Yet emotions did not attract strong attention in the classic sociology of the end of the nineteenth century, nor did they play a central role in the structural functionalism or the rational action theory of the twentieth century. In recent decades, however, we have seen a surge in research and theory on emotions, ranging from neurology and evolutionary biology to psychology, anthropology, and sociology. Research in these different fields profited greatly from mutual attentiveness. The results have been substantial.[1] And they are critical for our understanding of social action.

Emotions and their expression are central to any kind of sustained interaction and solidarity. The generation of appropriate emotions is therefore an abiding concern in all social formations. At the same time, emotions have a strong potential for disrupting social relations and for blunting rationality. They thus engender attempts at social control and give rise to social arrangements that make it possible to live with emotional reactions that are recalcitrant to social shaping. Since they are criti-

---

[1] One might object to the characterization of the classic sociologists of the period before the First World War. After all, Weber's *Economy and Society* (1922/1978) opens with four elementary types of action, one of which is affectual action, and Weber's discussion of charisma is part of his lasting legacy. Durkheim's theory of religion (1912/1954) builds strongly on emotions and explores their role in linking religious symbols to group solidarity. And Pareto put great emphasis on sentiments and their "derivations" in the study of beliefs. Yet with the possible exception of Pareto, the most neglected theorist of that generation, the classics did not make the role of emotions a regular part of routine social analysis. That, in addition to a firmer grounding of the psychological and sociological study of emotion in neurology and evolutionary theory, is a recent achievement. See Turner and Stets (2005) for an overview in sociology.

cal elements in virtually all social structures and social processes, our discussion of emotions—seemingly the most individual of phenomena—will
occasionally have to "jump ahead," as was done in the chapters on knowledge, norms, and preferences, and offer at least a few indications of their
role in systems of inequality, in religious ritual, or in the creation of solidarities and exclusions.

Issues of Framing and Conceptualization

Emotions have a special place in our examination of the internal dimension of social action. The subjective aspects of action—the beliefs of
actors, their preferences, and their normative orientations—are critical for
social analysis, it will be recalled, because human behavior is less determined than that of other animals by "instincts," clear-cut behavior dispositions built into the body. This creates room for the role of knowledge
and illusion, varying wants and desires, as well as norms and values—for
the particular role of consciousness that defines human existence.

Emotions stand at the border between that space of flexibility we have
called the internal dimension of action and the body's automatic responses that regulate heartbeat, body temperature, immune responses,
food and water intake, as well as other needs and drives. Positioned
astride this border between consciousness and the body's systems of self-
regulation, emotions mediate the determinate automatism of somatic responses and the realm of greater flexibility that is critical for the constitution of human social life in all of its variety. Emotions, together with
deep-seated needs and drives, bound this sphere of flexibility, they in-
trude into it, and they are in turn nurtured and shaped by it. Only partly
accessible to conscious monitoring and control, emotions stand in consequential interaction with the dynamics of preferences, cognition, and
normative orientation.

The neurologist Antonio Damasio (2003) sees emotions and the automatic regulatory systems of the body as closely related.[2] He bases this
view, among other findings, on the fact that emotional impulses and the
information about states of the body that shapes the body's self-regulating
response system are processed by the same parts of the brain. Damasio
distinguishes involuntary body-based emotions from accompanying con-

---

[2] For the following discussion of the nature of emotions I found it useful to consult the
treatments of Damasio (1994, 2003), who uses introspective reports as clues for neurological research and theory but emphasizes the latter, and of Elster (1999), who offers a comprehensive analysis but focuses on the phenomenology of emotions as revealed in philosophy
and literature.

scious feelings. In the interest of simplicity and continuity with common usage, I prefer the concept of emotion to embrace both the body-based emotions of Damasio's narrower definition and the feelings these touch off. His distinction is, however, analytically useful for developing certain arguments and insights. Among other issues, the cultural variability of emotions is more easily understood if their feeling component is analytically distinguished.

Feelings are in Damasio's conception mental states that are consonant with emotions in the narrow sense which underlie them. Feelings, he argues, complement the self-regulation of the body as they build on metabolic regulation, basic reflexes, and immune responses; on pain and pleasure behaviors; on basic drives and motivations; as well as on background emotions (reflecting the state of the organism), primary emotions (e.g., fear and anger), and social emotions (e.g., envy, gratitude, admiration).

Emotions are touched off by an event or object such as the satisfaction of a desire, a threatening situation, or an insult. This is technically known as an "emotionally competent stimulus." It may be actually present or mentally recalled. It typically—and perhaps always—involves beliefs; thus fear may vanish once the perceived threat is revealed as innocuous. The body responds to the initiating stimulus with a pattern of chemical and neural processes that find physical expression in the face and other parts of the body. Within split seconds, these responses engender various degrees of pleasurable or painful feelings as well as a readiness to act in certain ways.

The immediate reactions to an appropriate stimulus are programmed by the human brain as it has evolved. They are thus shared across cultures. However, the initiating stimuli are not confined to a preprogrammed set. They may be learned and thus can and do vary by culture, subculture, and individual disposition. The same goes for the feelings instigated by the neural processes and for the readiness to act in certain ways that is brought about by the full emotional response. In varying degrees, these behavioral inclinations are open to individual self-control as well as to social and cultural influence. Anthropological research on emotions has underlined the tremendous variability of the feeling side of emotions. To cite but one dramatic example, researched by Wikan (1989, 1990) and retold in an excellent overview by Reddy (2001), "Bali was listed as the single place (in a survey of seventy three cultures) where death was not followed by mourning." "A calm cheerfulness prevailed in social life with almost complete uniformity." This was achieved, if need be, by "ferocious efforts at concealment and mastery" (Reddy 2001, 60).

Emotions play a peculiar linkage role in the internal dimension of action. They link preferences, ideas about reality, and normative orientations to each other, often to the point of fusion. We encountered this phenomenon in the chapter on knowledge. Studies of ideologies as well as of mentalities and "habitus" (Bourdieu) found a strong propensity toward a fusion of cognition with evaluation and preferences. Factual beliefs as well as cognitive frames tend to be intertwined with normative orientation and desires unless a special effort is made to separate them; as the oral tradition of sociology has it, Howard Becker (the elder) famously quipped about the effort required for social research: "The scientific handstand is a part-time job." Tendencies toward a close linkage seem to derive from the fact that emotions and the associated behavior dispositions are grounded in the self-regulating system of the body, which requires integration of "sight, judgment, and action." Such linkages—and ways to counterbalance them as well—are the subjects of much commonsense observation and reflection: on "wishful thinking" as well as on "the urge to face the truth," on the desire to be at peace with what the community expects as well as on commitments to stand up to social pressure, and on the strength of norms derived from a reasoned understanding of their rationale but also on the corrosive effects sometimes produced by insistence on such rationales.

Emotions not only integrate the different components of the internal dimension of action, what people believe, what they feel obliged to do, and what they are after. Further—largely because of this integration—emotions are also a critical element in relating individuals and groups to each other and in establishing strong solidarities as well as social aversions and divisions. Social attachments and aversions in turn play a linkage role in the internal space of action similar to that of emotions themselves. This is most obvious in close interaction; but the symbols representing collectivities that transcend face-to-face groups—"imagined communities," to use the felicitous phrase Benedict Anderson (1983) coined for national identities—also gain a powerful hold on people if they are infused with strong emotions; it is through these emotions that wider collectivities acquire muscle and vigor in relation to their members. Emotions, then, not only energize and sustain individual existence; they do the same for social relations, small and large. Generating appropriate emotions is an ever-present concern in all social formations, a concern that tremendously varies in content across cultures.

Emotions may differ considerably in the intensity of their outward expression, ranging from rage and jubilation to a quiet and perhaps inconspicuous sense of well-being or malaise. However, emotions of less conspicuous intensity must be recognized as significant if we want to bring the whole range of emotional effects on behavior into view. Many subtle and powerful effects of emotions will be missed if we focus only on the more dramatic emotional outbursts.

EMOTIONS AND PREFERENCES

Preferences and their ordering derive in part from bodily needs and appetites, and they are also shaped by conscious processes—by the perception of the pursuits of others, for instance, by the awareness that some pursuits are honored while other objects of desire are forbidden fruits, or by the insight that pursuing a given preference has negative effects on the satisfaction of other needs and wants. How do emotions enter into the dynamics of preferences?

Emotions give force to desires as well as to aversions. Being engaged in any pursuit involves emotions. Emotions can shorten the distance from opinion and attitude to action, unless they are deflected by inhibition or ambivalence (which in turn are emotion-based). Emotions can also blunt and control even strong desires. Given a certain intensity, they will rearrange the structure of preferences, focusing, for instance, on hurting a hated person or helping a friend in need at the expense of other wants and desires.

Yet perhaps the most significant contribution of emotions to preference formation is that they—often in quite subdued form—aid in the ordering of preferences by marking past experiences and the elements of an imagined future with feelings. "The past, the now, and the anticipated future are given [by feelings] the appropriate saliences and a better chance to influence the reasoning and decision-making power" (Damasio 2003, 178). Earlier, Damasio (1994) had related that patients whose responses were emotionally flat because of brain damage had trouble making efficient decisions. His conclusion: "The powers of reason and the experience of emotion decline together" (1994, 54).[3]

If emotions play an essential role in "normal" processes of ordering preferences and weighing the costs of a given pursuit, that also explains the common observation that strong emotions—fierce anger, for instance, or intense feelings with a positive valence—may disturb and disrupt the rational consideration of alternative courses of action. Intense emotions can weaken and even suspend the cost-benefit calculus. In the extreme case, they inspire actions without regard for any consequence but the immediate outcome passionately desired.

If we accept the view that emotions are part of the self-regulating system of the organism, it may be tempting to see them essentially as adding force to self-regarding preferences. This temptation might be reinforced

[3] Elster (1999, 291–98) disputes Damasio's stronger hypothesis that the reduction in emotion may be the *cause* of the difficulty in decision making, though he concedes that "when the data are in Damasio may turn out to be right" (298). The logic of evolution gives Damasio's claim a considerable degree of plausibility.

by the fact that the trenchantly insightful French moralists of the seventeenth century—most prominently Pascal and La Rochefoucauld—made love of self, *amour-propre*, the center of their discussion of emotions (Elster 1999, 76–107). After all, their skepticism about unselfish virtue inspired Bernard Mandeville and, indirectly, later economists to opt—in the name of realism—for a theory based on self-interest alone.[4] Yet this would be a fundamental mistake because it overlooks that, as we have seen already when discussing preferences, the readiness to cooperate with and give consideration to others is almost certainly one of the complex behavior tendencies built into the human gene structure.

Whatever the exact shape of the underlying evolutionary processes, human beings have a strong emotional need for bonds of various kinds with others. Thomas Scheff (1990, 1997) sees the maintenance of social bonds as the most powerful human motivation. And this emotional need is nurtured by strong features of many social relations. This reminds us again of Durkheim's view that close social ties—at once constraining and enabling—are the critical antidote to what he considered a major pathology of modern societies, anomie, a claim that he famously explored in his comparative analysis of the incidence of suicide (1897/1951).

What are the circumstances that give emotional force to prosocial behavior and create the variety of relations and bonds which make up people's social world? A first answer is simple: uncoerced interaction tends to foster positive sentiments among the people involved, feelings that accentuate other-regarding preferences (Homans 1950). A less mundane hypothesis derives from Durkheim's analysis of religious ritual. Durkheim made the understanding of religious ritual central to his theory of religion. Ritual focuses on sacred symbols and in the process intensifies the bonds uniting the community. This mirrors Durkheim's view that religion as a whole is closely tied to moral solidarity. It symbolizes and represents the power of society. Several elements come together in ritual: the presence of the congregation, a common object of attention, shared expression of emotion, symbolic objects that represent the sacred and—indirectly—the group, intensified emotional energy, and hostility toward disturbances of the occasion and its symbols (Durkheim 1912/1954; Collins 1988, 187–228).

Durkheim's view of religious ritual as a source of solidarity has been broadened to elucidate formally similar if much attenuated forms of secular rituals in everyday life—by Erving Goffman (1967), Randall Collins

---

[4] See Horne (1978). It is worthy of note that this was not the position of Adam Smith, the author of *The Theory of Moral Sentiments*; but it became the dominant mode of analysis in economics after the middle of the nineteenth century. See, however, Ben-Ner and Putterman (1998) on the current state of the discussion of these issues in economics.

(1981, 2004), and others.[5] Even a simple conversation or a casual greeting can be seen as a ritual involving the presence of two or more people, a common focus of attention, and a shared mood. "Natural rituals [as distinguished from intentional ceremonies] are any form of interaction which can be characterized by some degree of co-presence, common focus, and common mood. Hence any experience of social interaction produces a high or low degree of membership symbols, emotional energies, and pressures to conformity, depending on the amount of co-presence, focus, and mood" (Collins 1988, 227). For extremely routinized encounters of this kind, the theory of interaction ritual coincides with our simple initial claim that uncoerced interaction generates positive sentiments among people. In fact, the theory of interaction ritual could explain that near-commonsense proposition. But importantly Durkheim's theory of ritual as a source of solidarity includes as a critical element *symbolic objects,* pointing beyond the immediate occasion and the actually present congregation. This allows the solidarity-creating effects of ritual to transcend the confines of face-to-face interaction.

Attachments are, as noted in the chapters on knowledge, norms, and preferences, particularly stable and consequential social bonds. Bonds such as family ties, group relations of a specially intense solidarity, and commitments often felt toward ethnic groups or nations are accompanied, modulated, and reinforced by emotions. Groups that are defined by dissent or deviance from the mainstream—extreme political or religious groups or gangs of alienated youths—often stand out for the intense emotional loyalty of their members.

The emotions evoked by and in turn shaping attachments may be quite subdued. And attachments of passionate intensity are often subject to routinization over time. But the taken-for-granted character of many emotional bonds must not be mistaken for weakness. They can reveal their power if challenged. Thus emergency situations may give a salience to family and friendship relations as well as to ethnic, racial, or national attachments that make them consequential indeed.[6]

That conflicts with others outside a group constitute a major emotion-mobilizing mechanism has long been recognized. It is at the core of the

[5] An early voice, temporally and intellectually close to the Durkheim circle, is that of Johan Huizinga. He discussed play as a critical element in culture, pointing to its solidarity-generating character and emphasizing the lack of an instrumental utilitarian orientation that sets it apart from the pursuits of "real life" (Huizinga 1944/1970).

[6] It has been pointed out, for instance, that the annual transfer of a significant fraction of the West German domestic product to East Germany after the fall of Communism cannot be understood without a recognition of national attachments; transfers of the same magnitude to the Czech Republic or Poland seem simply inconceivable (Jürgen Kocka, personal communication). This in spite of the fact that national or patriotic feeling was neither very widespread nor especially intense in post-Nazi Germany.

well-understood in-group–out-group dynamic. The in-group–out-group dynamic is an important reminder of the disruptive potential of intense and passionate emotions. Most commonly recognized is the association between nationalist passions and war. Ashutosh Varshney (2002) made the important discovery that civic associations bridging ethnic and communal boundaries in India—in contrast to those bonding people within communities—dramatically reduce ethnic conflict.

EMOTIONS AND COGNITION

That emotions interfere with cognition seems an obvious commonplace. Emotions engender wishful thinking and, when passionate, blind us to many features of the situation and to the consequences of rush actions. That should settle the case, and for a long time it did. The reality is more complicated. Aristotle, who even defined emotions by their effects on judgment, recognized nevertheless that "the causal connection is contingent. People may be angry or ashamed without having their judgment distorted by the emotion" (Elster 1999, 55). Emotions may define and "protect" the unthinkable; but passionate search for the truth is driven by emotions as well.

Actually, extensive evidence shows that both positive and negative emotions influence—and distort—assessments of reality in ways that are congruent with the emotion (Berkowitz 2000), though a number of these experiments identified an interesting asymmetry: positive emotions influenced perceptions and assessments more than did negative emotions. These findings were given a number of competing but possibly complementary explanations. One, the associative network theory, focuses on the "priming" effect of emotions: "If we have to evaluate someone or estimate the likelihood that a particular event will occur, our prevailing mood will prime, or bring to mind, feeling-congruent relevant memories, ideas, concepts, and modes of information processing." Another explanation treats moods as information: the mood evoked by the person or issue to be assessed is treated as a shorthand heuristic cue for the overall assessment. Finally, there are more complex theories that see these processes as complementary and add yet others, such as strong emotional pressures toward a given result as well as active and differentiated cognitive efforts.[7]

The experiments surveyed by Berkowitz show, however, important corrective tendencies as well (Berkowitz 2000, 130–35). If the experimental

[7] Berkowitz (2000, 121–30; the quoted passage is on 124) refers to works by Gordon Bower (associative network theory), by Norbert Schwarz and Gerald Clore (mood as information), as well as by Joseph Forgas and Berkowitz himself (for multiple process analyses).

subjects were made aware of their good or bad moods, or even if they were just distracted from them, the effect on their judgments disappeared. It is reasonable to extrapolate from these observations that the influence of stronger emotions will be less easily counterbalanced, but also that the corrections will be more powerful the higher the stakes for an accurate assessment. Equally important, the interest in accuracy itself often has strong emotional support.

Self-correction for the sake of accuracy may also explain why bad moods—perhaps more noticeable in their distorting potential—had less of an effect than did good moods. Alternatively, some researchers have raised the question whether happiness makes for mental laziness. There is indeed some evidence suggesting that positive moods lead to faster and more stereotype-based judgments, a tendency that would, however, presumably be subject to a similar self-correction if the stakes for accuracy were raised (Berkowitz 2000, 138–42).

Elster devotes an extended discussion to complementary findings that he puts under the heading "Sadder but Wiser" (a title taken from Alloy and Abramson 1979). The claim is that the emotional state most favorable to cognitive accuracy is not one of neutral valence, but rather one of mild depression. "To get it right, one has to sink into depression. Of course, the depressed are not very motivated to do anything. The reason why there is no sand in *their* machinery of action is that the engine is idling" (Elster 1999, 300). This seems too strong a claim. It is, after all, possible to have a serious emotional stake in getting it right, whatever the "it" is. The search for the right assessment itself has an emotional base. Action-oriented emotions may often induce hasty judgments, and strong emotions can make a person myopic. But emotions can also concentrate the mind on what is critical to know and to explore; most people who read this book know that from their experience of complex data analysis or the close study of scholarly literature.

Damasio presents a picture of contented and sad feelings that is not altogether different from the studies which cast doubt on the cognitive effects of positive emotions; but his conclusions about their overall mental effects differ dramatically. His more positive assessment of the emotion-cognition nexus rests ultimately on trust in the adaptive capacities favored by evolution and on the fact that support for dualistic conceptions of body and mind continues to weaken (2003, 84, 85).

What, then, can we say about the role of emotions in cognition? I suggest two results: First, the relationship is similar to the impact of the social conditions surrounding a belief's creation on its truth value. The early sociology of knowledge assumed that all social influences were inevitably damaging to the validity of beliefs. Later reflection arrived at a different conclusion, obvious in retrospect: both true and false or distorted beliefs arise under identifiable social conditions. The question then becomes: which conditions and influences have distorting consequences and which do not? The same can be said about emotions, and we are beginning to have some specific ideas about detrimental and favorable effects of emotions on cognition.

The second conclusion is equally important, given the long history of intellectual distrust of emotions: On balance, emotions play not just an important but a primarily positive role in the cognitive orientation of actors.

Before closing this section, I turn briefly once more to a subject that has preoccupied us repeatedly: the importance of emotion-based social attachments. The chapter on knowledge made clear that there is a significant tension between attachments and cognition. This accords with the first, but qualifies the second conclusion, though it does not invalidate it. To the rationalist view, the effect of emotion on beliefs is mysterious: "Given the fact that one cannot decide to believe, this [redefining a situation] cannot be a conscious operation. Somehow—we do not know how—the mind manages to come up with an interpretation of states or events that takes some of the emotional sting out of them" (Elster 1999, 408). If it is strong social bonds that for many make life worth living, it is not surprising that they are protected by these "alchemies of the mind" that work partly through unconscious and not very well understood mechanisms. The special place strong bonds hold in our lives is in many different ways socially recognized. They are often accorded a particular respect and tolerance. Many legal systems excuse spouses from giving testimony against each other. Conflicts between strong loyalties and norms and values are viewed as involving hard choices. And erring in judgment because of attachments is more easily excused than other cognitive distortions. Often this kind of acknowledgment insulates and contains the cognitive distortions caused by strong social bonds, though that is not the case when such distorted views gain a hold in a whole community or country, because then detached third-party views become easily marginalized.

EMOTIONS ARE SOCIALLY SHAPED

Emotions are subject to social control. This is not surprising, given that emotion-based actions can disrupt social relations and challenge power and privilege, overturn prudent and rational choice of behavior, and distort our views of reality. Moreover, many emotions are socially generated in the first place. Social control, then, must be understood in a broad sense. It not only restrains emotions; it also prescribes which emotions and expressions of emotions are appropriate for the occasion, be it one of celebration, of mourning, or of caring.[8] And many social mechanisms generate emotions and in the process shape them.

The social "management" of emotions aims both at the emotions themselves and at their expression. As emotions are closely intertwined with corresponding behaviors, regulating emotions is part of regulating behavior. It is a safe guess that the latter is more effective than the former. Thus the lament of moralists through the ages that "the hearts of men are evil; madness fills their hearts all through their lives" (Ecclesiastes 9:3). But one must not underestimate the effect restraining or encouraging the expression of an emotion has on the emotion itself.

The social control of emotions works in large part—though not exclusively—through norms. Anger and envy, fear and self-pity, and even pride are commonly censored, though there is considerable variation across cultures and subcultures as well as over time. The middle-class culture in our own society, for instance, has become increasingly tolerant of individuals' expressing whatever they feel. Yet even here a good deal of the efforts of parents is still devoted to keeping the emotions of their offspring within acceptable limits.

In the efforts at socialization the ground is being prepared for feelings of guilt and shame that subsequently act as internal self-censoring and self-controlling mechanisms. Guilt and shame are—to recapitulate from the earlier discussion of norms—generalized tools of social control. Both are grounded in a personal acceptance or internalization of norms. Shame arises when a person is confronted with social disapproval or even just with other people's awareness of his or her inappropriate behavior, while guilt is aroused even without other people's knowledge if one's behavior deviates from an internalized norm.

Both guilt and shame are themselves emotion-based. This brings to mind the claim of Spinoza in his *Ethics* (cited in Barbalet 1998, 181) that "emotion can neither be hindered nor removed save by a contrary emotion" (though taken literally this is surely an overstatement). Jona-

[8] Rules about the display and restraint of emotion are common in occupational work, especially in service work that involves person-to-person interaction. Hochschild's *Managed Heart* (1983) pointed to this regulation of emotion with a strong critical thrust. Much earlier, C. Wright Mills observed that white-collar people "sell by the week or month their smiles and their kindly gestures, and they must practice the prompt repression of resentment and aggression" (Mills 1951, xvii; cited by Barbalet 1998, 18–19). The effects of such emotion management on the workers' emotional experience and job satisfaction vary, however, a great deal. In an empirical comparison of different jobs Wharton (1993) has shown that autonomy and involvement with one's work are far more important for job satisfaction and emotional exhaustion than is the incidence of regulation of emotion; see the critical discussion of Hochschild's claims by Barbalet (1998, 177–83).

...an Turner (2000) has plausibly speculated that in the long course of evolution an increased capacity for sadness, fear, and aggression gave rise in humans to guilt and shame as powerful mechanisms of social control. Emotions, then, are not only socially shaped and subject to social control. Rather, emotions are themselves centrally involved in these two major forms of social control. They are critically important for sanctioning and for reactions to sanctions.

A complementary mechanism, whose origins are not well understood, though it almost certainly is partly rooted in socialization, comprises the impulses that bring many to make others feel guilty and ashamed. While often enjoined by other norms, these impulses also seem to have deep emotional roots, which means that the corresponding behavior carries its own rewards. If so, this would solve the puzzle of apparently unrewarded norm-enforcing behavior, which has detained many rational action theorists.

Internal and external social controls are not the only means of a social "management" of emotions. As emotions of different kinds play a part in all of social life, these other ways of dealing with emotions take an almost endless variety of forms. Two or three illustrations must therefore suffice.

A first pattern is to provide spaces in which the expression of emotions is allowed to play itself out in greater freedom than is usually acceptable. The best-known example may be the institution of carnival before the austerity of fasting. Structurally more important are the simultaneous developments of greater bureaucratic discipline in schools and workplaces and a deepening intimacy in family life. Bureaucracies demand emotionally austere operations—an absence of anger and zeal (*sine ira et studio*) as well as of a holistic acknowledgment of the other as a person. At the same time that bureaucratic discipline was in the ascendancy, the modern family became a place of greater emotional openness, a development that may have weakened its stability but also increased its capacity to nurture the emotional life of its members.

Another set of arrangements express collectively—and thereby deflect and "tame"—emotions that otherwise might get out of control. Institutions of mourning—gathering in memory of the deceased and relating the loss to ultimate beliefs and values, the funeral itself, and the joining with relatives and friends afterwards—is the paramount example. Commemorative rituals for the war dead and those who served in armed conflict are another. In fact, it may be that most, if not all, collective rituals respond to situations and memories that without such provisions would engender emotions that could veer out of control. At the same time, they become occasions for reaffirming beliefs and values and for grounding them anew in emotional experiences. If such ceremonies can leave the impression of an empty performance, this points to the fact that often the professed sentiments seem to some hollow or absent and their prescription hypocritical, while for others they are awesome indeed, if not necessarily sacred in a religious sense.

The Causal Impact of Emotions in Social Structure and Process

If emotions accompany and modify virtually all individual experiences and actions, it is not surprising that they also define the conditions that give shape to larger social patterns and developments. We have encountered—in this and earlier chapters—a variety of instances where this was the case. These ranged from the very functioning of social control to the experience of religion and its secular equivalents, from the creation and maintenance of strong social attachments to intergroup conflict, and from the dynamics of in-group–out-group divisions to the creation and symbolic maintenance of overarching social harmonies.

I will round out these pointers and give them a bit more substance by discussing briefly two instances of the causal impact of emotions in large-scale social structures and developments. Emotions make a critical difference in people's participation in matters of common interest and the emergence of social movements. And they play a crucial role in structures of social inequality. Both of these are large and complex topics; but at present, my only interest is to illustrate the important role emotions play in these two very different contexts.

First, a few observations on social participation and the development of movements. In the opening chapter, I mentioned Elster's (1989a, 9) juxtaposition of two contrasting and—in the abstract—equally plausible responses of people to the participation of others in a matter of mutual interest. Others' cooperation could diminish one's sense of obligation, but it might also conceivably increase it. If others cooperate, I should do my share too; yet, also, if others cooperate, there is little need for me to do so as well. As noted earlier, it is likely that this equal plausibility gives way to more predictable reactions if we look into preexisting commitments to the cause in question, related social attachments and affinities, and preoccupation with competing concerns. Strong feelings about fairness and discrimination, personal relations with members of a discriminated-against minority or even just a sense of affinity with that group, and ample resources of time, treasure, and power make it far more likely that a person gets involved in the defense of the civil rights of a minority than is the case if that person has never thought about social discrimination, has no social affiliations that link him or her—directly or indirectly—to the minority, and has to struggle with satisfying more urgent routine needs and wants. Strong preexisting commitments, social attachments, and the claims that competing interests have on one's limited resources are, of course, all matters of more or less strong emotion.

Emotionally infused inclinations to care about a cause can be activated by appeals from others. A good deal of social engagement in nonroutine shared interests is brought about by personal and often highly emotional appeals of others. It's worth noting that the "activists" who make such appeals are themselves typically motivated by emotionally supported commitments.

Finally, there is the chance that the spread of involvement is due not just to appeals in the course of informal interaction among people or to organized forms of appeal that give a more formal cast to the spread of affiliation. It may also benefit from leaders capable of appealing to a much wider audience, beyond the reach of one-on-one or small-group persuasion. What Weber (1922/1978) called "charismatic" authority most dramatically involves strong emotions. It builds in turn on conditions that are not very well understood. Weber just refers to some extraordinary qualities that set the leader apart. These he saw as frequently, but not necessarily, grounded in religion or magic.[9] Charismatic leadership is intrinsically nonroutine, in the extreme case revolutionary; it breaks with the established order. Correspondingly, the readiness of followers to impute charisma to a leader is often associated with crisis conditions, subjectively with deprivation and frustration. Another corollary is, of course, that charisma is inherently unstable. It continuously has to cope with the reassertion of routine interests of its followers.

The second area that I choose to illustrate the role of emotion in large-scale social structures and developments embraces the systems of social and economic inequality.[10] Here I will pick out just two themes. The first is one aspect of the dynamics of social status and prestige. In contrast to differences in power and economic resources, differences in status are peculiarly based on—in fact, they are virtually constituted by—the views of people in various social positions. True, these views are shaped by socialization, indoctrination, and habituation as well as by displays of power and submission and the evidence of poverty and wealth. But status

[9] Edward Shils (1968, 386) gives charisma a definition that retains but broadens the religious core: an imputed quality that is grounded in "the presumed connection with 'ultimate', 'fundamental'", 'vital', order-determining powers . . . with ultimately 'serious' elements in the universe and in human life."

[10] Among the studies of emotion in structures of inequality, the work of Kemper (1978, 1984), Collins (1990, 2004), and Barbalet (1998) stands out. What follows is largely sociological common sense rather than an exploitation of the most sophisticated ideas in this literature.

differences are in a particular degree—and to a far greater extent than power and economic advantage—based on voluntary consent. This core of a voluntary assessment combines cognition with normative evaluation. Thus it is no surprise that the views that constitute status differences are infused with emotions. Their emotional content ranges across a wide spectrum: from feelings of ease and comfort evoked by interaction among equals to contempt for disorderly and unskilled people and fear of those who disregard norms of "middle-class" civility, from identification with admired people of the higher ranks to disrespectful rejection of claims to elevated standing if these are seen as presumptuous. It is impossible to understand the way different status systems function and are experienced without taking such emotional correlates of status relations into account. In the last analysis, this is due to the fact that the approval and regard of others is a motivator of human action that is rivaled only by the search for material advantage.

The peculiar evaluative character of the status dimension of social inequality is also related to the second theme illustrating the role of emotion in systems of inequality. Differences in wealth as well as in power can easily induce envy and resentment. This may be limited and restricted by norms condemning such sentiments, norms that are indeed common across societies, though perhaps not universal. A probably more powerful way of containing envy and resentment comes about if the distribution of power and wealth is consistent with the gradations of a widely accepted status order. In that case, the evaluative core of the status order indirectly lends moral support to differences in power and wealth. In turn, where such legitimation is missing, the tensions about advantage and disadvantage are likely to be more severe.[11]

A Closing Note

Emotions play a strategic role in our conception of the internal dimension of action. Grounded in the body's systems of self-regulation, they animate, affect, and integrate the other three features of that space of con-

---

[11] One must, of course, not give too much emphasis to the evaluative dimension of structures of social inequality. This is, in my view, what Talcott Parsons (1949) did in his early essay on stratification (ironically written in recognition of the hundredth anniversary of the *Communist Manifesto*). The "realistic" advantages of wealth and power have tremendous staying power even in the face of discordant evaluations in many quarters and despite widespread resentment and disapproval. This will become clear by contrast when, in the next chapter, we consider "stratification" in small groups, where what is usually at stake is only personal regard and influence, while differences in wealth and coercive power are absent. Nevertheless, Parsons's analysis brought out aspects of structured inequality that are very suitable for demonstrating the role of emotion.

sciousness—preferences, cognition, and normative orientation. I have focused the discussion systematically on these interactions. As a critical part of this ensemble, emotions are indispensable to the understanding of elementary social action and interaction.

If, as in the case of preferences, what could be offered amounts to less than a coherent and effective theory frame for the study of emotion in social life, these considerations can nevertheless add significantly to the understanding of emotions in interaction with cognition, norms, and preferences. They are of help, first, in being aware of the pervasive presence of emotion. They, second, direct attention to the "quiet" roles of emotion—in marking preferences, in weighting experience, in supporting cognitive self-correction, in strengthening or weakening normative commitment—and balance the all-too-common focus on the more dramatic and passionate display of emotion. They underline, third, the "linkage effects" of emotions, which account for integration of the internal dimension of action as well as for potentially problematic fusions of cognition, norms, and preferences. Through these linkage effects and by themselves, emotions are, fourth, a critical ingredient in the construction of social relations, be they lasting or passing relations, intensive or ephemeral contacts, attachments or aversions. Given their pervasive presence and involvement with all aspects of social action, it is—fifth—to be expected that emotions also play a causally relevant role in larger social structures and developments. And, finally, emotions are an object of social nurturing as well as of social control and normative shaping. Different forms of structural "management" of emotions complement normative regulation where direct control seems inefficient or inappropriate.

Chapter VII

"THE HUMAN GROUP" REVISITED

I begin this chapter on a personal note. *The Human Group* by George C. Homans (1950) was the first whole book I ever read in English. It was a case of amazing luck. I was to report on a book in a small-group seminar at the University of Cologne. Homans's volume, probably because of its 484 pages, was the only book on the list that had not yet been chosen by others when I came late asking for an assignment. It was by default, then, that I came across this book at the beginning of my graduate study, one of the works that set the stage for the grand development of sociology after the Second World War.[1]

Returning now to this book and its sequel, "Psychological Aspects of Social Structure" (Riecken and Homans 1954), is less of an antiquarian exercise than it may seem. This chapter is indeed an homage to an outstanding work done more than half a century ago, but it also serves strategic purposes in this volume. First, analyzing face-to-face groups moves our focus from action to interaction, showcasing the interrelations among the subjective dimensions of action in a particularly transparent setting. Second, it helps us to see how cognition, norms, preferences, and emotions are constitutive elements of group structure and process. Third, Homans's work is one of the rare cases of a developed sociological theory— a set of falsifiable hypotheses that are logically interrelated and have a clearly defined domain of application. Finally, interaction in face-to-face groups is the most commonly experienced aspect of social reality. As we

---

[1] Two judgments will make clear that this is not an extravagant personal opinion. Robert Merton concluded his introduction to the volume: "Not since Simmel's pioneering analyses of almost half a century ago has any single work contributed so much to a sociological theory of the structure, processes, and functions of small groups as George Homans' *The Human Group*" (Homans 1950, xxiii). More than fifty years later, Barrington Moore, Jr., known for his acerbic skepticism about many renowned works in sociological theory, commented, "I think Homans' book on the group is one of the few permanent acquisitions of social science" (Moore in Munck and Snyder 2006, 93–94)

My own reaction was awe, and a resolve. The resolve was to use this book and related studies as a foundation for my own work. In my dissertation, I imported the rigorous empirical research on small groups into the sociology of knowledge, an area of inquiry that was remarkable for flights of speculative imagination and for its affinity with nonempirical issues in epistemology and the philosophy of history (Rueschemeyer 1958a; cf. Merton 1941/ 1968d and 1948/1968e).

will see, the dynamics of groups, as spelled out in the theory, emerges as a multipurpose causal mechanism—or, better, a cluster of mechanisms—with a wide range of relevance.

A Theory of Small Groups

The Human Group opens with a brief theory frame stating the initial elements of the analysis—activities, interactions, and sentiments—to be used in the review of five accomplished empirical studies. Other core concepts—above all norms and values—are added as the argument proceeds. The criteria for selecting these concepts are threefold: they must unambiguously relate to observations, both of visible actions and of verbal expressions; they must be general, applicable to groups of different character and purpose; and they must fit our best hunches as to how different aspects of behavior are related to each other. The five studies that Homans uses to develop and present his theory deal with an industrial work group (Roethlisberger and Dickson 1939), a slum street gang (Whyte 1943), the family in Tikopia (Firth 1936), a New England rural community in decline (Hatch 1948), and the upper echelon of an electric company (Arensberg and Macgregor 1942). Each is first described in as "neutral" a way as possible and then subjected to an analysis in terms of the conceptual grid developed.

We have already encountered a few of Homans's hypotheses: Uncoerced interaction leads to mutual liking, and, in turn, mutual liking increases interaction. Or: Wherever people interact frequently with each other, they develop normative expectations about each other's behavior. The core of Homans's achievement lies in the systematic identification of the complex interrelations among the selected core variables. From this he develops hypotheses that explain ranking, influence, leadership, social control, subgroup formation, conflict in groups, and their decline as coherent social entities.

Homans defines a group as "a number of persons who communicate with one another often over a span of time, and who are few enough so that each person is able to communicate with all the others, not at secondhand, through other people, but face-to-face" (1950, 1). He begins his analysis with the activities "imposed" on a group by its external environment, such as factory production or fishing. These generate the "external system" of the group's functioning. The "external" activities are also the takeoff point for analyzing the internal functioning of the group, the "internal system" of interrelations among activities, interaction, and sentiments. Yet the externally induced activities are themselves givens; they are not the theory's object of explanation. Other given factors are the composition of the group along various lines, including age and sex; the norms and values that members bring into the group; and the history of the group, ranging from one or two previous meetings to an existence spanning generations or even centuries.

Activity and interaction stand in the same relation of mutual dependence as do interaction and sentiment. "In fact, it takes an uncomfortable effort of mind to separate them only to put them together again." Many activities, from work in industry to child raising, require interaction; and from dense interaction and mutual liking flow in turn other activities. "A great deal of social activity—dances, parties—is enjoyed less for the sake of the activity itself, which may be trivial, than for the possibilities of social interaction it affords" (Homans 1950, 119).[2]

The mutual dependence of activity, interaction, and sentiment constitutes the core of Homans's theory. It explains tendencies toward similarity and even uniformity of activities, interaction, and sentiments in undifferentiated groups, and it offers an understanding of the emergence of norms. Conformity with norms derives not only from a person's readiness to embrace the normative expectations of other members (because she finds group membership attractive or has accepted the norms for reasons that lie outside the group); but it is also due to the negative reactions of others in the group to norm violations and their increased valuation of those who live up to the group's standards. Homans shows this "social control" to be simply a consequence of the normal interrelations among activity, liking, and interaction. Living up to expectations or not meeting them has predictable consequences in the sentiments, interactions, and activities forthcoming from others. Conscious "sanctions" and "rewards" are, then, merely a special case of the broader dynamics of the internal system.

[2] It is the hypotheses spelling out the mutual dependence of activity, interaction, and sentiment that the later winner of the Nobel Prize in economics, Herbert A. Simon, formalized mathematically in 1952. Homans recognized this possibility in principle but dismissed it as unattainable: "The logical problem we are wrestling with is, in the end, the mathematical problem of setting up and solving a system of differential equations. Our system cannot be as elegant as that, but it can at least take the mathematical system as a model of what it would like to be" (1950, 117). Simon responded differently: "To a person addicted to applied mathematics, any statement in a non-mathematical work that contains words like 'increase,' 'greater than,' 'tends to,' constitutes a challenge" (1952, 202). He demonstrates that an ingenious use of differential calculus can squeeze interesting and important conclusions out of crude and uncertainly quantified statements. He arrived at new explanations of aspects of the stability and dissolution of groups and generalized the formal structure of his argument to a variety of quite different circumstances, circumstances where "(a) an external (positive or negative) motivational force toward some activity, and (b) a secondary 'internal' motivational force induced by the activity itself" are present.

The reactions to people's behavior as measured against shared norms lead over time to a ranking of group members. Yet in groups that display such stratification for some time it is often observed that not only, as one would expect, do people of lower rank conform less to shared norms but also that people with the highest rank take some liberties. Once established, the accepted rank order gives them a certain degree of freedom.

This is closely related to issues of leadership. On the one hand, it is the high status in a group that undergirds influence, giving a person's initiatives as well as his responses to others greater weight. On the other, any significant innovation disturbs the status quo, upending not only established practices and anticipations but often also the normative expectations of group members. Deviation and innovation are—in the context of group dynamics—closely akin. And they provoke similar reactions. Without some independence from group consensus, innovation and leadership are hampered and, in the extreme case, impossible.

The norms of a group are not necessarily consistent with each other. That raises the question whether we shouldn't expect different rankings of members and divergent, even contradictory opportunities for influence and leadership. While some mechanisms compensate for such tendencies toward heterogeneity—for instance, people largely see and evaluate each other as wholes—this question opens insights into several aspects of internal differentiation within groups.

Many studies noted that persons who assumed a leadership role in dealing with specific tasks were typically not the best-liked people. This phenomenon of duality of high status seemed linked to different fundamental dimensions of group life, such as the contrasting concerns of getting things done and getting along with each other, the difference between "instrumental" and "expressive" activities (which we encountered earlier in the context of norms and motivations for compliance), as well as Homans's distinction of an external and an internal system of group dynamics. Since in many groups people have an interest in reaching specific goals as well as in making life with each other attractive, it is reasonable to look for mechanisms that reconcile the two types of concerns (even though it would be naive functionalism to expect such mechanisms with certainty). Depending on the group's situation, one side may take precedence of the other. Over time, norms may crystallize into roles that make for special allowances and give distinct responsibilities to different members. A simple ad hoc resolution was observed in student discussion groups where task leaders were not identical with the best-liked persons: people in the two kinds of high status often supported each other. The similarity with traditional family patterns has given rise to interesting speculation, which, however, tends to essentialize this mechanism as well as some phases in family history.

Up to this point, our discussion implied that the members of a group basically share the same norms. That may be the case, but often it is—despite tendencies toward uniformity—an unrealistic assumption. The very tendencies toward uniformity can contribute to the creation of subgroups that share separate norms where several group members with such inclinations support each other and develop a distinct solidarity. The underlying causes for such subgroup formation may lie in rankings that in effect exclude some from the rest of the group or in particular separate interests, which may derive from "external" givens. The dynamics of subgroups are otherwise subject to the same set of hypotheses regarding the mutual dependence of activities, interaction, and sentiments as well as the emergence and maintenance of norms. Within the group as a whole, subgroups may create the same kinds of tension as task leadership and other differentiated positions, and they may—but do not necessarily—induce similar integrating mechanisms such as mediating positions and roles, shared ideas that regulate and legitimate the differences, and others.

A last aspect of group structure and process worth considering is the patterns of communication. Shaped by what is required for reaching a group's goals and by the degree of group cohesion, these, too, follow from the same core propositions of Homans's theory. Members who like each other communicate with each other more than with others. In goal-oriented groups, higher-ranking members initiate communications more often than do others, and they more frequently address several others at once. In turn, people direct their communications more often to higher-ranking members. Qualitative differences complement these quantitative contrasts. High-status members more often offer information and suggest group decisions, while lower-status members more often ask for information and express support or disapproval. In effect, rank ordering induces a centralization of communications. This is especially the case where communications focus on reaching goals. Dense social communication emerges more easily among equals in rank. Furthermore, in groups with a more established rank and leadership structure, the activities and interactions of the incumbents of top positions seem to decline over time, giving rise to positions of "lieutenants" and "experts."

The content of what is communicated also affects communication patterns. While mutual sympathy favors communication of the most varied kind, the relevance of a message for particular other members shapes more specialized communications. Information that reinforces shared attitudes within the group is spread faster and wider than are discordant messages or those about which attitudes are mixed. A special case is the communication patterns induced by norm violations. They often first induce increased communication, followed by relative isolation if the violation persists.

The different communication patterns keep some members well informed and in a position of greater influence, while others are left "out
of the loop." This has consequences for the group, for its efficiency in
reaching goals as well as for its cohesion and the satisfaction of its members. Centralization often favors efficiency; but it may diminish the satisfaction of the more peripheral members of the group.

Small Groups and the Internal Dimensions of Action

Small groups have long served as social psychology's stand-in for the
larger society, because they are more easily manipulated or at least observed with considerable precision. Thus we have learned a good deal
about the impact of group dynamics on cognition, normative orientations,
motivation, and emotions. In *The Human Group*, Homans focused on
norms and emotions, leaving cognition and preferences to more indirect,
though nevertheless important attention.[3] Yet the dynamics of all four—
knowledge, norms, preferences, and emotions—follow a pattern that is
quite compatible with Homans's theory, and this was spelled out by
Riecken and Homans (1954). All four are constitutive of emergent group
features, and all four are transformed by the impact of group processes.

The impact on *cognition* was studied with particular intensity in social
psychology, perhaps because it contradicted common intuitions. Among
the most famous are early observations by Muzafer Sherif (1935) using
the "autokinetic" effect, in which a point of weak light seems to move,
because there is no way to relate its position to other objects. The perceived extent of this movement is strongly influenced by the judgments of
others. This influence is the stronger, the denser the previous interaction
among the experimental subjects and those seeking to influence them, and
the stronger their mutual affection; mutual antagonism had the opposite
effect. A similarly famous study with similar results had people judge the
clearly different lengths of several lines (Asch 1952). When numerous
coworkers of the experimenter offered plainly wrong judgments, a significant number of experimental subjects followed them if they found
themselves in a minority of one. Both studies demonstrated that even elementary perception—and not only expectations, memory, and interpretation—were subject to group influence. Sherif employed an inherently ambiguous visual stimulus, while Asch removed any ambiguity but
dramatically increased the social influence. Other research introduced
subject matter more complex than elementary perception as well as more

---

[3] "In order to retain as much economy as we can, we shall not study all ideas but only
the special class of ideas sociologists call norms" (Homans 1950, 122).

complex relations within the group, including ranked status, leadership, and different structures of communication. All of these studies about the interconnections of cognition with other aspects of group process were smoothly integrated via the core of Homans's theory about the interdependence of activity, interaction, and sentiment and the resultant tendencies toward uniformity, as well as his analysis of leadership, social control, and the dynamics of communication (Riecken and Homans 1954).

The effects of group process exhibit a fundamental similarity whether we consider ideas about reality, values and norms, sentiments, attitudes and behavior dispositions, or actual behavior. The most important extension of the mutual interdependence of activity, interaction, and sentiment is what Homans has to say about *norms*. Accounting for their emergence and enforcement by simply deploying the core propositions about activity, interaction, and sentiments points to group dynamics as an emergent social phenomenon with causal effects of its own. Other emergent properties of groups are the trust and mutual support, as well as the shared interests and beliefs they generate under specifiable conditions.

Preferences and their variation are present but do not occupy a place of centrality in *The Human Group*. For the internal group process Homans focuses on the desire for approval and liking. Most other needs and wants are introduced as elements of the "external system," as for instance the interest of workers in Roethlisberger and Dickson's Bank Wiring Observation Room to make a living with their labor or the concern with fishing and planting in Tikopia. The theory claims that a group's "internal" functioning will produce new activities and will affect the way a group deals with its environment. However, how the new activities come about and the ways in which they are imposed on those who resist the change are not a central concern of Homans's analysis. An exception is the restrictions of output beyond a decent day's work in the industrial group. Here, a specification and change of preferences, responding to external pressures, becomes a major theme as it is treated as a paradigmatic specimen of the development and enforcement of norms.

Other small group research of the same period was very much concerned with how group processes interacted with tastes, behavior dispositions, and preferences. For instance, Coch and French (1948) showed that group participation in planning job changes, as compared to the conventional method of just ordering the change, diminished the anticipated disruption of production. Lewin (1947) reported that attempts to change food tastes introduced via discussion groups were far more effective than those initiated through lectures. And Lewin, Lippitt, and White (1939) found that different styles of leadership in boys groups—authoritarian, laissez-faire, and democratic—induced unforeseen differences in aggressiveness. Other studies covered the whole range of different aspects of group functioning as they shape motivation and preferences. And they, too, were consonant with Homans's theory, as is evident from reviews at the time (Riecken and Homans 1954, but also Kelley and Thibaut 1954).

Emotions, finally, occupy as "sentiments" a critical place in the very core of Homans's theory. And sentiments are the main element driving the emergence of norms, the formation of rank order and leadership, and the evolution of communication patterns. Yet the sentiments of Homans's theory have a peculiarly conventional, even anemic character. This may serve the theory quite well, as far as that goes; but it omits important features of face-to-face interaction. It gives no hint of the potential intensity and destructive negativity that are also inherent in face-to-face interaction. This can border on torture even in such benign contexts as family life, not to speak of harsh interrogations or the critique and self-critique sessions with which Soviet Communists responded to ideological deviation. More recent work on small groups has much more to say about the emotional dynamics of face-to-face interaction as well as about their grounding in neurological and evolutionary processes (Turner 2002).

SMALL GROUPS WITHIN LARGER SOCIAL STRUCTURES

Small groups play a critical role in all societies, in the most simple as well as in the most complex. There are, first of all, the varieties of family and household forms, the location of bringing up children and, ideally, of surrounding grown-ups with solidarity and nourishment, both physical and emotional. Small group theory is indeed enlightening about the functioning of families and their change. Of particular importance for understanding family change is one central feature of Homans's theory—the role of the external system, the activities linking families to the larger society, which then shape and in turn are shaped by the internal functioning of the group. Homans failed to predict—taking off from a comparison of the family of Tikopia and the urban middle-class American family in the late 1940s—the resurgence of the women's movement and the spread of middle-class women's work outside the house; but he identified strong tensions within the middle-class family as likely wellsprings of change, with new norms to be expected (1950, 276–80).[4]

---

[4] This deserves a moment's further reflection. Homans's theory did generate a prediction—that the continued tensions would generate new norms. His failure was, strictly speaking, a failure not of prediction but of *forecasting*, of anticipating correctly what a large variety of concrete conditions (including some that were not part of his theory) would combine to produce. This failure was widespread. It was dramatized by the fact that Betty Friedan's *Feminine Mystique* (1963) critiqued the then current functionalist sociology of the family. The failure of forecasting may point to a deficiency in historical perspective, in sociological imagination, or just in common sense. Turning back to Homans's small group

The high visibility of close interaction in the family, intense emotion, and huge power differences combine to make early childhood socialization effective. Here is clearly a process that cannot be done, assembly-line fashion, in a large and impersonal organization. Needless to say, early childhood socialization creates—in a second birth, one might say—the very subject of voluntaristic action, the individual person who is capable of pursuing goals with reflection. At the same time, it instills critical parameters of preferential choice and normative orientation.

If family formations represent abiding similarities—despite stark contrasts—between agrarian and industrial, knowledge-based societies, small groups are also pervasive in the impersonal bureaucratic structures characteristic of the latter. This is true at the managerial top, in departments of experts as well as in industrial work groups. The latter attracted disproportionate attention because—close as they are to the lines of potential class antagonism—they can strongly affect productivity. Their informal norms may support and strengthen or qualify and oppose both formal corporate rules and the goals of managers and owners.

In American high schools, informal norms of student groups often give the decisive nod to one or the other side of competing goals the surrounding culture sets for secondary education. One such tension is that between straight academic excellence and an emphasis on physical fitness, competitive sports, and the cooperative loyalty team sport inspires (Coleman 1961). Another influence derives from the intrusion of delinquent adolescent subcultures symbolized by distinctive behavior or dress and the threat of violence.

Delinquent gangs demonstrate the transformative power of small groups as they set themselves apart from mainstream society. They create a peculiar "social reality" (Festinger 1950, 1954) and normative outlook of their own that allows them to neutralize norms and understandings of the kids' earlier lives, as Gresham Sykes and David Matza argued in a perceptive early essay (1957).

Extensive analyses after the Second World War highlighted the importance of small groups both in the American armed forces and in the German Wehrmacht. Even though both sides stressed the larger stakes of the conflict and cultivated wider symbolic identifications—with the flag, the regiment, certain commanding officers—it was the loyalty to the immediate group of fellow soldiers that was of the greatest importance for the will to fight and to endure deprivation (Shils and Janowitz 1948; Shils 1950).

---

theory, the vagueness of his prediction highlights the formalism of that theory, which leaves the substance of activities, goals, and sentiments out of consideration. But this happens to be a limitation that almost certainly was also a condition of the successful construction of the theory.

The critical role of small groups in modern societies is indeed pervasive, as Harrington and Fine (2000) have recently reminded us. It ranges from neighborhood interaction, friendship relations, and the large variety of groups with particular interests that constitute the local base of "civil society" to important contributions to the political orientation and activation of citizens. Intense interaction among a few is often found at the beginning of broader social movements, and it is an important factor in keeping movements alive.

More routine face-to-face interaction filters and modulates the information and the appeals received through the mass media, as was early claimed by Katz and Lazarsfeld in their model of a "two-step flow of communication" (1955). Since face-to-face interaction often involves higher levels of trust, it helps people more generally to compensate their often low levels of political information by suggesting shortcuts to overall assessments and political stances.

As we have seen earlier, it is possible and even likely that—owing to the way our biological nature evolved—other-regarding and norm-regarding preferences may be more easily instilled and maintained among close associates in face-to-face groups. If this is right, complex societies with their vast impersonal organizations will have "alternately taken advantage of and finessed our social instincts" (Richerson and Boyd 2005, 230–31)—that is, they concentrate critical processes of orientation, achievement, education, and control in small groups.

It is equally important, however, to recognize that much of the substantive functioning of small groups is determined by the larger context within which they are located—by war, for instance, by the organization of economic production, by the institutions of learning and communication, or by the system of inequality. It is indeed for good reason that "the external system" is assigned such a prominent part in Homans's theory. These external circumstances also provide an opening for the inherent historicity of small group functioning. The processes Homans analyzed take off from very varied givens, adding sequences and a set of equilibria that can be understood and anticipated with the help of his theory. Broadly conceived, the relations between substantive external givens and formal internal processes and outcomes prefigure recent analytic work on path dependence, a theme to which we will have to return in the next chapter.

Conclusion

Small group interaction is the most common experience of social life. Therefore it is no small thing to have a viable theory of small groups that explains a good deal of what goes on in that interaction. It does not tell all we may want to know. For instance, it does not tell us much about what substantively goes on in groups—when gang behavior turns violent or which kinds of political messages fare better in the filtering of the "two-step flow of communication." But the way it develops the internal group processes—norms, sanctions, status differentials, communication patterns, leadership, subgroup formation—out of external givens and the interrelations of activities, interaction, and sentiments makes it a full-fledged theory with strong, if circumscribed implications.

In the context of our inquiry in this volume, Homans's theory serves a particular and important purpose. We are moving—in a fashion that is perhaps experienced as hesitant and slow—from the foundational theoretical framework of social action through a consideration of four critical components of the internal dimension of action to larger social structures and processes. Revisiting Homans's theory after the quartet of chapters on knowledge, norms, preferences, and emotions gave us an opportunity to see all four components integrated in the functioning of small group interaction. This complements the anticipatory arguments that inevitably referred to larger social structures and processes in each of the discussions of cognition, normative orientation, needs and wants, and emotions. This integration benefited from the tight theoretical structure of Homans's theory. Even though he himself focused more on sentiments and norms than on knowledge and preferences, cognition and motivation were studied in related research that came to parallel and fully compatible results.

Homans's theory is a systems theory. It looks at the interrelations of a few central elements and raises questions about equilibrium states (though it does not offer definite answers to these questions). This gave at the time strong encouragement to systems theory in all social analysis as well as to inferences from small group processes to larger and more complex social structures and processes. As spelled out earlier (see chapter 2), my judgment is that while interdependence of causal relations is common throughout social life, larger social phenomena are, if they can be called social systems at all, almost always much more loosely structured systems than small group interaction.

If that assessment is right, taking small group processes—implicitly or explicitly—as models for all social structure and process can easily mislead. For instance, stratification in small groups is likely to be a fundamentally different phenomenon from more comprehensive systems of inequality, if for no other reason than the fact that in most small groups only status and the appreciation of others are at stake, not inequality in the means of making a living or power differences that shape people's life chances. This does not mean, however, that structures and processes that are visible and intelligible in small groups cannot serve as an analogical basis of inspiration for hypotheses about broader social phenomena. It is at least plausible that such an inspiration by research on small groups will be more fruitful than analogical speculation that takes off from the biological organism or from cybernetic circuitry and computers.

More important than such analogical uses is the fact that research on small groups in various social locations—ranging from households and work groups to urban gangs and military units—has pointed to amazing similarities of effective social support and trust as well as strong social control and influence. What emerges from the juxtaposition of these studies of small groups in diverse settings is the underlying importance of group dynamics as a multipurpose causal mechanism. Calling it a mechanism in the singular conceals that groups, as emergent social phenomena, come in many different forms, and that these differences will affect the outcomes they produce. But it also points to similarities in outcome that refer us back to the core of the theory discussed. And the theory does give us indications of how to anticipate different causal outcomes from differently constituted groups.

Chapter VIII

MIDPOINT

In the preceding chapters, we have explored the four major components of the "internal" or subjective space of action—knowledge, norms, preferences, and emotions. These elements of social action play a fundamental analytic role in three ways. First, singly as well as in their interrelations, they are *constitutive elements* of social action and of more complex social formations. In this first sense, their causal relevance is indirect: they help constitute groups, role clusters, or organizations to which we may come to attribute causal powers. Second, knowledge and ignorance, norms clustering in different ways, changes in preferences, and passionate as well as calm and steady emotions may—singly or jointly—*exert causal effects themselves*, enabling certain outcomes and making others difficult or impossible. And third, we explored how *causal relations also run in the opposite direction*: larger social formations, while themselves building on the elementary features of social action, in turn influence and mold cognition, normative orientations, needs and wants, as well as emotions.

The study of face-to-face groups offered a particularly transparent view of how the four components of action are involved in elementary interaction patterns, and how they generate small-scale structural results that in turn shape individual social action. Moreover, small groups play particular and particularly important roles in larger social structures. Groups turn out to be emergent social phenomena with causal powers that cannot be directly explained by characteristics of individuals and their actions.

It now seems time to pause and reflect on what has been learned so far, and to look forward to questions beyond the microlevel, questions of meso- and macroanalysis. First, I will consider the implications of our reconstruction of social action in the chapters on knowledge, norms, preferences, and emotions.

BROAD RESULTS OF EXPLORING THE SUBJECTIVE DIMENSION OF ACTION

I argued at the outset that the simple core model of rational action theory needs to be supplemented by theories on how actors understand their situation, which norms they accept as constraints, which needs and wants they pursue, and how emotions support and energize (or inhibit and disturb) cognition, normative orientation, and the choice and pursuit of preferences. The "quartet" of chapters on knowledge, norms, preferences, and emotions explored this subjective space of action. These chapters did not yield full-scale theories. Some—the chapters on norms and knowledge—arrived at relatively specific and coherent theory *frames*. The other two chapters fell short of that, though they also offered ideas and insights that, while more fragmentary, can be built on, both in constructing specific hypotheses and in further work aimed at coherent theory frames for the study of preferences and emotions.

Yet these results on the dynamics of knowledge, norms, preferences, and emotions allow us to proceed with causal arguments. For example, the analysis of clusters of norms yields important clues about the effectiveness and the stability of norms. Likewise, considering what shapes the search for knowledge tells us a good deal of what to expect and—equally important—what not to expect from the cognitive maps that guide individual and collective actors of different kinds in the various situations under investigation. In fact, even the very distinctions among cognitive, normative, and appreciative orientations and the supplementary focus on the role of emotions can serve as a springboard for explanatory hypotheses as they highlight the question of how the four dimensions are interrelated—how, for instance, what people need and desire focuses their attention but also can distort their perception and understanding, or how an understanding of their condition can constitute an element in how people adjust their preferences.

Often the theoretical propositions that we are able to formulate on the basis of these insights will "just" serve as causal explanations of particular descriptive findings in contrast to more fully developed sets of hypotheses with clearly specified conditions and a circumscribed scope of applicability. And such explanations may furthermore be "just" plausible accounts rather than robust statements of causation. Yet if such hypotheses and arguments make sense and can be further investigated, this suggests that causal explanation remains a viable project.

Where does this "yes, but" outcome leave us? It has, I submit, a number of powerful implications. I begin by relating it, on the one hand, to simple—one might say simplistic—rational action theory and, on the other, to radical varieties of the linguistic and cultural "turns" with their retreat from explanation to the hermeneutics of meaning and indeterminate interpretation.

First to rational action theory. If we cannot predict with confidence what people know and which norms they treat as binding, and if we are in a similar or worse position when it comes to preferences and emotions, either a radical version of rational action theory is naive, or it represents a nearly empty *format* of a theory. For many problems it is not enough to make simple assumptions about what people are after, what they know, which norms will or will not influence their behavior, and when emotions interfere with or reinforce rational choice. Such assumptions can be successful only if we deal with spheres of social life in which answers to these questions are clearly established and institutionally secured, or if we are closely familiar with the particular attitudes and past behavior of people regarding the problems we seek to analyze in one or a few populations.

Such favorable research situations do exist. One is the economics of behavior in a market economy whose institutions work smoothly. Similarly, the behavior of elected officials has been shown to be shaped strongly by reelection chances.[1] Often it is possible to make "local" predictions about the motivation shaping, say, migration or fertility decisions in a particular social and cultural setting. Here, simple assumptions are likely to be adequate for rough, overall assessments. They work in a probabilistic way, leaving more detailed and subtle questions unresolved.

Once we move beyond institutional spheres with well-established behavior patterns or try to make predictions about the decisions of people whose particular social and cultural situation is not fully understood, adequate assumptions are harder to come by. Yet what emerged in the quartet of chapters on ideas about reality, normative orientation, preference structures, and the role of emotion can give some guidance about what to expect. The results may be helpful to fill in with theoretically informed guesswork what cannot be simply taken for granted or readily found out in a given research site. They can identify circumstances in which effective norms and trust-based expectations may constrain self-regarding preferences. They can offer preliminary estimates of where cognitive inattention, distortions of perception and understanding, or more or less precise knowledge is likely to prevail. In combination with the empirical indications that are available in a given research site, this may lead to plausible hypotheses about the role of knowledge, norms, preferences, and emotions.

A second implication of our "yes, but" bottom line is a mirror image of the first. If the exploration of the dynamics of cognition, normative orientation, preferences, and emotions resulted in usable theoretical ideas that leave the search for causal explanation a reasonable if difficult goal, this stands against the retreat from causal argument represented by the most radical "culturalist" approaches as well as against the relativist no-

---

[1] To pick a less well-known instance of this extensive literature, Swers (2002) has demonstrated in a quantitative analysis that women members of Congress manage to pursue policies favorable to women's interests but do so within the constraints of electoral considerations as well as party affiliation.

tion that everything social may be considered a "text" that is open to multiple interpretations.

The difficulties that gave force to the linguistic, constructivist, and interpretivist movements are real indeed. They are rooted precisely in the complexities of the subjective dimension of action that we have examined; and I have no intention of denying or diminishing them. It is the commitment to the goal of causal explanation that separates the position advocated here from interpretivist resignation and certain radical postmodernist programs. To be sure, cultural studies focusing on interpretation can make very valuable contributions to nuanced understandings of the meaning situations and actions have for the participants. What is rejected is not such hermeneutic work that points to irony, hyperbole, or to the focusing and truncating effects of dialogue and debate. This is most welcome. What is rejected is a retreat from causal argument. Our ways part radically if everything social becomes the subject of willful imagination.[2]

Reflections on Strategies of Theory Development

Our explorations of the dynamics of preferences, knowledge, norms, and emotions also suggest conclusions that go beyond this rejection of extreme versions of rational choice theory and postmodern cultural approaches. In particular, they throw a clarifying light on strategies of theory development. Some, which have already been advocated, can now be better understood. Others, more limited pragmatic suggestions, are yet to be introduced.

[2] The retreat from causal argument often remains ambiguous. It may be merely implied in critiques of "positivistic" social science. Thus Seidman (1994, 120–21) seeks to replace a "sociological theory" that "articulate[s] a language of social action, conflict, and change in general" with a morally committed "social theory," presented as diverse narratives that are proud of their particularistic roots. But the retreat from causal analysis can also be explicit, as in Clifford Geertz's substitution of interpretive understanding and "thick description" for a dismissed "laws-and-causes social physics" (Geertz 1973, 5; 1983, 3; see also, earlier, Winch 1958). The ideals of interpretive description and of social theory rooted in diverse moral commitments are radicalized in claims that social reality itself is but a text, and that "theoretically . . . a given text is open to as many different interpretations as there are articulate readers" (Brown 1994, 233; Brown 1987; see also Derrida 1981)

The refraining from causal argument is often inconsistent. It is not easy to sustain, especially when the primary impulse is moral critique. It is hard to advance critical arguments about repression and emancipation without making claims about the causal mechanisms involved in these issues of domination and subordination.

Our theoretical focus on action and intention (as well as on interaction and unintended consequences) revealed the complexity of the subjective dimension of action and a great subjective variability. Here seems to be a major condition that accounts for multiple outcomes of very similar initial constellations.

This subjective variability is, however, to some extent socially shaped and constrained. That this shaping exists is beyond doubt, even though our understanding is still limited. Moreover, the social shaping of the subjective aspects of action goes together with the formation of social structures, large and small. Thus groups or states represent emergent social structures that may—and often do—have causal power. They themselves vary in the particular forms they take and, accordingly, in their causal effects; but their variability is typically more narrowly bounded. Subjective variability, then, translates into social variability in particular locations—a variability whose understanding often remains time-space bound because the causal components of our explanations vary in character, and their scope conditions often remain unclear. Plausible explanation of closely studied developments may be possible, while generalization and prediction remain stymied. The attempt to formulate general "laws" that hold under specified conditions for a wide variety of concrete instances often founders against stubborn "local" variations.[3]

It is a good guess that the complexity of the subjective dimension of action and the lesser, though still significant variability of social structures and causal mechanisms are the main reasons why social scientists have been more successful in developing *theory frames* than in creating sets of adequately specified hypotheses that fully deserve the name of theory. Yet as argued earlier in chapter 1, detailed and coherent theory frames represent the results of past research; they are a—and perhaps *the*—major vehicle for theoretical continuity and accumulation in the social sciences as they really exist; they are open for revision and respond to new insights; and even though they do not provide for the direct derivation of further, more specific hypotheses, they can guide the

---

[3] It is useful to distinguish two meanings of claiming a proposition's or theory's "generality." Seidman (1994) and others confound them when they reject sociological theory "as a language of social action, conflict, and change in general" (121). The two meanings of generality I insist on separating are nearly the opposite of each other: One assumes that all forms of "social action, conflict, and change" fundamentally take the same forms and arise from the same conditions. The other claims causation for carefully identified outcomes in relation to specific causal conditions, and these claims hold only for a well-defined scope of background conditions. If the first type of assertion borders on the absurd, the second claims generality precisely if and only if conditions and outcomes can be carefully specified. That the second type is often hard to achieve does not change its character.

generation of such hypotheses in diverse research sites and help make sense of empirical findings.

"Local" variability and uncertain scope conditions for the hypotheses that we do develop also constitute the reason for a major and closely related premise that underlies this whole volume. This is the emphasis on the need for do-it-yourself theorizing. If our best theoretical tools often and perhaps typically remain on the level of theory frames, interpretations and explanations of descriptive findings as well as attempts at theoretical generalization and prediction require on-the-spot theory construction that can learn from, but is rarely able just to apply, hypotheses and theories developed in other contexts.

Finally, our explorations of knowledge, norms, preferences, and emotions also yield some more limited pragmatic suggestions for potentially fruitful ways of proceeding with theory development. The subjective variability that arises from the ontological premise about the role of the subjective dimension of action may give a certain advantage to structuralist approaches as an alternative to theorizing directly from consideration of the subjective dimension. This can take two main forms. Theory construction can confine itself to hypotheses about structural regularities, neglecting the complexities of the individual level. And it can focus on ways in which social structures and developments shape individual dispositions and actions.

First, structuralist approaches can bypass subjective variability. An example is the work of Peter Blau on structural differentiation, inequality, and organizational structure (Blau 1970, 1977). This kind of analysis, which has its antecedents in the work of Durkheim and Simmel, focuses on regular interrelations among such structural features as heterogeneity and size of a social formation, and seeks to explain structural correlates and outcomes such as intermarriage rates or the extent of specialization. It neglects individual motivation and the microfactors that condition it. Another example of structuralism is found in network theory, which in its strong version holds "that the world is made up of relations first and individual entities second" (Gould 2003, 242; see, e.g., Wellman and Berkowitz 1988). Gould's own work on mobilization in the Paris commune (1991) also demonstrates the importance of a more moderate and less dogmatic version.

Structuralist approaches to theory development are also encouraged in a second, broader way. If social structures and institutions constrain subjective variability, if they stabilize and privilege some orientations and discourage others, it makes sense to favor theory development on this front. This line of theory development received strong support in recent institutionalist work, both of the historical and the rational choice variety (Steinmo, Thelen, and Longstreth 1992; Katznelson and Weingast 2005);

but it has been practiced long before. Thus the impact of structures of inequality on the outlook, mentality, and "consciousness" of people in different class locations has long been noted.[4]

The detailed variability of individual attitudes and actions may become pragmatically irrelevant, given reasonable empirical assumptions. Often it is not necessary to get these assumptions right for all people involved as long as they are right for many. If a majority or a significant minority of individual dispositions is all that is required for predictions on the meso- or macrostructural level, the macroanalysis can often sidestep questions of individual variability. Thus Theda Skocpol could assume in her study of social revolutions that peasant dissatisfaction was pervasive in agrarian bureaucracies. Rural poverty and widespread exploitation made grievances against landlords common. This left her analysis free to focus on fractures in the system of domination, and on conditions favoring or disfavoring collective organization of peasants (1979; see also Goldstone 2003).

To focus theory development on the impact larger structures have on individual functioning and microprocesses is in an important sense the inverse of the dominant project of social action theory, and of rational choice theory in particular—to explain complex social structures and developments by reference to individual action. Yet if I argue that the problems of subjective variability give promising opportunities to structuralist approaches, I do not mean to argue for an ultimate dominance of structuralist approaches. There is no warrant to give up on the complementary strategy that seeks to explain institutions and large-scale structures taking off from individual agency and elementary interaction. Balancing both of these directions of causal inquiry is in my view a pragmatic way of dealing with the issues of agency and structure that pose vexing questions—and often rather scholastic answers—when the solution is sought on a meta-theoretical level (see, e.g., Giddens 1984).[5]

---

[4] Consider, for instance, this assessment by Adam Smith (1776/1937, 734–35) of the "mind" of the working class in eighteenth-century Britain: "The understandings of the greater part of men are necessarily formed by their ordinary employment. The man whose whole life is spent in performing a few simple operations . . . has no occasion to exert his understanding. . . . He . . . becomes as stupid as it is possible for a human creature to become. The torpor of his mind renders him not only incapable of relishing or bearing part in any rational conversation, but of conceiving any generous, noble, or tender sentiment, and consequently of forming any just judgment concerning many even of the ordinary duties of private life."

[5] The result of these considerations about hypothesis formation and theory development is, then, not a retreat from opting for an overall frame of reference based on social action. As a comprehensive ordering device it seems to be of unsurpassed utility. It remains a fundamental intuition about human life that individual action is the ultimate foundation for understanding social structures and social change. As Peter Hedström puts it, "The most rea-

The Subjective Dimension of Action
and Larger Social Structures

The quartet of chapters on knowledge, norms, preferences, and emotion not only gave us insight into the complexities of social action and the beginnings of an understanding of how these components of the subjective dimension of action are shaped by larger structures and processes. They also made clear that here are, in turn, some of the foundations of these larger social formations. The dynamics of knowledge, of norms and values, of preferences, and of emotions are critically important for complex and persistent patterns of order and conflict as well as for change in these patterns. They are constituent elements of emergent social structures.

That norms and values are building blocks of larger and persistent social structures is quite clear. We have seen how norms form interdependent clusters and define roles and role sequences. They also represent nodal points in the construction of organizations. And they are the central component of social institutions such as the rules of contract and property. Finally they are deeply implicated in maintaining inequality. Norms seek permanence, even if they never fully attain it; yet compared to simple victories in contests of interest and will, a norm secures the approval of third parties and often the consent of those whose behavior it seeks to regulate. In view of all this, calling norms the "cement of society" (Elster 1989b) seems justified.

Perhaps less obvious but equally important in the constitution of more complex social patterns is the role of ideas about reality. This, of course, is especially true of conceptions of social reality, of categories of people, of social forms such as complex role configurations and large communities, or of structures of inequality. Yet ideas about inanimate nature can have equally far-reaching consequences in social and cultural life, as is evident from the responses to the discoveries of Galileo and Darwin, but also from the impact of technical innovation on work and economic production as well as on relations of power.

Preference structures, too, have powerful consequences for more complex social formations. People's desires and inclinations shape which social arrangements are possible, which work well, and which only with difficulty. This becomes quite clear if we just consider the varying incidence of self-regarding, other-regarding, and norm-regarding preferences and the consequences of their distribution in different social locations.

sonable ontological hypothesis we can formulate in order to make sense of the social world as we know it is that it is individuals in interaction with others that generate the social regularities we observe" (2005, 19).

Without other-regarding and norm-regarding preferences, or with only a weak presence of them, many forms of solidary and norm-obedient social life will fail or be extremely fragile. On the other hand, any comprehensive social formation has to accommodate strong tendencies toward self-regarding preferences. All three types seem to have a biological foundation. And it is perhaps partly due to this grounding in our biological evolution that small social formations seem to be especially suited for cultivating prosocial behavior. If that is right, biologically grounded preference patterns have profound implications for the functioning of complex societies.

The implications of preference structures go, however, beyond the consequences of our biological nature as constituted by evolution. Preferences, after all, share with the other components of the subjective dimension of action in the particular flexibility of biologically grounded dispositions that is characteristic of the human species. Yet the diverse preference structures that characterize different cultures and subcultures may also evince great stability. Acquired tastes, too, often do not change easily. Food preferences and food taboos are well-known examples of this. Finally, long-term preference changes, such as those associated with the loosening of traditional behavior patterns, clearly have far-reaching consequences.

Emotions, lastly, are no less implicated in the constitution of complex and persistent social configurations. Emotions constitute collective memory, and strong emotions often fixate grievances as well as positive views of others over time. Even more important, emotions are a critical element in the emergence of close social bonds, attachments, as well as of hostile relations and lasting enmities. Finally, emotions invest symbols with great and even binding power. This link between symbolization and emotion is the basis of people's relations to larger communities and their values. Without such symbolism, grounded in emotion, social life would be much more confined to face-to-face relations than it is.

SOME CONDITIONS OF STRUCTURAL PERSISTENCE

It may be useful at this point to ask a simple, yet wide-ranging question: what are some of the mechanisms that make for persistence and stability of social patterns? The fundamental import of this question for the understanding of larger social structures should be obvious: whatever persists of the results of previous interactions and social processes becomes a structural condition affecting later developments. The conditions of maintaining a structural pattern are often simpler and less demanding than the conditions of its origins. The dimension of time, then, is critical for an understanding of the micro-macro nexus.

Gathering a number of hypotheses about causal mechanisms underlying stability and persistence—many perhaps with incompletely or uncertainly specified conditions—will highlight ideas that apply to many themes at the meso- and macrolevels of social analysis to which we will turn after this chapter. Strong collective memories, for instance, can trouble or energize a political community, an army at war, economic enterprises, or kin groups. Certain stabilizing mechanisms may equally apply to the maintenance of value orientations, to the protection of material advantage, and to the integrity of institutions.

Which constellations and developments, then, favor structural persistence? I begin with one of the simplest, the creation of a *precedent*. Consider three quite different developments:

- specifying a norm while settling a dispute, which can have paradigmatic significance;
- developing a new product with as yet uncertain consumer demand; and
- making claims that highlight a previously latent ethnic or other social identity.

All three can turn into precedents. As such they share a number of noteworthy characteristics. They are inevitably bound up with the particular historical situation of their origin and presumably reflect its conditions in their features. At the same time, they create a perspective for the future. Precedent setting is usually seen primarily as a matter of specifying norms and urging a following. But if successful it will almost certainly modify preferences. And it also has a cognitive aspect. The very creation of the precedent and its initial success, however modest for the time being, dispel the fog of uncertainty that often inhibits innovation. This cognitive side of precedent setting is far more important than is generally acknowledged. The temptation to take new developments, once they have occurred, for granted as useful and even necessary makes us too easily forget the sense of openness and uncertainty that prevails when we ponder an oblique future.

In the chapter on knowledge we encountered an extension of the same idea: *tradition*—relying on a complex set of precedents—may be seen as a reasonable response to uncertainty, an uncertainty about the consequences of changing one, a few, or many of the ways in which things have been done before with acceptable results. Tradition as a response to uncertainty—and perhaps often just as a convenience—represents another mechanism that makes for persistence in social life. It is a mechanism of great importance, widespread not just in those societies that we call with gross simplification "traditional societies" but in our own as well. Tradition normally involves, of course, much more than this response to uncertainty. Above all, it is often secured by norms as well as by deep emotions. In conjunction, these can remove any rationale for the traditional pattern from explicit consideration. But the cognitive dimension of tradition, the respect for a complex that works but whose components are difficult to disentangle and assess in their separate and joint consequences, remains an important and undertheorized feature.

From studies of interaction and small group research, we know many instances of *self-reinforcing sequences at the microlevel*. These may have wider relevance, either because they become duplicated on a large scale or because they occur in strategic locations within wider structures. Relations of leadership and authority are maintained by the successful exercise of influence, which can in part build on the leader's confidence grounded in the experience of higher standing. In turn, leadership tends to wither with nonuse and is undercut by unsuccessful attempts to lead. Similarly, relations of trust are reinforced by the experience that trust was justified, while they themselves make that experience more likely. By contrast, there is the vicious circle of disappointment, resignation, and disengagement. Resigned withdrawal will in turn reduce the chance of successful action, quite aside from other factors that contribute to frustration.

A simple entry point into the analysis of persistent patterns at the meso- and macrolevel is gained when we consider likely moves of a winning party to conflicts that matter—of a firm that recently gained a dominant market position, a party that won an election in an as yet unsettled democracy, or an agrarian ruler who expanded the territory controlled. A common strategy will be to use the newly acquired resources to reinforce and protect the gains. This defense of advantage by use of the spoils can take many different forms—among them investments, creation of organizations, promotion of favorable ideas and understandings, promulgation of norms and the establishment of institutions, as well as preparations for coercive measures. Each one of these modes—and various combinations of them—can account for complex persistencies.

Economic investment is a powerful and often used means of stabilizing a social arrangement. The particular goals pursued with the investment may vary greatly. One paradigmatic case is the endowment whose proceeds cover the maintenance of a college or other organization. Another is the use of economic resources to build a following and "buy" support, though there may be norms constraining such an exchange of material advantage for compliance and loyalty. And then there is, of course, investment by business firms as a means of maintaining and broadening their position in markets.

Normative stabilization is a tool of ubiquitous use. As they need for their full effect acceptance and acquiescence, if not voluntary consent, norms and values as tools of social reproduction require that partisanship be to a certain degree transcended or at least muted, even if strong interests are involved in advancing or opposing such stabilization. Here ritual and symbolization will play an important role as supportive mechanisms. The intellectual counterpart to them is explicit formulations justifying the values to be secured. If fully developed, these take the form of ideologies.

The use of *coercion* defines in some sense the opposite of a stabilization of social arrangements through values and norms. Yet an established, predictable, and largely accepted monopoly of violence is a major linchpin of social stability. Other mechanisms, especially the promulgation of norms and organizational provisions, such as those securing "law and order," may grow up around it. The critical role of force and coercion becomes most visible in periods of transition. Thus the withdrawal of the guarantee of armed force that the Red Army had extended to Eastern European regimes until 1989/90, the war after the United Nations' partition of Palestine in 1947/48, and the violence that accompanied the separation of Pakistan from India in 1947 set in motion both new stable institutional forms and persistent patterns of conflict.

Several different mechanisms of stabilization come together in the phenomenon of *social institutions*. Here economic resources and power as well as ideas and intellectual authority are joined to rules, norms, and values. This may be, but is not necessarily, related to the state and statelike orders. We will consider different stabilizing mechanisms associated with institutions in greater detail when we discuss institutions in a separate chapter. In particular, we will have occasion to examine again the phenomenon of "overdetermination," where reproduction and stability are more than guaranteed by the combination of multiple sufficient causes, "redundant" causal mechanisms.

I will close this incomplete list of ideas about sources of social reproduction and persistence with a pattern of stability that involves neither powerful interests nor strong normative commitments. What might be called a "calendar model of social stability" suggested itself to me when years ago a newly appointed president of Brown University failed repeatedly in efforts to change the academic calendar so that the fall semester would finish before the holiday season at the end of the year. The difficulties of changing the calendar rested on a concatenation of lesser considerations. Each could be changed in principle; together they proved resistant to change. There was the convention that summer activities end with Labor Day; there were the schedules of sports events, to be planned one or two years ahead; there were established times for professional meetings, and so on. As with a calendar schedule, many social arrangements can accrue around a social pattern once chosen. None of them need be backed by strong interests; none need involve profound value considerations. In each case, the particular arrangement does not matter much. Yet their inter-locking has the unplanned effect of securing the pattern in question.

This "calendar model" is akin to similar interlocking constellations in which interests and values do play a role of varying weight. I discussed such mutually reinforcing configurations in the case of norms, where clusters of norms and linkages between norms and values as well as between norms and social attachments give strength to any one element (or, if inconsistency and tension prevail, weaken it). Similar linkages were noted in the discussion of preferences. Such cases where values and interests of different strength are involved represent the more frequent version of this phenomenon of stability due to interlocking configurations. Yet considering calendar change is particularly instructive because it isolates the effect of interlocking from the stabilizing or, in the case of dissonance and tension, destabilizing effect of strong interests and normative concerns.

Mechanisms that create and sustain persistence over time are critical for moving from micro- to meso- and macroanalysis. Without persistence and reproduction beyond elementary action and interaction, meso- and macrostructures are not imaginable. Simply invoking inertia is not an adequate explanation of social structures extending in time. The same mechanisms, however, that we have considered in order to get a handle on social patterns persisting over time are also relevant for understanding social change, both dramatic and abrupt change and incremental transformations. This was already evident in the discussions of, say, norms or preferences, and it will again become clear in the coming chapters.

History Matters

The simple fact that structural persistence often extends over decades and centuries and is frequently rooted in conditions quite different from those that later maintain and reproduce it represents one major ground for the claim that history matters for causal explanation in the social sciences, a ground that should not be dismissed as trivial because it is well known. There are others. Some outcomes of interest are the result of long-term developments so drawn-out that they are not easily visible in their entirety and require historical reconstruction. "Example: displacement of personal armies, feudal levies, militias, and mercenary bands by centrally controlled national standing armies took several centuries to occur" (Tilly 2006, 421). Yet another reason: major differences in outcome may depend on the sequence in which causally relevant processes took place. For example, in a historical comparison of the German and the American legal professions in the nineteenth and twentieth centuries I argued that drastic early contrasts and limited later trends toward convergence could in large part be explained by the relative timing in the growth of state control and the expansion of market exchange (Rueschemeyer 1973, 146–84). In these and other ways, the historical past represents a context that is causally significant.

If history matters in causal analysis, this frustrates what might be called causal and functional "presentism"—the parsimonious inclination to take only current conditions and recent developments into account when considering the causes and consequences of what is under investigation. Giving the historical dimension of causal analysis its full due does further complicate the search for theoretical propositions that hold under specified conditions across diverse concrete situations. It is critical, however, to understand that what is invoked here is the *historical dimension of causation*, not historical particularity, perhaps turned into a "thick description." As Paul Pierson puts this difference in the conclusion to his ingenious explorations in *Politics in Time* (2004, 172):

> In this emerging literature "context" takes on a particular meaning. It becomes a point of entry for thinking about how events and processes are related to each other in social dynamics that unfold over extended periods of time. It is decidedly not a matter of treating each social setting as unique and infinitely complex. Instead, these inquiries urge us to recognize that any event is environed by its temporal location, its place within a sequence of occurrences, and by its interactions with various processes unfolding at different speeds.

That history matters was an insight widely embraced both in sociology and in political science when they were still closely intertwined with historical studies. In the middle decades of the twentieth century, when these fields became separately institutionalized as disciplines in their own right, the idea was forgotten by many and rejected by quite a few. It was scholars such as Reinhard Bendix, Barrington Moore, Jr., and Charles Tilly who restored historical depth to the search for social explanation. Following their lead, comparative historical analysis has made great advances. It has developed specific analytic tools, methodological innovations, and a wealth of substantive theory frames and causal analyses (Mahoney and Rueschemeyer 2003, Adams, Clemens, and Orloff. 2005).

Developments in methodology make clear that comparative historical analysis accepts the same fundamental standards of inquiry as any social or political research. The developments include renewed attention to the search for necessary and sufficient causes, in addition to theoretically oriented narrative, and comparative work focusing on partial causation (Mahoney 1999, 2003; Ragin 1987, 2000; see also most recently Mahoney, Kimball, and Koivu 2009, and Mahoney 2008). One major advantage that results from this broadening is that it eases the problem of "too many factors, too few cases," which many see as inherent in comparative historical work. The determination of necessary and sufficient causes—as well as the rejection of such claims—requires much smaller numbers of cases for statistical significance. Furthermore, when comparison across macrostructures such as nation-states is combined with theory-relevant observations within cases, the small-N problem is further relieved because what counts in the assessment of validity is the number of relevant observations, not the number of macrounits compared. Such observations are typically quite numerous in analytically oriented comparative historical work. This is especially the case when within-case processes are traced with a rich array of theoretically plausible mechanism hypotheses (George and Bennett 2005; Hall 2003; Rueschemeyer and Stephens 1997).

The refinement of analytic tools for exploring the historical dimension of causation is equally important. The simple starting point was the observation that there are patterns that cannot be understood but as "survivals" of an earlier time. These survivals are not just trivial items, as for instance the frequently cited buttons on the sleeves of jackets, but have considerable interest for understanding the present. Reinhard Bendix was fond of quoting Schumpeter:

> Social structures, types and attitudes do not readily melt. Once they are formed, they persist, possibly for centuries, and since different structures and types display different degrees of the ability to survive, we almost always find that actual group and national behavior more or less departs from what we should expect it to be if we tried to infer it from the dominant forms of the productive process. (Schumpeter 1947, 12–13; see Bendix 1964, 8–9)

By itself, however, this observation does not much advance our causal understanding of the present except that it blocks a purely "presentist" route of explanation (represented in the passage quoted by inferences from the dominant forms of production). Being aware of important survivals offers little help in fashioning more comprehensive explanations unless we can answer a series of obvious, but difficult questions: When and under which conditions were the survivals created? What determines the different degrees of their ability to survive? What can modify this persistence and under which conditions is it likely to end? These questions have not been answered, but models and theory frames have been developed that bring us much closer to the formulation of testable hypotheses. Analytic reflections on "path development" are the most important of these.

Arthur Stinchcombe (1968) made a critical contribution with his discussion of "historicist explanation." He contrasted explanations of persistent phenomena by sets of repeated causes, where "this year's phenomena are produced by a system of constant causes, the same causes that produced last year's phenomena" (101), to explanations that point to a historical dimension. For instance, "it is well known that the results of the movements and wars of the Reformation still determine which European countries are still predominantly Catholic, which predominantly Protestant" (102). In historicist explanation, "the problem of explanation breaks down into two parts. The first is the particular circumstances which caused a tradition to be started. The second is the general process by which social patterns reproduce themselves" (102–3). He then proceeds to develop a rich set of ideas about the mechanisms of reproduction, ranging from the self-replication of elites and their influence on the values, beliefs, and activities of others to the creation of permanently available resources, be they physical capital, cultural capital or skills, useful organizations, or institutional structures.

In more recent years, Paul Pierson took off from dramatic changes in economics and economic history, where long-term divergent developments were explained by initial decisions that were reinforced by increasing returns. These self-reinforcing developments then constrained future choices. The previously often neglected phenomenon of *increasing* rather than *declining returns* on an innovation or investment had been demonstrated to be a major factor in technological developments (Arthur 1989), in the location of industries and cities (Krugman 1991), in the concentration of international trade among rich countries (rather than among countries with sharply contrasting resource endowments and comparative advantages), and in the study of economic development (North 1990). Pierson reanalyzed the major constellations economists found conducive to increasing returns in the distinctively different context of politics and developed a wealth of orienting ideas for studying path-dependent processes in political science and macrosociology.[6]

It is evident that the discussion of path dependence is full of unsettled conceptual problems. However, "it bears emphasis that these debates are

---

[6] If Stinchcombe and Pierson see path-dependent development as a frequent and often important phenomenon, James Mahoney (2000) adopts a more restrictive definition and sees path dependence as fairly rare. His model of path-dependent sequences begins with initial conditions that are contingent, eluding explanation in terms of the pertinent theory frames. It then posits a deterministic process of self-reproduction as well as conditions that end this sequence of reproduction, both of which are amenable to theoretical explanation. He contrasts four sets of reproducing mechanisms, corresponding to the major theoretical orientations: utilitarian, functional, power, and legitimation mechanisms

Mahoney (2000) also proposes to add another type to the family of sequences called path dependence. Here each later step in a sequence of events is a reaction to the preceding one. While this clearly is another way in which the past history can powerfully affect the present, it is very different in character from self-reinforcing processes. Furthermore, the stipulation that the sequence in question be close to deterministic seems to make this a very rare phenomenon.

not merely semantic matters; they intersect with major themes concerning explanation in the social sciences" (Mahoney and Schensul 2006, 457). In spite of this unsettled state of the discussion, the various overlapping attempts to come to terms with the analysis of historical processes have advanced our understanding greatly beyond the simple acknowledgment that long-past events must somehow be taken into account in causal explanation. They have yielded strong orienting ideas and the beginnings of coherent theory frames for historical sequence analysis. More than could be shown in these brief remarks, the development of these tools has gone hand in hand with a veritable wealth of empirical comparative historical studies—of state formation and regime type, of revolutions, of colonialism, of international development, and of social welfare policy, to name only a few major themes (Mahoney and Rueschemeyer 2003; see also Adams, Clemens, and Orloff 2005). We will revisit some of these issues in the coming chapters.

Looking Forward

In the second half of this volume we will consider social and political analysis beyond microaction and face-to-face interaction. Rather than deal with the substantive study of family and kinship, ethnicity, law, politics and the state, the economy, religion, and the vast array of varied historical constellations and transformations, I propose to organize my discussion by focusing on very few major analytic aspects of meso- and macroanalysis. I will concentrate on problems of aggregation of small units, on the difficulties of launching collective action, on organizations and institutions and their relations to power and domination, and on the creation of social identities. The two chapters preceding the conclusion treat larger social structures as causally relevant locations for individuals, groups, and organizations and examine the role of culture and ideas. All of these chapters, but especially the last two, will review a number of theory frames that deal with such macrohistorical themes as states and social structures or class formation.

Chapter IX

AGGREGATIONS

Aggregating individuals and small units into larger sums may seem a simple way of moving from the micro- to the macrolevel. And it is indeed commonly used that way. This chapter deals with two radically different kinds of aggregation: In one case, outside observers add up individual opinions, attitudes, and actions on the premise that these sums adequately characterize communities, ethnic groups, classes, and nations. The other case, which I will call *socially grounded aggregation,* points to a major feature of complex societies.

Except for the simplest sums, such as the number of people in a country or a city, aggregating individuals, their attitudes, their motivations, and their actions is a poor way of gaining insights into larger social phenomena. This is the *fallacy of simplistic aggregation.*

The reason is twofold and elementary. First, groups, organizations, communities, and large social formations are composed not literally of individuals but rather of people in their capacity as members who occupy specific locations in these formations. Multiple memberships and social locations have an influence on their cognition, normative orientation, motivation, and emotional involvement. That was evident from our examination of the components of the internal or subjective dimension of action. Later we will explore how social action in different spheres of life is institutionally structured (see below and chapter 12); the role of institutions is not for nothing at the center of both social and political analysis. The second reason complements the first. Recognizing the structure of small and large social formations makes visible the inevitably unequal ways in which certain motivations, actions, views, and commitments come to prevail in a collective. Averages, even averages of more circumscribed groups and social sets, are a poor guide for the reconstruction and understanding of these social processes.

There are, however, a number of areas of social life where decentralized decisions have significant aggregate consequences. Examples are voting results, fertility rates, and market prices. What is at issue here is different from simple aggregation by an outside observer. Rather, since the actions of individuals or small social units have socially recognized consequences, both these decentralized decisions and their aggregation come about in the context of complex institutional foundations. The results of voting, fertility decisions, and market choices are *socially grounded aggregations*. Their institutional foundations make uncoerced voting, individual fertility decisions, and market exchange socially feasible in the first place. And they entail aggregate outcomes that may or may not be acceptable to prevailing or powerful interests.

At the same time, the institutional contexts have another effect that is of interest. As they shape relevant ideas, norms, and preferences and to some extent homogenize them in a given area of social life, they create different "zones" of social life that are set off from each other by distinctive motivational patterns—such as organized politics, life with family and kin, and economic exchange.

One of the most important of these zones in modern capitalist societies is the sphere of economic behavior. Understanding the motivation of economic activities as distinct from the predominant motivations in other spheres of life is a critical tool of social and political research. Equally important, without an adequate comprehension of what is achieved by market exchange, it is not possible to come to a realistic appreciation of how complex societies work. I will therefore offer in this chapter an extended discussion of what markets do.

THE FALLACY OF SIMPLISTIC AGGREGATION

The tendency to characterize social phenomena simply or primarily as aggregations of individuals and their characteristics is amazingly widespread. Such misplaced aggregations include the prediction of political developments based on randomly surveyed opinion, conjectures that derive cultural templates from averages of individual attitudes, and many judgments about individual responsibility of the many for the deeds and misdeeds of large collectivities.

The most trivial fallacy is also one of the most common. Inferring macro-outcomes—that is, often, macrofutures—from simple aggregation of individual attitudes works, if at all, only by coincidence. For instance, in the spring of 2006 substantial majorities of Israelis and Palestinians favored negotiations for peace. Yet the just-elected Hamas majority in the Palestinian parliament refused to acknowledge the right of Israel to exist and refused to forgo the use of violence against civilians, while the new centrist Kadima Party of Israel campaigned for a unilateral withdrawal from the larger part of the West Bank and an unnegotiated annexation of the land occupied by the main settler centers. To point out that majorities of random samples on both sides have persistently favored negotiations can serve all kinds of purposes; to take it as a basis for confidently predicting that the disconnect between popular opinion and representative collective action would soon—or for that matter, eventually—disappear is surely, given the long history of that disconnect, to make a dubious claim.

The inverse use of mistaken aggregation is nearly equally widespread. Here simple narratives of how many individual citizens may have reacted to certain events are used to explain changes in policy stances of the government. The two cases differ only in the specifics of the initial piece of information and the direction of the inference: from mass public opinion to complex political decisions or from policy choice to underlying aggregate views, attitudes, and actions of common people.

What is neglected in both cases? Both inferences set aside the most elementary complications in the processes of collective decision making and the ways in which these are affected by inequalities of knowledge, status, influence, and wealth; by differences in goals and values held with varying intensity; by the multitude of views and cognitive frames that are grounded in parties, government offices, and communal agencies; and by the exigencies of dealing with organized opponents and friends. That "the many" have a difficult time converging in joint action even if they share common interests, views, and attitudes is at the heart of the ubiquitous "collective action problem" (see chapter 10). If anything, it is a better bet that "elite" opinion will prevail in the longer run than that it will be shaped by popular opinion. However, opinion formation among people in interrelated elite roles has its own dynamics as well.[1]

It may be useful to understand why these elementary insights are so often set aside. Exploring what makes for this inclination reveals how our hunches take shape. The main reason for this inclination toward simple aggregation seems twofold: the sensible premise that ultimately all of social life is the result of actions and interactions of individuals, and the undeniable fact that much of the common sense we derive from our immediate experience is social psychological in character. The small-scale base of common sense foreshortens the insights to be gained from the individual action premise, while the plausibility of the principle of individual action as the fundamental starting point of social analysis protects misleading common intuitions. Beyond that, there are perhaps three further explanations. First, many people take too simple a view of individual action and interaction, assuming that individual action will not be subject

[1] A dramatic example of a disjunction of elite and popular opinion was the persistent positive evaluations of President Clinton by random samples of citizens during the Monica Lewinsky affair, which diverged sharply from the prevailing judgments among political elites and the press.

to complex influences on cognition, normative outlook, preferences, and emotion, and that people will stand by a position once taken and act to see it prevail. Furthermore, the unanticipated effects of actions and interactions are often neglected. Second, many people view collective decision making simplistically and assume—probably influenced by idealized models of democratic politics—that majority opinion prevails in the long run, even in highly authoritarian organizations and countries. Finally, both simplifications are most tempting where ignorance is combined with some pressure to deploy a theory. Both, that is, are most likely where positive or negative stereotyping suggests itself.

Socially Grounded Aggregation of Decentralized Decisions

Not all aggregations of individual actions and characteristics, however, do violence to what we know and surmise about the construction of more complex social processes. Many social and political phenomena of great interest are indeed aggregations of the dispersed decisions and actions of individuals or households, businesses, and other, often small units. And they are recognized as such. Aggregations of voting decisions determine election outcomes. If many actors buy and sell goods and services, they generate prices and thus affect production and consumption. And decisions about childbearing shape the composition and size of whole populations.

In all of these cases, the decisions are made by many units—individuals or (typically small) groups and organizations—but they add up to qualitatively distinctive aggregate results. Constituting in their aggregate social phenomena of great consequence, they are surrounded by the complex institutional infrastructures of family and kinship, of politics, and of market exchange. These institutions shape norms and moral orientations, beliefs and understandings, as well as wants and desires. They define the options available to individual actors and outline modalities of decision making. In some social formations, they may reduce individual decision to virtually zero. In others, they give it the much greater but not unregulated range to which people in complex societies are accustomed.

The aggregation of individual decisions may or may not meet with universal or widespread approval, but it usually has powerful support or did so in the past. The three instances selected—market choice, voting, and fertility decisions—significantly differ from each other in the way the aggregate outcomes are judged. I will further discuss each of them below but will give special attention to the case of capitalist market exchange.

FIELDS OF ACTION

As noted, effective institutions not only represent and enforce norms but also mold relevant ideas and preferences. This gives rise to relatively homogeneous patterns of motivation—preference structures that are normatively sanctioned and joined to shared understandings and "definitions of the situation." These patterns set different spheres of social life apart from each other. Most commonly recognized is the contrast between the predominance of self-regarding preferences in economic market exchange and the stronger claim of other-regarding norms on the interactions among family members and friends. This relative standardization of motivation renders choices and actions in each area more predictable.[2]

That institutional underpinnings create a relative homogeneity of motivational patterns in different spheres of social life is of interest beyond their role in socially grounded aggregations of individual decisions and actions. In a given society and a given historical situation, we may be able to come to reasonable expectations about prevailing clusters of norms, common understandings, and preferences in different spheres of life. If that is possible, it will aid considerably in explanatory hypothesis formation, even if the exact boundaries and conditions of such time- and place-bound expectations remain not fully identified.

A few suggestions about distinctive motivational "zones" in the social life of rich democracies may illustrate the point. The contrast between the motivation of economic activities in capitalist societies and the more strongly solidaristic norms for family and kinship in the same societies is only the most obvious and dramatic example. There are zones of allowed and encouraged hostility, suspicion, and flat stereotypical cognition in racial and class relations, even though this hostility may be incompatible with publicly expressed views and widely held ideals, and may therefore be accompanied by ambivalence and a certain lack of ease. There are zones of middle-class life in which strangers treat each other with genteel politeness and helpful friendliness. There are zones of behavior marked by a relatively open flow of emotion or by affective restraint. There are zones of a somewhat vague civic idealism concerning behavior in the com-

---

[2] Aggregate analyses of many individual actions—market behavior, fertility decisions, voting—seem to have a special affinity with rational action theory (as the late Herschel Grossman, a well-known macroeconomist on the Brown faculty, once noted in discussion). The multitude of individual and small-scale collective actors make an individualist approach plausible. This is reinforced by the prevalence of certain kinds of motivational patterns. And the importance of the interests involved (which admittedly varies across the three instances selected) strengthens the inclination to decide and act deliberately. The affinity with rational choice theory is indeed reflected in the—sometimes implicit—methodological and theoretical assumptions of many voting analysts, economists, and demographers.

mons. This may be strengthened by middle-class norms of orderliness and decency to the point that "We never do that!" only rarely has to be backed up by "What if everybody did that?" Finally, there is the peculiar zone of politics, defined in this country and in other rich democracies partly by Harold Lasswell's "Who gets what, when, why?" (1936) but also by a nonpartisan longing for the common good. Both of these contradictory orientations may be alive even in the same political actors, collective and individual. This ambivalence engenders disgust with "politics" as endless conflict and even plain self-enrichment; but it also drives volunteering, devoted expert service, and genuine attempts at compromises for the common good.

That different norms, preferences, and cognitive understandings co-alesce into contrasting motivational patterns, some of them strongly grounded in emotion and social attachments, has of course long been recognized. An older language simply referred to "different spheres of social life." Currently, both the action theory of Pierre Bourdieu and the new sociological institutionalism in organizational analysis offer more differentiated conceptualizations of contrasting "fields" of action. Focus-ing often on organizations as actors, both explore the role of power and conflict in the emergence of more or less homogeneous fields of action, and both emphasize the impact of given cultural templates as well as di-verse prevailing "scripts" and routines, an emphasis that sets them apart from rationalist theories of action.[3]

The Motivation of Economic Activities and the Role of Markets

Economic activities and their integration through market exchange are prime examples of a socially grounded aggregation of dispersed decisions

---

[3] See, for instance, Bourdieu (1998, 1999) and Powell and DiMaggio (1991). The collec-tion of Powell and DiMaggio includes a set of early foundational statements, as well as some applications to specific fields of action and organizational activity. A recent example of the latter that builds on Bourdieu, as well as on the new sociological institutionalism in organization theory, is Rohlinger (2007)

Bourdieu and the new institutionalists in organization theory share with each other, as well as with other important theorists (e.g., Giddens 1984), a systematic emphasis on unre-flected routines and continuities in social life. They see this claim as sharply at odds with theories of purposive action. I have taken a different starting point, suggesting that with some critical modifications—in particular a fuller exploration of the subjective dimension of action—a conception of purposive action can usefully serve as a comprehensive theory frame (see chapter 2). In my view, it seems quite possible to account for persistent nonratio-nal features of social life once the part played by knowledge, ignorance, and uncertainty, by norms and normative commitments, by the dynamics of preference formation, and by emotions, as well as attachments to people and social symbolizations, is fully recognized.

and behavior. Understanding them requires the consideration of two
broad questions: How are economic activities and their motivation institutionally shaped and set apart from social action in other spheres of life?
What do markets do by way of integrating dispersed decisions?

Identifying the motivation of economic activities in market-based economies seems simple enough: what stands behind all of them is the rational
pursuit of self-interest. Yet this pursuit is bounded by legal regulation as
well as by nonlegal norms. It is bounded by the legal institutions of property, contract, tort liability, provisions for the creation of corporate entities, and complex legal regulations. And it is also bounded by social customs, understandings, and commitments that underlie the relations of
trust required for smooth and low-cost economic transactions.

This, in simplified form, is the most common account. It is adequate
for many immediate purposes. Talcott Parsons viewed it as insufficient
when he set out on his long career of theory building (1940). Perhaps
surprisingly, given the reputation of Parsons's work as an unhelpful elaboration of abstractions, his insistence on putting the motivation of economic activities into a broader framework yields insights of pragmatic
utility in social and political research. The common view of economic
action sketched understates the role of institutional structuring, and in
particular it fails to convey that economic activities share with other legitimate activities a grounding in overarching social institutions.

Economic behavior is regulated by a set of institutions not limited
to specifically economic ones. It shares with other legitimate activities
approval and support from wide sections of society. And this broader
institutional infrastructure of economic activities not only legitimates the
pursuit of self-interest while setting boundaries to it, but it also defines
that pursuit as the socially approved center of economic roles. Most people with strong commitments to generosity and solidarity in dealing
with others do not feel at all inhibited in negotiating a "good" price for
their new house. The institutionalized rational pursuit of self-interest in
economic life belongs thus to a world conceptually different from that
embracing such categories of individual psychology and morality as ego-
tism or greed.

Institutions are (as noted repeatedly) often more than just a complex
of norms and regulations. They are frequently aligned with dominant
preference structures and supported by beliefs and understandings that,
in the strongest forms of institutionalization, are completely "natural-
ized" and taken for granted. Effective institutions not only enjoy wide
approval and support, but they control substantial resources to enforce
norms and regulations and to grant rewards for conforming behavior.
These rewards—both material and immaterial—shape the system of stratification, the unequal distribution of economic resources as well as the

hierarchies of status. Clearly, economic inequality or even the status system of a society is not simply a function of conformity or deviance in roles and pursuits that are considered specially important. But ideas of desert are rarely divorced from the facts of inequality. Both often reinforce each other. That economic and social inequality can become issues of social justice at all testifies to the linkage between inequality and normatively oriented reward and punishment.

The rational pursuit of self-interest in the economic life of capitalist societies is, then, far more deeply embedded in the institutional structure of these societies than it appears to be when we see it as merely a feature of human nature that is given an outlet in economic life, bounded by certain norms and regulations. This is true even if Parsons's account does not pay sufficient attention to the contradictions, tensions, and frictions between different "zones" of social life. After all, even in successful capitalist countries many people have strong ambivalent and even outright negative feelings about outstanding successes—say of corporate CEOs—in the single-minded maximization of profit.

I turn now to the second question of how dispersed decisions are integrated through the market. What do markets do? The seemingly paradoxical claim that markets are aggregation and coordination mechanisms that turn the pursuit of self-interest by many independent actors into a contribution to the common good goes back to the eighteenth century. It is nicely expressed in the title of Bernard de Mandeville's book *The Fable of the Bees or Private Vices, Publick Benefits* (Mandeville 1714/1988). Mandeville's claim was part of intellectual arguments that anticipated the turn from political, coercive acquisition of wealth and privilege relying on martial passions to the more peaceful and more productive mode of capitalism relying on the pursuit of material gain (Hirschman 1977).

Instead of a more formal definition, I will just say that by markets I mean more or less competitive, money-based exchange relations, in which supply and demand result in variable prices. I will advance a dual claim: Markets offer tremendous benefits; above all, they have a remarkable capacity to steer and coordinate economic activities. At the same time, market functioning also has a darker side.[4]

Before I turn to markets as tools of coordination, there is a more elementary benefit to note, a benefit of great consequence in any view that values individual freedom: potentially, open markets empower individu-

---

[4] I intentionally couch the following in terms that are not normatively neutral. The reason: the discussion of markets is rarely done in a normatively neutral way. Thus it is easier to make my dual claim in explicitly normative terms. At the same time, the substance of my arguments is largely descriptive and analytical, and it is not particularly difficult to identify the underlying normative judgments and vary them as desired.

als. This egalitarian potential earned them pride of place in the original project of liberalism. Amartya Sen insists in *Development as Freedom* (1999) that markets are an inherent aspect of his normative conception of development rather than only a useful instrument. He points to persistent quasi-feudal dependencies to make clear that this is not just a remnant of liberalism's history.

In advanced capitalist social formations, flexible markets represent above all an amazing steering mechanism capable of coordinating many participants, their knowledge of dispersed local conditions, and their preferences. Without direct command, preplanned relations, or deliberative agreement, markets achieve a complex coordination among many actors. This coordination of intelligence as well as of desires enhances economic productivity. In a large, complex, and rich society with diverse needs and wants there is no substitute for this coordination. Consider the manifold consumption preferences you know from today's everyday life and contrast them to a situation where the issue is how to meet the most elementary needs of food, clothing, and shelter. It is only in the latter circumstances—under the impact of war and its devastating consequences, for instance—that overwhelming scarcity makes a central administration of economic production and distribution plausible. Otherwise, centralized command economies face insuperable problems of information and motivation.

Competitive markets provide strong motivation for producing goods and services for which there is demand. Markets join signaling information and preferences, offering incentives, and providing resources in the same process: First, prices signal relative demand and scarcity as well as the estimates of market participants about future conditions in their varied locations. Prices are an effective communication device about this, largely because they offer incentives and allocate resources at the same time as they deliver information. Second, prices provide incentives that induce responses to scarcity or abundant availability of goods and services. Higher prices constitute incentives to reduce demand and increase production, while lower prices have the inverse effect. Third, prices transfer resources that are needed for effective responses; thus rising prices channel resources from consumers to producers, declining prices from producers to consumers.

There are, however, other, darker and more problematic sides to this picture of a smooth and efficient motivation and coordination mechanism. Since most of them are also well known, I confine myself to very brief pointers. First, needs that are not associated with resources are not met. Specifically, under many conditions, competitive labor markets do not keep all working people from starving. Second, an initial unequal distribution of resources—no matter how it came about—is at best repro-

duced but not ameliorated, a consequence that is at odds even with the
libertarian criteria of justice that Robert Nozick (1974) once advocated.
In fact, an unequal distribution of resources is even likely to be accentu-
ated, depending on the legal order underpinning market exchange. Third,
there are "externalities," costs that are borne by society or some sectors
of society but that do not show up in the books of market participants.
An example is the pollution of air, water, and soil, unless special provisions are made to "internalize" these costs. More generally, not all needs
and wants are translated into incentives; and not all costs are translated
into disincentives.[5]

Other problems of market exchange are perhaps more subtle. One of
them is represented by long-term tendencies toward concentration, leading to monopolistic and quasi-monopolistic market power in many fields.
This reduces the responsiveness of production to demand, and it is another factor that makes increasing inequality likely. The major reason for
the propensity toward concentration is that the economic advantages of
economies of scale are at odds with the economic advantages due to the
spur of competition. Yet monopolistic market power does invite innovative competition, even though economies of scale also raise the bar for
newcomers to enter markets.

There are also significant short-term problems. In response to changing
conditions, markets can drastically overreact, creating price bubbles and
price collapses.

Quite aside from bubbles and troughs, market changes often come
about suddenly, and their consequences may be profoundly unsettling.
Desires for social stability are at odds with the "creative destruction"
wrought by capitalist markets (Schumpeter 1947). For this reason Polanyi
considered the pure market "a stark utopia" and argued that it "could not
exist for any length of time without annihilating the human and natural
substance of society; it would have destroyed man and transformed his
surroundings into a wilderness" (1944/1957, 3). Markets, then, become
viable only if they are regulated and "tamed."

Finally, if market functioning is taken as the most general, natural, and
legitimate steering mechanism in economy as well as society—an extreme
claim that is, however, advocated by quite a few ideologues—it margin-
alizes people, values, and practices that no society will want to do without. This was at the core of an earlier, European "neoliberalism" (now
sometimes called Ordoliberalism after a yearbook that was published in
the 1940s and 1950s), which was and still is dominant in continental
Europe. It seeks to make use of the market mechanism as much as possible

---

[5] It bears mentioning that the obverse is true as well: there are positive externalities when
benefits are the by-product of operations whose costs are not imposed on the beneficiaries.

but at the same time to protect people, families, communities, moralities, and cultural developments at least to some extent against the corroding pressures of markets.

The bottom line of these brief characterizations is simple: the market is an indispensable tool of well-being in complex and rich societies, but it also creates profound problems that engender political responses seeking to modify market outcomes. The institutional underpinnings of markets require a few additional observations.

Since the outcomes of market functioning are the results of many aggregate decisions rather than of the actions of a few known and visible actors, there is a tendency to consider markets and their results as "natural." This tends to give them the peculiar legitimacy of facts "one can't do anything about." But markets are not natural occurrences. They are complex social constructions that require for their sustained functioning and viability intricate institutional arrangements. Most prominent here are the legal institutions regulating property, contract, and the constitution of corporate legal actors; but this brief enumeration belies the complexity of formal and informal institutional support functioning markets require. There were those who thought that once the controlling layers of state socialist rule were removed from Eastern Europe in the 1990s, free markets would spring into existence. That proved to be wrong, especially in the countries with the longest history of centrally planned economies. And it was known to be wrong since the Edinburgh Enlightenment of the eighteenth century, since Adam Smith and his friends: markets require a complex institutional infrastructure.

Market exchange, then, requires preconditions such as the rule of law for its continued viability in the longer run, and these preconditions are not simply there, nor can they be created ad hoc out of nothing just because they are needed. Roman law was a critical resource in the medieval and postmedieval transformations in Europe. The requirement of a rule of law must not be overinterpreted. "Rule of law" connotes to many a fundamental equity; but the regulation of markets is rarely—perhaps never—a neutral set of rules that creates a "level playing field." Morton Horwitz has shown in his important *Transformation of American Law* (1977) how between the Revolution and the Civil War American courts—not legislatures—transformed a common law that retained strong traditional communal orientations into one that perfectly served the new competitive capitalism. This was done explicitly in the name of advancing economic development. It entailed, for instance, a transformation from affirming a contract only after finding it fair to upholding it on the merely formal judgment that a contractual agreement was reached. Or it involved absolving the employer of responsibility for injuries to the employees because the compensation for injuries was already anticipated in the wage agreement. Or it stipulated the famous principle of "the buyer beware!"—absolving the seller of responsibility for a defective product once the sale was completed.

The construction and maintenance of markets, then, is a matter of politics, be that politics by way of judicial decision, legislative enactment, or nonlegal social pressures. Inevitably there will be measures that favor some parties and disadvantage others, measures that moderate or increase the impact of creative destruction, and measures that seek to spread the motivational patterns associated with the market or contain them and explicitly "protect" other spheres of social life. Markets are indeed precious mechanisms whose performance requires careful maintenance. In addition, we see in all rich capitalist countries that market outcomes are variously counteracted and steered by social welfare provisions, macro-economic management, and tax policies.

Two Other Socially Grounded Aggregations

It is time to return briefly to voting and fertility decisions as cases of institutionally structured decentralized actions that have profound aggregate consequences. Both represent different ways in which attitudes and actions are institutionally structured on the microlevel and different modes through which macro-outcomes are aggregated.

The principle of "one person, one vote" is accepted in all mature democratic systems. Together with rules that protect the vote against coercion as well as threats of coercion and with provisions that ensure some degree of responsiveness of the ensuing policies, it represents and symbolizes one major condition of democracy: the separation of decision making—incomplete to be sure, and yet powerful—from the structures of economic and social inequality.

As noted earlier, a generalized version of this ideal shapes naive views of aggregation. Here is one of the main mechanisms encouraging the fallacy of a simplistic summation of individual traits, attitudes, and actions. It is an instance of a more general phenomenon, one that we have already encountered in the discussion of knowledge and beliefs (chapter 3): taken-for-granted ideals often shape—and in the extreme fuse with—views about how social life actually works. Reflection can break such naive links; but only trained awareness can really avoid the fallacy.

The aggregate outcomes of voting differ from the aggregation of market choices. Inevitably faced with disagreement, the institutions and rules surrounding electoral results empower pluralities, majorities, or qualified majorities; and they protect minorities. If strong enough, these institutions ensure that electoral results are accepted. But this acceptance is different from approval. It remains a "formal" matter. It does not imply that the choices made by the majority are approved in substance. By contrast, market prices are widely seen as true aggregations of all individual choices, even though it is clear that some carried greater weight than others, and that policies counterbalancing market outcomes are common.

This difference between the outcomes of voting and market functioning notwithstanding, it has been argued that the cognitive assessments that enter into both political and economic choices often represent a distinctive "wisdom of crowds" (Surowiecki 2004). This idea is worth exploring briefly. Aggregate views expressed by "the many" are indeed often more accurate than those of any expert. That insight applies to such diverse issues as the value of stocks, the chances of politicians to be elected, or the number of pebbles in a glass bowl. The idea is old indeed, though its rejection by such authors as Le Bon (1895/2002) or Ortega y Gasset (1930/1993) seems still more popular. Hofstätter (1957) cites Machiavelli's *Discourses on Livy* (1531/1996, 1:58, 117–18): "A people is more prudent, more stable, and of better judgment than a prince. Not without cause may the voice of the people be likened to that of God; for one sees a universal opinion produce marvelous effects in its forecasts, so that it appears to foresee its ill and its good by a hidden virtue." Hofstätter also points to Aristotle, who in the third book of his *Politics* speaks of the intelligence and the manifold perceptive capacities of groups.

The superiority of aggregations of many judgments rests on certain conditions. The individual judgments have to be (largely) independent of each other; they have to be—on average—somewhat insightful rather than completely ignorant or shaped by a common bias; and they have to find an aggregation that does not favor any one opinion or set of opinions. If these conditions are given, it follows from statistical logic that the larger the number of judgments, the greater the approximation to the true value. Large numbers may in many situations be hard to aggregate without distortion; but even smaller numbers often add up to judgments that are better than the best individual estimates. At the same time, it is clear that the independence of individual judgments is easily compromised. This is probably more often the case in political than in market judgments, since the role of social values, of shared collective interests, and of trust-mistrust relations is greater in politics, while the independence of economic assessments finds support in the competitive character of many economic relations as well as in the fact that individual profit and loss are at stake in market transactions.[6]

---

[6] Ober (2008) offers an important analysis of institutions that make the aggregation, alignment, and codification of citizens' knowledge more effective.

Fertility behavior is embedded in institutional structures governing gender roles and gender relations. Institutions, which regulate sexual behavior and define relations of marriage and cohabitation as well as family and kin ties, form the social context within which fertility decisions are made. Fertility behavior is not well understood if we simply collect information on individual attitudes, fears, hopes, and actions without seeing them in these institutional contexts.

However, in the case of fertility behavior the institutional grounding of individual attitudes and actions does not ensure aggregate outcomes that are equally acceptable as in the cases of electoral outcomes and price developments in economic markets (even if, as just noted, the acceptance of election outcomes differs substantially in character from that of market functioning, and market outcomes are often the object of correcting state interventions). Both in many rich modern countries and in most poor developing areas, aggregate fertility outcomes are seen as a social problem, at least in the short and medium run. China's one-child policy imposes burdens on families for the sake of more acceptable aggregate outcomes.

To render a complex picture in a very crude way, an established set of institutional structures favoring high fertility at the microlevel corresponded in many historical cases to high mortality. It compensated at both the individual and the aggregate level for high mortality. Early formulations of a model of "demographic transition," in which lowered death rates induce—albeit after a time lag—lower birthrates, had to be revised substantially. Not only did the time lags vary a great deal across countries and historical conditions, leading in many countries to rapid population growth and skewed age distributions, while in others it was observed that the declines in fertility *preceded* the major declines in mortality. In addition, many rich countries with low mortality exhibit fertility rates that stand well below the replacement rates for even the lowered rates of death. This has engendered counterbalancing population policies, which, however, do not meet with much success. The complex links between aggregate population outcomes and the mortality experience and fertility decisions of individuals and their close associates at the microlevel of social life have been well studied, though important questions are still open.[7]

Comparing the interrelations between microprocesses and aggregate outcomes in the three cases of institutionally grounded aggregation reveals interesting contrasts. After the old high-mortality/high-fertility equi-

---

[7] Of the extended demographic literature I cite only Coale and Watkins (1986), Hirschman (1994), and Caldwell (2006). It is worth noting that the disjunction between micro–fertility decisions and macro–fertility outcomes was a major theme in Garret Hardin's famous essay "The Tragedy of the Commons" (1968).

libria were upset, aggregate results of fertility behavior at the microlevel very often demonstrate that strong institutional grounding of individual decisions and actions does not guarantee macrolevel outcomes conforming to expectations that are widespread and powerful. This stands in sharp contrast to voting, where the outcomes are, at least in consolidated democracies, institutionally embraced. In fact, voting and fertility decisions are in one sense inverted opposites. Institutional grounding shapes in today's world the substance of fertility decisions in complex ways, but it often leaves the aggregate outcomes erratic. By contrast, electoral institutional arrangements focus at the microlevel on securing freedom from coercion rather than on civic virtue and the substance of voting decisions, while at the macrolevel they seek to ensure that the results are accepted despite continued division of opinion, and that electoral outcomes at least to some degree inform macropolitical policy choices.[8]

Market processes occupy a middle ground. The institutional grounding of microlevel behavior and of the coordinating features of markets is so strong that most people are inclined to accept market outcomes as "natural." At the same time, the institutional underpinnings of markets vary across countries, and the states of all advanced capitalist countries steer market functioning through tax policies and countercyclical macroeconomic management and engage in more or less comprehensive modifications of market outcomes through social welfare policies.

Conclusion

This chapter dealt with the apparently simplest move from micro- into meso- and macroanalysis, the aggregation of individual small-scale social actions into larger sets. On closer inspection, that move turned out to be not so simple after all. We saw, on the one hand, that aggregations of individual dispositions and actions by outside observers often provide a poor way of understanding more complex social phenomena. The temptation to pursue this approach anyway easily leads into the fallacy of simplistic aggregation.

[8] Some philosophers and political theorists hold that stable democracy requires above all individual civic virtues, commitments, and value orientations such as mutual toleration, openness to factual information, and devotion to the common good. Yet while there is some evidence that institutional features in some consolidated democracies engender certain levels of trust and civic virtue (e.g., Rothstein 1998), the guarantees of "negative liberty," of freedom from coercion and undue pressure, seem in virtually all rich democracies far stronger than are institutional underpinnings of civic virtues that would link microlevel political decisions to macro-outcomes such as democratic consolidation, as claimed by some political philosophers.

On the other hand, there are socially grounded aggregations of individual decisions and actions that constitute social mechanisms of the utmost importance. The aggregation of individual economic decisions through market exchange constitutes a major example of this. It is a phenomenon whose understanding is critical for a wide range of social and political research issues.

Socially grounded aggregations rest on institutional infrastructures that shape both the decentralized small-scale decisions and their aggregations. This can take very different forms, as became clear when we compared voting, fertility behavior, and market choice. Meaningful and acceptable aggregation may be difficult to achieve, as is evident in the difficulties of adjusting aggregate fertility rates. Electoral outcomes in democracies and the aggregation of market choices in market economies represent different but clearly more widely accepted aggregate results, even though market outcomes are often the object of remedial policies.

Finally, we noted a serendipitous side effect of the institutional structuring of the motivations and actions evinced by individual and collective actors in different "fields" of action. This has a fortuitous consequence for much social and political research: it can significantly enhance the chances of explaining and even predicting social behavior in different settings.

Chapter X

COLLECTIVE ACTION

THE PROBLEM

If many people share a strong interest, nothing seems more plausible than to assume that they will join together and work to protect and advance that interest. This had long been a common—though often implicit—premise in social and political theory. That changed with the publication of Mancur Olson's *The Logic of Collective Action* (1965).[1] Olson argued that rational actors would not contribute to efforts to attain collective goals except under special conditions. People would opt not to participate if they expected so few others to join that the collective effort was doomed to be futile. But they also would not join if they could expect to benefit from a successful effort whether they participated or not, as is in the nature of "collective" or "public" goods. They would then opt to take a "free ride." People would participate in collective efforts only if the individual benefits of participation exceeded its costs. That may be the case because individualized, "selective" incentives for participation (or punishments for nonparticipation) make participation worthwhile. These selective incentives can be material rewards and deprivations, or they can be social incentives involving acceptance and honor or social rejection. Another condition favoring active work toward a collective good obtains if an individual's share in the results of success is large enough to cover the costs of participation. Thus parents who cope with housework while their adolescent children do not do their share may gain sufficiently from what they accomplish despite frustration with the lack of cooperation.

One upshot of these considerations is that small groups can more easily win the cooperation of their members—because members can more easily monitor and sanction each other and because the individual share of the common benefit might be quite substantial. For larger groups and social

---

[1] This is not to say that Olson was the first to identify conditions that make group formation based on common interests difficult. Marx's and Marxian theorizing about class formation, to which I will return, treated the emergence of "class consciousness" and class organization as a central and problematic issue (see, e.g., Dahrendorf 1959). However, Olson was right in claiming that group formation resulting from common interests was often taken for granted, as it was in pluralist interest group theory in American political science. And more complex theories—Marx's included—were often more "optimistic" than warranted.

categories, however, the conclusion remains that participation in the pursuit of common interests, and thus the transition from latent group to actually cooperating group, are problematic. Across widely varied conditions, participation in large collective undertakings should *not* be expected even though the collective good at stake might be important—the creation of an effective trade union, the maintenance of an irrigation system, the care of common property, the erection of a legal order easing economic transactions, or an uprising against an unjust regime. This "collective action problem" is an ever-present issue, central to all social and political analysis.

Some objected that Olson stipulated for all social action a strictly self-interested calculation of the costs and benefits, and that his argument was informed by a simplistic version of rational action theory. As one graduate student put it, "he assumes that everybody acts the same way as small businesses operate in a competitive market." This is not quite correct. First, we must observe that much behavior outside the market is also governed by self-interest. This is the case especially when it comes to defensive actions, avoiding serious loss and punishment. Second, the sense of futility about one's contribution to what requires large-scale cooperation is independent of self-interest. It impedes other-oriented and norm-oriented participation as well: "Even if the member of a large group were to neglect his own interests entirely, he still would not rationally contribute toward the provision of any collective or public good, since his own contribution would not be perceptible" (Olson 1965, 64).

Collective action, then, came to be seen as problematic. Olson successfully put the "collective action problem" on the agenda of all meso- and macroanalysis in the social sciences. And yet his analysis of the conditions favorable for collective action seemed too restrictive. The fact is, of course, that collective action often does succeed, even under harsh adverse conditions. The *Solidarnosc* trade union of Poland is a famous example. Albert Hirschman called attention to a historic irony: "Mancur Olson proclaimed the impossibility of collective action for large groups (just as Daniel Bell proclaimed the 'end of ideology') at the precise moment when the Western world was about to be all but engulfed by an unprecedented wave of public movements, marches, protests, strikes, and ideologies" (1982, 78).

There is, then, reason to explore further the conditions under which active groups emerge from social categories with common interests; the conditions under which, that is, collective action comes about. The more than thirty years that have passed since the publication of *The Logic of Collective Action* have indeed seen a good deal of ingenious work with important results. Game theory, which explores strategic interactions among rational actors through modeling, first came to conclusions as negative as Olson's. In the Prisoners Dilemma game, rational actors will choose not to cooperate if one cannot count on the cooperation of the other, even though cooperation would make both sides better off. That outcome is changed quite dramatically if some of the game's premises are changed. Later studies showed how even single-mindedly self-interested actors can avoid the pitfalls of their self-interest producing negative collective outcomes. Above all, the likelihood that the question of cooperation will pose itself repeatedly in the future makes it rational to try out cooperation and to stick to the option if the try has been successful. If, however, a definite end of the relationship is anticipated, noncooperation becomes again the rational choice. Similar variations flow from assumptions about reputations, the ability to negotiate and to make credible commitments, different distributions of "payoffs," and so on. Looking at models with such less radically restrictive assumptions led to important hypotheses about the "evolution of cooperation" (Axelrod 1984), balancing the darker views of the collective action problem (see also Hardin 1982; Taylor 1987; Lichbach 1995, 1996). The substance of these contributions goes far beyond what I will describe here. I shall pursue one particular line of qualifications that may usefully complement the game theoretic work on cooperation.

Some Qualifications and Solutions of the Collective Action Problem

As noted by Albert Hirschman, historical developments following the publication of *The Logic of Collective Action* in the 1960s made it very clear that Olson had underestimated the role of moral and ideological commitments and the direct, individual appeal of certain collective goods. Olson realized that retreating to the premise that any action—and thus even the sheer response to normative responsibility—by definition presupposes a "utility" generating the action would make his argument tautological. Therefore he acknowledged that groups working for "lost" causes contradict his theory, as do mass movements for "utopian" goals as well as all ideological elements in politics. He claimed, however, that his theory was vindicated by the fact that such nonrational behavior was so rare as to be insignificant, at least in "stable, well ordered, and apathetic societies that have seen the 'end of ideology'" (1965, 162). Yet these empirical judgments, to which he added an observation about potential peace movements that might have interested Lyndon Johnson ("there are multitudes with an interest in peace, but they have no lobby," 166), put his very narrow claims about the possibilities of collective action in large potential groups into question.

In most large-scale collective action episodes whose goals transcend routine economic advantage, normative commitment and ideology are central factors. This is especially true when the costs and risks of active engagement are high and the outcome remains uncertain. In the face of a possible loss of livelihood, imprisonment, or even death, passionate commitments rather than prospects for limited material gain are decisive. In the broader context of a collective action's genesis, commitment and ideology are critical for motivating initiators who can become models, leaders, and organizers. This applies also to unionizing, as it typically combines the effort to create economic advantage with an appeal for justice. Such moral and ideological motivations cannot be fully understood as individualized "benefits" responding to the private urgings of conscience; they manifestly derive their strength from the appeal of the collective good itself.

It is true that those who act on conscience and commitment represent even in the most successful collective actions a small number compared to the vast mass of noncooperators. And part of the reason for this is found in the factors pointed out by Olson: a less passionate strength of concern and the sense of futility about broad spontaneous cooperation. But the active minority often constitutes the critical number necessary and sufficient to get the action going.

It is also true that passionate commitment is vulnerable to "burnout." As Max Weber pointed out in his discussion of the related phenomenon of charisma, the reassertion of the routine concerns of everyday life tends to transform and "normalize" charisma and passionate engagement. But while the engagement lasts, it can make a decisive difference.

The role of value-oriented engagement of a minority in certain forms of collective action suggests that "collective action" is an underspecified concept; some distinctions seem in order. Olson had made halfhearted efforts to confine his analysis to collective action aiming at economic benefits for the latent group, maintaining that the theory could be extended to other forms of collective action as well, though it would be less useful there because these other forms were based on nonrational or irrational behavior.[2] This was a move in the right direction but hardly a successful reconceptualization.

In principle, an outcome to be explained—the "dependent variable," in the language of quantitative research—should be conceptualized so as

---

[2] This judgment of nonrationality indicates, if interpreted narrowly, just that certain acts are not exclusively guided by an individual cost-benefit analysis. Taken more broadly, however, it points to a rather impoverished conception of politics. It is hard to see why committed work for attainable political goals should be irrational, in contrast to the rationality of joining politics for the prospects of office and personal enrichment (Olson 1965, 162–65).

to maximize the plausibility that a certain set of causal conditions bring it about or obstruct it—without, however, making the outcome certain by way of tautology. Reformulating Olson's intuitions, we may distinguish collective goals that in routine fashion aim exclusively at material advantages for a set of people from other collective goals that invoke nonmaterial values and therefore can arouse value-oriented passion. In the former case, selective individual incentives and the size of the group are crucial factors in overcoming the collective action problem. This is the way the automobile manufacturers' lobby works or, to a large extent, the American Medical Association and the American Bar Association as well. Olson's logic of collective action is smoothly applicable here. The alternative case describes most of the instances of collective action to which Hirschman's historical observation refers—peace movements, civil rights movements, but also collective action for educational reform (the signature event of the sixties at Brown University was a sustained mobilization of students to transform the curriculum) and action to establish unions as collective bargaining partners. Here the direct appeal of the collective goal is important; individual incentives are far less central, and concern for them can even seem to demean the cause; group size tends to be large; and unconditional passionate initiatives are often critical. Olson's logic of collective action still identifies difficulties of collective action but is not useful for explaining the success of such collective outbreaks.

Other differentiations of the broader conceptions of collective action are probably needed. Thus the maintenance of established behavior, which is secured by common understandings, widely held norms, and individual as well as collective habits, is most likely subject to quite different configurations of causal influence than is the success of initiatives that seek to establish new shared behavior patterns. Collectively refraining from action that would interfere with the current cleanliness and safety of the commons is very different from collective action to make public spaces in a current slum clean and safe. Similarly, maintaining a given level of readiness to owe and pay taxes is a very different matter from introducing de novo the ethos of a tax-contributing citizenry. Differences in the uncertainty of uphill efforts, differences in the role and efficacy of positive and negative sanctions and of material and immaterial incentives, and differences in the resources needed and available for the effort are only a few of the likely relevant features.

If I refrain here from attempting to sketch a complex typology of different forms of collective action, it is in deference to a sturdy pragmatic rule of thumb, which suggests that conceptual refinement be guided by specific

---

Clientelism and corruption can appear as the normal form of politics only if one neglects the institutional arrangements that give politics a different cast in most rich democracies.

causal problems and hypotheses, and warns against a proliferation of conceptual types that are only loosely connected to hypothesis formation. Instead, I will further assess the theoretical claims and suggestions made by Olson.

At the core of Olson's theory about the creation of collective goods lies a sharp distinction between small and large groups. Olson offers here significant insights contributing to Georg Simmel's early twentieth-century program of inquiry on "the bearing which the number of sociated individuals has upon the form of social life" (1950, 87). We are familiar with the characteristic power of face-to-face groups to influence their members through subtle as well as drastic sanctions based on nuanced mutual knowledge—social pressures that function in Olson's language as selective incentives.

Olson adds the argument that the individual benefit derived from a collective good may be sufficient to motivate members of small groups to contribute, while in a very large group futility would block cooperation. Compare the contribution a few households may make to keep a limited-access road snow-plowed with what Olson deemed the "absurd" idea that "the individuals in an economic system would voluntarily curtail their spending to halt inflation, however much they would, as a group, gain from doing this" (Olson 1965, 166). In certain cases, the individual benefit for some may even be large enough that a single member of a group will provide the collective good at his or her own expense, leading to the paradoxical outcome of the weaker members of a group exploiting the strongest. Together, these two arguments underline the distinctive character of small groups.

Olson claims that effective social incentives—in contrast to selective material advantages and disadvantages—work only in face-to-face groups. Yet he concedes that on occasion many different small groups induce their members to contribute to the achievement of collective goals that only the whole, "federal" group or collective can bring about. This is an important but undeveloped idea to which I will return. It begs for inquiries into the structural conditions under which different small groups come to nurture similar concerns in wider social formations.

Equally important, Olson overlooks here that many and important social norms are established and enforced with effective sanctions in large groups as well. Political voting can best be explained by broad-based norms of civic duty. And such communitywide, nationwide, or subculturewide norms are not rare, even though their enforcement may be uneven in its effectiveness. Significantly, one of the more common social norms is the injunction against free riding, against enjoying a benefit without contributing "one's share." Normative valuations of wider obligations and social attachments to larger groups build on symbolic mediation that transcends the immediate face-to-face environment. This supports the pursuit of different collective goods and makes at least minorities respond with uncoerced and unrewarded contributions; examples are individual and unobserved self-restraint in using natural resources, charity giving as well as volunteering for civic work or service in the armed forces. Where the effect of such broad-based norms, values, and social attachments is much diluted so that active cooperation does not come about, they can still create a distinctive receptiveness for appeals and generate sympathies and passive support.

Subjectively embraced norms and values supporting collective goods have noteworthy cognitive correlates. They tend to magnify the value of a single contribution (so that some people deliberate at length as to how to cast their single vote in a "strategically smart" way), and they tend to induce the belief that many other people will act in line with the same norms, reducing the sense of futility that figures prominently in Olson's argument.

The actual existence of large-scale collective action suggests that under certain conditions large "latent" groups may be mobilized by initiating and organizing leadership. What are some of the conditions that make such mobilization attempts successful? The chances of finding resonance are shaped by complex structural and subcultural variations.

The most elementary structural condition for mobilization is some interaction and mutual awareness among members of the latent group. Marx found here the reason why the most numerous class of nineteenth-century France, the small independent peasants, did not become an organized force. As he put it in his essay *The 18th Brumaire of Louis Bonaparte*: "The small independent peasants constitute an enormous mass, the members of which live in the same situation but do not enter into manifold relations with each other. The mode of production isolates them from each other instead of bringing them into mutual intercourse. This isolation is strengthened by the bad state of French means of communication and by the poverty of peasants" (Dahrendorf 1959, 183).

By contrast, this condition was largely met among the working and urban middle classes in Europe and the United States when industrialization concentrated production in factories, and when vast increases in urbanization coincided with a decisive improvement in the means of communication. That is the background of the emergence of complex political systems in rich democracies with their dense arrays of parties, unions, and interest associations. The differences across countries and among parties and interest organizations are, on the one hand, due to differences in political institutions, such as electoral systems and the relations between the executive and elected representatives, and they derive, on the other hand, from variations in the landscape of interest configurations and the social and cultural conditions favoring or inhibiting mobilization attempts of different kinds.

For the chances of working-class organizations, a number of factors were particularly important. The experience of conflict in strikes, in fights for the right to form "combinations" in the first place, and in struggles to gain full voting rights made many more concerned with wider issues than they would have been otherwise. Such local experience of conflict has important consequences. It gives emotional force to—first small, then wider—solidarities, and it can articulate with the ideas and interpretations offered by a mobilizing leadership. Whether such a melding of local solidarities with the help of a common ideology is successful depends to a large extent on whether the ideas offered by the initiators harmonize with the mentalities and ideological inclinations of different parts of the constituency. Here enters a factor of critical importance: the ethnic, religious, and racial composition of the latent group may favor or obstruct a growing unification under a single interpretation of collective needs and goods. Related factors are the degree to which membership in a class location is seen as long-term and perhaps lifelong and the extent to which one's present situation is seen as due to chance and "structurally irrelevant" factors, such as "delinquency, extreme lack of talent, personal mishaps, physical or psychological instability." In the latter case, "conflict group formation cannot be expected" (Dahrendorf 1959, 187–88; see also chapter 14 on status and class).

These considerations can be generalized. With appropriate changes, they can guide investigation into a wide variety of appeals for collective action. The major points correspond to the core of the current political process approach to social movements. The emergent focus on political opportunity structures, structural conditions underlying the chances of mobilization, and framing processes has greatly advanced our understanding of social movements and, more generally, of the dynamics of collective action (Tarrow 1994; McAdam, Tarrow, and Tilly 1997; McAdam, Tarrow, and Tilly 2001; Goodwin and Jasper 2004). This success lends credence to the qualifications of Olson's logic we are developing (see also chapter 13 on social identities).

The move from small, localized concerns and readiness to act to broader mobilization could be considered as an instance of Olson's concept of "federal groups," larger groupings that consist of a range of small face-to-face groups. Yet it is important to see that local networks and small groups can nurture concerns for a long time without any automatic "federation." Rather, such a melding may well occur only as the result of successful mobilization by initiators and organizers and their interpretation of causes and possibilities, and this process of mobilization may go far beyond the concerns harbored by individuals and small groups initially.

When it comes to gauging the receptiveness of latent groups to mobilizing appeals of many different kinds, the same sorts of factors as just indicated seem broadly relevant:

- the emotional charge derived from dramatic experiences (which under current conditions may be conveyed by mass communication, often mediated by personal relations and intimate small groups);
- normative orientations, both of the formal ("Do your part and don't be a free rider!") and of different substantive kinds (such as patriotism, social concerns, or civic reform); such orientations may be established in varying degree in different subcultures and latent groups;
- the division or homogeneity of a latent group in terms of ethnic, religious, racial, and other identifications, which generate sympathies and antipathies that are often as decisive as shared or contrary interests (and sometimes more so); and
- the way these features of the "target landscape" articulate with the manner in which mobilization attempts are framed by an analysis of causes and prospects and their ideological assessment.

These are major factors that determine failure and success of mobilization for collective action. They modify the impact of the conditions emphasized by Olson, but they do not eliminate them.

I now return to Olson's core conceptualizations of collective goods, individual costs, and individualized, "selective" benefits and sanctions. First a closer look at individual costs. It is plain that these can and do vary a great deal, ranging from major risks under repressive conditions to small expenditures of time or money. More important is the fact that participation may carry its own rewards. It may be fun and entertainment. (This was the charge conservative observers raised about the motivation of activist students in the sixties.) More profoundly, joining the like-minded may be deeply gratifying. Albert Hirschman adds the observation that in public action striving and achievement are peculiarly fused, and that this makes people spurn a free ride: "The sudden realization (or illusion) that I can act to change society for the better and, moreover, that I can join other like-minded people to this end is in such conditions pleasurable, in fact intoxicating, in itself" (1982, 89). These arguments not only put the costs of certain kinds of participation into question; they also maintain that individual gratification and motivation for the sake of collective goods are often fused with each other.

Individualized "selective" incentives, both benefits and negative sanctions, are clearly important in motivating people to contribute to a collective good. This is so because some collective goods will not generate strong motivations to act even among a minority, and the sense of futility about infinitesimally small contributions to the solution of far-flung problems often squashes individual initiatives aside from that. Threatening coercion makes people cooperate where they otherwise might not—laboring on common projects, serving in armies, obeying laws and regulations, and paying taxes. Individualized benefits may do the same. But about both we must ask: who has the resources to threaten sanctions and offer individual positive incentives? If these resources are just hoped for or promised as a result of successful collective action ("After the coup, we will reward you with lucrative positions"), the motivating power of individualized incentives may not differ so greatly from that of the collective good ("regime change") itself.

Olson develops a supplementary "by-product theory of pressure groups": large latent groups will be represented by organized lobbies only if the organizations have the capacity to coerce membership, offer valuable economic benefits, and/or provide social benefits; together, the value of these benefits has to exceed the individual contribution to the common cause. An example of what this theory stipulates is the American Association of Retired Persons, which offers public lobbying for a small fee while generating major resources from insurance activities. Olson claims in a wide-ranging overview that this by-product theory is supported by the facts.

A brief look at the professional associations with which many readers will be familiar, the American Political Science Association and the American Sociological Association, points to complications. Membership in these organizations is not directly or indirectly coerced. It is urged by social norms that are legitimated by the value of common concerns. The selective benefits—journals, insurance offerings, and access to meetings—hardly explain the membership, especially since all except the meetings are available in different ways. Participation in meetings, which requires additional contributions, results in some benefits that can be seen as primarily individual (presenting a paper that enlarges one's record of performance, making useful personal contacts), but in the eyes of many it is also motivated by collective benefits—the public representation of what political science and sociology have to offer, and the airing of debate that is significant for intellectual understanding and the emergence of consensus or polarization. Here, then, we encounter again a peculiar intertwining of motivation by individual gain and the direct appeal by the collective good.

Such interconnections between motivation by individualized incentives and the appeal of collective goods themselves have some theoretical significance. This is especially true for social incentives and sanctions. Olson's neglect of these interconnections corresponds to his impoverished view of norms. The clustering of norms, values, and attachments that emerged as a critical phenomenon in our discussion of norms hardly comes into view in his discussion. A strong valuation of a collective good typically stands in the background of positive and negative social incentives. Most coercion would be illegitimate without it.[3] This does not mean that illegitimate coercion is necessarily ineffective; but illegitimate coercion may generate opposition and diminish subjective commitment to the goals it seeks to advance.

An extension of Olson's by-product theory of representation of collective interests suggests that multitask organizations have a special role in overcoming the collective action problem in the pursuit of public goods. Often it is far from clear which collective good is apt to satisfy an emergent set of interests. This is frequently the case in public policy. It is obviously difficult to mobilize cooperation for an as yet unclear cause. However, existing organizations that have the capacity either to provide a variety of collective goods by themselves or to induce people to participate in their creation can explore different solutions for new problems and then proceed to mobilize resources once a promising course of action is identified. This typically requires strong institutional backing. States are prime examples of such institutionally grounded multipurpose organizations that can directly provide solutions or activate collective action once a goal has been determined. They and their nonstate counterparts (such as, for instance, religious bodies) might be considered prefabricated problem solvers, as it were.

The thrust of Olson's analysis was that genuine collective action on behalf of large latent groups had poor prospects indeed. The qualifications that have been argued and others not reviewed here give somewhat better chances to solutions to the collective action problem. But the genesis of collective action in large latent groups remains a complex and not fully understood problem. The conditions analyzed by Olson are important:

- collective action as the by-product of the provision of individual goods and services;
- collective action grounded in industrial and political relations conducive to membership (as in unions that have attained recognition as partners in collective bargaining and in politics);
- collective action founded on the capacity and authority of states to make cooperation compulsory.

---

[3] Coleman (1990, 21) speaks of "a collective right to exercise social control over certain actors' actions, via norms enforced by sanctions," and notes that the establishment of this right comes about "through some poorly understood process."

The evidence about successful mobilizations for collective action suggests that Olson neglected the direct appeal of collective goods. This is relevant both for committed action of minorities and for a more muted responsiveness in larger groups. The conditions that generate both of these include configurations of interest as well as of established norms. The valuation of potential collective goods also constitutes a context that makes different selective incentives—from social persuasion and pressure to concealed or outright coercive means—more or less effective.

THE INHERENT AMBIGUITY OF COLLECTIVE ACTION

Collective action may not lead to the results expected and hoped for. Bringing about change, or protecting interests, against opposition is difficult and may be less than successful. But a prior question is equally important: what goals will be pursued once a degree of cooperation for collective action is secured?[4]

Whatever the route by which collective action comes about, the goals are not self-evident. There are different interests that have to be considered and combined; priorities have to be set and rankings established; and the ways of best realizing collective goals have to be determined. For example, a union may or may not make higher wages its top priority. Other goals may concern employment security, fringe benefits, social relations at work, or different degrees of sharing authority in production. Political goals may also come into play. Moreover, there is the question of defining the collectivity to be represented: building electricians in a given construction site? all construction workers? all blue-collar workers in a country? white-collar workers too? or even the "Workers of the World"? In unions as well as all other collective representations of interests, shaping the actual goals of collective action is inevitably a process of social construction, a process that may—and is likely to—become a matter of conflict and contention.[5]

The determination of the goals actually pursued typically takes place in the process of mobilization and organization. A small number of activists will therefore have a strong influence on the choices made. This influence becomes consolidated as the core of the group becomes solidly organized. Robert Michels turned this insight, which he gained from his

[4] The following builds on the discussion of class formation in Rueschemeyer, Stephens, and Stephens (1992, 53–57).

[5] That collective action can be a source of division and conflict is in the perspective of rational individualism obvious to the point of tautology: "Diverse wants and values with respect to a collective good are a basis for conflict, whereas different wants with respect to individual or private goods are not" (Olson 1965, 173).

frustrating experience as an untypical member of the German Social Democratic Party, the strongest prodemocratic form in imperial Germany, into
his famous "iron law of oligarchy": "It is organization which gives birth
to the dominion of the elected over the electors, of the mandataries over
the mandators, of the delegates over the delegators. Whoever says organization says oligarchy" (Michels 1911/1949, 410). The activists in charge
of the organizational core of a party, interest association, or movement
are skilled politically. They have at their disposal the advantage inherent
in systematic rational organization. They control the financial assets of
the group. And they are in command of its media. Their influence will be
especially large when compared to that of the least affluent, least educated, least informed, and least respected members. That the latter have
virtually no chance of making their interests heard might well be called
another "iron law" of power relations, one that holds across a wide variety of situations. But not all rank-and-file members are in so dependent a
situation. They may be quite well informed and have the means of making
their different views heard and considered. They may also trust the leadership and be content with its decisions. This is especially likely if the leadership is seen as competent and the group finds itself embattled in conflict.
That the internal disparities of power and influence vary across associations and are further dependent on the social and political context was
shown in the brilliant investigation of a democratically functioning labor
union, the International Typographical Union in New York, by Lipset,
Trow, and Coleman (1956). Michels and his many followers, including
Lipset, Trow, and Coleman, focused on the structural deficit in democracy. They did not emphasize, as I do here, that the goals actually pursued
on behalf of large constituencies are shaped to a large extent by small
organizational elites.

Organizational leaders have to deal not only with their constituencies
but also with other power centers, with the state as well as with the representative elites of other organized interests. If they are highly independent
of the rank and file, they can use this autonomy to come to arrangements
even with representatives of starkly opposed interests. Such cooperation
may be further smoothed by shared cultural and social commonalities.
Different degrees of "oligarchy" make possible different degrees of elite
cooperation and co-optation. In the extreme, this includes the possibility
of betrayal. Pondering this possibility, it seems reasonable—from a grass-
roots point of view—to speak of an "inherent ambiguity of collective
action." Given that collective organization is a power resource of distinctive importance for the many, this is a sobering insight.

Each link in the extended causal chain we have just sketched—from
the difficulty of coming to collective action in the first place, through the
oligarchic tendencies inherent in organization and their effect on the col-

lective course of action chosen, to the effects of elite interaction that constrain or even contradict many common members' impulses to join—is shaped by complex conditions. Each can compromise the initial interests. But each can also be counteracted significantly. If it is difficult to imagine large organizations without any trace of oligarchy and co-optation, the neglect of members' interests also has its limits. Even an organization that relies on compulsory membership must serve some interests of its rank and file if it is to retain any internal life. Otherwise, the activities of the rank and file exist largely on paper, and the nominal members become, as the German phrase has it, *Karteileichen*, corpses on file.[6] But as a broad conclusion we can hold that large groups with multiple potential interests are faced with far more complex problems of interest representation than small groups with sharply defined interests.

CONCLUSION

Mancur Olson's *Logic of Collective Action* put a problem of tremendous importance on the agenda of political science and meso- and macrosociology. Following a long history of commentary and qualification during four decades, I have critically examined his arguments. All of my critiques have one common denominator: they point to necessary qualifications where Olson's original position was, even though he tried to argue it in a nuanced way, too close to a simple rational action theory that neglects the determinants and effects of varying norms, values, and attachments, of strong and of becalmed emotions, as well as of changeable preferences and beliefs. This is illustrated by the main qualification I proposed, that passionate commitment to collective values can generate effective mobilizing elites. In a minority, individual motivation may respond to collective goods in much the same way as others would pursue individual goods. Correspondingly, common norms, values, and attachments shape the likely responses of different latent groups to appeals of the mobilizing minorities. Strongly held norms and values also shape beliefs, such as those about how many others will value things in similar ways and act accordingly. Finally, we saw that the goals pursued once large-scale mobilization is successful are subject to further complex causal determination.

---

[6] Marilyn Rueschemeyer has shown that work collectives, the lowest level of union organizations in the former German Democratic Republic, served their members by mediating between the demands the enterprise made on them and their varied other needs and interests. This gave the collectives an organizational life that contrasted with the flat levels of involvement characteristic of many other East German organizations at the time (Rueschemeyer 1982, 1982–83; Rueschemeyer and Scharf 1986).

A critique of this kind does not yield more definitive predictions; in fact, the outcomes of attempts at collective action appear ever more complex. But our critique does point to conditions under which norms, values, beliefs, and emotions can override Olson's stark predictions. Yet recognizing the problem Olson highlighted was and remains a vast step forward, even if we are not in a position to spell out all conditions under which it does or does not hold.

Chapter XI

POWER AND COOPERATION

Cooperation and coordination stand in close interrelation with the creation and use of power. Most forms of cooperation, especially lasting forms, require some exercise of power, be it directly or indirectly. And, in turn, power is generated and enlarged when lasting cooperation and effective coordination are brought about. This nexus between power and cooperation is a key to major problems of meso- and macro–social analysis.

Maintaining that cooperation and coordination require the exercise of power is not simply to repeat the claims of Hobbes, who posited powerful authority as *the* alternative to a war of all against all, though powerful authority can indeed be one important means of achieving cooperation. Contemporary rational choice theory has focused on models in which cooperation arises from mutual agreement among rational actors. But since unequal bargaining positions are common, mutually agreed understandings and rules often rest on a consent that would not have been given under equal conditions. In a different vein, shared meanings as well as common values and norms have been invoked by Parsons and other functionalists as conducive to cooperation. Yet such common views and normative orientations often are created and secured by asymmetrical relations of influence and power. Moreover, effective norms are *enforced* even if they do not meet with the support of all concerned. Even spontaneous conventions tend to become, as we have seen, enforced norms if disagreement and contention arises about them. Finally, while one of the most important coordination mechanisms—namely, competitive market exchange—does not involve the exercise of power in a direct way, it could not function were it not undergirded by strong power-based guarantees.

In turn, cooperation and effective coordination typically create resources that can be—and frequently are—captured by minorities and turned into a source of power. One prototype of this outcome was identified by Robert Michels's "iron law of oligarchy" (see chapter 10). More generally, the division of labor, which arises with cooperation and enlarges its results, entails the creation of roles that differ in status, economic advantage, and power. Michels's oligarchy is only one special case of that. Those privileged in this specialization-inequality nexus will mobilize their resources to protect their advantaged positions. Even those who have a less advantageous place in the social division of labor may benefit sufficiently from the results of cooperation to support—or acquiesce in—the division of power and authority that goes with the division of labor. Egalitarian cooperation that does not create differential power and influence is difficult to achieve and perhaps still more difficult to maintain. Even competitive market exchange has strong tendencies toward monopolistic and oligopolistic concentrations of power and advantage.

In either direction of the causal arrows that link power and cooperation, neutralizing power has been the goal of idealisms of the ideological Left and Right. However, while cooperation which is not based on power and cooperation which does not generate power are social configurations that cannot be ruled out, it appears easier to overlook or conceal the role of power than to realize and maintain a level playing field of power and yet achieve effective cooperation and coordination.

What Do We Mean by "Power"?

At this point, it is necessary to consider different meanings of "power." Different aspects of what we call power—highlighted by distinct conceptualizations—give a particular cast to the relations between power and cooperation. In the widest understanding of power, the nexus between power and cooperation stands out with special clarity. Here power is the capacity to get things done, or, as Michael Mann put it in the introduction to his historical anatomy of power, "power is the ability to pursue and attain goals through mastery of one's environment" (1986, 6). In its social aspect, this ability hinges crucially on the capacity to create lasting cooperation and coordination. In this broadest conception of power, then, the link between power and cooperation is acknowledged in the very definition of power.[1]

[1] Technically this renders hypotheses stating the power-cooperation nexus tautological—true by definition. However, that pitfall can be avoided if we use more specific definitions of power when developing hypotheses about the mechanisms involved in that nexus

The problems of concept formation that become apparent here are well to keep in mind: the temptation to include general insights into definitions seems strong, even for many experienced scholars, because it is a handy way of giving certain relationships prominence. This is reinforced by the widespread inclination to view definitions as capsule statements of the "essence" of a phenomenon (the source of many endless and often fruitless discussions about the "right" definition). In empirical research, it is more rational to view definitions just as a means to identify distinctively certain phenomena under study. Yet if we reject arguments formulated with "essentialist" ideas in mind as just tautologies, we may often discard sound insights. Reformulating the concepts more specifically can often avoid arguments that are true by definition and lead to the generation of promising propositions.

Max Weber was skeptical of the utility of broad conceptions of power. He called the concept of power "sociologically amorphous," because power can derive from a virtually endless diversity of conditions, even though his own definition—"the probability that one actor in a social relationship will be in a position to carry out his will despite resistance"— narrowed the broadest meaning and emphasized power *over* others rather than a generalized capacity to attain goals. For his own work, Weber preferred the concept of domination—the chance of finding obedience to one's commands (1922/1978, 53).

Comprehensive conceptions of power are, however, reasonable, provided we can identify—perhaps only in rough outline—important consequences that such more broadly conceived phenomena may bring about. This is indeed the case. Mann's still incomplete but already massive two-volume analysis of the sources of power in history (1986, 1993) represents one persuasive piece of evidence for that. It focuses on the interrelations between different broad conceptions of power and various forms of cooperation and coordination.

There are two remedies to the amorphous character of the broader conceptions of power: inquiries into the diverse resources of power and, second, the creation of more specific concepts of power—conceptual differentiation. Weber offered a beginning of such differentiation with his concept of domination. Its focus on asymmetrical authority-command relations must be complemented by other specific concepts, in particular concepts that point to more diffuse and indirect forms of power, such as those that underlie and enable market transactions and their results.[2]

Consideration of diverse sources of power also helps to make overall concepts of power less amorphous. It is easy to think of different bases of power. They are indeed multifarious, but each has its own pattern of genesis, of accessibility to various actors, and of use in different exercises of power. The ability to deploy physical coercion and destructive violence, property of economic resources, possession of specially desirable skills or of knowledge that is useful to others, religious and magical capacities,

---

[2] Mann's work has given wide currency to the concept of "infrastructural power." This refers to diffused forms of power in the hands of a state. In contrast to what he calls "despotic power" ("power by the state elite *over* civil society"), infrastructural power "denotes power of the state to penetrate and centrally coordinate the activities of civil society" (1988, 7; see also Soifer and vom Hau 2008). I refrain from relating the full set of concepts Mann develops, nor will I try to present a set of power concepts of my own. The reason is, again, my conviction that the construction of more specific concepts should go hand in hand with the formation of specific hypotheses. At this point, my argument can proceed with the distinction between diffused power and command power (or, roughly, Weber's domination). Mann replicates this distinction, when he discusses the power of the state, with the concepts of despotic and infrastructural power.

authoritative voice on norms and values, control over means of communication, command over an established and efficient organization, capacity to bring others together to form collaborative associations—these and many others come to mind. Some are inherited (in the biological or in the socioeconomic sense); others depend on performance. Some derive from imputations of capacity that outside observers may view as illusory; others—as, for instance, lethal violence—have a core of effectiveness that is independent of social construction. Some, in fact most, are available only to select groups of people, while merely a few—such as collective organization—are accessible to "the many" (and that only under specially favorable circumstances). These passing indications of differences in origin, accessibility, and use may be sufficient to suggest that the very variability of sources of power can be a springboard for interesting hypotheses about the resulting forms of power.

Michael Mann pulls this diversity together under four summary labels—ideological power, economic power, military power, and political power. Each involves complex and contrasting organizational forms that are interrelated with each other and, under different conditions, take precedence over each other. Together they form the foundational grid for his long-term historical analysis. Throughout, he sees social formations and their diverse forms of cooperation and coordination as constituted by overlapping organizational power networks.[3]

This chapter will take a different tack. I will proceed from a rough comparison of social formations that rely largely on family and kin ties for structuring diverse activities and others in which formal organizations, nonkin associations, and market exchange are available for a much greater number of pursuits. In the latter, indirect and enabling forms of power are of special importance. The difference between these two broad institutional types puts contrasting forms of the power-cooperation nexus into sharp relief. Remarkably, it also throws a revealing light on the process of women's emancipation.

CLASSIC DUALISMS AS A POINT OF DEPARTURE

Proceeding this way is inspired by theoretical ideas common among the classic social theorists of the nineteenth and the early twentieth centuries, ideas that later gave birth to modernization theory. I build on these ideas in a critical spirit. On the one hand, it seems foolish to simply cast aside

---

[3] Rarely if ever, he argues, do these networks of power coincide in such a way as to make the common understanding of *societies*—as more or less self-contained comprehensive social structures—a useful foundation of macroanalysis.

the insights of Comte, Spencer, Durkheim, Toennies, and Weber, which took off from what they saw as a break in the social order of European countries that became visible toward the end of the eighteenth century. Their rough consensus, expressed in the form of polar opposites, pointed to important transformations.[4]

On the other hand, these dualistic conceptions became associated with evolutionary views that assumed a unilinear development of all societies through universal stages. And this engendered stereotyped and unrealistic ideas about the prehistory of European societies as well as facile expectations for the future of "developing" countries. Normatively, the evolutionary perspective encouraged seeing European and "Western" societies as the apex of world development. Evolutionary theories also suffered from being vague about the mechanisms that pushed social evolution forward. And this deficiency carried over into modernization theory. Modernization theory, too, was stronger as a global description of broadly contrasting social formations than as an analysis of forces that generated transitions from one to the other. It was fashioned out of the earlier dualistic views when decolonization after the Second World War required answers about the possible and desirable future of "new nations."[5]

Despite the flaws of the classic dualisms, of nineteenth-century theories of social evolution, and of simplistic versions of modernization theory, in a long-term perspective it seems nevertheless reasonable to set the last two centuries of world history apart from several millennia in which social life based on agriculture predominated, and to explore what is new and

---

[4] Most readers will be familiar with the classic dualisms of militant and industrial society (Spencer), social formations based on status or contract (Sumner Maine), mechanical and organic solidarity (Durkheim), or *Gemeinschaft* and *Gesellschaft*—community and association (Toennies)

Max Weber made a critical move when he turned the latter distinction into pure types of relationships whose features are in reality typically mingled. Communal relationships are, he says, "most conveniently illustrated by the family. But the great majority of social relationships has this [communal] characteristic to some degree, while being at the same time to some degree determined by associative factors" (1922/1978, 41). Talcott Parsons later developed Weber's distinction into a set of contrasting features of social relationships that he called "pattern variables," distinguishing achievement vs. ascription, universalism vs. particularism, specificity vs. diffuseness, emotional neutrality vs. affectivity, and collectivity vs. self-orientation as such relationship features. Clearly one pole in each of these pairs may preponderate in a social relationship; but in reality they combine in complex ways, and it is very unlikely that a whole social formation will be characterized by pure and unmixed features, as is claimed in simplistic models of "traditional society," in which all social relationships display unmixed ascription, particularism, and diffuseness.

[5] It is, however, worthwhile noting that the major points of critique indicated above were made early on by authors who are still often associated with modernization theory; see, for example, the set of papers by Bellah, Eisenstadt, Moore, Parsons, and others in the June 1964 issue of the *American Sociological Review*.

distinctive in our world. It is in this broader picture that a comparison of family- and kin-based social organization in agrarian societies with "modern" institutional formations, in which nonkin-based social relations play vastly more important roles, comes to the fore.

The years of 1776 and 1789—the years of the American Revolution, of Adam Smith's *Inquiry into the Nature and Causes of the Wealth of Nations*, and of the French Revolution—mark and symbolize a fundamental shift in the character of human societies. This shift had been in preparation in Europe since the Renaissance and earlier, and it is rapidly completing itself globally in our own time. It involves a number of interrelated transformations:

- from agrarian to far more productive industrial and knowledge-based economies;
- from slow changes in science and technology to rapid developments that transformed economic production, culture, and everyday life;
- from limited exchange relations to more and more encompassing market exchange;
- from monarchic and oligarchic political control to a "fundamental democratization" (Mannheim 1940) that may enable democracy in the narrower sense but also can encourage mobilization under authoritarian auspices;
- from limited state power, in which command power predominated (whether embedded in asymmetric forms of traditional mutuality or not) to vast increases in indirect, enabling, or "infrastructural" state power, potentially paralleled by equally enlarged command power (which may, however, be balanced by countervailing power in civil society and constrained by the rule of law);
- from an extremely one-sided distribution of economic and social privilege to status and class relations that tend to be more fluid and less unequal, though far from egalitarian (Lenski 1966);
- from a narrowly localized social life of the vast majority of people to the opportunities created by continuing expansions of transportation and communication; and finally
- from a social organization primarily based on family and kin relations to one that displays a great variety of formal organizations and associations which are detached from family and kin relations.

This list of contrasts focuses on the interrelations between power and cooperation and highlights four broad interrelated kinds of change: first, change in technology and productivity; second, change in the triple dimensions of structured inequality—in class, status, and power (Weber

1922/1978/; Bendix and Lipset 1953/1966); third, change in the geo-
graphic mobility of people, goods, and ideas; and finally, change in prevailing forms of cooperation and coordination. If I do not include cultural
changes more prominently in this list, this is not to denigrate the causal
role of religion and culture in social life generally (see chapter 15). Yet
cultural difference may well "cut across" the dividing line under discussion: there is a good deal of cultural variation among different parts of
the world before as well as after these transformations set in, and there is
also a good deal of cultural continuity in different countries, regions, and
groupings despite these profound structural changes.

CONTRASTING FORMS OF POWER AND COOPERATION

In the emerging new institutional formations, the family is no longer the
nearly all-purpose organizational form that in agricultural societies was
used for production as well as consumption and education, and that—
partly through its extensions in kinship—also played a central role in the
creation of wider solidarities, in religious practice as well as in structuring
systems of rule. The new institutional patterns support not only vastly
expanded market exchange, but also a much larger number and variety
of voluntary organizations and secular social movements and, above all,
formal organizations from schools to hospitals and from government departments to business corporations.[6]

The family still represents an important mode of cooperation, but its
internal inequality of power—between men and women and also between
generations—has been dramatically reduced. Among the most apparent
causes of this reduction are the decline of economic production within
the family-based household and a softening of the pressures of scarcity in
the material necessities of life. Public and private corporate actors, independent of family and kinship, are responsible for vastly expanded new
forms of cooperation, and these formal organizations now constitute the
major type of cooperation that involves command authority. However,
that these command structures of cooperation can be stable and effective
independent of family and kinship rests on the indirect guarantees offered

---

[6] This claim is critically debated. Many family sociologists reject older formulations of a
"loss of functions" suffered by the family and point to the many new demands that are
made on families in Europe and the United States. Some of these demands have their origin
in the very features often used to define modern social structures, such as increasingly meritocratic education and employment or the requirements of jobs that often do not take the
functioning of family life into consideration (Thornton 2005, 93–95). But such arguments
in no way detract from the fact that nonfamily modes of coordination and cooperation play
a much larger role in "modern" societies than they ever did before.

by the coercive might of the state. These guarantees define the identity of corporate actors, their basic internal structure, and their obligations and rights. They relate them to the law of property, contract, and myriads of detailed regulations. And they articulate them with the nonlegal bases of the law. The same new institutional infrastructure that makes the flourishing of corporate actors possible is also critical for the other two proliferating forms of cooperation and coordination, market exchange and purposive voluntary associations, often congealing into social movements.

In the "old order"—or, better, "old orders," for there was great diversity—the social life of most people was largely family-based. Above all, households provided the primary organizational form of economic production. With family relations at their core, age and gender differences offered a grid for the division of labor. This also remained true in "patrimonial" households, which included apprentices, servants, and possibly many other nonkin members. Authority differences based on age and gender—reinforced by the requirements of discipline in work and consumption inherent in agricultural production and life under harsh scarcity—assured effective coordination. The visibility of life in small groups made social control robust. The stability of these organizational forms was secured by mutual dependence, which resulted in a rough sharing of the fruits of the household's labor (though this was compatible with a good deal of inequality), by the difficulty of finding a place in social life independent of family and kin relations, and by widely accepted norms that were often protected from critical reflection and sanctioned by religion.

The family-based household as an all-purpose organization took a great many different forms in historical social formations grounded in agriculture and horticulture. Thus the extended family was, contrary to earlier assumptions, not common in northwestern Europe, nor was it characteristic of agrarian societies in general, though it was typical of certain areas and historical periods. Similarly, the inequality between men and women, though associated in an overall fashion with agriculture, varied (and varies) a great deal in its severity across agrarian social formations. Work in historical demography and family history during the past half century strongly suggests that quite different patterns of family and kinship are compatible with similar modes of economic subsistence, as this research uncovered substantial continuities in English and northwestern European family life that reach from around 1800 as far back as to the thirteenth century. By contrast, the last two centuries have seen dramatic changes in Europe and its "Western" cousins as well as in other parts of the world, though there remain important contrasts between East and West. These changes include declines in childbearing, increases in age at marriage, the increase in the autonomy of young people, growing egalitarianism between women and men, increases in divorce, independent living among the elderly, increases in sexual activity and cohabitation outside of marriage, and the growing emphasis on individual rights as opposed to the norms and regulations of the larger community (Thornton 2005, 9).[7]

Family relations share—in the old as well as in their new forms—a personal character, which contrasts fundamentally with relations in markets, formal organizations, and purposive associations. They are inherently relations between particular persons, while formal organizations are constituted by positions that are in principle independent of the people who fill them.

The positions in a formal organization—as well as the social relations in market exchange and in purposive associations—are specialized. They are designed for achieving specific goals, and their incumbents are chosen, evaluated, and possibly replaced by criteria of success and failure. Formal organizations as well as market relations and voluntary associations are, in principle, rationally constructed social phenomena.

Family members, by contrast, have encompassing and persistent, unconditional obligations toward each other. Not remaining together is experienced as a rupture and a failure, not as a normal response to insufficient performance. While the participants in formal employment, market exchange, and purposive association are autonomous individuals in contractual relationships with others, family members are part of a collective whose joint and multidimensional welfare is the reference point of their mutual obligations and shared orientations. Though family life, too, is subject to change, and though this change often reflects adjustments to changing circumstances, family structures and people's roles in them are experienced as givens. Most participants do not treat them as objects of rational construction and reconstruction.

These contrasts remain important even if corporate enterprises often seek to induce generalized commitments in their employees, if many purposive associations rely on the intrinsic satisfaction of related activities in small groups as well as on identifications with broader social groupings and the values associated with them, if market exchange is often embedded in somewhat personalized relations, and if—on the other side of the

[7] Thornton's book makes a strong case that the "developmental paradigm," which has shaped social thought for 250 years, led in the study of the family to mistaken historical conclusions from cross-sectional evidence ("reading history sideways," as the title of his book puts it). These "family myths" were based on the assumption that patterns observed in less-developed countries must have been characteristic of the historical past of advanced countries as well. Thornton gives an impressive summary of the findings of the last sixty years that dramatically contradict those ideas (2005, 83–102). I am less convinced about the second large claim of his book—that the high valuation of certain family patterns constitutes itself a major causal factor in the spread of the "modern" family patterns.

divide—family relations take on some of the characteristics of contractual relations between autonomous individuals. Aristocratic wedding strategies of old and today's prenuptial agreements of some wealthy partners represent radical forms of such variation, while some developments in modern family life constitute more subtle changes in that direction.[8]

Modern families do not encompass the whole life of their members in the degree that they did in many agrarian social formations. This means that family life loses much of its controlling power, which was often based on its confining character: there were few feasible exit options. Put differently, "the invention [of formal organizations independent of family and kinship] was a critical development, for it had the effect of freeing persons" (Coleman 1990, 427). Marion Levy, generalizing from observations in China, makes the same point from the perspective of kin-dominated social formations when he describes the access to new forms of association and cooperation as a "universal social solvent" acting on "relatively nonmodernized" family, kin, and village structures (1966, 741–64).

The epochal transformations under discussion, then, resulted in radically different forms of the power-cooperation nexus. Family and kin ties do not any more structure most of economic production, and they also play a less significant role in the creation and maintenance of larger social units and in their governance. At the same time, the domination exercised within the family has significantly diminished.

The deployment of "infrastructural" power of states has given nonkin forms of cooperation and coordination stability and effectiveness independent of family ties. Together with other causal conditions—most prominently advances in communication and transportation—this brought about the proliferation of formal organizations, of market exchange, and of voluntary associations. The formal organizations of public and private corporate actors are now the main locus of command forms of domination.

THE HALTING EMANCIPATION OF WOMEN

The emancipation of women is one of the central processes in the epochal transformation of the past two centuries. It is central because it is interrelated with the main forces driving the transformation. It is also central because it represents—by itself as well as symbolically—one of its main

---

[8] In other words, while the contrast is strong as well as important, expressed in its strongest form it is a contrast between pure (or "ideal") types. See n. 4 above on the transformation of Toennies's concepts of community and association introduced by Max Weber.

outcomes: reshaping the power-cooperation nexus by setting people free and making them available for a wide range of activities.

Considering this centrality of women's emancipation, two questions suggest themselves: What are the causal conditions eroding the subordination of women? And what are the main obstacles to a full emancipation of women? Given the complexity of the issues, it may seem problematic to even raise these questions here; but reflecting on the power-cooperation nexus in the context of the transformations under discussion may be enlightening.

The subordination of women has been associated with social life based on agriculture, though there were and are variations in this subordination and perhaps even exceptions to it. It makes good sense to believe that the subordination of women was less common throughout the forty to fifty thousand years before the Neolithic revolution transformed life in small bands of hunters and gatherers into the social forms of life associated with gardening and agriculture. In turn, the decline of agriculture as the main mode of production seems at least associated with the decline in women's subordination.

Some of the factors that erode gender inequality seem to stand out clearly, though on closer inspection each one turns out to be more complex in its preconditions and consequences than I can even indicate here. What I can offer, then, is a bare explanatory sketch.

In social structures with a differentiated social division of labor, being confined to activities related to and compatible with childbearing and the nurture of small children is a severe obstacle to attaining equality of status, of economic advantage, as well as of power and influence. In social formations of some complexity, then, even rough forms of equality between women and men presuppose a radical reduction in the social division of labor by gender. Therein lies the critical importance of the facts that having children is no longer a potential source of wealth for the family, as was often the case in family- and kin-based agricultural production, and that—whatever the motivation for having children—radical declines in child mortality have reduced the number of needed pregnancies as well as the time devoted to nurturing small children. Given that life expectancies beyond the childbearing years have increased also, this means that a large proportion of women's lives has been freed for activities other than childbearing and baby care. The impact of biological differences between women and men on their respective life tasks—however modified and modifiable in different social arrangements—has been dramatically reduced by these developments.

The same generalization suggests itself when we consider changes in the nature of work. In economies driven by high energy use, technological innovation, and large capital investment, the earlier premium on upper body strength has been replaced by emphases on intelligence, mental discipline, and diligence, characteristics that are in principle gender neutral, though they may favor one gender over the other in given historical circumstances. (Thus women in Western Europe and the United States currently do better in education than do men.)[9]

As argued earlier, family and kin ties play a much smaller role as a generalized tool for social organization of any kind, having been replaced by relations based on, in principle, voluntary agreement and legal guarantees. That also means that gender relations are, overall, less defined by family and kinship. The purposive relations in markets, organizations, and associations open spaces for the independent pursuit of women's life interests outside the family. And equalized opportunities outside the family strengthen equality within.

Productivity is vastly higher in industrial and knowledge-based economies than in the older forms of agriculture. This means that many households live well above the minimum needed for survival, reducing the need for tight discipline and—on the assumption that there is a link between struggle and hierarchic decision making—the resort to authoritarian relations in the household. Higher productivity also offers some leeway for experimentation with new social arrangements, both in households and in factories and offices. This space is expanded if the household or work organization finds itself in an advantaged market position. Finally if public policies treat gender equality as an important collective good, their sponsors can mobilize resources and devise regulations for such supports as affordable child care, affirmative action, and flexible work time. These supports can significantly contribute to achieving a rough equality of women and men in their pursuits outside the family.

If major religious and cultural orientations seem not to be closely synchronized with the epochal transformations, there are some cultural changes that do stand in a more direct relation to these processes of structural change. The freeing of human labor from fixed allocations due to family and extrafamilial domination, the increased mobility of people and ideas, and meritocratic principles in formal organization and market exchange tend to strengthen individualism and egalitarian ideals. Ascriptive advantage and disadvantage—unequal treatment because of who a person is and to whom she is related rather than because of what she does, did, and can do—have lost much of their legitimacy outside family and personal relations. To be sure, such changes in normative ideals also have

---

[9] Cultural disruption, often associated with migration, and in particular warfare tend to favor men. Whether this is grounded primarily in biology or in historical configurations shaping gender roles, the effect is strongly suggested both by anecdotal historical evidence and by quantitative comparison (Sanday 1981).

independent and older roots, and they may have an appeal quite beyond the reach of supportive structural developments: the promise of equality is embraced by many women in different parts of the world long before realistic chances of social transformation are in sight.

The forces and developments enabling equal gender relations are powerful indeed. But so are the obstacles to the elimination of male advantage. There is first the fact that no previous society has existed without a gender division of labor. And, as noted, there are good reasons for the claim that at least beyond a minimum level of social complexity any form of social differentiation entails inequality. A gender-based division of social activities leads in a complex social order nearly inevitably to a continuation of gender inequality. Changing the division of labor, however, is a much larger task than is abolishing a number of specific "unfair practices" (such as unequal pay for equal work), opening mobility chances into upper management, or revaluing housework. The absence of historical precedents for a comprehensive social order without a gender-based division of labor makes repeated large-scale experimentation necessary, and much of that experimentation is likely to be less than fully successful.

The absence of historical precedents is reflected in patterns of path dependency with different strengths of momentum. Social structures favoring men in the pursuit of status, wealth, and power tend to be interconnected with structural arrangements such as those protecting and regulating property or the management of private and public affairs, from banking and government administration to policing and the military. These structural interrelations, a major factor stabilizing norms and institutions (see chapters 4 and 12), have a subjective and cultural counterpart in deep-seated and change-resistant ideas and values surrounding gender roles. Often shared by both women and men, they profoundly shape socialization and personality formation as well as the legitimation of established institutions.

Finally, there are powerful vested interests in maintaining the status quo in gender relations. These exist in families, in work organizations, in associational life, in religion, in public and private systems of governance, and in politics. Even where these vested interests are not directly and consciously hostile to women's advancement—and often this is the case—they frequently stand in the way of changing the status quo because change seems also to interfere with established and apparently gender-neutral institutional goals—a consequence of the complex interdependence of structural arrangements just noted.

The coexistence of strong forces eroding the status quo in gender relations and powerful obstacles explains why the advances of women's emancipation in the last 150 years were the result of persistent struggle and political movements. If one judges the forces that brought about a

decline in the subordination of women to be in the long run stronger than
the obstacles to changing the status quo, this coexistence also yields a
suggestion for the future: the struggle for gender equality will persist and
lead to important further transformations, but it will do so by repeated
political mobilization. As an unintended consequence, women's struggle
for equality may well come to be one source of renewed energies that
strengthen civic participation in democratic politics.[10]

INDIRECT, ENABLING POWER AT WORK

Market exchange, formal organizations, and voluntary associations have
in common that they receive strong support from the "infrastructural"
power of the modern state. This takes above all the form of the impersonal
rule of law, which, grounded in the structure of the modern state itself,
offers guarantees to relations between private parties and restrains personal and discretionary uses of political power (Lange 2005).

In market exchange, the state regulates the actors, the substance, and
many modalities of the exchange and then lends its coercive power to the
partners in private contracts to enforce their agreements. Formal organizations—whether public or private—use contractual agreements that are
similarly empowered to create long-lasting forms of cooperation. Voluntary associations rely on the rule of law in a somewhat more indirect way.
They, too, may be seen as constituted by implicit or explicit contracts. It
is equally significant, however, that these "horizontal" social relations
become more important forms of cooperation as hierarchic relations of
personalized authority—such as lord-vassal and patron-client relations—
are weakened by the impersonal rule of law. At the same time, associations and secular movements respond to the deepening penetration of
economy and society by the modern state.[11]

The legal infrastructure of competitive markets, formal organizations,
and voluntary associations works smoothly only if it rests on a much
broader basis of compatible nonlegal foundations. When Durkheim

[10] This was the central argument of Rueschemeyer and Rueschemeyer (1990). In the
above, I drew on that paper and the literature cited there. We found Sanday (1981) particularly instructive; but my discussion here emphasizes structural factors more than she did.
Sanday had moved in her theoretical explanation of gender inequality from a materialist
position to one that stressed the impact of long-term cultural traditions.

[11] The relations between voluntary associations and the modern state actually have a complex and ambiguous history. Before they became beneficiaries of infrastructural state power,
associations and "combinations" were—even in relatively free countries such as the United
States and imperial Germany—often outlawed or restrictively regulated, unless they could
be co-opted and controlled. In the dictatorial regimes of the twentieth century, mass organizations lost their voluntary character and served as instruments of central domination.

(1893/1964) called attention to the "non-contractual bases of contract," he pointed to the deep institutional grounding that not only undergirds competitive market exchange (as was discussed in chapter 9) but also provides a foundation for formal organizations and voluntary associations. This institutional grounding at once identifies, generalizes, and constructs several presuppositions as socially recognized "facts":

- that individuals are free agents, not precommitted in their actions by custom, family ties, and local systems of domination;
- that important social relations can be rationally constructed and reconstructed; and
- that impersonal, highly specific, possibly quite temporary relationships, in which merit considerations outweigh who a person is and whom she knows, can be trusted to be reliable and stable.

It is this complex of norms and values, implicit preference structures, and cognitive premises that underlies the world of purposive social organization of which market exchange, formal organizations, as well as voluntary associations and secular social movements are the major manifestations.

The functioning of formal organizations deserves particular comment before we turn to some of the results created by the new prevalence of different forms of purposive social organization. I will first briefly consider Weber's famous model of "bureaucracy" and then set it side by side with ideas of the new economics of the corporate firm. Of both, however, I can offer only the barest sketch.

We have encountered Max Weber's "ideal" or pure type of bureaucracy several times (1922/1978; see chapters 1 and 3). Rather than merely treating it as an extreme construct to which more complex realities can be compared (the original purpose of ideal types), one can interpret it also as a model of rational organization (see Kalberg 1994, chap. 4). As such it stipulates:

- specialized positions that can be rationally designed and articulated with each other; they become fungible modules of organization to the extent that they are separated from outside involvements and from other roles held by the incumbents; this is accomplished through such devices as full-time appointment, sharply defined specific tasks, and norms of emotional neutrality;[12]

---

[12] Using sharply defined specialized roles as fungible building blocks of organization aids rational action. As noted repeatedly, focusing attention on one or a few matters facilitates rationality as it excludes from consideration multiple consequences of one's action for other concerns. This is the precise obverse of one major condition of traditionalization. Traditional action is reasonable if several different persistent issues—each with its own optimal

- positions that require merit in hiring and promotion, though merit considerations are tempered by job security so as to instigate and maintain loyalty;
- positions whose remuneration is partitioned over time in the form of salaries and wages rather than given as a lump sum, as in feudal or postfeudal grants of local rule and exploitation rights;
- positions that are subject to strict supervision, which is aided by the specificity of tasks;
- positions that are integrated into a corporate whole by rules and rule-based lines of command;
- cohesion among core positions, supported by honoring the incumbents' place in the surrounding society as a distinct "status group" and by fostering an esprit de corps among them.

This model was, above all, devised to make a broad historical judgment: bureaucracies are the organizational core of an impersonal form of rule that Weber called "legal-rational." As such, they are far more efficient instruments of large-scale administration than are the organizational instruments of personalized rule—bands of followers of a charismatic leader and the staffs embedded in the households of patriarchal or patrimonial rulers.

The model combines, if only in embryonic form, considerations of rational design, effective governance and coordination, monitoring performance, incentives, and nonrational sources of motivation and cohesion. Even though it acknowledges nonrational aspects, it emphasizes how bureaucratic administration differs from traditional—patriarchal and patrimonial—forms of organization. In Weber's actual use of the concept, however, it is clear that the informal and nonrational elements that give stability and life to bureaucratic structures also constrain their fungible use for any and every purpose organizational elites may choose, and constrain their flexibility in adapting to changed circumstances. Internally, bureaucratic structures rely more on established routines than the model stipulates. Weber's conception of bureaucracy thus foreshadows the two major strands of analysis in organization theory and the economics of the firm that during the last two generations have greatly advanced our understanding of organizations.[13]

---

solution that may well be inconsistent with what serves other purposes best—have to be dealt with in a single social arrangement, such as family and kin groups in agrarian societies.

[13] See, for instance, the retrospective appreciation of the work of Chester I. Barnard (1938) edited by Oliver Williamson (1995). Several contributors stress that Barnard "attempted to straddle two apparently different and irreconcilable views of organizations:" On the one hand, he stipulated that "it is the deliberate adoption of means to ends which is the essence of formal organization." And on the other, he claimed that "informal organizations

Weber extended the reach of his model from the political realm to private formal organizations as these historically took off from public administration. It is interesting to see that the recent economic analyses of business firms have inspired attempts to rebuild that bridge from the other side, drawing lessons for public bureaucracy from the modeling of firms while recognizing the fundamental differences that separate public and private formal organizations (Moe 1984, 1995).

Coleman (1990, 422–24), influenced by the remarkable developments in the economic analyses of firms, saw Weber's analysis as fundamentally flawed. It treated, he argued, only the ruler as a purposive actor and neglected that employees have interests of their own. Coleman points to problems that he claimed the Weberian model misses or underemphasizes, problems of accepting command authority, of the exchange of compliance for inducements, and of the balance between the value of compliant performance and the costs of the inducements, of delegation and the use of subordinates' initiative, of the resultant issues of "principal-agent relationships," and of the associated problems of monitoring and controlling agents. This critique overlooks that Weber was primarily interested in highlighting the epochal changes underlying the more detailed problems of organizational functioning and that he focused on public organizations rather than private firms.[14] It also misses the ways in which the Weberian model, as it can be reconstructed from its actual use, anticipates the duality of formal and informal, rational and nonrational, legal and nonlegal elements in the functioning of organizations. However, Coleman does indeed point to the major innovations that the rational choice approach to organizations has brought about.

For neoclassical economics, the entry point into these issues was the question asked by Coase (1937): Why are there firms in the first place? Why is the coordination of activities through competitive markets not enough? The answer—that firms reduce transaction costs as these occur in the real world in contrast to the idealized environment of perfect competition models—still underlies the most comprehensive treatment of

---

are necessary to the operation of formal organizations as a means of communication, of cohesion, and of protecting the integrity of the individual." (The first quotation gives the judgment of Scott 1995, 40. The next two are Barnard's formulations, 1938, 186 and 123, as cited by Scott.)

Two excellent outlines of the rational choice theoretic analyses of organizations are Moe (1984) and the introductory essay of Putterman and Kroszner (1996).

[14] Research on today's development issues gives an indication that Weber identified a crucial factor. Evans and Rauch (1999) showed that in a sample of developing countries state organizations of economic administration, which were judged to hire by meritocratic criteria and to encourage performance by substantial long-term career rewards, were associated with strong growth of per capita GDP even with controls for human capital and initial GDP per capita.

firms, which we find in the various publications of Oliver Williamson (e.g., 1985). There were other entry points. Simon (1947) took off from issues of uncertainty and the difficulties of maximizing and pointed to solutions found in "satisficing" routines, learning, adaptations based on experience, and the like. This approach proved to be more compatible with sociologically oriented organization studies that emphasized nonrational and informal elements in formal organizations (e.g., Cyert and March 1963; March and Olsen 1975). Alchian and Demsetz (1972) made the problems of monitoring performance and protection against shirking central to their understanding of the firm. They answer the question of who sets up a structure of monitoring and who ultimately monitors the monitors by positing a central arbiter who, while making decisions about structures and processes of supervision, is rewarded by legal title to the firm's results. Putterman and Krozner (1996) put this side by side with the older argument of Knight (1922) who focused on the risks of enterprise and the "insurance" offered by the risk-bearing entrepreneur. The insuring owner-entrepreneur has to be given ultimate decision power unless the security offered is abused by shirking employees.

One common feature of these diverse strands of argument is their grounding in contractual agreements. They explain hierarchy as a result of a free choice that is imputed in their models to the contracting parties. While this reasoning, quite clearly reminiscent of Hobbes's argument, may not take cognizance of often quite drastic limitations of free, autonomous choice in social reality, it identifies in pure form issues and problems that may well—and are likely to—occur even if all preexisting inequalities did not exist. They illuminate issues and problems such as shirking, monitoring, incentives and sanctions, delegation, and control of agents.

Formal organizations, then, are inevitably more or less hierarchical arrangements, even though they are modeled to emerge from the good judgment and free consent of all concerned. The contractual relations on which the command authority in formal organizations is based are guaranteed by the infrastructural power of the state, by the rule of law and the nonlegal understandings underlying and empowering contractual agreements. The contractual relations presuppose formally free partners. The respective bargaining positions of employers and employees, shaped partly by their exit options, determine whether and how much this formal freedom translates into a substantive equality.

The actual constraints on the free choice of individuals are decisive for the severity of the domination exercised in public and private formal organizations. This may be mitigated by the substance given by different states to the very institutional foundations of indirect power embodied in the rule of law, here the law of labor relations. It may also be alleviated by the unparalleled overall wealth of rich countries, which gives even people in less privileged positions exit options that were not imaginable in the same societies only two or three generations ago. But the threat of unemployment, which is a permanent institutional feature of all capitalist economies, still entails hardships that induce routine workers to submit to forms of authority many would hardly accept otherwise.

It remains to indicate briefly some of the wider outcomes of the new configurations of power and cooperation. I have already discussed the halting emancipation of women as a major result of the epochal transformations of the last two centuries because it was closely related to changes in the role of the family. Other outcomes are perhaps less complicated but no less consequential.

There has been a tremendous increase in efficiency, above all in market functioning and in formal organizations, but also in purposeful associations. Of course, claims of efficiency must always be examined closely as to which goals and which beneficiaries are served. There is no question that neither associations nor formal organizations nor competitive markets simply serve an idealized common good, however defined. Not only is there a pervasive tendency for the interests of the already privileged to be better served in all the three forms of cooperation and coordination that rely on indirect enabling power. It is also true that these social mechanisms tend to be blind to many goals and needs unless they are forced to take cognizance of them. Still, there are many interests that are very effectively served by markets, formal organizations, and purposeful associations.

A corollary of this huge increase in efficiency is continuous streams and, on occasion, cascades of innovation. Again, all three of the newly prevalent forms of cooperation and coordination are involved in this. As is recognized in the feature of capitalist economies that Schumpeter called "creative destruction," this, too, is not an unmixed blessing, though images of bucolic calm and serenity in earlier phases of human history often turn out to be longing fantasies of later generations or descriptions of relatively privileged niches.

"Civil society"—conceived as an ensemble of associations in a very broad sense, forms of association that are not grounded in government, productive organizations, or kinship—represents a new element in political process. The instrument of purposive association is of special importance for disadvantaged, subordinate interests, because association for collective action is, as briefly noted earlier, the prime power resource of the many, while wealth, coercive power, persuasive argument and wide-ranging voice are the privilege of the few, of those owning capital, controlling armed force, shaping public communications, and enjoying high status and trust. Collective action by subordinate interests can be a major factor in making politics and—indirectly—markets and administrative organizations more responsive to otherwise underrecognized and underserved concerns.

Whether a lively civil society favors a democratization of rule depends on its composition, on the relations among its component organized interests, and on their linkages to the apparatus of the state. A potential partner as well as opponent of the state, a lively civil society may protect the interests that find organized expression in it from being overwhelmed by state power, but it may not be open to the inclusion of subordinate class interests. If it does include strong representation of subordinate class interests, it can indeed be of crucial importance in the introduction and maintenance of democratic rule and in the interplay between state power and social needs and demands (Rueschemeyer, Stephens, and Stephens 1992; Huber and Stephens 2001).

As noted earlier, a "fundamental democratization" (Mannheim) results from the freeing of human beings from preemptive fixations of their activities, preferences, and goals that were the mark of agrarian social formations. This can become the foundation of democratic rule when it is joined with restraints that protect the rights of citizens and, in particular, of minorities. However, it can also entail mass mobilization as a transmission belt for the power of political elites. The very efficiency of purposive association can become an instrument in the hand of state elites. Furthermore, the efficiency of formal organization as well as technological advances in transportation, communication, and surveillance can also serve "despotic power" of small political elites over society. If the chance of democratic rule is one of the unique possibilities of "modern" configurations of power, so is totalitarian and harsh authoritarian rule.

We must not forget that the twentieth century was not only the time when in rich countries democratic rule as well as social welfare policies became mature and stable. It was also the century that saw something radically different on an unprecedented scale. It saw the seduction of "advanced" populations by totalitarian and authoritarian elites and massive repression of any opposition by efficient state and party machineries. The same century saw wars whose destructiveness built on technical advances and administrative efficiency. "Total war" unleashed lethal violence against civilians. And the worst cases of genocide, above all the destruction of European Jewry by Nazi Germany, also belong to the record of this century, in which "modernity" came into its own.

Conclusion

Pursuing the nexus between power and cooperation has led us into very broad comparisons across human history. We have returned to major themes that constituted the substance of modernization theory and reconstructed them as contrasting forms of power-based cooperation and coordination. This put into sharp relief the peculiar role of indirect, enabling power in the forms of cooperation and coordination whose expansion at the expense of family- and kin-based forms is a core characteristic of modern social formations. Market exchange, impersonal formal organization, and purposive association made human and other resources more freely available, resources that in most agrarian social formations had been preemptively allocated to uses shaped by the family and local forms of nonfamily domination. The epochal changes in the nexus between power and cooperation are also illuminating about the halting emancipation of women.

Command power is in modern social formations concentrated in public and private formal organizations. Their analysis has made great strides as economic analysis has concentrated on the previously neglected theory of the firm, and as bridges were built between rational choice modeling and approaches that emphasize nonrational and informal features in really existing formal organizations.

The three major institutional forms of cooperation and coordination that rely on indirect infrastructural power—market exchange, formal organization, and voluntary association—engender consequences that are critical for the understanding of large and important features of modern economies, politics, and social life. Yet even brief reflection reveals a profound ambiguity when these consequences are evaluated normatively.

Chapter XII

INSTITUTIONS

Institutions undergird, enable, and regulate the interaction of individuals and organizations in particular areas of life. Thus conceptions and rules of corporate agency, property, contract, and credit are critical for economic life; conceptions and rules of marriage, descent, and kin obligations shape family life; new conceptions and rules of purposeful association and organization underlie the formal organizations and the voluntary associations characteristic of modern societies; and conceptions and rules of science set apart, regulate, and protect the world of research. Concerned with issues that are given great importance by powerful people and organizations, institutions can marshal and are supported by substantial resources.

Institutions ultimately derive from the actions and reactions of individuals, though tracing their roots in individual agency often runs into long sequences of complicated interactions and unforeseen consequences. Once established, however, institutions shape preferences, beliefs, norms, and emotions. They therefore are, as noted earlier, a major factor in structuring the variability that we encountered in our examinations of the subjective dimension of action into shared and more or less stable practices.

At the meso- and macrolevel, institutions not only mold the functioning of broad areas of social life—of economic production and distribution; governance, consent, and compliance; land holding and use patterns; capital-labor relations; or sexual reproduction. They also affect the deep structures of conflict and solidarity in a social formation, as they create, maintain, and restructure social categories with similar, neutral, or opposed interests.

The recognized social importance of institutions, their enabling consequences, their backing by major material and immaterial resources, and their impact on social structures as well as on the subjective orientations of people make the understanding of institutions a strategic entry point for social science research. This was early acknowledged in the institutionalist orientation of political economy, before that comprehensive field of inquiry branched into separate social science disciplines. The same recognition is also—perhaps paradoxically—the reason why we are now confronted with a variety of conceptions of institutions, which developed along different paths of inquiry. Yet these alternative conceptualizations are instructive, pointing to different features of institutions and offering alternative perspectives on them. Outlining that intellectual territory seems therefore useful before I formulate a concept of institutions that will guide our own discussion, and then consider the origins, conditions of change and stability, and consequences of institutions.

Diverse "Institutionalisms"

The early concern for institutions in political economy dates back to Adam Smith and the economics of the Scottish Enlightenment. When capitalist economies were in the process of establishing themselves, interest in the institutional underpinnings of market exchange and in the interrelations among economy, politics, and society was heightened precisely by this rise of capitalism, which took a particular form in different countries. Economics as a separate discipline left these concerns behind, when the marginalist revolution ushered in modern "neoclassical" economics. On the one hand, the historical school of economics in continental Europe had lost its way in diverse detailed investigations, or so it seemed to the new mainstream of the discipline. On the other, ahistorical model building took the institutional foundations of capitalist economies for granted and yielded dramatic advances in illuminating the logic of microeconomic decision making and in macroeconomic equilibrium analysis.[1]

The earlier insights into the role of institutions were better preserved in sociology, especially in those works that followed in the footsteps of Durkheim, who had stressed the role of noncontractual foundations of contract in his arguments against "the utilitarians," and of Weber, who tried to reconcile marginalist economics with institutional sociological analysis. By the middle of the twentieth century, it could be argued that the theory of institutional integration of social action "is essentially socio-

---

[1] The marginalist revolution replaced theories of economic value grounded in production and distribution (such as the labor theory of value) with an understanding of economic value derived from exchange, scarcity, and subjective utility. It got its name from the focus on the *marginal utility* of exchanged goods. Dismissing Continental historical economics as largely pointless descriptive detail studies was plausible when this approach was assessed against the goal of a comprehensive and parsimonious theory; but this overlooked the achievements of such giants of an integrated historical social science as Gustav Schmoller, Otto Hintze, and Max Weber. In the United States, institutional economics accepted the critique of European historical economics and sought to combine a concern for institutions with the analytic advances of neoclassical economics (Commons 1931). Yet it did not gain much influence in the field. Arthur Stinchcombe, who after the Second World War became acquainted and enamored with this "old institutionalism," notes, "I became a sociologist in order to make a living as an institutional economist, since it was clear that I would make a poor living at that among economists" (1997, 1–2).

logical theory," and that it defines "the place of sociological theory in the sciences of action." Parsons, who made these claims, saw institutions as sets of norms and values that, when aligned with subjective preferences and commitments and enforced by effective positive and negative sanctions, shape role complexes of strategic significance. He argued that any theory of instrumental action had to be embedded in an institutional analysis that gave due regard to norms and values (1951, 36–45).

Against this background, three dramatic new developments have arisen since the 1970s—one changed the emphasis Parsons had given to values, but developed self-consciously in relation to his precedent; another emerged with the resurgence of historical social science; and a third came from economic theory and its rational choice offshoots. Following a seminal review by Hall and Taylor (1996), we can label them sociological institutionalism, historical institutionalism, and rational choice institutionalism. Together, these three strands of theory have put institutional analysis at the center of social and political research on the meso- and macrolevels.

The new *sociological institutionalism* is centered in the sociology of organizations (Powell and DiMaggio 1991; Scott 1995). In comparison to the older sociological view of institutions, it shifts—in a proclaimed "cognitive turn"—the central analytic reference from values and norms to cognition and shared beliefs. Yet similar to the value-centered conception it claims that responding to widely held classifications, scripts, routines, and beliefs (including beliefs about rationality) generates legitimation. Moreover, the perceived and interpreted environment is viewed as shaping the identity of individual and corporate actors. If the shift toward an emphasis on cognitive approaches to culture—conceiving culture as an available "tool kit" (Swidler 1986)—makes the new sociological institutionalism more compatible with rational action theory, the contrast to rational choice models remains pervasive in other ways. This sociological approach underlines specifically diverse sociocultural constructions, the prevalence of habits in contrast to purposeful rational action, and taken-for-granted, unreflected practices.

Historical institutionalism focused, in the tradition of classic social theories, on large-scale structures and their transformations, especially those related to the emergence of Western modernity. These studies constructed and examined theories—often inspired by Marx and Weber—on the links between modes of production and the dynamics of class, on the expansion of market exchange, on state formation and warfare, on revolutions, and on transformations in the character of states. Increasingly, they paired strong analytic interests with an intense concern for historical particularity. Institutions—meaning formal as well as informal rules and conventions embedded in the practices of major historical players—became central in their analysis of continuity and change. Often stable over long stretches of time, institutions are in this view frequently created and changed in particular transformative constellations, in "critical junctures." Effective institutions influence—at the individual as well as the collective level—beliefs, normative commitments, and preferences. Their major effect at the macrolevel is to create and maintain power disparities and to broadly structure shared and antagonistic interests.

The new *economic institutionalism* is the most remarkable of these analytic innovations. It is remarkable above all because it emerged within the very discipline that abandoned the earlier institutionalism of political economy. It emerged when the neoclassical approach faced problems that challenged its conventional premises: Given the efficiency of competitive market exchange, why do firms exist and how do they function? How can differences in long-term economic growth be explained? And how useful are rational choice models for the understanding of social processes outside of markets and outside the economic sphere of social life? We have seen in the previous chapter how the economic theory of the firm turned to institutional analysis. Douglass North (1990), a Nobel Prize–winner who took off from economic historical studies, found that recognition of institutions is critical for explaining long-term economic growth. And the application of rational action analysis outside of the established scope of economics has brought about a strong appreciation of institutions in game theory.

Rational choice institutionalism is set off from the other two "new institutionalisms" by several distinctive features. The first is deductive modeling, often based on radical premises: actors pursue with instrumental rationality a set of imputed preferences; they act strategically with a knowledge and information that surpasses realistic conditions; and they do not care about expectations of other actors that are not strategically relevant, nor about constraining social norms and values (except that some restraints, required for orderly transactions, are often silently assumed). This kind of modeling is at odds with widely accepted standards of scientific inquiry (Moe 1979). Unconcerned with realistic description or the detection of empirical regularities that can be theorized as causal relations, it is not able to explain or to predict. But it is not without value. It can put problems into sharp relief and indicate solutions that would work even under adverse conditions. These problems and solutions may transcend the extreme conditions of the model and have wider relevance.

Dealing with the collective action problem and similar issues has led rational action theory to an appreciation of institutional structures. The fact that the logically produced dilemmas of theoretical games are often avoided in social reality drove multiple and successful attempts to model the emergence of norms and shared understandings from the interaction of rational, self-interested actors. Remarkably, rational choice theorists have tended to model the interaction of equal partners, often leading to happy-end outcomes of productive solutions as well as harmonious, consensual relations among the interacting parties. This may be astonishing, since imposition by parties with better power resources seems a simple enough assumption to build into a model of strategically interacting parties. Yet given a starting point of socially unconnected individuals, differential power may seem like an arbitrary deus ex machina assumption. And the convention of looking for a Nash equilibrium, a state of affairs in which no actor has an option that would improve his situation, favors models with outcomes that at least can be interpreted as consensual. Moreover, the welfare-maximizing postulate of the economic conception of efficiency drives a search for the "best" collective outcomes. Still, in principle rational choice modeling should be quite capable of integrating power consideration into its repertoire of institutional features stabilizing interaction (Knight 1992; Moe 2005).

These three lines of scholarship on institutions clearly contrast with each other; but they interestingly highlight different features of the phenomenon. That economic analysis returned to the importance of institutions after sidelining these issues for a long time represents in itself a first such highlight.

Yet the different lines of theory work and research on institutions do not really contradict each other. They represent different approaches but do not hold on to hypotheses that other research has empirically rejected. If their disagreements and disputes are sometimes referred to as a "war of paradigms," we can observe that all three of the new institutionalisms have remarkable points of contact and overlap. In some cases one can reasonably speak of a promise of convergence.

Katznelson and Weingast (2005) argue in the introduction to their volume on rationalist and historical institutionalism that rational choice analysts in political science have built increasingly realistic assumptions into their models. For instance, the preferences that drive the behavior of American legislators—above all, a concern for reelection—are modeled as they emerge within the institutional constraints created by themselves and their predecessors, a structural pattern that sets U.S. politics apart from, say, its British counterpart. Instead of simply positing certain kinds of preferences, then, these rational choice models increasingly work with preferences that earlier studies have shown to be endogenously induced. This is a critical step toward crossing the chasm that long separated deductive model building based on usefully simple but empirically arbitrary premises from research seeking to understand how institutions shape preferences, and how institutional continuity and change come about empirically. Katznelson and Weingast see a complementary change in comparative historical work. In the older works of historical social science, blanket assertions about the preferences and interests of bureaucrats, peasants, or Protestants were largely taken for granted. This, they argue, constituted a form of imputation similar to the premises of rational choice modeling. "People and their preferences tended to be collapsed into categories established by the interplay of theory and history" (13). More recent historical institutionalist work has moved to much more fine-grained assessments of the impact of institutions on preferences. Here, too, then, they see a change from roughly imputed to historically induced preferences.

There are in fact a number of successful historical studies that deploy rational choice modeling but whose assumptions build on realistic historical inferences. Rational choice models serve here as analytic frames for inductive historical studies. One such work is Gerard Alexander's (2002) comparative research on democratic consolidation in Western Europe, which demonstrates that the beliefs of the political Right about the security of their interests were the decisive factor in consolidating democratic rule. An earlier set of intriguing historical studies was offered by the analytic narratives project of Bates, Greif, Levi, Rosenthal, and Weingast (1998). Here, too, rational choice modeling was combined with inductive determinations of the options and the likely outcomes and utilities as assessed by the primary actors. Similarly, Mahoney (2005) presents a rational choice analysis of the options and preferences of liberal elites in nineteenth-century Central America, complementing his earlier monograph on how their decisions shaped the long-term trajectory of four political regimes (Mahoney 2001a).

The second form of contact and intersection between different lines of research on institutions is much more clearly a case of convergence. In the previous chapter on power and cooperation I have described how the economic theory of the firm retained rational model building but operated with increasingly realistic assumptions, similarly bridging the gap between deductive modeling and empirical research on organizations (Williamson 1995; Putterman and Kroszner 1996). This has engendered an open-ended cooperation between the economic theory of the firm and research on organizations along the lines of the new sociological institutionalism. Even the nonrational elements emphasized by institutionalist organization theory are partially absorbed by the transaction cost economics of the firm.[2]

---

[2] Williamson emphasizes three aspects of the relationship: "The first . . . is that transaction cost economics has been (and will continue to be) massively influenced by concepts and empirical regularities that have their origins in organization theory. Secondly, I sketch the key concepts out of which transaction cost economics works to which organization theorists can (and many do) productively relate. But thirdly, healthy tension survives—as revealed by

The relationship between historical institutionalism and the new sociological institutionalism grounded in organization theory is the least problematic. This is mostly due to the fact that historical institutionalist work
is eclectic in its theoretical orientations. It certainly is open to focusing on
cultural templates and their impact on institutional patterns. However,
while less problematic, this relationship has not been a venue of intense
interaction. Organizational research in the institutionalist mode is not
especially engaged in historical work, even though this arguably might
bear ample fruit. And the particular emphases of the new sociological
institutionalism, while not controversial, are not prominent among the
ideas shaping historical institutionalist research.

The rapprochement among the new lines of institutionalist scholarship
is partial and proceeds along several dimensions. It seems reasonable to
interpret these three approaches as alternative theory frames that are at
once incomplete, partly overlapping, and complementary. Yet it still remains to settle on a useful conceptual baseline for our own discussion.

A Concept of Institutions

Following a consideration argued repeatedly, the best choice would be a
concept that is narrowly defined but open to propositions that relate it
to various phenomena one might want to see included in a more comprehensive concept. Arthur Stinchcombe's deft formula points the way: "By
an 'institution' I mean a structure in which powerful people are committed to some value or interest." He expands this into two more formal
definitions: "Then we could define 'institutions' as the values and norms
which have a high correlation with power (which seems to be Parsons'
preference), or as the concentrations of power specially devoted to some
value (as seems to be the tendency of common speech)" (1968, 107 and
183–84). I prefer a narrower definition whose core might be called
"norms with teeth":

> *Institutions are clusters of norms with strong but variable mecha-
> nisms of support and enforcement that regulate and sustain an im-
> portant area of social life.*

Some comments are in order.[3] Taking clusters of norms as the center of
the concept is a deliberate choice, though the additions of strong mecha-

---

an examination of phenomena for which rival interpretations have been advanced, remain
unsolved, and provoke controversy" (1995, 208).

[3] I take here space for an extended conceptual discussion because the problems of conceptualizing institutions are not only at the center of political and social theory; they also seem
paradigmatic for other issues of concept formation.

nisms of support and enforcement and of concern with important spheres of life specify this core. Strong mechanisms of enforcement and support are critical for this conceptualization, but exactly how strong the mechanisms are is left open. Also left open are the relative role of internal and external sanctions, the kind and forms of support, as well as the social actors involved in sanctioning and support.

To leave the core concept open to variable additional features of what we call institutions is in my view critical because these variable features can be linkage points for specific hypotheses. Therefore I avoid putting an unrealistic pure model of complete institutionalization into the center of the discussion, as Parsons came close to doing. In his conception, complete institutionalization is realized when a value pattern is so fully internalized that the preferences of the people involved coincide with what the values demand of them; moreover, full institutionalization requires that all reactions by others to the behavior of an actor support and reward the realization of the value in question and impose prohibitive costs on contraventions. The main argument against such a construction is that it is contradicted by a fundamental quality of the human condition that Isaiah Berlin made a central theme of his philosophical reflections on history: different human values can be and frequently are incompatible with each other (see, e.g., Berlin 1997). This often leads to the delineation of separate institutionally ordered "zones" or spheres of social life; but even where such differentiation is successful, it does not eliminate contradiction, contamination, and tension among different institutional realms.

In reality, different institutions exhibit different degrees of institutionalization. Many are quite dilapidated. But if institutions are effectively enforced and supported, they often become well established and yield predictable patterns of social practice. Much of their normative character then tends to be taken for granted. Still, I consider a definition via norms to be more useful than a concept based on established practices because it is narrower and does not preempt hypotheses by making the effects of strong enforcement and support part of the definition.

The proposed definition pairs enforcement with support for the institutional cluster of norms as well as for the sphere of social life it enables and regulates. Enforcement and support are often intertwined. Strong support—say, for scientific research, for competitive economic wealth creation, or for the maintenance of a slave economy—raises the stakes for the maintenance, protection, and enforcement of norms; it mobilizes resources for the mode of social life in question; and it engenders large advantages for the major players. In the case of very strong institutions, the reactions to appropriate and inappropriate behavior may contribute significantly to the inequality of status, of economic advantage, and of power among conforming or deviating actors.

Immaterial supports may involve shared values that infuse specific norms or the whole complex with importance and strength. Similarly, cognitive understandings—whether based on empirical evidence or on myth—spell out the rationales for the institution and portray how it originated and how it is related to other parts of social life. By treating values and cognitive understandings as potential and variable supports of institutions, we sidestep the controversy between the old and the new sociological institutionalism over values vs. cognitive orientations as the primary cultural reference points of institutional analysis.

Finally a comment that should be obvious, though it may be useful to spell it out anyway. The importance of the sphere of life regulated and sustained by an institution is not a feature to be assessed objectively by the researcher. Whether such objective assessments are possible—a premise of functionalist theories—we can leave open. For present purposes, importance is defined by the views of influential actors. It may be useful to focus on different views of different sets of actors and on conflicts between them.

VARIETIES OF INSTITUTIONS, CLUSTERS,
AND INCONSISTENT PATTERNS

In view of the ubiquity of institutions at the macrolevel of social and political analysis, which is reflected in the fact that virtually all current theoretical approaches make analogous concepts of institutions central to their analysis, it is useful to remind ourselves of the great variety of phenomena covered by this concept. Substantively, I have repeatedly referred to rules of marriage and kinship, to rules of democratic electoral choice, to the provisions guaranteeing contract, property, and the constitution of corporate actors, and to the rules and provisions undergirding scientific research. The range is, of course, much wider. It includes the normative underpinnings of many forms of one-sided advantage and disadvantage such as slavery and colonial rule. It includes the regulation of the use of violence by armed forces, various forms of an establishment of religious belief and practice, as well as provisions for religious diversity and choice, informal institutions about neighborhood life and friendship, and many, many other normative structures of social life.

While some institutions—for instance, those regulating political contestations or marriage and family life—seek to structure the practices in a given area of social life, other institutions may *offer* rules and regulations that actors can accept and use or leave alone and look for alternatives. Examples are institutions that regulate a service, such as vocational training (Thelen 2004), conflict settlement, or credit provision. These institutions depend for their success on the use of the regulated activity, which can be withheld. If the potential users have feasible alternative options, the new institutional provisions will take their interests into account or be confined in their utilization. This is illustrated by the early state-sponsored adjudication of disputes over commercial transactions, when cooperative arrangements among merchants offered competing forms of resolving those disputes. For institutions making such offers of regulation, increasing use becomes a measure of success. At the same time, dependence on voluntary use will make the institution more responsive to the needs of the intended user constituencies.

The concept of institution adopted here covers different types of institutions often considered separately. For many purposes it is important to distinguish formal, consciously adopted and revised institutions from informal ones. Paul Pierson (2004) limits his consideration of the peculiar role of institutions in politics to formal institutions that are legally binding. "Discussions that attempt to cover all types of 'institutions' run a high risk of overgeneralization and necessarily obscure many features distinctive to the study of formal institutions" (34 and 104 n. 1). This limitation to formal institutions articulates well with rationalist modeling, enabling a critical dialogue in Pierson's treatment. It is also true, however, that informal clusters of norms often stand in important relations to formal ones, affecting their stability as well as their effects. This is at the heart of the cooperation between transaction cost economics and studies of organization inspired by the new sociological institutionalism. Moreover, it is only with such a wider lens that one can do justice to the fundamental insight of Durkheim that formal agreements and regulations are grounded in an underlying *conscience collective* (only the French expresses in one formulation its normative as well as its cognitive character) or else become vulnerable and fragile.

Institutions are interrelated with each other, and—as we have noted in the chapter on norms—this has consequences for their stability as well as their vulnerability. Many institutional clusters are smoothly connected to others, sometimes "nesting" within them. Institutions surrounding birth, death, and life transitions are often—even in predominantly secular societies—embedded in religious institutions. Scholarly research is typically intertwined with different levels of education and with professional applications of knowledge. Recognition of these multifarious interrelations has engendered "consensus" models of society in which different institutions link up with each other to form one coherent pattern. But in reality institutions are also often at odds with each other. The question of tension or reinforcement among them must be left open. The interrelations among institutions—their clustering and nesting as well as their mutual contradictions and frictions—are important for assessing the effectiveness of institutional rules as well as their stability.

Where two institutional complexes are inconsistent with each other, improvised noncompliance as well as institutionalized evasion of norms will be common. In turn, if functioning institutional arrangements reinforce each other, especially if formal institutions are reinforced by strong informal institutional supports (as claimed by Durkheim for well-oiled contractual relations), compliance may morph into taken-for-granted routines.

The compatibility of an institutional arrangement with other institutional demands, which may be equally strong or stronger, shapes its acceptance as legitimate, useful, or at least tolerable among the affected people and groups. This acceptance—ranging from mere tolerance to strong support—is also dependent on the material, moral, and cognitive support that can be marshaled for an institutional innovation.

If institutions whose effects are at odds with each other coexist without being confined to specific areas and without effective mediating mechanisms, the mutual interference creates noteworthy consequences. This may generate some doubt and uncertainty on either side of the divide; and it may bring about demands for institutional change. Or it may lead to a greater separation of roles in the two realms of life, to more effective mediating arrangements, or to efforts to help and heal where damage is done. However, incompatible institutions may also continue to coexist without significant change.

The results of institutional incompatibilities are often experienced as personal troubles and crises rather than as the effects of structural arrangements. For instance, institutions concerned with the use of armed force encourage unquestioned command-obedience relations and cultivate an indifference to the use of violence. Both of these are at odds with fundamental norms of civilized life in many societies. Yet where flagrant breaches of these norms become public or where posttraumatic responses of soldiers or police to the experience of violence are diagnosed, they are treated as individual matters and are rarely seen as problems of institutional incompatibility. Arguably such "privatizing" interpretations reflect the fact that cognitive beliefs supporting the normalcy of both institutional complexes are often well protected indeed.

The relations between work and family offer another instance of tension between institutional realms. In almost all modern societies the norm complexes regulating work and those regulating family life display stark inconsistencies. These tensions are more often recognized as targets for institutional remediation; but in the absence of successful provisions ensuring better compatibility, the weaker parties—often women—are expected to absorb the tensions and strains.

What Do Institutions Do?

Institutions set and enforce the rules of the game in spheres of social life that are viewed as important. Often this regulation is so effective that, as noted, some consider institutions as established practices rather than as sets of norms and standards. Effective institutions make actions and reactions predictable. They structure incentives and disincentives and even shape the underlying preferences of people. They open up avenues for successful and rewarding conduct and close or limit access to other routes. They thus have major consequences for the patterns of structured inequality in status, economic resources, as well as influence and power.

Institutions frequently also have other consequences for the sphere of social life they maintain and regulate—for scientific research, for the rational organization of economic production, for market exchange, for marriage and family, for deployment of armed force, or for political contestation. Institutions typically encourage a high evaluation of the practices regulated; they mobilize resources for a significant part of these practices; they often protect the core activities from outside interference; in turn, they frequently contain them within defined boundaries; and they provide mechanisms that mediate between one sphere of life and another.

A major "product" of institutions is the provision of organizational forms that make it unnecessary to invent useful coordinations of activities for every concrete occasion. Organizations of any complexity and stability are impossible without appropriate institutional underpinnings. Even innovative organizational efforts utilize modules of role clusters as well as ready-made command-compliance relations and their legitimations. We saw in the previous chapter that what has been discussed as "modernization" can be understood as the rise of new institutions based on indirect, infrastructural power. Innovations in the institutions governing marriage, family, and gender roles went along with the rise of institutional foundations for vastly expanded market exchange, for private and public formal organizations, and for a great variety of purposeful voluntary associations.

Another range of institutional effects is critical for the dynamics of subsequent social change: institutions and their transformations are often conducive to the emergence or redefinition of collective actors. One entry into understanding these consequences is to consider the effect of institutions on preferences. As individual and collective actors reconsider their interests in a changed institutional landscape, it is plausible that they will look out for, recognize, and engage with new allies and antagonists. Institutional innovation and change do not automatically create new collective actors; but they do change the landscape of latent groups or potential collective actors. Moreover, the restructuring of existing collective actors and the arrangement of new coalitions among them can often diminish the problems bedeviling the creation of collective action among many unrelated individuals (see chapter 10 on collective action).[4]

These effects of institutions on collective actors are heightened if the results of several institutions coincide with each other and if some of the advantages and disadvantages created have a strong and visible symbolic dimension. For example, a newly forming industrial working class, governed by employment rules and labor market conditions not of their own making, will more easily gain collective agency if class position coincides with religious or linguistic boundaries, and if electoral rules add insult to injury by withholding civil rights on the basis of class position.[5]

Two broadly divergent effects of institutions figure prominently in the literature. A first claim, advanced especially by the new economic institutionalism, is that institutions of various kinds enable cooperation and coordination. They make it possible that actors "who are self-interested and opportunistic overcome collective action problems to cooperate for mutual gain" (Moe 2005, 216). The second broad claim—prominent in historical institutionalist studies—holds that institutional arrangements stabilize asymmetries of power, one-sided economic advantage, and differences in status. In these two divergent perspectives, the old division of consensus vs. conflict views of society reasserts itself in new form.

Aside from game theoretic inquiries into the conditions under which self-interested actors can keep individually rational pursuits from yielding collective losses, the first claim can invoke the remarkable effectiveness of market exchange. Given its complex institutional infrastructure, competitive market exchange coordinates many decentralized actions without the use of direct command or coercion (see chapter 9 on aggregations). The second claim can first of all point to institutions of major historical importance that maintain one-sided advantage, such as those undergirding slavery, serfdom, colonialism, autocratic political domination, as well as command-obedience relations in business firms. Beyond that, it builds on the insight that the stabilizing effects of institutions and their reliance on

---

[4] In the conclusion to his examination of the long-term effects of colonialism on development in Latin America, James Mahoney makes the important claim that the collective groups created by colonial institutions—in mercantilist colonialism, above all subordinate indigenous populations set off from monopolistic merchants and landed estate owners—were "the agents through which the long-run effects of institutions are transmitted" (forthcoming, 406). This insight transcends the particular issues of colonialism and development in Latin America and is a critical addition to the views of institutions in the rational choice and sociological equilibrium traditions.

[5] For the last point see Katznelson (1981).

strong positive and negative sanctions inevitably tie effective institutional rules to structures of inequality.[6]

The two broad claims stand in tension with each other; but they are not radically incompatible. They can be read as divergent emphases in the analysis of a most variegated phenomenon. All effective institutions create a measure of predictability in a sphere of social life. When predictability is joined by acceptance, institutions can enable peaceful cooperation among individuals and groups. Yet acceptance and predictability do not entail truly voluntary consent, and they are far from yielding equal or equitable results. No regulatory system can establish a really level playing field, because all rules—even intentionally evenhanded rules— inevitably have unequal effects on actors with unequal resources. As a sarcastic nineteenth-century Parisian observed, "The law in its majestic equality forbids the rich and the poor alike to sleep under bridges, to beg in the streets, and to steal bread" (Anatole France, *The Red Lily*, 1894).

Whether the mutual gain through cooperation or differentials of power and advantage are emphasized, institutions have more elementary effects through which these overall outcomes are realized. Here we must return once more to the role that knowledge, preferences, norms, and emotions play in the workings of larger social structures and processes (see chapter 8). Effective institutions build on these elements of the subjective dimension of action, but at the same time—and partly for this reason—they shape knowledge and beliefs, they structure preferences, they affect norms other than those represented by themselves, and they often are capable of mobilizing strong emotions. It is through these more elementary effects that outcomes of special interest to meso- and macroanalyses are brought about. And it is through these effects that institutions create zones or fields of action in which the individual variability is in a certain sense standardized.

Beliefs are constitutive of institutions.[7] And they are, in turn, a critical result of institutional functioning. Thus beliefs about the sources of productivity and affluence offer rationales for meritocratic employment

[6] The discussion of norms (in chapter 4) has already highlighted strong inequality effects of norms and clusters of rules.

[7] The social constructions of cognitive underpinnings for institutions may turn out to be very intricate. An instructive example is offered by the legal historian Morton Horwitz. He examined the changing rationales for the legal construction of corporations and showed that a "natural entity" theory, ultimately rooted in interpretations of medieval corporations, won out over theories built on contractual relations among partners and others that saw incorporation as a grant of states. The reasons were tied to major interests. Partnership theories did not—among other reasons—protect shareholders sufficiently from liability claims, while the state grant theories made corporate rights too dependent on the government. The intellectual struggle over this complex theory-interests nexus was not easy. It lasted for forty years, from the late 1880s to the end of the 1920s (Horwitz 1992, chap. 3).

norms as well as for relying on competitive markets as the decisive mechanism in the allocation of economic resources. As these institutional norm clusters gain a stronger hold, the corresponding beliefs gain in appeal and acceptance as well. They can turn into unquestioned truths if the cluster of norms is taken for granted. When the scope of institutions is contested, beliefs easily become instruments of ideological struggle resulting in extreme cognitive claims.[8]

All institutions of any effectiveness shape *preferences*. It is not only that their sanctions offer significant rewards for some lines of action while steeply increasing the costs of others; but the more basic preferences that underlie goals and actions shaped by shifts in costs and benefits will be affected as well. Thus profound changes in the rules of political contestation—say, from a system dominated by an authoritarian executive to a parliamentary democracy—will restructure the fundamental goals as well as the strategies of most political actors in a country.

Norms constitute, in the view proposed here, the core of institutions. The strength of material and ideational supports enjoyed by institutions will influence the effectiveness of norms, their subjective acceptance, and the degree to which they are taken for granted. That norms other than those which define the substance of an institution will be affected by institutional change follows from the fact that norms tend to form complex linkages. Those that are in tune with an institutional complex in the ascendancy will be strengthened; others that are at odds with it will be weakened. This can be most easily illustrated if we focus on questions of boundaries between institutional realms. While fundamentalist believers in the market see virtually all value as best determined by competitive individual choice, their opponents point to the virtues that are endangered when the reach of market valuation is extended, such as caring for people and things for their own sake.

The mobilization of *emotions* is a critical factor in the functioning of most norms, the more so, the more important the regulated practices in the eyes of monitors and bystanders. Emotional involvement is also specially intense if strongly held norms are publicly violated or if the role and scope of an institutional complex is a matter of contest. If norms are buttressed by taken-for-granted beliefs, not accepting these cognitive underpinnings is often met by charges of madness or evil.

It is fusions of norms, beliefs, preferences, and emotions that result in shared and stable practices. They create in different spheres of social life more similar, more compatible, and more predictable motivations

---

[8] Thus F. A. von Hayek asserted in *The Road to Serfdom*, published at the end of the war against Fascism and just before the beginning of the cold conflict with Communism, that central economic planning would lead to totalitarian rule, even in democratic societies.

among many, if not all people. At the collective, cultural level they constitute the *conscience collective* Durkheim postulated in his discussion of
the noncontractual foundations of contract, which also underlies other
specific institutional clusters, though Durkheim overestimated the reach
of that conscience collective across all social and cultural divisions in a
social formation.

The more elementary effects of an institution on norms, beliefs, preferences, and emotions frequently duplicate and reinforce each other. They
are redundant, rendering certain outcomes "overdetermined." Such re-
dundancies are important stabilizing mechanisms. The same overdetermination can emerge if different institutions reinforce each other and bring
about similar results, stabilizing and reproducing, for instance, different
forms of inequality of opportunity.

Origins and Transformations

If institutions are "the humanly devised constraints that shape human
interaction" (North 1990, 3), one might well anticipate that institutions,
especially formal ones, are consciously created with specific purposes in
mind. This possibility has engendered a body of ideas about "institutional
design" (Goodin 1996). Consciously conceived goals are indeed common.
Whether they lead to a corresponding institutional creation is, however,
very much an open question.

The recent history of Brown University offers a striking example of
a vastly successful institutional innovation that was initiated by a well-
thought-out plan but then turned into something radically different—
Brown's Open Curriculum of 1969. Three students produced the original
plan and mobilized strong support for it in the student body at large.
Undergraduate students were to be liberated from grade pressure and the
mechanical guidance of a common core curriculum of required courses.
The first year would consist of ungraded freshmen seminars. Free choice
of courses, an unlimited option for ungraded but individually evaluated
courses, the chance to major in an individually designed field of concentration, and intensive capstone work in this field during the last year were
major features of the plan. The faculty approved the plan after several
days of continuous meetings; but what was implemented was a very different matter. The extensive provisions for the first and last year, though
critical for the original plan, were scotched by the university leadership
because the cost—for an unloved innovation—was too high. After a
short-lived student enthusiasm for ungraded courses, nearly all courses
were taken for grades again. What was left were great flexibility of choice
and a liberal openness to the self-guidance of students. This proved to be

extremely attractive to prospective students, but it remained a blemish in the eyes of many conservatives, including many on the "Corporation," Brown's board of overseers. Yet with minor adjustments the open curriculum was left in place because it attracted more and more as well as better-prepared applicants. Within a short time, success of graduates in applying to law, business, and medical schools soared. What resulted, then, was a pattern nobody had anticipated. But that outcome proved very successful, the more so as other universities and colleges withdrew from similar but less far-reaching experiments, leaving Brown and a few other colleges with similar curricula to dominate a niche in liberal education.

Three things stand out in this episode. Different actors, with different power resources and partly antagonistic concerns and goals, interacted in bringing about this innovation. The result did not realize the goals of the student activists, the faculty majority, the university administration, or the board of overseers. Owing to unanticipated success in the competitive market of undergraduate education, the innovation stabilized and became acceptable to the reluctant partners in its creation.

"Nations stumble upon establishments, which are indeed the result of human action, but not the execution of any human design." Taking off from this observation of Adam Ferguson (made in his *Essay on the History of Civil Society*), Paul Pierson has composed a nested list of complications and obstacles that stand in the way of successful "design." First, institutions have multiple effects. That means different initiators may have quite different motivations to advance an innovation, resulting in heterogeneous design coalitions. Second, designers may not act instrumentally but may copy institutional patterns they consider "appropriate" rather than construct solutions to particular local problems as they understand them. Third, designers may—and often do—have planning horizons that are shorter than the likely duration of the institutional innovations. Fourth, the effects of an institutional arrangement may not be adequately foreseen. Fifth, the effects of an institution may change as its social environment changes. Sixth, the actors who initiated an institutional innovation pursuing certain preferences may be replaced with second- and third-generation actors concerned with different interests. Pierson completes these arguments with a skeptical assessment of the chances of later corrections due to learning from experience and competitive elimination of ill-conceived arrangements. In sum, for a causal understanding of institutions, a focus on institutional *development* seems more promising than centering attention on *design* (Pierson 2004).

Yet there are instances where long-term institutional developments seem best explained as the result of the persistent pursuit of clear-cut goals, even when this involved a succession of actors. Nitsan Chorev has described how the advocates of free trade and economic openness suc-

ceeded in the United States in removing decision making about trade restrictions first from the legislature to the executive and then from the
national government to adjudication by the World Trade Organization
(Chorev 2007). One may well argue that this was aided by a number of
exceptional conditions, among them the existence of a long-established
tradition of advocating and monitoring free trade policies—the *Economist* newspaper has filled this role since 1843—as well as the success of
relatively free trade among the Atlantic economies after the Second World
War, which followed the disastrous decline of economic openness in the
Depression of the 1930s.

Another instance of a long-term institutional "design" involved even
more complex institutional arrangements as well as an even longer period
of time. Morton Horwitz (1977) analyzed how, in the time between
the American Revolution and the Civil War, American private law was
changed from eighteenth-century English and colonial precedents into a
system of law fit for the rising competitive capitalism. Guided by ideas
of facilitating economic growth, judges in state courts—rather than legislatures—transformed the meaning of property, contract, and tort law in
radical ways, often aiding actors seen as indispensable and decisive
for economic growth at the expense of farmers, workers, and consumers. This was achieved in sequences of smaller steps; but the results
were dramatic and clear-cut. When the transformation had run its course,
contracts—to take a major example—were considered valid and enforce-
able once it was established that the parties had come to an agreement,
while the older law required the judiciary to inquire whether the
agreement was equitable. Here, again, it is possible to point to a context
that may well have been decisive for these innovations, above all the
revolutionary establishment of "the first new nation" (Lipset) and its
constitutional innovations.

Select instances favored by extraordinary circumstance do not change
the fact that purposive design of institutions is extremely difficult. Yet the
impressive list of obstacles to institutional design—Pierson calls it "actor-
centered functionalism"—must not obscure the fact that institutional arrangements often favor, broadly but systematically, certain outcomes,
such as increases in efficiency, the protection of dominant interests, or—
a frequent occurrence—a combination of the two. This suggests a modicum of successful design and revision, however imprecise in detail. The
obstacles to successful institutional planning may in most cases make any
close fit between design and result illusory. But a rough approximation of
broadly shared goals, such as protecting dominant interests, is frequently
not beyond the power and resources of the initiating and sustaining
actors. Moreover, mistakes can often be corrected, at least in a rough way,
and changed circumstances can be taken into account. Beyond that, the

very strength of institutional arrangements—their material and immaterial supports and the positive and negative sanctions enforcing
their norms—tend to link and harmonize power and privilege with the
effects of institutions.

Historical studies of institutional innovation have often focused on
"critical junctures" that initiated new patterns of institutional persistence
(Moore 1966; Krasner 1984; Collier and Collier 1991; Thelen 1999).
Recent models of path dependency take off from this work (Pierson 2000;
Mahoney 2000). Focusing on critical junctures makes attempts at instrumental design more visible and—at least for a while—more plausible.
However, it is easier to identify such decisive configurations in retrospect
than in situations whose aftermath has not yet played itself out. Furthermore, though war and economic crises are frequently invoked, what exactly leads to a critical juncture is still not well understood.[9]

It is also often unclear which avenues of innovation are opened by a
critical juncture, and which features of the status quo remain untouched
or continue in adapted form. After the Second World War Germany experienced what was certainly a critical juncture by any standard. In both
parts of the then divided country many institutional features of political
and economic life were transformed; but a decade or two after 1945,
West Germany saw many complaints about "restoration" policies,
claiming that the chance of a fresh start had been missed. Rejecting a
single-minded focus on critical junctures and "punctuated equilibrium
models," Kathleen Thelen suggests generally that "there often seems to
be too much continuity through putative breakpoints in history, but also
often too much change beneath the surface of apparently stable formal
institutional arrangements."[10]

---

[9] Barry Weingast (2005) has offered a model of discontinuous political change, which he
applies to the American Revolution as well as to current political developments. It identifies
mechanisms that make new radical opinions successful. Their acceptability depends (1) on
confirming developments that are beyond the control of their advocates and (2) on the
stakes of the controversy in the eyes of pivotal actors, i.e., on the degree to which predicted
developments threaten major life interests of dominant opinion holders. If the stakes increase, the readiness to accept new ideas gains ground. This explains why advocates of
radical ideas are often "prophets of doom." If Weingast's construct amounts to less than
"the microfoundations of a macroscopic concept" (i.e., of critical junctures), as the essay's
title promises, it certainly represents an intriguing mechanism hypothesis about one type of
critical configurations. It also constitutes a welcome addition to the body of work pairing
modeling in the rational choice tradition with comparative historical analysis.

[10] Thelen (2003, 211). Thelen has sought to illuminate this combination of continuity
and change in her work on the German occupational training system with the inductive
conceptualizations of "institutional layering" (or partial renegotiations of institutions) and
"institutional conversion" (or turning existing institution to new purposes); see Thelen
(2003, 225–30) as well as her important comparative treatment of skill training in Germany,
Britain, the United States, and Japan in Thelen (2004).

Critical junctures, then, may be important research sites for the analysis of institutions; but they rarely pinpoint origins. They may indeed engender dramatic transformations. Yet these dynamics are as yet ill understood. There is a good chance that they may be shaped in ways that are largely similar to those that produce less dramatic changes, to which I will return below.

Focusing primarily on critical junctures seems even less appropriate if we look into the origins of informal institutions—such as friendship or revenge—and the informal foundations that make formal institutions, such as contractual market exchange, possible. The latter include rules of reciprocity, standards of civility in impersonal transactions, as well as differentiated norms about the place of seeking advantage in social life. Such informal institutional patterns depend on the concurrence of many decentralized and often unconnected views and decisions. They therefore are extremely unlikely to emerge full-blown from critical constellations of events, or to be created purposefully with new institutional outcomes in mind. They are much more likely than formal institutions to conform to Adam Ferguson's formula: nearly without exception, they are "the result of human action, but not the execution of any human design." This does not, however, mean that change in informal institutions necessarily takes a long time. Even institutions that are grounded deeply in personal conscience and close social control—such as those governing premarital erotic and sexual behavior—have changed in the span of one generational turnover or less.

Informal institutions may, however, be ruptured rapidly, and such breakdown may be due to critical junctures. War, civil war, severe economic crises, but also political repression banning autonomous action and open discussion can weaken institutions of civility in dealing with strangers to the point of breakdown, while others—such as those building on the solidarity of kin, clan, and religion—may gain strength in response to the same situations. The condition of Iraqi social life in the aftermath of the second Gulf War seems to illustrate both tendencies. More generally, breakdowns of informal institutions seem to be associated with quite different causal conditions from those underlying their creation, re-creation, and transformation.

If successful institutional design is rare and if even in critical junctures the causal conditions of change in formal as well as informal institutions are not at all well understood, is it possible to offer reasonable hunches about institutional development rather than design? Paul Pierson's list of obstacles to successful design constitutes a first set of points from which one can develop more specific hypotheses. Considering the consequences of heterogeneous coalitions, noninstrumental orientations, short planning horizons, limited foresight, adverse developments in the social envi-

ronment, and generational turnover point indeed to a set of factors that
shape the outcomes of diverse attempts at institution building.

Another baseline for developing hypotheses about institutional development can be found in the theory frames of the three current versions
of institutionalist analysis. They point to (1) efficiency considerations in
the pursuit of given preferences, (2) the balance of power, and (3) cultural
conceptions of what is appropriate. Kathleen Thelen suggests that "each
of these perspectives contains an implicit theory of change: if institutions
rest on and reflect a particular foundation (whether efficiency-based,
power-based, or cultural) then they should change as a result of shifts in
those underlying conditions" (Thelen 2003, 211–12). These are diverse
and broad, but instructive perspectives.

The first, rational choice institutionalism, is instrumentally oriented toward the consequences of action. Changes in the environment, changes
in the understanding of the environment, and changes in technical options
for reaching given goals will occasion institutional change. Some of the
factors discussed earlier as reshaping the institutional structure of gender
relations fit into this perspective on institutional change. Better survival
chances of children, decreased economic advantages of large numbers of
children, and the changing role of brain and brawn in economic production were critically important for institutional change that increased
women's options.

The third approach, the new sociological institutionalism, is oriented
to relevant cultural premises. Changes in what are considered relevant
cultural precedents and changes in the way these are embodied in effective
institutions as well as functioning organizations and groups will shape
the pace and direction of institutional development. Again the change in
gender relations offers an illustration: both the resistance to institutional
change in gender roles and the repeated waves of movements for reduced
gender inequality invoke normative and cognitive elements of culture,
often deeply anchored in indigenous tradition but in some cases derived
from comparison with what other cultures hold in high regard.

The theory frame focusing on the balance of power holds a distinct
place. Power—in the sense of the chance that an actor can carry out his
or her will despite resistance—is closely related to the controlling character of institutions. Shifts in power resources will weaken or strengthen the
effectiveness of institutions. In addition, the use of power will often be
decisive in changing the substance of institutions, in building and shaping
coalitions, in persuading broader constituencies of the need for change,
or in blocking the influence of other interests. In turn, as noted repeatedly,
institutions create power advantages and disadvantages, and they reproduce patterns of power over time.

A power approach is quite compatible with the other two theory frames, and it can build on them. But there is a particular reason for giving a special place to considerations of power. The other two approaches are inconclusive if power is not taken into account. Efficiency arguments and their associated cost-benefit assessments inevitably lead to the question: Efficient in terms of which—and whose—preferences? Whose costs and whose benefits are being assessed? Furthermore, diagnoses of a changing environment are far from self-evident once spelled out. Rather, they are subject to social and cultural construction and thus to the influence of—possibly contending—intellectual, moral, and political authorities.

Power plays a similar role in the cultural-sociological theory frame of institutional analysis. Which cultural precedents and constructions can be invoked successfully? And which can be brought to bear on and embodied in the codes of everyday life and the functioning of groups and organizations? This depends in large part on the influence and cultural power of contending actors. And that power clearly relies significantly on social and political power, and not merely or primarily on a deep knowledge of cultural traditions and options. The change in gender relations can serve once more to illustrate this pervasive role of power balances in institutional change. Even if part of this change is clearly due to changes in technology and economic production, and if cultural invocations constitute another important component in the transformation of gender relations, it took intellectual, social, and political clout to achieve the reductions in gender inequality that are now part of the institutional landscape in many countries.

Emphasizing the balance of power in the study of institutional change also has the desirable effect of focusing attention on the various actors involved in institutional development without at the same time engaging in a simplistic "actor-centered functionalism." Who acts on behalf of an institutional complex—as initiator and sponsor, as guarantor and enforcer, as monitor of its functioning and reformer of its provisions, and finally as supporter or detractor? It may be harder to identify these actors working on behalf of institutions in some cases than in others; by and large, this is more difficult in informal institutions than in formal ones; but their existence and actions are critical for institutional analysis.

A corollary of a broader emphasis on power also highlights the role of opponents of the institutional innovation as well as that of the people and groups adversely affected by the institution in question. Unless opponents and losers were weak to begin with, are radically weakened subsequently, or are afforded some protection of their interests in the new situation, they are likely to encourage noncompliance, weaken monitoring, and inhibit enforcement. For example, laws seeking to control anticompetitive behavior in oligopolistic and monopolistic markets have engendered such subversive reactions repeatedly. Other examples—including the phenomenon of "institutionalized evasion" of norms (see chapter 4)—are abundant because this constellation of interests and power resources is common indeed.

Interests and groups that are put at a disadvantage by an institutional innovation may also recoup and find new strength. This is a major mechanism reflected in simple (and perhaps too simple) ideas claiming with some regularity that "the pendulum will swing back again" as well as in sophisticated (and perhaps too sophisticated) claims about an inherent "dialectic of history."[11] It is indeed prudent to watch out for future developments advancing the interests of groups subdued earlier; but there may also be a good chance that a new institutional constellation damages the interests it subdues permanently and even progressively.

Finally, opposed interests may adjust to each other in lasting ways. One major source of institutional stability lies in the partial accommodation and co-optation of weaker interests. Indeed, if we look at the longevity of major historical empires—ranging from the Middle East through South Asia to China, Japan, and Korea—there is little question that complex compromises between relatively rational institutions at the political center and local and regional rule based on a very different institutional logic survived for time periods that far exceed the life span political institutions of modern capitalist countries have achieved so far.[12]

Conclusion

In this chapter, I found it necessary to preface my own comments on the dynamics and the effectiveness of institutions with an extended review of alternative approaches to their analysis. This reflects a seemingly paradoxical state of affairs: Institutional analysis is now broadly recognized as the key to social and political structures and their dynamics. At the same time, the different approaches, grounded in divergent theory traditions, are not fully consonant with each other. These approaches

---

[11] Rooted in Marxist ideas, recognition of the existence and possible resurgence of subdued groups and strata became a central argument of conflict theory against the consensus models of structural functionalism; but it was not confined to conflict theory (see, e.g., Dahrendorf 1959, but also Eisenstadt 1964). For a brief review of recent work on "losers" bringing about institutional change, see Pierson (2004, 135–36).

[12] See Eisenstadt (1963) and, among more recent treatments, Islamoglu and Perdue (2001), who refer to two workshops at New York University in 1999 and 2000 titled "Shared Histories of Modernity: State Transformation in the Chinese and Ottoman Empires, Seventeenth through Nineteenth Centuries." See also Karen Barkey's *Empire of Difference* (2008).

can best be understood as theory frames that, despite significant trends toward rapprochement and even convergence, still diverge from each other; they use different analytic strategies and encourage different empirical procedures.

However, building on the earlier discussion of norms, I have sought to show that the different "institutionalisms" can in effect be used jointly as a single theory frame, if a somewhat kaleidoscopic one. As an ensemble, they do offer rich suggestions for the development of specific hypotheses; but they do so from different angles, pointing to different outcomes and trajectories of institutions, identifying different factors as most important, and giving different reasons for these hunches and suggestions. It is possible to deplore this state of affairs and to continue with well-known meta-theoretical polemics. It is also possible—and possibly more fruitful—to accept, at least for the time being, a deficit in systemic elegance and to use the current richness in orienting ideas to best effect in theoretically oriented research.

Chapter XIII

SOCIAL IDENTITIES

With Matthias vom Hau

Social identities are relations of membership recognized as significant by members and outsiders. They are constituted through processes of self-identification and external categorization et al. (Barth 1969; Jenkins 1997). Drawing on analytical tools from the first part of this book, we develop ideas about "social identities" as social and cultural patterns interconnecting institutions, organizations, and the subjective dimension of action. Social identities carry awareness and a sense of loyalty; they are affectively charged and engender emotional commitment; and they entail both obligations to and claims on other members. Social identities may or may not crystallize into strong attachments to a particular, bounded entity, whether an ethnic group, a class, a nation.

Social identities matter in important ways. They shape collective self-understandings and constitute a source of meaning (Giddens 1991). They pattern the experience and the public representation of groups, movements, and organizations (Castells 1997; Tilly 1996). They define rights and obligations. They create social solidarities, in particular solidarities that transcend direct interaction. They reproduce social boundaries. And at such boundaries they may activate the in-group–out-group mechanism, turning people on either side into friend or foe.

As a consequence of these and other effects, social identities are closely related to the chances of collective action. The meaning of social identities and the strength of identification with them define the propensity of "groupness," or sense of belonging (Brubaker 2002), and shape the chances of mobilizing them into movements and organizations (see chapter 10 on collective organization).

There is a rich literature on particular social identities, their constitution in social conflict, and their role in collective action. Students of social provision have shown that distinct welfare state regimes had major ramifications for gender identities in everyday life, and shaped the power resources and framings employed by women's movements (e.g., Huber and Stephens 2001; Orloff 1996). Scholarship on race relations has explored how distinct trajectories of nation-state formation (e.g., Marx 1998; Wimmer 2002) and different modes of colonial economic organization (e.g., Winant 2001, Mahoney forthcoming) instigated distinct meanings and experiences of race in the postcolonial world; and these works have looked at the consequences of those different racial identities for the organization and goals of antiracist movements. Focusing on social identities helps to bridge these distinct literatures and develop a theoretical frame that cuts across gender, race, and class to approach the interplay of collective framings and sentiments of belonging with issues of power and organization.

CONCEPTUALIZATIONS

In their broadest sense, social identities encompass face-to-face groups, local communities, as well as large groupings that transcend any conceivable form of direct interaction, as do ethnic groups, social classes, and nations. A narrower version of the concept, which is the primary concern in this chapter, includes only groupings that go beyond direct relational connectedness. Broadening a felicitous formulation of Benedict Anderson (1983), we can call all such social identities that transcend face-to-face interaction *imagined communities*. The peculiarity of imagined communities is their capacity to engender powerful imageries and feelings of communality even in the relative absence of direct networks and relational ties.

Social identities are distinct from *social categories*—sets of people with certain characteristics that are defined and recognized by outside observers, perhaps only by the social analyst herself. Social identities must be recognized by those involved and named in the vernacular. Age and income groupings are commonly just social categories;[1] but when we speak of generations, age groups that have shared important experiences such as the Second World War, the Great Depression, or even just a birth date in the years of the baby boom, we shift from social category to social identity.[2] Social categories become social identities when they are recognized and embraced by members and others as meaningful and worthy of identification. This process can be self-initiated; but it can also be instigated from the outside, as people and organizations frequently impose categories on others, especially when these "categorizers" are backed up by powerful material and symbolic resources.

[1] Far-flung interaction networks and even small face-to-face groups may be examples of social categories as well if they are not recognized as significant identities by members, significant outsiders, or both. De facto interaction patterns without such recognition are exactly analogous to sets of people in an age or income bracket that is arbitrary in their own view.

[2] Mannheim (1928/1952) presents a famous sociological treatment of generations.

Analyzing the relationship between social categories and the formation of social identities has a distinguished pedigree in class analysis, where sets of people who are categorized by their position in the system of production, in the distribution of wealth, in rankings of power and influence, or on a scale of status and prestige are distinguished from social classes in the fuller sense, which require a developed consciousness, solidarity, and perhaps organization.[3] By comparison, the study of nationalism and ethnicity has been more prone to conflate categories and identities, and to simply assume the existence of ethnic groups and nations as reified entities (Brubaker 2002). Yet this domain of social analysis has now also become more attuned to thinking of ethnicity and nationhood as constituted in a process of transforming categories into identities.

The contrast with social categories highlights that social identities are socially constructed. The meaning and experience of membership in an ethnic group, a social class, or a nation congeal through complex mental and social processes of perception, interpretation, and assessment. People identify and categorize self and others and thereby create and reproduce distinct ways of seeing, interpreting, and judging the social world. To boot, social identities also define the very entities of which people are claimed to be members, using a variety of criteria. For instance, in relation to social inequality they may focus on status, on various aspects of economic position, or on power and influence, and they may identify narrowly circumscribed status groups, such as power elites and fragments of the working class or large inclusive groupings. At the same time, the variability of social identity construction is subject to constraints. Social identities are entwined with a specific social position. As such, they are inevitably linked to power differentials, organizational resources, and larger structural dynamics. Social identity formation thus can never fully escape its conditions, which are reflected in the frames, habitual dispositions, and subjective experiences of their members.

Social identities are in the first place cognitive maps constitutive of particular perspectives on the world (Brubaker, Loveman, and Stamatov 2004). These frames and classification schemas—often engrained in the habitus of people (Bourdieu 1990) and only sometimes self-reflexively employed (Giddens 1991)—provide a grid for making sense of lived experience. In charting the social landscape, cognitive processes of classification and labeling are often fused with evaluation and norms. Social identities not only designate particular understandings of one's self and social location; they also work through normative orientations and prescrip-

[3] Dahrendorf (1959), Katznelson (1986), and Wright (1985) develop varieties of Marxian conceptions of social class. The similarities and contrasts of working-class formation in Britain, Germany, France, and the United States are explored comparatively in Zolberg (1986).

tions. Similarly, social identities are entwined with preferences. They structure people's needs and wants by defending interests that are indicative of one's membership or by advancing preferences that are explicitly targeted against the interests of "outsiders."[4] Emotions play an equally central role. Social identities focus emotional needs for collective belonging and structure sentiments of proximity and distance and sensations of liking and aversion (see Scheff 1990, 1997). Thus social identity formation fuses the subjective dimensions of action.

Attachments determine the salience, importance, and commanding character of different social identities and the affinities and commonalities expressed by them. Attachments charge certain cognitions, norms, preference structures, and emotions with subjective meaning and fuse them into specific reference points for social identity. Attachments crystallize into specific boundary markers. This means that attachments function as an overarching organizing principle of social identities and powerfully shape the motivation of people.

It is critical to think of social identities in the plural. Different identities vary a great deal—in their origins as well as in the substance and intensity of obligations and claims they entail. That is intuitively evident if we compare membership in a kin group with membership in a local community, a political party, or a nation of millions. Moreover, any individual will have a multiplicity of—actual and potential—identities. This raises complicated issues of their relative salience—of, say, being at the same time—black, a doctor, a woman, a resident of a gated community, and so forth—issues that in turn have decisive consequences for the effects of any given social identity.

The inherent plurality of social identities points to the potential of identity conflicts. Individuals may be attached to contradictory worldviews and normative orientations, sustaining conflicting obligations and claims of solidarity. Tensions among different social identities are most likely to occur when one particular social identity dominates perceptions of one's place in the world across a variety of institutional and organizational contexts, and challenges other ideas of belonging and commitment. For instance, the lived experience of Kyrgyz migrants in post-Communist Moscow is primarily shaped by their status as "illegals," a social identity that stands in tension with the imagery of the city as their capital during the Soviet era, and their self-understandings and practices as workers and parents (Reeves 2008). Conflicts among social identities have real-life consequences especially when membership claims are tied to legal recognition and access to power resources.

---

[4] The nexus of identity and preference formation is such that some authors see the fundamental preferences of actors as an expression of their social identity.

Conditions of Identity Formation

It is possible to distinguish conditions favorable to social identity formation. There are, first, dense interaction patterns that just need a spark
of recognition to initiate processes of identification. This condition was
identified by Homans (1950) in the context of small group research, and
gained further prominence through Tilly's (1978) idea of "netness" in the
context of social movement studies. The situation is more complicated in
the case of "imagined communities" with minimal or no direct interaction. These require multifaceted symbolic mediation. Symbols (e.g., Kertzer 1988), myths (e.g., Smith 1986), narratives (e.g., Somers 1994), and
collective archetypes and stereotypes (e.g., Gutierrez 1999) are critical
for engendering powerfully imagined self-understandings and feelings of
belonging. In turn, these means of symbolization have to reach far and
wide. Thus print media were important in the historic emergence of nations (Anderson 1983), while mass media, education systems, consumption conduits, and family structures play a central role in the dissemination of social identities today.

The special role of symbolization is immediately clear when we consider a list of shared characteristics commonly understood to be conducive to mutual identification. These range from common behavior codes
and shared language to a common fate—memories of the past, anticipations of the future, or both—and also include common major life interests,
common values and ideals, and common religion.

A distinction of long standing in the study of identity formation is the
contrast between ascribed and acquired characteristics, between, for instance, family membership and occupational status. A controversy has
flared up around the labeling of identities based on ascribed characteristics
as "primordial," which is often understood as quasi-natural. It is indeed
misleading to see some identities as "natural" and others as culturally
determined (Geertz 1963). Yet rather than dismiss the whole distinction,
we might ask under what conditions social identities are perceived and
experienced as primordial elements of collective life (see Eisenstadt 1998).
For instance, it makes sense to take account of the consequences of how
early a given aspect of one's social existence is treated as relevant, the ways
in which it shapes later experiences, and the degree to which it is or becomes a matter of choice. Family membership, on these criteria, clearly
stands apart from occupational performance, though many acquired characteristics—be it success in education or conviction of a criminal offense—
can take effect early as well and do not easily change later. The degree to
which social identities are conceived of as a matter of choice also plays
into collective action. The perception of identities as "primordially" given
facilitates the mobilization of shared attachments.

While it is possible to pinpoint generic conditions favorable to identity formation, it is equally important to realize that specific preexisting social identities play a critical role. They can be extended or contracted, intensified or flattened. And they can be used as models for a variety of new identity formations. The proclamation of *fraternité*—brotherhood—as the paradigm for collective solidarity in the French Revolution is perhaps the most famous instance of the latter, providing the grid for the modern idea of nations as horizontally integrated communities that transcend class and status differences (Anderson 1983; Greenfeld 1992). Preexisting identities also affect changes in the meaning and intensity of identification as they entail collective memories of critical events, of shared glory, of shared frustrations, and of past developments in in-group–out-group relations. This is precisely what Anthony Smith (1986, 1991) suggests when he emphasizes the continuities between *ethnies*, with their specific cultural and historical attributes, and the "myth-symbol complexes" of modern nations. Finally, the malleability of preexisting identity formations is to an important extent shaped by their particular modes of social closure (see Wimmer 2008). "Horizontal" identities, such as local or regional affiliations, probably lend themselves more readily to recomposition and transformation, whereas "vertical" identities, such as race and gender, are less easily reconstructed into new social identities.[5] In either way, the peculiar role of preexisting identity models makes clear that *historicity*— historical singularity and the peculiar intertwining of continuity and change—is of abiding relevance in the study of social identity formation.

Another way of looking at how identities form and change in relation to what is on offer by past developments is to view cognitive maps of the social landscape as presenting a "repertoire" of identities. Social contexts not only classify and sort individuals into categories—such external imposition is indeed one major form of initiating identity formation (Jenkins 1997)—but they also provide a variety of identity options, historically grounded scripts and models that make certain subjective processes of identification more imaginable than others. Identity formation is both constrained and enabled by previously established cognitive maps. If social identities are unambiguously inscribed in cognitive maps so as to deny reflection, they are most persistent; the facts of social construction are then hidden.

Processes and Actors

Conceiving of identity formation as a matter of social construction inevitably raises the question: who are the agents that do the constructing? A

[5] Thanks to Michael Woolcock for pointing us to this distinction.

first distinction separates outsiders and insiders. Discrimination by others, be it positive or negative, plays a major role in constituting and strengthening social identities. The centrality of this process has been highlighted in a variety of domains, including research on migration (Portes 1995), racial formation (Winant 2001), and indigenous mobilization (Yashar 2005). The joint experience of enjoying positive recognition and of suffering negative discrimination engenders solidarity on which individuals and organizations that claim to speak in the name of the designated identity can build with interpretations, suggestions of common reactions, and proposals of norms to be adopted. If we take external categorization and internal identification together, it is clear that conflict holds a very special place in the emergence and consolidation of social identities, creating lasting collective memories, restructuring evaluations and preferences, and mobilizing emotions.[6]

The list of relevant actors involved in social identity formation is virtually endless. Among the more important are educational bodies, news and entertainment organizations, as well as religious establishments and groups. Here we focus on three kinds of actors—on the leaders of identity movements who engage in mobilizing potential constituencies to embrace a particular self-understanding, on people embedded in established organizational positions who make it their business to monitor and nurture the reproduction of a given social identity, and finally on modern states that constitute particularly powerful agents of identity formation.

The work of identity "entrepreneurs" is multifaceted. They define and police the boundaries of a social identity, offer reasons and incentives—symbolic and possibly material—for accepting identification, develop historical narratives, lay out visions of the future, and devise roles ensuring that whatever momentum has been created is maintained. In order to do this, they need not only political and moral authority but also the capacity to reach a wide and dispersed audience as well as to acquire material and symbolic resources. The foundations of this authority, the means of communication, as well as the kinds and origins of resources influence the way social identity formation proceeds. For instance, in late nineteenth-century Mexico, local intellectuals (i.e., notables, low-level administrative officials, teachers, and elders) were more effective in advancing their alternative visions of national identity if they were able to build a support coalition among villagers, marshaled cross-regional ties to other identity movements, and effectively linked their framings to familiar notions of national identity (Mallon 1995). Thus it makes a difference whether such identity leaders find support from other sources, whether their goals—

---

[6] This is one of the many "functions of social conflict" Lewis Coser (1956) discussed in his magnificent elaboration of Simmel's (1908/1955) ideas on social conflict.

and thus their support—are primarily economic, cultural, or political in character, and which symbols, collective memories, and desires they are invoking in their appeals.

Eventually the work of such identity entrepreneurs shades over—in a process that Max Weber has ideal-typically analyzed as the "routinization of charisma"—into the monitoring and maintenance activities of established functionaries who make a living from "identity work." Without such established supports, wider social identities do not have very good chances of flourishing, though many of these roles and organizations may support the cause along with other goals. For example religious functionaries, teachers, but also tourism promoters and entertainers may be vigorous supporters of certain ethnic identifications, even when the institutional and organizational contexts they are working in are not explicitly oriented toward social identity formation.

Modern states play two roles in the creation and reproduction of social identities. The first centers on states as identifiers and classifiers. Nationalism plays a central role in the legitimization of state power. Modern states take a strong interest in how their societal constituency conceives of itself, and how it relates to the apparatus of rule. As a matter of fact, through the cultivation of national identification states tend to constitute the very societal constituencies whom they claim to represent. National identity creates a collective self-portrait, instills a sense of solidarity, establishes rights and obligations of membership, and defines the boundaries that set the nation in question apart from others. Key institutional underpinnings of national identity formation may include primary education systems (Gellner 1983; Hobsbawn 1990), public ceremonies and rituals (Kertzer 1988), but also mundane administrative practices such as issuing passports (Torpey 2000), making maps (Anderson 1983), or building roads (Weber 1976).

State involvement in social identity construction is not limited to "nationalizing" discourses and practices (Brubaker 1996). State administrative practices set in motion the creation and re-creation of a wide range of social identities. The legitimacy of modern states rests to an important extent on the exercise of "symbolic power" (Loveman 2005), the capacity to name and categorize people more generally. States routinely sort their subjects according to a variety of criteria, including gender, religion, ethnicity, caste, class, health, and criminality (Scott 1998). A stark example here is the construction of modern-day caste in colonial India, when the classification activities of British authorities superimposed a supposedly traditional caste structure on a complex web of social relations of difference and deference (Dirks 2001). Official categories, of course, do not seamlessly translate into social identities with cognitive and emotional relevance. States generally cannot create social identities in this literal sense. As the gradual transformation of "Hispanics" from census category into collective identity illustrates (Kertzer and Arel 2002), state-sponsored modes of categorization encourage identification primarily by becoming the common language both state and nonstate actors refer to and struggle over (Brubaker and Cooper 2000).

The second role modern states play in the structuring of social identities is more indirect. It derives from the fact that each system of rule inevitably affects the chance of various societal actors to acquire meaningful social identities and shapes the character of those identities. This holds true for racial and ethnic groups, religious affiliations, different groupings based on status and economic position, as well as local and regional communities.

Examples of how state action shapes boundaries, salience, and character of diverse identities are abundant. Attaching legal consequences—privileges as well as disabilities—to religious, ethnic, racial, and occupational groupings is common across countries and has been so throughout the history of modern states. For instance, the difference between white-collar and blue-collar workers in nineteenth- and twentieth-century Germany was not just defined by—inevitably shaded—differences between office and factory, clean and dirty work, as well as closeness to and distance from ownership and authority. It was also delineated by legal measures, for instance by different social insurance provisions with contrasting levels of support and rules of access; not surprisingly, this long corresponded to separate unions for white- and blue-collar workers. It is similarly clear that any legal system of reverse discrimination or affirmative action gives greater salience as well as sharp boundaries to the racial and ethnic identities involved (Marx 1998).

Likewise, modern states shape social identities by providing the broader institutional framework for the collective organization of nonstate actors. As Riva Kastoryano (2002) illustrates in her work on immigration and ethnicity in France and Germany, it is the institutional infrastructure of states that privileges certain social identities around which collective organization and interest representation take place. For instance, a state following a corporatist model of interest mediation provides a different set of "institutional channels" (Ireland 1994) for social identity formation from that provided by a state following a more open model of interest negotiation. An even more obvious example of institutional frameworks configuring social identities is local communities. These owe, in modern countries, their very constitution as corporate actors with defined boundaries to state action.

The two roles of states in identity formation interact with each other. Different identities within a country are affected by how states handle the cultivation of a national community. Legally, the latter is often grounded in the structures of citizenship. In addition to political citizenship, which defines people as formal members of the political community with civil and voting rights, we find in all modern states diverse forms of social citizenship that gives access to various kinds of social provisions—to schools, health care, pensions, and the like. These state provisions of social welfare imply that national solidarity overrides differences and rivalries that might otherwise divide the citizenry. Aside from this symbolic effect, state-sponsored social provisions may well diminish divisive fights for sparse resources. In turn, however, if rival identifications are in fact stronger than national solidarities, the evenhanded provision of social supports across ethnic, religious, and racial lines may come under attacks that are motivated by these identifications and aversions. If the state provides evenhanded services on the basis of political and social citizenship, this not only can shape a coherent political community, but it can transform relations between different identities in a country. The perceived fairness of the state vis-à-vis a diverse society is one of the most important factors creating a culture of trust in a social arrangement.[7]

The identity work of states does not unfold in a vacuum. State-sponsored identity projects are inherently contested. As the domain of nationalism illustrates, the nation and its boundaries, the obligations and rights it creates, its historical narratives, its visions of a common future—all this is subject to political struggle. Too often national identities are thought of as unidimensional: a right-of-center concern that ranges in intensity from mild patriotism to extreme forms of nationalism, which generate hostility toward other nations. Even a superficial review of history reveals, however, many forms that differ along various dimensions. Civic nationalisms that sought to stimulate public service and to assimilate heterogeneous populations into a culturally homogenous national community; ethnic nationalisms that advanced the image of an already existing ethnocultural nation to achieve statehood; and "homeland" nationalisms that sought to defend the interests of conationals abroad—these are only a few examples of the rich variety we can observe in nineteenth-century European history (Brubaker 1992, 1996). In early twentieth-century Latin America liberal nationalisms adopted a political-territorial understanding of the nation, envisioned national unity as achieved through the spread of "civilization," and viewed national history as driven by elites, while popular nationalisms promoted a cultural understanding of the nation, imagined the assimilation of the resident population into a homogeneous na-

---

[7] See, e.g., Rothstein (1998). It is usually argued that socially, ethnically, and racially homogeneous countries can more easily provide generous social supports. But the opposite hypothesis about the direction of causation—that evenhanded public provisions are one of the most important foundations for trust among groups in society—holds as well.

tional identity, and viewed the masses as driving national history (vom Hau 2008b). All of them were the result of political struggles in which state elites and various political contenders sought to impose their vision of national identity. These distinct conceptions of national inclusion varied in their political significance and broader resonance, with major implications for a variety of outcomes, including political development, citizenship regimes, and the politics of redistribution.

RESONANCE

Why are social identities—and in particular imagined communities of an ethnic, religious, political, or class variety—accepted and embraced? Contending identity entrepreneurs can create, re-create, and diffuse social identities, but the response to these identity projects is not under their control. The dynamics of acceptance, indifference, or rejection may be—and often are—quite different from identity production and attempts at institutionalization by elites. The ultimate conditions of acceptance are of course manifold, reflecting the variety of potential identity repertoires and past identities available to actors as well as the specific characteristics of the identity in question. Among the underlying factors shared by many different social identities are, as noted earlier, common experiences affecting major life interests and such symbolically central commonalities as language and religion, as well as publicly recognized myths, stories, and archetypes. Given these bases of possible appeals, there still remains the question whether we can identify some factors that make for acceptance, indifference, and rejection across very different kinds of possible identifications.

One central consideration is without doubt what any rationalist theory frame would first suggest: What are the perceived costs and benefits of identification? How appealing is an affiliation and which disadvantages does it bring? Often, and perhaps typically, the costs and benefits of social identities are of a symbolic-emotional and not a material nature. That may make it more difficult to assess them with precision, but it does not diminish their impact.

Yet while acceptance of, indifference to, and rejection of a social identity are to a considerable extent the result of a cost-benefit calculus (however implicit), a simple rational choice explanation has its limitations. It tends to underemphasize the role of attachments in choices about identification, which may make rational assessment difficult. It also overlooks that "costs" and "benefits" are subject to social construction and redefinition, especially when the issues are highly charged with emotion, or when the particular social identity in question is perceived as primordial. For example, in case of negative discrimination based on race, religion, or ethnicity, avoiding identification, for many a rational response, may be difficult and even impossible; but instead of trying to escape being identified or play the identity down, many may—given some emotional and cognitive support for this different response—embrace it as a matter of pride.

Appeals based on ascriptive criteria rather than on choice and performance deserve special consideration. Such appeals make claims of membership on grounds that often have been removed from conscious reflection by being taken for granted since early in life. Discrimination based on ascriptive criteria is generally framed as insulting and arouses strong emotions because it rejects long and often cherished personal experience, and because it is at odds with standards of merit and fairness. This may help to explain a puzzle that has preoccupied many on the left and that is not easy to account for in a simple rational choice frame—that identification based on ethnicity, race, religion, and nationality is often more stable, and easier to mobilize, than is identification based on class positions marked by shared interest in material resources and power.

Processes of identification also have a temporal dimension. Acceptance or rejection depends to a considerable extent on *when* identity entrepreneurs appeal to a particular identity project. The creation and routinization of social identities are embedded in political contestations, organizational resources, and institutional frameworks, just to mention a few of the relevant causal conditions developed in more detail above. As such, the broader resonance of social identities needs to be analyzed vis-à-vis the temporal dynamics of theoretically relevant contexts (see Pierson 2004). For instance, the acceptance of new official national identity projects may be more likely when their re-creation unfolds simultaneously with state development. By contrast, a new national identity project may face more indifference or rejection when it confronts an already well-established state institutional infrastructure (vom Hau 2008a). Thus timing and sequencing constitute another causally relevant condition of social identity formation.

The relative resonance of identities matters especially because all people participate in multiple identities. The fact that any individual may draw on many different—compatible or divergent—social identities is often overlooked. But even the most salient social identity is never the only social attachment that counts. This raises difficult questions of causation, especially about the relative weight and importance of contradictory identifications. If clan, village, kin group, and family reinforce one another as a set of concentric circles, one must expect a very different outcome from that produced by simultaneous affiliations with identities that make divergent suggestions and demands. Focusing on background conditions and on the specific processes and actors involved in identity production and institutionalization can generate some hypotheses about the relative strength of these influences.

EFFECTS: WHY SOCIAL IDENTITIES MATTER

For a close interaction network it may make only a small difference whether it is recognized and embraced as a membership group. For wider social categories the transition to acknowledged social identities is essential. It turns conceptual and statistical abstractions held by a few outsiders into social realities with consequences for the outlook, attitudes, and behavior of the members who accept the identification.

It is important to emphasize the relative autonomy of social identities. They are entwined with organizational and structural dynamics, but not coextensive with the social structures and organizations that may build on them. Whether states and their organizational bodies, churches, political parties, hometown associations, or terrorist groups, they represent themselves as speaking and acting in the names of specific social identities. Yet these social identities are not to be equated with those organizational claims. Even national identifications, often created with the aim to legitimize state power and backed up by substantial material and symbolic resources, do not entail acceptance of the state political apparatus or the self-organization of its civil society. A more feasible strategy is to explore the resonance of specific social, cultural, and political projects through which organizations and identity entrepreneurs seek to foster identification. When social identities gain broader salience and acceptance, they constitute a readiness for participation and for responding to activation by identity entrepreneurs and organizations. This readiness derives from the sense of attachment that corresponds to cognitive and emotional self-understandings, from the recognition of symbols representing the identity, from the concern for shared life interests, and from embracing obligations and claims that go with membership.

Social identities shape responses to appeals for collective action. This is of critical interest because it affects the recruitment of personnel, the generation of organizational resources, as well as the willingness to respond to leadership. The way incipient movements articulate their claims with the normative, cognitive, and emotional outlook of established social identities is of decisive importance for their success in mobilization. For example, social movements may be more effective in their mobilization efforts if their framing strategies appropriate and reinterpret already-popular stories and symbols (Jansen 2007). The historical trajectories of the targeted social identities make some trajectories of group organization and representation more likely than others.

Quite similar considerations apply to structuring the relations with outsiders. In order to cultivate attachments and solidarity, it is necessary to define boundaries and to distinguish members from others. This can activate the in-group–out-group mechanism that sees the others as foes. Hostility toward "the other" often springs up spontaneously. It is a frequent correlate of the creation of solidarity, an affinity that casts a shadow of moral ambiguity on solidaristic ideals (see Wimmer 2002). However, whether the emergence of solidarity goes hand in hand with hostility toward others, and if so in what measure this is the case, depends largely on the dynamics of categorization and identification, which is partially shaped by conceptions of the more comprehensive identities,[8] as well as the content, salience, and boundaries of the identity in question.

One mechanism that softens conflicts between mutually exclusive social identities derives from the fact that individuals carry multiple identities, which may make competing claims on them. For example, attachments of class and occupational status may connect people of different ethnic loyalties, and vice versa. Such cross-cutting loyalties are likely to modify both solidarities and reduce the chances of unqualified hostility toward both class antagonists and ethnic others. In turn, as we have observed earlier, both loyalty and hostility may become reinforced if ethnic, linguistic, or religious boundaries coincide with lines that separate wealth and poverty, power and subordination, or high and low occupational status (Coser 1956, 78–79; Dahrendorf 1959, 213–18). A closely related effect of multiple identities with divergent claims and obligations has been identified by both Durkheim (1893/1964) and Simmel (1908/1955). Advancing social differentiation, which brings about an increase in the (actual and potential) social identities, induces greater and greater individualization. Individuals who respond to many different identities will develop greater autonomy and independence in their beliefs and normative orientations.

CONCLUSION

In this chapter we have sought to develop a theory frame for the analysis of social identities. As collective creations, social identities help to shed light on individual behavior as well as social outcomes, most importantly solidarity and conflict. Social identities are especially critical when analysts seek to understand the chances of collective action.

[8] See Jeffrey Alexander (2006) on the "civil sphere" as well as the utopian ideas of Karl Marx on "species consciousness."

We have found it useful to draw on the four subjective dimensions of action to generate suggestions and hypotheses about social identity formation. Social identities are most importantly a cognitive phenomenon. They recognize certain membership relations as relevant. But cognitive identification and classification schemas are often entwined with evaluations and norms. They are also associated with restructured preferences and marked by frequently powerful emotions. In social attachments, cognitions, norms, preferences, and emotions are fused into specific reference points of self-identification and external categorization.

A variety of actors and processes are involved in the creation and re-creation of social identities. The list of relevant causal conditions includes commonalities that link up with major life interests, and that can be articulated with available symbols, self-understandings, and memories; recognition by others, both wanted and unwanted; social conflict with outgroups; initiating entrepreneurs and continuous organizational support; links to socialization and upbringing, from the earliest formative influences to formal education; the development of norms once the identity has been formed; the systematic cultivation of ritual and symbols; and the temporal order of all these processes.

This causal background not only shapes the content, salience, and boundaries of social identities; it also determines the institutionalization of social identities as regular products of organizations as well as the resonance of an identity's hold on people. Conceptualized this way, social identities crucially link cultural patterns of allegiance and solidarity (as well as of discrimination and rejection) to the actions and dispositions of individuals, groups, and organizations and to macro–background conditions such as comprehensive cultural patterns, social inequality, and overarching institutions.

Chapter XIV

MACROCONTEXTS

Individuals, groups, social networks, organizations, and social identities exist within more comprehensive social environments. These macrosettings include cultural templates, overarching institutions regulating social, economic, and other spheres of life, as well as factual, nonnormative conditions such as power relations, conditions of war and peace, population composition, horizons of available knowledge, available technology, and past economic accumulations. Such encompassing social conditions are in many ways causally relevant for the lives of individuals and small groups, while they themselves are often beyond the reach of smaller social units and their dynamics.

There tends to be, then, a rough asymmetry in the causal relations between the micro- and the macrolevels of social life. This asymmetry is not without significant exceptions;[1] but to anticipate its likelihood when developing hypotheses is important because it runs counter to our common sense, which tends to neglect macrostructures.

Emphasizing the asymmetry may also seem counterintuitive in view of the axiom that ultimately all social structures are the result of actions and interactions of individuals. Yet this axiom can be upheld only if we admit of complex indirect effects of the actions and interactions that shape stable relationships and structures. It certainly does not entail that individuals and small groups—and even large organizations—can *on their own* change comprehensive institutional complexes, broad economic conditions, or wide-ranging established power relations. Some individuals and groups may indeed have a significant influence on comprehensive large

---

[1] We encountered, for instance, an unequivocal exception in our discussion of collective action. I argued that both strong initial leadership and a readiness to respond positively to the initiators' framing arguments and mobilizing symbols may be nurtured in sets of small groups and interaction patterns.

However, aggregate effects of individual actions that confront the actors with unintended and undesirable collective outcomes are only apparent exceptions to the idea of a causal asymmetry between the micro- and macrolevels of social life, because—though rooted in individual actions—the aggregate results become intractable but effective macroconditions of action. Thus developments in the age structure of a large population cannot be much influenced by small numbers of individuals and groups, but they have considerable consequences for competition in the education and labor markets, for the prospects of a secure old age, and for other conditions affecting major life interests.

social structures and developments, but this influence is contingent on specific social, cultural, and political locations that render their actions influential. Individuals and groups in less favored locations typically have just a marginal effect on the overarching social environment. Yet as we have seen earlier (in chapters 3–7) social action at the microlevel is grounded in knowledge, normative outlook, and preferences as well as in emotional reactions and social attachments that are influenced, if not fully shaped, by the larger social environment.

Broader social formations also offer or deny material and immaterial resources for individual lives and achievements. The impact of social and economic inequality is well known. The role of contrasting broad social formations is equally powerful or more so: Western success stories of entrepreneurial initiative, scientific insight, or medical intervention depend on opportunities and support structures that are not available to similarly competent individuals and groups in other, simpler and poorer social environments. Differences in the environment beyond the reach of most individuals and small groups in one case render native ability and effort impressively successful and in another leave the same effort and ability blocked and frustrated.

Other micro-macro asymmetries are grounded in power differences that derive from increasing size of social units. Significant participation in collective decisions is limited by the size of the collective. As size expands, the need for representation and intermediation grows. This may let representatives and intermediators pursue goals at odds with the interests and concerns of their constituencies, a possibility that casts a shadow of ambiguity on all collective action with large constituencies, as we noted earlier (chapter 10 on collective action). This size effect can be moderated by functioning democratic arrangements and safeguards. Where these are weak or just not available—as in many groups and private corporations, in many countries, and in worldwide operations of multilateral public bodies such as the World Trade Organization—the influence of most individuals and small groups is so feeble as to be negligible.

Corporate organizations, organized interests, parties, and other social formations at the mesolevel often stand in a doubly asymmetrical relation to macro- and micropatterns and processes. They are constrained and influenced by more comprehensive settings over which they frequently have little control; and they are causally relevant for micro–social relations within them, which in turn often have little chance to shape their mesolevel contexts.

This has interesting implications for research design. In research that remains within the confines of a single macrocontext, mesolevel social formations deserve special attention as independent causal factors because the more comprehensive macroconditions are held constant. Thus meso–social formations such as parties, their policy orientations, and their relation to constituencies and interest groups may be of decisive importance for political developments. This remains a reasonable expectation if different broad social formations are compared, especially if the relevant macroconditions are roughly similar. And even if cross-national analysis focuses on contrasts and similarities in macrofeatures, it is wise to pay close attention to how these work themselves out through different intermediate structures and mechanisms. For example, it may well be the case that political participation is more shaped by how political parties are linked to politically relevant associations, by the realistic chance to gain desirable results through political activity, or by the responsiveness of public administrative bodies than by countrywide histories of democracy and authoritarianism (e.g., Rueschemeyer, Rueschemeyer, and Wittrock 1998).

A correlate of the typical asymmetry of causal relations between the macro- and microlevels of social reality is the fact that macropatterns (and meso- ones as well) are often quite stable even if the individual actions and dispositions underlying them are much more variable. This is counterintuitive but clear on reflection. The existence and stability of comprehensive institutions and of overarching relations of power may rest on significant minority backing and not depend on overwhelming consent and support among all individuals and groups involved, even though cumulative developments of dissatisfaction may blunt the effectiveness of institutions and limit the exercise of power through suasion and leadership. The same holds true of mid-level organizations.

The claim of a causal asymmetry between larger-scale social formations and smaller structures and processes does not mean that the larger patterns are more important than what happens at the meso- and microlevels; it means only that here is a set of new causal factors that shape the included levels, and that are themselves less influenced by common meso- and microdynamics. Their impact must not be understood as an overpowering determination of micro- and mesoprocesses. Such causal relations are often quite loose. Furthermore, it is a mistake to assume that the different components of large social structures—say, power relations and overarching institutions of different kinds—have always mutually reinforcing effects; they may very well be at odds with each other, opening degrees of variability and "freedom" at the lower levels.

The endeavor to get a handle on causal influences that run from overarching social contexts to a variety of less inclusive structures and processes is the major reason why the consideration of large social structures as environments of individuals, groups, and organizations is important. Another reason is closely related: looking at different overarching social structures brings varieties of human social existence into view, a diversity that would be concealed if our analysis were exclusively concerned with the social worlds in which most social science research happens to be carried out.

Varieties of human social existence constitute the first subject to be taken up briefly. I will then try to sketch a few theory frames that can guide more specific theory building about large social structures, their change, and their impact on smaller patterns and processes. Finally, I will turn to problems of method peculiar to the comparative analysis of overarching large social structures.

VARIETIES OF HUMAN SOCIAL LIFE

To be aware of the significant variations of social life in different comprehensive contexts is of great importance for social and political theory. It stimulates the theoretical imagination. It exposes unrecognized premises about what is "normal," notions that easily creep into the construction of hypotheses. And it raises questions that may be difficult to answer, but that are important to keep in mind, such as: what is possible? what impossible? what patterns are incompatible with each other? and which combinations involve trade-offs, which synergies?

In the longest view of human existence, one may distinguish just a few major social forms. These broadly contrasting social formations differed above all in the means of subsistence. After a long period of evolutionary gestation, human beings lived for dozens of millennia in small groups and survived by hunting and gathering. The so-called Neolithic revolution introduced more complex tools as well as the domestication of plants and animals. It ushered in social formations based on gardening and agriculture. This made sedentary life possible and eventually resulted in larger, more complex, and typically more hierarchical social formations. The changes that brought about today's energy- and knowledge-based social formations are of much more recent origin. They had an incubation time of several centuries but became dramatically visible only during the last 250 years.

In important respects, the long-term trajectory of human social existence was not at all a unilinear development. We have seen already that the role of family and kin structures varied in complex ways within otherwise broadly similar social structures (in chapter 11 on power and cooperation). And if we look at structured inequality, agrarian social formations were more unequal in their distribution of power, status, and wealth than either hunting-and-gathering bands or industrial and postindustrial political economies (Lenski 1966; Nolan and Lenski 2006).

Despite the radical changes that occurred during the two most profound transformations of the human social experience—the Neolithic and
the industrial "revolutions"—it is worth noting that the inherited biological equipment of individuals did not change significantly. That means that
human existence in small hunting-and-gathering groups, in medieval
peasant villages, and in today's urban centers remains grounded in much
the same biological nature of human beings. Analyzing social action and
social patterns in relation to body and brain as shaped by evolution may
well lead to profound advances in human studies, but we must not lose
sight of the immense flexibility of human nature that is demonstrated
by these epochal variations in human social life, and that predates all
developments about which we have any historical knowledge.

Detailed descriptions of contemporary forms of simple societies have
greatly expanded our views on how human social life can be arranged.
In the twentieth century, this was a major achievement of anthropology,
symbolized perhaps best by the name of Margaret Mead, whose work
had such a dramatic impact on educated understandings of social life.
These studies made it impossible to view what we take for granted in our
own society as the direct expression of human nature.

Comparative politics and macrocomparative sociology have done
similar work on complex modern social formations and on developing
areas. But the influence of these comparative studies—for example, the
work on "varieties of capitalism" (Hall and Soskice 2001; Kitschelt et al.
1999) and more generally findings about the limits to a convergence
of all societies on one single pattern of "modernity"—has been much
more muted, both within the social sciences and beyond the boundaries
of the academy.[2]

Yet the substantial differences among rich countries raise important
questions about social and political possibilities as well as about causal
factors that sustain current patterns. These questions do not easily present
themselves if the analysis is confined to one—typically the analyst's own—
country. Nor can we begin to answer them without systematic comparative analysis transcending one's own society. Why do the northern and
continental European countries have more generous social provisions than
does the United States? Why do some established democratic systems limp
along with half the adult population abstaining from the vote, while others
have much higher rates of political participation? Why does the popular
culture of the United States have an unrivaled appeal around the world?

---

[2] One reason for this more limited impact may be that one's own country and its institutions tend to set the frame for social and political discussion. This suggests that the resonance of anthropological work in the twentieth century was largely due to developments in
American culture and society.

Macrocomparative research also can shatter silent assumptions about what is "normal." With some exceptions (e.g., Giddens 1987), the atrocities of the past century—above all two world wars and the Holocaust—are bracketed as exceptional and delegated to special literatures. The view of the French Enlightenment, that a country "is only healthy—that is to say, in its natural state—when it is at peace" (expressed in the eighteenth-century *Encyclopédie,* cited in Bell 2007) still seems to inform much of today's social science. Such a focus on normality impoverishes social and political theory as it neglects not only the devastations of war and genocide but also breakdowns of major institutions and state failures. These in turn are instructive for a comprehensive understanding of the dynamics of institutional order.

The varieties of social formations that come into view in macrocomparative research finally shed light on large empirical problems related to normative questions. Most sociologists and political scientists will abstain from questions about political ideals and good societies; but whether they do so or not, they should be able to make some contribution on pertinent questions of fact and the related dynamics of things social—questions about what is realistically possible and impossible and questions about trade-offs between partially incompatible ideals. Our students and our broader audience are as much interested in these big questions as were the readers of Montesquieu, John Stuart Mill, or Tocqueville. Aside from agreements or disagreements about the desirability of equality, social scientists should have a judgment—based at least roughly on factual information—why close approximations to an equality of outcomes are impossible, in what ways and to what extent many forms of inequality can be reduced, whether equalizing policies and different forms of individual freedom are at odds with each other, and under which conditions such incompatibilities and trade-offs are especially pronounced or relatively well mitigated. Questions of this nature abound. The chances of containing the use of force within and between nation-states and of mitigating the in-group–out-group mechanism that pairs solidarity on the inside with hostility to outsiders are just two further examples. Macrocomparative work on the variety of large-scale social formations is a good place to search for at least initial and rough answers to such questions.

It will be useful to approach the study of large, comprehensive social structures with relevant theory frames in mind. A few of these are already familiar from earlier chapters. Understanding the dynamics of comprehensive institutions is clearly of central importance. The way modern societies are characterized by three social forms that rely on indirect, infrastructural power—market exchange, formal organizations, and purposive associations—yields far-reaching insights into the character of comprehensive social structures. This leads, by extension, into a closer examination of large corporations and their wide-ranging power or of the internationalization of markets that makes them less subject to public control than are local and national markets. In the following sections I will briefly sketch just two further theory frames—on social inequality, specifically on social class, and on states and state-society relations. Neither will offer ideas that go beyond what is widely understood; but these two themes deserve at least a rough, if largely review treatment because of their special relevance for the analysis of large social structures and their change.

Social Inequality: Transformations of a Theory Frame

Sociology—and to an extent political analysis as well—developed in its modern form in response to the stresses and strains that European societies experienced as capitalism took hold, and the Industrial Revolution transformed economy and society. Fundamental questions revolved around the nexus of poverty, new wealth, and exploitation; around the subversion of established orders of status, honor, and respect; and around contestations of autocratic rule. The "social question," as the core issues were then labeled, informed social and political analysis as the social sciences transformed themselves at the end of the nineteenth century. Studying systems of inequality has remained at the center of sociological research since then, and it is never far from many of the issues studied by political scientists. The reason is clear when we realize that cumulative social inequality concerns the distribution of what is near-universally desired—economic resources that cover for many the material necessities of life; social appreciation, respect, and honor; and social influence and power safeguarding autonomy and determining success in even modest undertakings. Given the centrality of the study of inequality, it is no surprise that there are several different approaches to stratification analysis (for one overview see, e.g., Wright 2005). I will offer here only the sketch of a theory frame about the causes of social inequality that is indebted to the ideas of Marx and Weber and to recent work in that tradition.

Focusing on the social organization of production, Marxian thinking about class gives center place to the concept of exploitation. The exploiting class derives its advantages at the expense of the exploited class; it gains *because of* shortfalls in the compensation of the exploited. Exploiters, Marx claimed, use their control of land, capital, or other productive resources in such a way that the exploited are deprived of the full value of their labor. Exploitation serves in the Marxian view to explain not only strong inequalities, but also the development of class consciousness and class organization, as well as broad-based class conflict and resultant social changes.

The concept of exploitation was initially tied up with the labor theory of value, which stipulated that economic value was created singularly by human labor. This was superseded in economic theory as the marginalist revolution in economics defined the relative contribution of labor (and of other factors of production as well) by the utility of the last unit added, representing both use value and scarcity under competitive market conditions. This eliminated the option of contrasting the actual remuneration of work with the "true value of labor" as defined by the labor theory of value. But the concept of exploitation did not vanish with the abandonment of that theory.[3]

It is perhaps astonishing that Marx never developed a single full-blown theory of class but just used the concept in different analyses. Yet from this emerges an interesting lesson: the concept of class takes varying shapes depending on the specific problems investigated. To illustrate with the number of classes distinguished:

> Marx implicitly suggests that the number of classes to be defined depends on the reason why we want to define them. This is why he mentions three classes in *Capital*, two in the *Manifesto*, and seven in *The Class Struggle in France*. In *Capital*, a study in economics, he could not fail to distinguish three fundamental kinds of social agents that economics always differentiates [i.e., landowners, capital owners, and workers]. . . . In the *Communist Manifesto*, a work in political theory, . . . Marx wanted to show that the class struggle is the motor of history; in other words, that social change is the result of class struggles. . . . In *The Class Struggle in France*, a historical study, the point is to describe a concrete situation in its complexity. This is why more classes are distinguished in this work. (Boudon and Bourricaud 1989, 341)

The lesson at hand transcends the particular example. Concept formation is an integral part of hypothesis formation. It will always—and ought to—correspond to specific problem formulations and hypothetical solutions.

Max Weber followed leads of Marxian class analysis more closely than is understood by those who see his essay *The Protestant Ethic and the Spirit of Capitalism* as proclaiming an antimaterialist counterposition to Marx. Yet Weber (1922/1978) differentiated the conceptual frame for studying inequality thoroughly, and he was more skeptical about the circumstances under which socially organized classes become collective historical forces. He insisted on organized power as a separate and poten-

---

[3] Among the attempts to formulate a theory frame of exploitation without its initial context in economic theory are Roemer's *General Theory of Exploitation and Class* (1982) and Tilly's *Durable Inequality* (1998); I will return to the latter below.

tially autonomous dimension of inequality; and he distinguished a narrowly economic conception of class from status hierarchies of honor and prestige. Bendix and Lipset gave these reorientations a pointed formulation in the title of their influential volume *Class, Status, and Power* (1953/1966).

As he did with the conceptualizations of *Gemeinschaft* vs. *Gesellschaft* (see chapter 11, note 4), Weber turned global characterizations of historical stratification systems into universal features that occur in different combinations in any or most systems of inequality. From broad contrasts of class societies and status societies he developed the concepts of status and status groups and a more purely economic concept of class that captures the distribution of advantage and disadvantage in the markets for labor, capital, land, and the like. Elements of both class and status are likely to be found in the same social formations, and they interact with each other in intricate ways.

The concepts of status and status groups point to different and far more complex phenomena than the rank on a scale of prestige. They are relational concepts rather than variable characteristics of individuals. A person's status does involve evaluation and esteem; but, based on a mode of living shared with others, it defines the chance to be heard, to be persuasive, and to be believed; it includes or excludes from different forms of interaction; and it determines membership or nonmembership in a status group. Sharing a common status eases understanding and anticipating the reactions of others.

Common descent, shared education, like occupations, and similar wealth are among the major foundations of status groups. Status groups are, of course, an important form of social identities (see chapter 13). They are major carriers of effective cultural orientations. Understanding their formation and their effects can become a resource for making reference group theory more determinate (see chapter 1). In the analysis of social inequality, it is important to note that status groups often buttress themselves through social closure, establishing collective monopolies that reserve opportunities and advantages to members while excluding outsiders.

Weber's concept of class is in one sense diametrically opposed to status groups, yet classes and status groups are at the same time closely interrelated empirically. Based on market relations and their competitive dynamics, classes are inherently unstable formations unless they take the form of *social classes,* which are defined by ease of internal mobility and virtual closure to mobility at their boundaries. If we add to that—as neo-Weberian analysts have done (Giddens 1973; Stephens 1979a)—a particular frequency and ease of internal interaction that breaks off at the boundaries of a social class, it becomes clear that the character of social classes derives from a fusion of the pure versions of class and status group.

In Weber's conception, it is the tendency toward exclusive closure of status groups that defines sharp boundaries of social classes, while the market-based class features engender more graded as well as more fluid divisions. It is due to their quality as status groups, entailing similar attitudes and shared culture, that social classes have the chance to become collective actors. In this respect, much depends on the strength of commonalities of past experience and on the consequent intensity of identification. At the same time, this capacity for acquiring class consciousness and class organization is diminished if other status characteristics such as ethnicity or narrower occupational identifications divide a social class internally and make it heterogeneous in outlook (see chapter 10 on collective action).[4]

Charles Tilly has made a noteworthy contribution to the study of inequality that takes off from the ideas of Marx and Weber. "Durable inequality," in his titular (1998) phrase, "builds a bridge from Max Weber on social closure to Karl Marx on exploitation, and back" (7). This work represents the fruition of a significant shift in Tilly's work. After immensely successful research that pursued large historical questions in a theoretically oriented way, he turned to a more formal, though still historically informed use of universally applicable mechanism hypotheses as tools of causal explanation. *Durable Inequality* focuses on social categories that profoundly shape social arrangements and that separate people with different life chances, categories such as gender, race, ethnicity, religion, and stable class position. It is social organizations, including economic corporations, that build and maintain categorical inequalities. The two major mechanisms producing categorical inequality are *exploitation* and *opportunity hoarding,* denying outsiders the full value of their contribution and reserving valuable resources for insiders. Often these mechanisms are by-products of the solution of organizational problems other than the maximization of returns. The grounding in organizational problem solving gives great importance to two supporting

---

[4] That tendencies toward closure are characteristic of status groups is a critical insight for the understanding of communal conflict and violence. Ethnic groups are, after all, status groups par excellence. Varshney (2001, 2002) found in India that conflict and violence between Hindus and Muslims was significantly mitigated if networks of civic engagement crossed the in-group–out-group boundaries. This was true for informal day-to-day interaction as well as for formal associations bridging the ethnic divide. But he made the remarkable further discovery that organizational bridges across the communal divisions were clearly more sturdy in the face of polarizing appeals. Varshney is now engaged in a large multinational test of the contrasting relations between different forms of civic engagement, on the one hand, and communal conflict and violence, on the other.

mechanisms, *emulation*, or copying arrangements established elsewhere, and *adaptation*, or developing social routines based on categorically unequal patterns.

Tilly's answer to the question of how exploitation can be established independent of the discarded labor theory of value invokes the same procedures that are used to establish causal relations in the social sciences:

> We must handle the counterfactual by the usual methods of nonexperimental disciplines, making comparisons among otherwise similar firms whose systems of exclusion differ significantly, inspecting the extent and character of covariation between exclusion and inequality of rewards, examining what happens as exclusion increases or decreases within particular firms, and breaking into elements the causal chain connecting returns to effort in order to single out the effects of exclusion. To the extent that discrepancies in rewards within firms correspond to categorical boundaries and that these discrepancies correspond to differences in control over the firm's central resources, we acquire evidence that categorically organized exploitation is itself generating inequality.[5]

Weber's insistence on the distinct character of class, status, and power as dimensions of inequality raises interesting questions about their interrelations. In what ways and under which conditions do class and status translate into power, power and class into status, and status and power into class? We touched earlier on the role of status and class as sources of power (see chapter 11), and we have just seen how status differences can sharpen and stabilize, but also compromise, class cohesion. Among the many other questions thus instigated are some of the most complex problems of macrocomparative analysis. What, for example, enhances or diminishes the autonomy of power concentrations in the state from the impact of dominant class interests? Or: which historical conditions make political power a major path to wealth acquisition, and which contrasting conditions underlie the opposite flow of advantage, from wealth to political power?

---

[5] Tilly (1998,131–32). Tilly's resurrection of the concept of exploitation without recourse to the labor theory of value is plausible; it certainly is defensible. It does not, however, achieve the purpose that was critical for Marx's use of the concept—to join inequality to the chances of collective action and to identify in this outcome a—if not *the*—major force of historical change. The late Aage B. Sørensen noted that this feature of Marxian class theory was lost with the demise of the labor theory of value and with what he deemed the corresponding demise of the concept of exploitation. Sørensen proposed instead a theory of exploitation grounded in rents that deviate from returns in competitive markets. This was critically discussed in a "Symposium on Class Analysis" (Sørensen et al. 2000).

STATES AND THEIR SOCIETY: ELEMENTS OF A THEORY FRAME

States are a major concentration of power. Especially power of the kind that Weber made central to his social and political analysis—domination or the chance to get obedience for commands. Specifically, states are defined as sets of organizations capable of making binding decisions for individuals and organizations in a given jurisdiction and of putting them into effect, using force if necessary.

The emphasis of the Weberian tradition on the independent importance of politically organized power, the internal dispute among Marxian theorists about the degree and character of the capitalist state's autonomy vis-à-vis dominant class interests, and empirical macrocomparative historical work on states and their transformations were the major sources for renewed interest in state analysis in the last third of the twentieth century (Evans, Rueschemeyer, and Skocpol 1985).

In the definition adopted here (which is not undisputed), states are above all distinguished by the threat as well as the use of force and coercion. They share this characteristic—as well as conditional services to those who comply—with organized crime, as Charles Tilly (1985) has pointed out. Closely related is his observation that at least in Europe state making has been closely interwoven with war making (see, however, Centeno 2002 on Latin America). At the same time, making good on threats of force and coercion carries high costs, higher than soliciting voluntary compliance. Therefore state systems of domination will also offer material incentives, appeal to ideal motives, and—beyond both threats and incentives—cultivate beliefs in their legitimacy (Weber 1922/1978, 213).[6]

The extent of force and coercion used (though not their presence as an option) varies significantly across actually existing states. This is one of several dimensions on which states can differ sharply from each other. Among the other dimensions are the following:

- States vary greatly in their ability to extract material and personal resources from the society they rule as well as in their capacity to shape—directly and indirectly—social and economic life.

---

[6] As every social science student knows, Weber grounded his analysis of systems of rule on three pure types of legitimation rather than the old classification of rule by the many, the few, or a single monarch. The distinction of rational-legal, traditional, and charismatic legitimacy is offered as fruitful because it signals other differences as well: "The type of obedience, the kind of administrative staff developed to guarantee it, and the mode of authority, will all differ fundamentally. Equally fundamental is the variation in effect." Weber adds in a note: "The choice of this rather than some other basis of classification can only be justified by its results" (1922/1978, 213). It was a theory frame innovation of unparalleled utility.

- While all states are interrelated with—and indeed constitute an important part of—the overall pattern of power and domination in a society, they vary in their autonomy vis-à-vis dominant interests. The Marxian conception of states as an instrument of ruling classes highlights an extreme point on this scale of variation.
- Closely related is the degree to which state actors view themselves and are seen by others as pursuing the "common good." Such claims may invoke different standards; but these are "inherently contestable" (Gallie 1955–56) and subject to ideological pretense and propaganda. Even so, appeals to the common good represent a near-universal touchstone; they fit the commonsensical, yet justly famous Thomas theorem: "If [people] define things as real, they are real in their consequences" (Thomas and Thomas 1928, 41).
- Given their power and influence, states are inevitably arenas of conflict among contending social and economic interests. The degree to which this is the case identifies another dimension of variation among states.
- States have an interest in corporate unity so that different departments and policies do not undo what others seek to accomplish. The degree to which striving for this capacity of corporate action is successful points to yet another dimension of variation.
- Effective corporate action by a state also requires that the individuals acting for the state are competent, and that they align their own interests and commitments with the goals of state action (see chapter 11 on power and cooperation). The solidary character of the corps of state agents, their recruitment and training for competence as well as their ethos of loyalty and commitment, may be quite strong, or it may fall well short of enabling consistent and effective state action.

Some of these different dimensions of variation are mutually reinforcing; others stand often in tension with each other. Thus the state's being an arena of conflict is at odds both with consistent corporate action and with the claim to represent universal interests. Similarly, widespread self-serving actions of state agents undermine both corporate action and claims of pursuing the common good. Loyalty may have to be cultivated at the expense of competence. As they vary on these partly contradictory dimensions, states will only rarely approach the extreme positions, and often they will seek to balance contradictory options. Sometimes these balancing acts produce remarkably stable outcomes.

What accounts for the impact of states on society? As we saw earlier (in chapters 10 and 11, on collective action and on coordination), states can facilitate cooperation, and they can do so on a large scale.

> Cooperation in the effort to achieve common goals has been responsible for most human achievements, and the state offers one way of securing this. It is certainly not the only way, but at present it is the dominant way. (Strayer 1970, vi)

States have the authority and the capacity to make cooperation compulsory. States also often have substantial resources to offer incentives for cooperation. And—especially in their modern, rational-legal form—states are able to create rules and practices that enable cooperation among private parties as they form the infrastructure of market exchange, formal organizations, and voluntary associations.

At the same time, states also take from society. They extract economic resources as well as personnel. And they may take for very partial reasons, be it for corrupt enrichment of state agents or for one-sided policies. In fact, too many versions of compulsory cooperation amount to taking from, rather than giving to, society. Therein lies the point of comparing states with organized crime.

A state that is both effective in its actions and unrestrained in its takings looms over society as a "Leviathan." What can tame this Leviathan, and why do states turn at all toward serving society? The simplest answer is that state elites engage in self-restraint as well as service to economy and society because that turns out to be in their own interest. But the simplicity of this explanation misleads. It does not highlight that it takes strong pressures by nonstate actors to contain the potential abuse by the state. And it hides the complex constellations of conflict, overlap, and coincidence of interests that lead to clashes, mutual accommodation of the more powerful, and stable arrangements.

The tamed opposite to an overwhelming and disruptive Leviathan rests under modern conditions ultimately on three foundations: rule of law, the market, and democracy (Evans 2005). Max Weber conceived of a model of early capitalism in which a limited state, formally rational law, and competitive markets formed a clockwork-like triad into which democracy intruded, disturbing the mechanism. Yet democracy can be seen as a counterpart to the modern service state, driving its development and shaping its form. The rule of law disciplines the bureaucratic state apparatus internally and imposes restraint and predictability on its actions in society and economy. Market signals "convey costs and benefits, facilitate the efficient allocation of resources and . . . make sure that goals remain consistent with available means" (Evans 2005, 30). And a plurality of collective social actors monitor, pressure, and constrain the state. When combined with well-known formal arrangements for voting, open exchange of information and opinion, and protection of civil rights, this approaches democracy in its different forms. Yet the combination of effective state services, rule of law, and concentration of state action on areas where it can be most successful is by no means an inevitable and convergent outcome of different historical paths.

Even if we have some understanding of how state, society, and economy can come into relations of synergy, the practical relevance of this knowledge is limited by two broad issues that remain open. First, aside from a fundamental appreciation of market coordination, there is intense ideological contestation of policy options, and there are unresolved questions about what makes different economic and social policies effective. At the same time, there is no doubt that significant state action is required for developing and maintaining productive economies, and that the different versions of modern social formations render far-reaching state action inevitable. Second, if a functioning state apparatus and synergic state-society relations have not been established in a country, they cannot be created quickly just because they are deemed necessary. Rather, their development typically takes time, often a period of time that goes beyond the time horizon of purposive political action (Lange and Rueschemeyer 2005).[7]

In addition to the tremendous impact of past and present state policies shaping economy and society, there is another side to the state's impact, which Theda Skocpol has called its Tocquevillean effects:

> States matter not simply because of the goal-oriented activities of state officials. They matter because their organizational configurations, along with their overall patterns of activity, affect political culture, encourage some kinds of group formation and collective political actions (but not others), and make possible the raising of certain political issues (but not others). . . .
>
> Thus, much of Tocqueville's argument about the origins of the French Revolution dealt with the ways in which the French absolutist monarchy, through its institutional structure and policy practices, unintentionally undermined the prestige and political capacities of the aristocracy, provoked the peasantry and the urban Third Estate, and inspired the intelligentsia to launch abstract, rationalist broadsides against the status quo. Effects of the state permeated Tocqueville's argument, even though he said little about the activities and the goals of the state officials themselves. (Skocpol 1985, 21)

Taken together, the effects of purposeful state policies (even if they may often have unintended or not fully intended outcomes) and the indirect, Tocquevillean consequences of the very presence of state structures and

---

[7] Of the large literature on the role of states in social and economic development, I name only a few works: Amsden (1989, 2001), Evans (1979, 1995), Kohli (2004), Migdal (1988), and Wade (1990).

policies leave no doubt that states and state-society relations constitute a powerful and influential environment for social and economic dynamics at the meso- and microlevels of social life.

Important macrocontexts extend beyond state-organized societies. In fact, a central insight of the renewed research on states during the last decades of the twentieth century was that states face power relations within their societies as well as power relations among states; it is largely from this fact—that they stand at the intersection of these two alignments of power—that states derive a potential autonomy rather than being driven by a combination of interests dominant in their societies (Skocpol 1979; Mann 1984).

The economic, social, and political relations that reach beyond nation-states and are not directly ordered by states have acquired a peculiar dynamic with the rise of capitalism. This was thematized early in Marxist and non-Marxist theories of imperialism and is today the object of manifold concerns under the label of "globalization." Some have argued that increasing globalization implies a general decline in the role of states. If that simply means that international economic and political relations have become more dense and influential, there is little reason to question the claim; but the argument overlooks that the very expansion of trade and capital mobility beyond national borders, which at the beginning of the twenty-first century has surpassed the levels reached a century earlier, relies on infrastructural guarantees provided by states and coalitions of states.

There is no doubt that worldwide contexts are of critical importance for current and future social and political developments. Obvious examples abound. Global warming, and the difficulty of coordinating multinational responses to its threats, and the emergence of China as the material workshop for the world, and the impact this has on consumption and production in richer countries, are just two instances taken from the current worldwide agenda. Cross-national comparative studies make clear, however, that the consequences of many global developments are more complicated than is often assumed. Economic globalization does not necessarily make social welfare provisions more skimpy but leaves ample room for political action to improve them. Openness to the international market does not uniformly increase poverty; in many cases it is associated with increased inequality but also with improved standards of living even for the worst-off. Greater involvement in international trade does not regularly have greater political openness and democratization as its correlates.[8]

---

[8] On economic globalization, state expenditures, and social welfare provision, see Rodrik (1998) and Garrett (2001) as well as Glatzer and Rueschemeyer (2005) and Haggard and Kaufman (2008). That economic openness can result in vast economic improvement but

Several theory frames have been developed to deal with macrocontexts that transcend the borders of countries. They were devised to focus on different questions and because of that do not directly contradict each other; but for the same reason, they resist easy integration. I will therefore just briefly point to them without attempting to fuse them into a single theory frame. There are four such frames. In political science, the field of international relations is dominated by old and new "realist" schools. In comparative history, world system theory has carved out a distinctive place (Wallerstein 1974, 1980, 1989). Closely related, but more focused on contemporary issues of development and underdevelopment, is dependency theory. And, finally, there are attempts to capture the impact of worldwide cultural and associational processes on change and stability in nation-states.

International relations theory has long constituted a predominantly rationalist analysis of conflict and cooperation among states. It acquired greater complexity in its central concepts along the lines advocated in this volume, when cognitive maps and preference structures, and in particular conceptions of sovereignty and the national interest, were explicitly reconceived as historically and politically constructed (e.g., Krasner 1978; Biersteker and Weber 1996; and Wendt 1999). An approach to worldwide patterns of culture and associations has been pioneered by John Meyer (Meyer et al. 1997; Meyer 2000). Closely related to the new sociological institutionalism (see chapter 12), it claims that similarities in the structure of nation-states result from diffusion of international models. In addition, worldwide cultural patterns also shape important internal processes, such as changing forms of, and access to, higher education. Yet many other features of state-governed societies have stubborn internal foundations. In combination with effective cross-national influences, this results in complex forms of structural incoherence.

World systems theory and dependency theory both built on earlier theories of imperialism. Both focus on relations of unequal power across nations that are grounded in the international division of labor and in turn have a profound effect on a country's chance of economic improvement. Early versions of both theories were more deterministic than later ones.[9] And both acted as scholarly movements, opening critical questions and highlighting the consequences of cross-national inequalities. Many of their concerns have come to be reflected in a variety of studies on the international political economy.

---

also greater inequality is illustrated by China, as is the failure of greater economic openness to advance political liberty and democracy.

[9] This is most clear-cut in the case of dependency theory. While earlier claims declared development in dependent countries to be virtually impossible, Cardoso and Faletto (1979) as well as Peter Evans (1979) speak of different paths of *dependent development*.

PROBLEMS OF METHOD IN MACROCOMPARATIVE ANALYSIS

Lastly I turn to methodological issues of comparative historical analysis. The dynamics of large-scale social structures are most directly studied through macrocomparative research. If we inquire about causal conditions and the consequences of their change, this comparative analysis will have to have historical depth. Yet many are skeptical that macrocomparative historical inquiry can yield causal explanation.

The study of large structures and developments does present special problems. These have often been discussed controversially between advocates of large-scale quantitative research, on one side, and proponents of qualitative work on a limited number of cases, on the other. In its extreme forms, that discussion turns into an argument between two fundamentally different modes of inquiry and causal assessment. Thus John Goldthorpe contrasts historical and theoretical explanations. He claims that a historical narrative, even if it remains confined to one particular sequence of events, "can itself constitute a form of explanation"(1997, 14 and n. 13). But historical explanations of this kind are fundamentally different from theoretical explanations, which hold not only for one particular historical development but also for other instances in a specified theoretical domain. Such a radical disjunction in the fundamental logic of different methodologies in social analysis seems unfortunate. Recent methodological work has emphasized to the contrary that quantitative and qualitative research, variable- and case-oriented work, should be subject to criteria of judgment that are in principle the same (Ragin 1987; King, Keohane, and Verba 1994; Bates et al. 1998; Mahoney and Rueschemeyer 2003). And, as I will argue shortly, the different concrete procedures used in qualitative and quantitative analyses can indeed be understood as meeting the same fundamental objectives of validity.

At first sight, the case for quantitative research seems overwhelming. Macrocomparative work often involves a great complexity of causal relations. Therefore a large number of cases seems necessary to disentangle and identify the different causal strands; but comparable macrocases are often in short supply. Variable-focused quantitative research designs can be conceived as a substitute for experimental analyses that are not available in macro–social research. Without a sufficient number of comparable objects of analysis—of revolutions, transitions to democracy, class formation, or state failure—it seems that the only result that can be achieved is a "historical explanation" of dubious qualification.

This common line of reasoning overlooks a fundamental point. What counts in making a causal explanation convincing is not the number of "cases" but the number of observations that are relevant for the research

question and the hypotheses entertained. Many of such theoretically pertinent observations can be made even within a single case (Campbell 1975;
Rueschemeyer 2003). Within-case causal assessment and especially
within-case "process tracing" have recently received special attention and
useful analysis (see George and Bennett 2005; Hall 2003; Mahoney 2003;
also Rueschemeyer and Stephens 1997). More generally, Tilly (1997, 48)
has made the case for assessments of hypotheses about causal mechanism
by confronting them with varied historical sequences in varied settings.
Why, he asks, do most students of state formation accept a number of
propositions about the nexus between warfare and state formation? and
answers: "because for a large range of times, places and situations they
can construct relevant, verifiable causal stories resting in different chains
of cause-effect relations whose efficacy can be demonstrated independent
of those stories." It is repeated hypothesis testing that gives credibility to
historical explanation, which then turns out to be just one variant of
causal assessment.

Many observations that are of critical importance for the understanding of class formation can be made within one historical case. This was
the achievement of E. P. Thompson in his *Making of the English Working
Class* (1963). His rich account of diverse developments in one country
showed convincingly that the conditions of class formation cannot be
"read off" from the bare economic facts of property and employment.

Going beyond a single case becomes imperative when the hypotheses
to be explored concern features of the comprehensive contexts that vary
from one broad historical situation to another. Does this mean that adequate causal assessments concerning macrocontexts require large numbers of cases that are often simply not available? Two further considerations can mitigate what otherwise remains a serious problem.

Within-case observations can give greater credibility to related across-
case explorations involving only a limited number of cases. Joining theoretically rich empirical work within cases to comparative analysis across
large-scale social formations may therefore go a long way to alleviate the
"small-N problem." This is a principal implication of the analytic strategy
advocated by Tilly, which focuses on mechanisms as universal causal links
that in different combinations account for diverse historical processes.

In addition, the nature of the theoretical question explored makes a
crucial difference for how small an N is too small to permit confidence in
theoretical conclusions. If the issue is to ascertain or to rule out a condition as a necessary or a sufficient cause, the required number of cases is
far smaller than that needed for the assertion of an ordinal association of
features. One or a few deviations from the hypothesis may be sufficient
to rule out a condition as a sufficient or necessary cause. Thus Theda
Skocpol (1979) dismissed relative deprivation as a sufficient cause of so-

cial revolution because it was present both in a handful of cases of nonrev-
olution, including England, Germany, and Japan, and in the run-up to the
French, Russian, and Chinese revolutions. Or Anthony W. Marx (1998),
in his three-way comparison of racial tolerance and repression in the
United States, South Africa, and Brazil, eliminates the factor of colonial
race discrimination in previous history as an explanation of later differences in racial tolerance, because it was present in all three cases.

By contrast to such categorical assessments of necessary and sufficient
causation, a probabilistic association of hypothesized causes and consequences requires a larger number of cases. Yet it is worth noting that
ordinal measurement of statistical association is less efficient in ruling out
alternative explanations, even if a reasonably large number of cases are
used in such cross-case analyses. It therefore often seems causally indeterminate (Mahoney 1999).

The dominance of quantitative designs in methodological discussion
has given ordinal measurement of association the most prominent place
in thought about causal assessment. It is time to broaden the recognition
of alternative modes of causal exploration. The assessment of causal
mechanism hypotheses in varied historical sequences and settings and the
exploration of necessary and sufficient causes (Dion 1998; Mahoney
1999 and 2003; Braumoeller and Goertz 2000) are the most important
of these alternatives. And both deserve closer consideration.[10]

What are the appropriate units for macrocomparative analysis? In most
quantitative work but also in a good deal of case-oriented qualitative
work, state-defined countries are taken without much argument as the
units of choice. This has been criticized. Thus Tilly speaks in one of his
recent obituaries for big-case comparisons (1997) of the "disintegration
of the state system" and argues that current trends "will eventually de-
stroy the plausibility and interest of comparisons among state-defined
societies" (47).

Quite clearly, which units of comparison are most appropriate depends
on the problem to be investigated and on the theory frame deployed for

---

[10] It is worthwhile to note here that the issues touched on in the preceding paragraphs
are not confined to an esoteric subfield of "comparative historical analysis" but have very
broad relevance in the social sciences.

If a good deal of quantitative research limits itself to a given country, leaving the impact
of cross-national and cross-cultural variation unexamined, these studies remain in that sense
single-case analyses. Furthermore, even within a country the better part of quantitative research focuses on individuals and their immediate environment. The analysis of meso–social
formations, of organizations or communities for example, is often based on only a few
cases. These mesostudies gain credibility if their conclusions are sustained by theoretically
relevant observations that are sufficiently large in number to rule out willfully speculative
interpretations. Their validity, then, rests on considerations very similar to those just discussed about macroanalyses.

its investigation. Thus Tilly concedes that "where empirically-identifiable states . . . actually constitute the object of study . . . social scientists have ample reasons to formulate ideas concerning their regularities and to undertake systematic comparisons among them" (46). And much comparative work does indeed focus quite reasonably on states, state policies, and social structures closely related to and affected by states and their actions. On the other hand, it has long been understood that the concept of "society," implicitly related to the notion of modern nation-states, not only abstracts in ideal-typical fashion from entanglements in wider social formations, cultural affiliations as well as transnational economic and political relations, but also tends to underemphasize the internal heterogeneity of countries.

Using state-defined countries as the unquestioned unit of analysis can be fundamentally misleading. For example, in the assessment of systems of economic inequality the best unit of analysis presumably would be defined by systemic economic interrelations, including international patterns of division of labor. If we content ourselves with measures of economic inequality within state-defined countries because here we have the advantage of government-produced income and property statistics, these statistics will often obscure the full span of economic inequality since they omit the economic situation of the poorest actors outside rich countries even though they are part of the international division of labor that is centered in the richest countries. Thus using national data on economic inequality is likely to give undeserved support to such well-known hypotheses as the claim of Kuznets (1955) that economic inequality first increases with economic development and then declines in the most mature rich economies.

Methodological decisions depend in a variety of ways on existing theory frames. Theory frames affect, for instance, whether within-case observations about the determinants of class formation can meaningfully link up to inquiries about class development across different broad social formations. In Thompson's *Making of the English Working Class* one of the central questions was whether the chances of class formation can simply be "read off" the objective conditions of economic inequality, and in particular the distribution of ownership of the means of production, or whether these chances also depended on preceding cultural developments including religious affiliation and the growth of community solidarities. Thompson's detailed historical investigations in England had vast implications for theory frames of class formation that claimed English developments as paradigmatic for other capitalist social formations. It transformed the twentieth-century Marxist theory frame for class analysis.

Conclusion

Macrocontexts shape what happens at less inclusive levels of social structure and change, and at the same time they have a great deal of independence from their meso- and microcounterparts. That gives them a strategic place in comprehensive explanatory understandings of social life. Not making macrocontexts problematic may not be very damaging to an explanation that stays within the same macrocontext, but in more broadly comparative analyses leaving the causal conditions and the consequences of large-scale social and cultural patterns out of consideration involves the risks that derive from omitting potentially powerful factors and conditions from the analysis.

Macro–social research and analysis are also of interest on their own. They explore the varieties of human social existence as well as the limitations to that variation. Both shape theoretical background assumptions and are indispensable for developing broader theory frames. Two more specific theory frames—on structured social inequality and on states and state-society relations—are offered in lieu of a large variety of available approaches to macro–social issues. Both took their inspiration from the work of Max Weber.

Studying comprehensive macrocontexts poses special problems, which have often been discussed by contrasting quantitative variable-based and qualitative case-based research strategies. Yet if a fundamental unity of the criteria of validity is taken as a premise, neither side holds the overwhelming advantage or disadvantage that some polemics would suggest. Among the insights that lead to this conclusion is first the simple observation that what counts is not the number of cases but the number of theoretically relevant observations. Other considerations concern the promise of causal process tracing, the examination of mechanism hypotheses in a variety of historical contexts, and the exploration of necessary and sufficient causal conditions that permit substantial conclusions with a smaller number of observations than are required for causal assessments based on ordinal measures of association.

Chapter XV

CULTURAL EXPLANATIONS

What causal role does culture play in social life?[1] If the core arguments informing this volume make any sense, there is no doubt that cultural patterns matter pervasively and decisively. This became clear in our four-fold treatment of the internal space of action, required for a suitable social action approach. Diverse forms of belief and understanding, norms and values, preferences and their ranking, emotions and attachments, as well as the multiplicity of codes of communication associated with them matter because they become constituent elements of social formations, and because they generate causal effects—by themselves and as elements of composite social mechanisms. As we examine culture and its effects, we return to the internal dimensions of action, now understood as patterns of beliefs, norms, preferences, and emotions.

Thinking of culture as a set of codes and patterns is a distinctive conceptualization. Culture in this sense does not mean the whole of one form of social life. It does not consist of actions, actors, or enacted roles. Rather, it is composed of templates, models, and paradigms that inform and shape some aspect of social action and interaction—religious teachings, superstitions, common understandings, empirical knowledge, values and aspirations that define the good life, law, as well as customs, folkways, and informal norms of various groups, patterns of desire, and various modes of symbolic exchange.

Cognition and beliefs, responsiveness to norms, preference structures, and symbolically mediated emotions all have innate foundations, but their varied forms are human creations—creations that, in their vast majority, transcend individual inventiveness. Individuals are not able to produce the ensemble of these patterns by themselves, though they do add to their change. In fact, no single generation is able to create a comprehensive set of such standards, codes, and meanings from scratch, as is obvious when we think of language. "We cannot interpret social behavior without acknowledging that it follows codes that it does not invent" (Alexander 1990, 26). Culture in its diverse patterns, then, is a collective creation arising from the subjective dimension of action.

---

[1] This chapter builds on Rueschemeyer (2006) and an unpublished earlier paper, "Reflections on Cultural Explanation in Macrosociology," whose first version was presented at the 1998 Congress of the International Sociological Association in Montreal.

Individual behavior and elementary interaction cannot be understood if these collective creations are not taken into account. And the collectively shaped components of the subjective dimension of action are, when they transcend immediate interaction, constitutive elements of social structures, whether these are small or large in scale, tension ridden or smoothly integrated, and whether they exhibit harmony or discord among groups. For instance, work and family roles build on particular beliefs and understandings as well as on accepted normative standards and patterns of preference and emotion. Similarly, contention about the fair or exploitative character of social relations typically involves a confrontation of different cognitive and moral premises held by the antagonists. All four components of the internal dimension of action are of critical importance here. Knowledge, preference patterns, and emotions are as much involved in the formation and architecture of social structures as are the complexes of norms and values to which Parsons gave priority.[2]

That cultural patterns are rarely or never invented de novo and in toto, as wholes and from scratch, does not mean that they reach into the past indefinitely and are immune to change. Some do change only slowly; language is a prime example. But even rapid change makes use of elements that are on offer from the past, urged by different groups within the same cultural context, or suggested even by distant cultures. Yet the fact that cultural patterns transcend individual action does point to their historicity, that they represent in large part sediments of past experience.

---

[2] In an influential paper, Ann Swidler (1986) has rejected a stylized version of Parsons's view that values, shaping the selection of ends, are the ultimate template for an understanding of social action. At this stage of understanding the impact of culture, I do not think it useful to assign or rule out a premier role for one set of cultural elements or another. A reasonable argument can be advanced for attributing this role to knowledge, ignorance, and distortion rather than to values (e.g., Rueschemeyer 1958a). At the same time, it seems contrary to current evidence and theory to deny that values and norms can significantly shape preferences as well as cognitive understanding and patterns of emotional response.

Building on Ulf Hannerz's (1969) anthropological analysis of an American ghetto culture, Swidler sees culture as a "tool kit," a repertoire of "symbols, stories, rituals, and world views" (273), which people use to construct and reconstruct their "strategies of action." These strategies or lines of action do not, however, indicate an instrumentalist view of social action; rather, they constitute different "approaches to life," shaped by diverse selections from the available repertoire of cultural elements (284). Instead of adopting a version of means-ends action theory as her broadest theoretical frame, Swidler takes off from more or less stable amalgams of cultural elements that fit a given social location, and that are evident in different approaches to life. These are conceptually close to the "habitus" of Pierre Bourdieu, whose brief definition is quoted: "a system of lasting, transportable dispositions which, integrating past experiences, functions at every moment as a matrix of perceptions, appreciations, and actions" (277 n. 11, referring to Bourdieu 1977, 82–83). The conception of culture I propose here does take off from a modified action theory frame, though it can accommodate contrary emphases of such authors as Bourdieu and Giddens (see chapter 2).

At the same time, it highlights diffusion, among subcultural milieus and between distinct cultures.

We do not, then, have to establish here *that* culture has causal relevance; it does shape social life. The task is rather to gain insights into *how* this influence takes place. A few ideas just sketched already suggest some such insights. For instance, the fact that cultural patterns do change and on occasion do so with surprising rapidity points to their heterogeneity, to the tensions among different parts, and to their connections with other features of social life. And the role of diffusion across time and different social contexts suggests mechanisms of how cultural patterns change, and how they grow or contract in social scale.

CONTENTION AND QUESTIONS ABOUT CULTURAL EXPLANATION

In spite of the arguments just sketched, cultural explanations are for many social scientists a matter of contest and a subject of skeptical questions. The contest involves fundamental assumptions about social reality. The skepticism concerns methodology.

Cultural studies and strong versions of cultural sociology claim that theory frames centered on culture hold the best promise for social and political explanation because they are best suited to deal with historical and cross-cultural variation. Prominent among alternative views are those that give causal primacy to material interests and to structural conditions that channel, favor, constrain, or block the pursuit of these interests. Controversies about the role of culture are deepened because the different sides build on contrasting ideological positions of long standing.[3]

The contrasting assumptions reflect to some extent the fact that different theory frames deal with different aspects and spheres of social life. This is most obvious in the case of economics; but it also plays a role in the analysis of contentious politics or in comparative historical work on political economy issues related to states, class structures, and class conflict. By contrast, the study of gender roles or comparative religion clearly requires attention to more than what a utilitarian focus on material self-interest would suggest (though excluding material self-interest would be unwise here too). Historical research with an institutionalist bent has highlighted complex variations and developments in preferences as well as in values and beliefs (Steinmo, Thelen, and Longstreth 1992; Thelen 1999). Earlier (in chapter 5), I noted that simple assumptions about pref-

---

[3] The names of Hegel and Marx are just the most obvious references. A similar polarity in American political thought is evident among the founding generation of writer-politicians. And comparable contrasts go back even further.

erences in economic analysis were significantly revised by economists
(Ben-Ner and Putterman 1998). Developments such as these may indicate
that the older hardened contrasts give way to more differentiated and
nuanced positions.

Methodological issues loom large in the discussion about cultural explanations. This is, in the first place, inherent in studies of culture (and
by extension in all social analysis that takes the internal dimensions of
action seriously). The subjective meanings of actors as well as cultural
patterns must be understood. This requires the "hermeneutic" work of
comprehending meanings. Such meanings—ranging from questions and
claims in constitutional law, social theory, and particle physics to political
discourse, invocations of custom, and the languages of loyalty, social affiliation, and love—come in different forms. Some are established and
institutionally secured; some are individualized, subjective meanings.
Law, "the language of the state," is an example of the former; religious
experience or the reading of poetry is often an instance of the latter. Many
forms of meaning fall between these two extremes. Frequently, the task of
explanation—for instance, in the case of charismatic political appeals—
requires relating publicly established meanings to individualized subjective understandings; the causal effects of charisma depend on multiple
appeal-response links.

Both established and individualized meanings may be easily accessible
or quite esoteric in character. We often rely on indigenous commonsense
understandings. These may fail or become a treacherous guide (but not
one impossible to improve) when we move across linguistic barriers or
into esoteric complexity. Here are important and difficult problems—
difficult because human dispositions and communications are often ambiguous and complex; and important because we have good reasons to
expect that cultural phenomena frequently acquire causal power. This
power we may not adequately grasp if we fail to understand the meanings
that guide actors.

These difficult and important problems of interpretation are, however,
not the main reason for skepticism about cultural analysis. In fact, they
are more appreciated by those focusing on culture than by those treating
it with simplistic neglect. Yet the genuine difficulties of identifying with
precision the content of often implicit ideas and less than fully articulated
sentiments are frequently aggravated by different forms of methodological inattention. These range from brazen neglect through simplistic solutions to a lack of concern about convincing skeptics.

Even if we leave aside the relativist abandon of the most radical postmodern cultural studies, we encounter too often grand assertions that are
built just on imperious say-so. An example may be instructive. One that

is not at all exceptional is Jesse R. Pitts's discussion of "a trait that seems fairly distinctive to French culture":

> This trait is a commitment to a nexus of authoritative ideas which incarnate the highest spirituality. In religious terms the nexus is the Church, in secular terms the Nation. There is a conviction that all behavior should have a clear deductive connection to this spirituality through rules, principles, and regulations which insure inherent value to the action. . . . Here we find the roots of French formalism, the demand for deductive chains of reasoning and hierarchy, the insistence upon the unity of the power center, and formulations where everything and everybody is *à sa place* (in its place). . . . Aspects of French social structure that seem to implement this doctrinaire-hierarchical theme are the centralizing and formalistic features of the civil service and its technocratic tradition. (1964/1990, 136)

No detailed comment seems necessary to highlight the problematic sweep of these assertions or the simplistic linkages between cultural features and social structure.

An alternative common mode of cultural analysis is more meticulous but no less problematic. Here, careful interpretations of the writings by a few authors serve to paint a picture of the prevailing views and values of a country at a particular period, its zeitgeist. Even if the conclusions are confined to the educated who read, this mode overlooks that the history of reading has quite different rhythms from the history of writing, and, equally critical, that one's reading does not define one's inclinations and outlook.

Another common mode is based on survey research. It measures and aggregates individual opinions and distills from them a cultural template that is used to explain particular features or developments. In skilled hands, the results can be impressive (e.g., Almond and Verba 1963, 1989). Often, however, this mode disregards what I have called the fallacy of simplistic aggregations (chapter 9). Moreover, it can result in virtually meaningless explanations because the danger of tautology looms large in this procedure, when what is to be explained also serves as the basis for inferring the causal condition.

Finally, some skepticism about cultural explanations corresponds to a widespread unconcern on the part of many proponents of cultural analysis to seek agreement and to convince the skeptics. Thus the editors of a recent collection on historical sociology with a strong cultural bent (Adams, Clemens, and Orloff 2005) are in their programmatic introduction more concerned with keeping innovations in historical sociology free of the "repressions" and "exclusions" that derive from a previous "do-

mestication" of historical sociology than with discussing standards of
method and convincing others about the validity of the work presented.[4]

In the end, however, since we have reason to assume that cultural elements have important causal relevance, such methodological problems
and unconcerns must be balanced by the consideration that omitting
major factors from an analysis has debilitating—and distorting—effects
on the analysis as a whole.[5] Yet the discrepancy between a potential causal
role of cultural patterns and the particular difficulties of identifying and
describing cultural phenomena reliably and with validity represents a dilemma that we will have to confront.

STRUCTURAL GROUNDING AND CULTURAL TRANSMISSION

The arguments developed in this chapter take off from one central proposition: *Cultural patterns become causally important when—and to the
extent that—they are grounded in groups, organizations, and institutions
and/or in the habits and customs of people's everyday life and in their
codes of communication.*[6]

At first sight it may seem trivial to assert that ideas, ideals, and other
cultural patterns have to be embraced, nourished, and supported by *social
carriers*. In fact, this corresponds closely to conceptualizing culture as an

---

[4] They incidentally seem to dismiss too easily the chance of causal explanations by claiming that the historicity of concepts and categories blocks the search for universal covering
laws (25 et passim). This overlooks that universal theoretical propositions in principle require specified scope conditions, that even propositions with historical (or simply uncertain)
scope conditions add to preliminary explanations, and that universal covering laws (which
are indeed rare) do not exhaust the possibilities of causal explanation, which also include
causal mechanisms or the (preliminary) establishment or exclusion of necessary and sufficient conditions.

The essay is also marred by an occasional neglect of the maxim *c'est le ton qui fait la
musique*. Consider this footnote: "Some might wonder if the machine terminology attached
to 'social mechanisms' is not at least partially an attempt to reclaim masculine intellectual
space, for example!" (56 n.127).

[5] Here the joke about the drunk who, when asked why he is looking for his keys under
the street lamp, answers, "Because here I can see," may serve instead of a complex explanation. In correlational analysis, this is referred to as "omitted variable bias."

[6] To add "habits and customs of everyday life" as well as "codes of communication" to
groups, organizations, and institutions may seem redundant because social customs and
socially relevant habits will typically have some grounding in groups, organizations, or institutions, and the same is true of codes of communication such as different versions of a
language. I have added these clauses in order to highlight that much of what underlies the
continuities of everyday life—including language, cognitive premises, ideals defining what
is desirable and what should take priority in cases of conflict, as well as paradigms of tastes
and of emotional response—tends to be taken for granted and is frequently seen by the
participants as independent of the care of social formations.

ensemble of patterns, though it is not tautologically true by definition. As we will see, the principle has a number of implications and corollaries that are anything but trivial.

Our orienting proposition takes off from Max Weber's famous image that likened religious ideas about salvation to "switchmen of history" as they direct similar spiritual concerns and energies in different directions— a hope for heaven, striving toward withdrawal from desire, work for God's kingdom on earth—much as railroad switches send engines and trains to their various destinations (1915/1958, 280). However, while Weber discussed the different ideas about salvation as characterizing whole civilizations and as more or less closely integrated with other cultural elements, it seems wise to leave the scale of acceptance as well as the integration of cultural patterns an open question. The proposition offered here is also not meant to be confined to religious ideas or the expression of values. Though different cultural patterns will relate in specific ways to the social formations that embrace or reject them, the principle applies to empirical beliefs, norms and values, preference ordering, and emotional response patterns as well.

Speaking of cultural patterns as being "grounded" in social formations or in the customs and habits of everyday life, as well as prevailing codes of communication, covers a good bit of territory. Considering its negative is perhaps less diffuse: an idea, even an empirical finding, the expression of a human value, a model of appreciation and taste, a paradigm of emotional response—any of these may exist in a library or be alive in somebody's mind and perhaps even offered to others. And yet they may not have any causal effect on social relations except that they are present and available somewhere. If, however, members of a group or those who control organizations and maintain institutions endorse, embrace, and expect others to embrace the ideas, ideals, norms, tastes, emotional responses, and symbolic tools in question, then these are likely to become infused with some causal force. Once cultural patterns become embedded in the habits and customs of everyday life, they function without the more or less self-conscious support of social actors, though such support may well be provoked by deviations from the taken-for-granted routines.

A number of factors will be relevant for the strength of this causal empowerment of cultural patterns. Among them are, first, the relation of a given cultural pattern to the material and immaterial interests and to the overall cultural configurations prevailing in the social formation in question; second, its relation to the interests of those equipped with particular resources of power and influence; and third, the structure of opportunities and constraints within which members of the social formation in question pursue their material and immaterial interests.

Formulations such as the "extent of grounding" and the "degree of causal power" may be intuitively plausible; but since both grounding and causal force depend on different particular mechanisms whose results do not simply add up along a single dimension, these notions of degree may serve as a shortcut; but on closer inspection they are problematic composite concepts that must be unpacked to be of further use.

As noted earlier, if we conceive of culture as an ensemble of patterns, and if their causal effects derive from grounding in social formations, questions of transmission from one unit to another acquire critical importance, both for the scale on which cultural patterns are embraced and for questions of cultural change. The following propositions about how cultural elements spread among and within groups and how they are received (or ignored and even rejected) are clearly selective and incomplete; but they may serve to illustrate the complexity as well as the importance of these transmission processes.

Cultural patterns are inevitably changed in the course of transmission from one group to another.

There is first of all the fact—known to any teacher—that transmission itself is an error-prone process. To take an extravagant example, the departmental organization of American graduate schools seems to have originated in misunderstandings by American visitors of what they observed in nineteenth-century German universities. They interpreted the hierarchical grouping of German students and junior scientists around a single professor as a relatively egalitarian collaboration among autonomous partners. They did so because they did not distinguish between the chair's hierarchical place in the universities' system of organization and the role of possibly the same person in the more group-oriented work in the national institutes of science (Ben-David 1971, chap.7 and 139–42).

More broadly, cultural orientations, modes of communication, as well as material and immaterial interests that prevail in the receiving group will reshape the meaning and will affect the force of the transmitted ideas and patterns in major or minor ways. This is why the functionalist anthropology of a Malinowski, insisting on the interdependence of different parts in a cultural whole, was more persuasive than an earlier simplistic ethnological focus on diffusion. True, cultural patterns are often at odds with each other, but they also show strong, if often selective strains toward consonance.

Receptivity is governed in complex ways by social status and recognized boundaries between collectivities.

- *The High Status-Receptivity Nexus*

Higher social status increases credibility and persuasiveness in cultural transmission processes. This seems at least in part due to the fact that status differences often entail a peculiar voluntary element—voluntary, that is, on the part of those who grant or withhold honored status. Though honor and deference are typically embedded in social rituals, though they are often subject to social regulation, and though differences in social status tend to be correlated with the wealth and power dimensions of social inequality, status distinctions often rely—in comparison to positions of power and wealth—less on objective facts, possibly secured by coercive protection, and more on feelings, attitudes, and behavior that have an element of spontaneity about them.[7]

However, steep status differences, especially those reinforced by socially recognized and emphasized boundaries, may limit and even prevent receptivity. German professor-student relations of old inhibited free exchange and thus limited learning. Nonimitation of high-status cultural patterns and practices may even be normatively secured.[8]

- *Status Similarity, Trust, and Receptivity*

Similar status encourages ease of communication; and uncoerced interaction generates positive sentiments and fairly generalized trust. Half a century ago, Katz and Lazarsfeld (1955) developed from these insights the famous two-step flow of communication hypothesis: the impact of mass communication is mediated by personal communication with people one trusts. That ordinary citizens with little political knowledge of their own can still make political choices that are roughly reasonable in light of their social position and their material and immaterial interests, is explained partly by the same mechanism and partly by affiliation with and trust in institutions and organizations, which in turn is often mediated by "horizontal" relations (Sniderman, Brody, and Tetlock 1991; Pierson, 2001; and Brooks and Manza, 2007, chap. 5; despite the findings of Converse (1964) and similar later research demonstrating widespread ignorance). The nexus among status similarity, trust, and receptivity works probably for quite a few different subjects of cultural transmission.

[7] These observations do not hold if status distinctions are regulated and protected much as are positions of wealth and formal power. For example, ethnic, caste, or racial inequalities that are socially as well as legally enforced are quite similar in character to coercively protected property and formal power. These inequalities will then partake much less in the peculiar voluntary characteristics of status relations, unless the latter are nurtured by adaptive and camouflaging responses to the imposed social disabilities. Such adaptations generating consent among the disadvantaged are often found in gender relations. (See the section on social inequality in chapter 14 and Tilly 1998).

[8] Making upward imitation and assimilation difficult—often by quite simple devices— has been and is a strategy of keeping a status order from being disturbed by an unwanted

Closer investigation of the link between similarity of status and receptivity can probably yield insights into the conditions under which very steep status differences negate the generalized influence often enjoyed by high-status persons and groups.

- *More Specialized Status-Based Influence*

The cognitive and moral authority derived from higher status is diffuse; yet it is in some ways similar to the credibility grounded in technical reputation and certification. Important aspects of the latter can be conceptualized as a specialized version of the higher-status effect; but now, say in the case of doctor's orders, both authority and receptivity are clearly delimited.

Likewise, the influence of similarly situated people and groups often seems to combine a generalized trust with an informal attribution of a certain "expertise," a special concern for and familiarity with, say, politics, the local economy, art and entertainment, or matters of fashion.

- *Divisions of Cultural Labor*

A combination of different status relations and very dissimilar involvement on the part of various actors can yield an elaborate "division of cultural labor." Think, for instance, of the interrelations among theorists, political leaders, field workers, influential rank and file, and loosely associated followers in an ethnic or working-class movement. The readiness of potential followers to respond to certain appeals involves very different mechanisms from those informing the inclinations of, say, union organizers. And the reactions of both are likely to follow a different dynamic from that driving the ideas of political theorists (Rueschemeyer 1976).

As an ensemble, such a division of cultural labor can significantly improve the stability of the overall pattern because of the built-in linkages of trust and authority. On the methodological side, being aware of such different roles and their interrelations can be very helpful in pinning down what exactly the cultural orientations of different sets of actors are and in interpreting how they affect, influence, and protect each other's ideas and outlook.

- *A Low Status-Imitation Nexus?*

Under particular—and not-well-understood—circumstances, higher-status groups are influenced by, and "borrow" from, groups of lower status. This seems of greater importance in matters of taste than in the normative and cognitive dimensions of culture, but it is not confined to

---

intrusion of newcomers, when that order had become less protected by law; see Goblot (1925/1967) and, more recently, Bourdieu (1984).

them. It often appears to involve playing out ambivalences and enjoying "forbidden fruit." The affinity of respectable bourgeois milieus and bohemian subcultures at the end of the nineteenth century offers one example (a suggestion Mark Elchardus made in personal communication). The upward mobility of jazz, of the Argentine tango, and of current hip-hop indicates others.

- *Definitions of "Otherness" Limit Receptivity*

If other groups and communities are evaluated as negatively distinct, as "others," the in-group–out-group dynamic may kick in, inducing active rejection of what the others stand for and reaffirmation of one's own contrasting positions. Thus the perceived and imagined horrors of big-city culture—of Berlin or New York—have reinforced traditional or retraditionalized orientations in the provinces. And separating themselves from the *Lumpenproletariat*, the underclass in rags, served the late nineteenth-century workers' movements of Europe to underline their own respectability and competence.

Yet under certain not-well-understood conditions, definitions of "otherness" may have a more neutral effect. Recognized delineations of collective boundaries may create what Clifford Geertz has called "contextual relativism": difference and otherness are then simply seen as less relevant. "That is what *they* do or believe; *we* are different." This protects against contamination and contains hostility.

The United States stands out among other countries for having cultivated a great degree of mutual acceptance of ethnic and racial otherness. While this is certainly not true of all parts of American society, and while it tragically still does not come close to delivering racial equality and justice, these developments have taken strong roots. A critical factor involved in this transformation has been changes in the conceptions of the societal community as a whole, within which incorporation and rejection take place. Jeffrey Alexander offers an important treatment of this in his *The Civil Sphere* (2006).

These quick notes on the relation between social status and cultural transmission should not be misread as belittling other more tangible resources for cultural influence. Even a cursory review of the history of rejection and exclusion reminds us of the critical role played by violence and coercion. Through collective memory, violence and coercion often continue to have an impact on intergroup relations much later, an impact that is not easily rivaled by other factors.

Moreover, cultural hegemony and counterhegemony (Gramsci 1928–37/1975) define a vast and perhaps undercultivated field of investigation. The following is just one orienting proposition that is taken from this discourse:

Control of organizational and institutional linkages and channels of communication has far-reaching consequences for the spread and the maintenance of cultural orientations.

Thus dominant interests and influential groups exert influence not only because they typically enjoy higher status as well. They characteristically also have at their disposal structural linkages, often specially designed for communication and influence. Religious organizations, hierarchical kin networks, schools, the armed forces, and voluntary associations represent such organized channels of influence.

Similarly, insulation from such hegemonic influence does not simply rely on negative contrasts between "us and them." Thus the organizations of subordinate classes—unions, parties, reading clubs, and the like—have often served to insulate them against the influence of dominant interests.

Looking at cultural transmission processes has prepared us to inquire more closely into a number of implications of the central principle. Cultural transmission processes are critical for an understanding of the scale of socially accepted cultural patterns, as well as for the often fragmentary and uneven acceptance of cultural elements. They also represent one major set of conditions for cultural change.

IMPLICATIONS OF THE GROUNDING PRINCIPLE

The grounding principle suggests, first of all, that we give special importance to mesoanalysis. It implies that we have to take a very close look at the groups, organizations, and institutions that are "carriers" of culture. How each of them relates to different cultural patterns, and how they go about their own central concerns in varied situations, will shape, constrain, and empower different elements of culture.

While I do not deny the possibility that comprehensive communities with a shared identity or even a whole national political system may be characterized by common values, shared cognitive interpretations, and a distinctive preference structure guiding behavior in different spheres of life, it is far more likely that such overarching cultural patterns reflect the heterogeneity of interest and outlook among the different carriers within larger social formations. This entails three consequences: The support for a given pattern may be much more scattered, uncertain, and therefore weaker than it appears at first sight. Second, such heterogeneity may put into question the reconstruction of consonant and consistent cultural wholes based on the inherent logic of separate cultural items that links them up with others. And third, we may find that some groups and organizations do embrace more or less coherent cultural patterns, but that these are held in explicit antagonism to others.

First, the support for given cultural patterns may be weaker than it seems. This has been evident, for instance, in the fact that large segments of the American population do not approve of the constitutional right to free speech, however unpopular; in the unwillingness of regional majorities to accept established scientific findings about evolution; or in the quite uneven acceptance of ethnic and racial "otherness" albeit in a country that stands out for this acceptance.

Second, uneven and fragmented acceptance of cultural items puts into question the common notion that cultural items are systemically interrelated. If this were regularly the case, it would indeed allow inferences about cultural wholes from more fragmentary evidence. Yet at any one time and in any place, the coherence of cultural patterns is limited. Converse (1964), in the essay to which I already have made reference, has pointed to one of the central lessons from public opinion research: only the well-informed few hold logically and cognitively consistent views on most subjects, though group membership (specifically class affiliation) and reference to groups (specifically to African Americans) were factors that increased coherence of views and beliefs. This can perhaps be generalized: cultural items are often quite loosely integrated with each other. Inferences made on the assumption of tight coherence are likely to be false. Furthermore, what is accepted as consonant or dissonant is likely to vary across historical constellations, though salient *social* affiliations seem to be especially important in organizing consonance between beliefs and ideals.

To illustrate the third point, in the comparative historical study of democracy of Rueschemeyer, Stephens, and Stephens (1992), we argued that class interests cannot be read off from the objective situation of class members but are constructed historically in the very process of organization. Working-class interests have been defined in this way by competing and differentially successful associations and movements—social democratic, Leninist, Catholic, even Tory in character. These historical definitions typically also include at the elite level interpretations of society at large, its history, and its possible futures. Here, then, are complex cultural creations, though each with a limited (and in various ways diluted) appeal to specific constituencies. Yet they are defined in distinction from and antagonism to mainstream ideas and ideals sponsored by dominant voices and interests.

All three consequences of the heterogeneity of cultural carriers outlined have further implications for cultural change. Fragmentary and uncertain acceptance increases the vulnerability to change. So do inconsistencies and contradictions within an overall cultural pattern once they are made explicit and are exploited by agents of change. Conflicts between groups with different outlooks and commitments add energy to change attempts, but the result may well be stalemate. Beyond that, these conflicts can indeed generate cultural effects, depending on which side is losing ground, be it to the other side or in the view of noncommitted "third parties." Or they can lead the two sides to new ground where the conflict is moderated or intensified.

Our insistence that cultural patterns must be linked to diverse groups, organizations, communities, and institutions makes things complicated for empirical research. But at the same time, there is a surprising methodological gain. The grounding principle points to potential and actual carriers—to groups, organizations, and institutions that concern themselves with the cultural patterns in question. And if it is not easy to find out what groups, organizations, and institutions stand for, it is—at least in modern societies, characterized by high levels of information use—far easier than to piece a cultural system together from different utterances of individuals high and low. If this argument holds, the grounding principle does double duty in a serendipitous way: it is a theoretically sound orientation thesis that can guide more specific hypothesis formation. And at the same time it eases the problems of identifying cultural patterns by directing research to the places where they are embraced and supported or ignored and rejected.[9]

Our discussion so far supports a number of corollaries of the grounding principle that are worth making explicit because they deny—or at least warn against—some of the most common misleading views of culture:

- *Culture is not identical with ethnonational culture.*

Many—including many sophisticated social scientists—think first, and primarily, of national and ethnic culture when the concept comes to mind. This tendency has a historical pedigree in romantic reactions against the Enlightenment, which shaped the discourse on ethnic and national culture. Yes: the early ("primordial") elements of culture transmission across generations—language, religion, morality, habits, rituals—do have a link to ethnicity and even nationality. Yet this insight is rarely used and systematically explored by those who see culture as primarily located at the ethnic and national macrolevel. What instead all too often informs the view of ethnonational cultures are simple stereotypes, perhaps cleansed of their most obvious self-laudatory and derogatory connotations (Sen 2004). Unless we deal with very small and homogeneous socie-

---

[9] Admittedly, this rough and tentative solution to the peculiar difficulties of identifying cultural commitments does not cover the last clause of the grounding principle; it does not help much to identify cultural premises of habits and customs nor the implications of prevailing codes of communication where these are far removed from the reflections of the actors involved.

ties such as hunting-and-gathering bands, cultural elements that are grounded in diverse organizations and institutions and that are intertwined with contrasting interests will result in a far more complicated picture. I am not just saying that "there are some of any kind in every society"; that's true even of hunters and gatherers. I am saying that we routinely overestimate, vastly overestimate, the homogeneity of such complex phenomena as New England, or French, or Irish, or Jewish, not to mention Mediterranean or Renaissance culture.

- *Culture is not necessarily consensual in character or contributing to harmony and mutual inclusion.*

This is fairly obvious once it is made explicit. Ideas and ideals tend to be intertwined with interests and consequently are often more conflictual than is assumed in consensus-oriented theories of a shared culture. Yet for many—again, including many sophisticated social scientists—giving less weight than they would to unifying cultural background assumptions and focusing on contrasting and mutually antagonistic cultural orientations, which are intertwined with opposed material interests, amounts to a "neglect of culture."[10]

- *Large cultural complexes—such as those built on a major religion or a system of rule with centuries of continuity—are heterogeneous in their meanings and consequences across different social formations and historical periods.*

This has become a mantra with respect to Islam in the world after September 11, 2001. Yet it is not trivial. If ideas, ideals, and other cultural elements become causally important to the extent that they are grounded in organizations and institutions, and in the routines and codes of everyday life, their effects will vary corresponding to institutional and material variations across societies as well as within societies over time. This puts a large question mark next to any assertion about the effects of Islam, Confucianism, or Christianity. Since many of us are most familiar with Western history dominated by Christianty, its dark as well as admirable sides, it might be a useful mental exercise to consider the many varied things that proved to be compatible with the Christian tradition. We might even ask ourselves whether there is anything that was so incompatible that it did not happen.

---

[10] This was our experience when we published *Capitalist Development and Democracy* (Rueschemeyer, Stephens, and Stephens 1992). It is to the great credit of Jeffrey Alexander that in his *The Civil Sphere* (2006) he avoids the harmonizing assumptions of Durkheim and Parsons about what they called *conscience collective* and the societal community. Comprehensive cultural templates can themselves, in conjunction with their changing structural

- *Cultural change can be quick and surprising. The stability of culture depends on its social grounding.*

Ideas and ideals tend to change as the organizations, institutions, and patterns of everyday life in which they are grounded change. Too often it is assumed that political culture constitutes an inherently stable reference point for political life. This is not only questionable when the views of unprepared survey subjects are used as evidence of "political culture." The assumption is equally problematic if political culture is more carefully assessed. The radical changes reflected in the two famous volumes *The Civic Culture* and *Civic Culture Revisited* (Almond and Verba 1963, 1989) should make that clear beyond any doubt. Cultural patterns are not more stable than social ones, even though one may easily be misled by language ("cultural *traditions*") or even by sophisticated social theory (Parsons's "cybernetic hierarchies") to make that assumption.

The Explanatory Power of Cultural Patterns

If culture comes in small parcels variously embraced by groups, organizations, and institutions; if its internal strains toward consistency and consonance may often be quite weak because cultural items adapt to the concerns of their "carriers"; if cultural templates do not necessarily harmonize but instead can deeply divide larger social formations; if culture changes over time as its social "carriers" change, possibly with great rapidity; and if it therefore often cannot offer an anchorage for social formations—what, then, is left of our claim that culture matters decisively and pervasively? This claim stands nevertheless. Earlier discussions, especially those about knowledge, norms, preferences, and emotions (see chapters 3–6), give the claim varied and complex substance; but it may be useful to offer a few additional considerations.

There are, first, large background assumptions that are shared across whole civilizations (e.g., Eisenstadt 2003). This is a difficult field of investigation, often too speculative for the comfort of most practicing social and political researchers; but the phenomenon is without doubt real. For instance, differences in the relative weight given to empirical and nonempirical—magical or religious—beliefs come to light only in wide-ranging historical comparisons. Another example is beliefs about the need to restrain self-interested preferences in different kinds of social relations. Yet another is the norms, preferences, beliefs, and emotional paradigms defining gender relations.

---

contexts, create deep divisions. Thus Alexander insists on the possibility that very similar aspects of societal solidarity can result in integration as well as in exclusion.

Such cultural differences and similarities do not coincide simply with differences in "modernity." Theorizing on "multiple modernities" grew out of cross-civilizational analyses, earlier comparative historical work that disposed of the claim that modernization inevitably leads to structural and cultural convergence, as well as the arguments based on demographic and family history Thornton (2005) advanced in *Reading History Sideways* (see chapter 11).

These comprehensive background templates overlap with the *premises* of the routines and customs of people's everyday lives. While one can expect with confidence that these will vary across different strata, communities, status groups, and other collective identities, what such more detailed variations share with premises that emerge from cross-civilizational studies at a higher level of abstraction is the accepted character of the premises and their typical exemption from continued critical inspection. The strength of these underlying beliefs, values, and commitments emerges with clarity when they are challenged. Socrates' fate stands as a symbol for the power of assumptions that are largely exempted from inspection.[11]

The major form in which cultural patterns are grounded in social structures is, of course, institutions. I have proposed to conceptualize them as complexes of norms with strong backing—efficient complexes of norms that shape, for example, economic behavior in the marketplace; the conduct of science and its place in society; or relations of marriage, family, and kinship. Significantly, the supporting resources accounting for the strength of institutions include knowledge and beliefs, the appropriate ordering of preferences, paradigms of emotion and attachment, as well as material backing and negative sanctions. Viewed from a different angle, perhaps more appropriate for the questions at hand here, institutions fuse all dimensions of culture into more or less coherent configurations. Institutions are the paradigmatic cases of a grounding of culture. Thus we often speak of a cultural configuration that enjoys a strong grounding as "well institutionalized."

At the opposite end of the scales of strength and grounding there are cultural patterns that are virtually devoid of "carriers"; but they still may have causal relevance because they constitute resources available for later use. With some simplification one might call this "culture in the library mode." This is the stuff out of which renaissances are made. The resurrection of Roman law out of Byzantine codifications, used to restructure

---

[11] The social sciences of today tread on ground similar to that Socrates trod, simply because they try to identify causal conditions and mechanisms that sustain disturbing problems as well as socially comfortable arrangements, be they sacred, just commonly accepted, or explicitly open to rational inspection.

church organization at the end of the first millennium CE and subsequently serving as the foundation for the Western legal tradition, is only one of many examples (Berman 1983).

Before closing this section, I offer a few comments on specific components of culture. After all, the dynamics and the effects of grounding are not the same for cognitive, normative, or appreciative cultural patterns. In each of the paragraphs that follow, the issue is similar. In each I will contrast the emerging complex frame for cultural explanation with simple commonsense understandings. For many, the appeal of knowledge is obvious, most important values are shared, and dominant preferences are set by human nature. These views are fundamentally mistaken, though they are plausible and persuasive within a firmly grounded and unquestioned cultural environment. In arguing against them, I can fall back on a variety of discussions throughout the previous chapters.

It is indeed a common belief that the basic preferences of human beings are set by "human nature." Yet as we have seen earlier (in chapters 5 and 9), preferences and beliefs about preferences vary, both within and across broad societal formations. In particular, the emphasis on, or permissiveness about, self-regarding and other-regarding preferences varies. And it does so not only across major cultural contexts but also across institutionally shaped areas of social life within the same cultural framework—from economic behavior in the marketplace to relations with family and kin and to the readiness to sacrifice one's life for "God and country."

Knowledge, especially when it comes with empirical proof, may seem to have an unquestioned authority, obviously affecting behavior and planned actions as well as influencing norms, values, and preferential dispositions. Yet even though empirical evidence does have a peculiar persuasiveness, the presumption of an unquestioned authority of empirical knowledge is true only with strong qualifications. These qualifications point again to institutional structures and codes of everyday life in which ideas about reality may or may not find acceptance and grounding. A scientific finding does not become socially operative just because it is true. Its acceptance as true and relevant—in different quarters and at different levels of sophistication and authority—is contingent on complex social and political processes (Rueschemeyer 1986, chap. 6). As we have seen (in chapter 3), modern science needs—and has in modern societies largely attained—institutional protection against interference and backlash. These strong institutional walls best protect natural science; but they also give institutional autonomy to social and political analysis and to the humanities.

But these protections are not impenetrable. Their importance is highlighted when a breach occurs. In 1933, when Hitler came to power in Germany, Jews were denied official positions, including positions in the universities and the Academy of Science. Some eminent scientists de-

nounced recent developments in theoretical physics as "Jewish science."
The anti-Semitic exclusions were devastating. "Among those forced out
were fourteen Nobel laureates and twenty-six of the sixty professors of
theoretical physics in the country." When an eminent physicist, Max
Planck, pointed out the damage to German science, Hitler's answer was:
"Our national policies will not be revoked or modified, even for scientists. . . . If the dismissal of Jewish scientists means the annihilation of
contemporary German science, then we shall do without science for a few
years" (Isaacson 2007, 207, 207–8).

New knowledge claims, especially if they are made outside the most
strongly institutionalized sphere of scientific inquiry, and if they affect not
only established ideas but also vested interests, have to gain acceptance
in a process that inevitably involves more than empirical evidence and
sound analysis. The fate of the doctrines of John Maynard Keynes, who
famously claimed that "the ideas of economists and political philosophers, both when they are right and when they are wrong, are more powerful than is commonly understood" (1936, 383), offers an interesting
case in point. Failing to persuade policy makers in his own Britain during
the 1930s, his theories and proposals had a quite different impact in different political economies, both during the Great Depression and after
the Second World War. Later, Keynesianism was largely rejected—especially in its broader implications for the interrelations of states, economies, and societies—even though important policy designs still bear the
imprint of his ideas. Peter Hall presents in the conclusion to the volume
on Keynesianism he edited (1989) a theory frame for explaining the differential impact of Keynes's ideas that highlights the role of politics.[12]

On values, much common sense offers a third version of the view that
some of the fundamentals of culture are self-evident. Aren't the basic values obvious and universal? It is true—and morally right—that on some
issues we insist on universalism, even if certain cultures diverge from what
we see as right. The extremes of mistreating women in some countries
provoke such judgments. The claims of this universalism derive from
strong beliefs in a shared humanity. However, core values that are held
high in one culture may contradict those praised in another. Isaiah Berlin
relates how he encountered this in the writings of Machiavelli:

> He thought it possible to restore something like the Roman republic
> or Rome of the early Principate. He believed that to do this one
> needed a ruling class of brave, resourceful, intelligent, gifted men

---

[12] To quote his brief opening formulation: "Four kinds of factors seem to have affected
the influence of Keynesian proposals: the orientation of the governing party, the structure
of the state and state-society relations, the nature of national political discourse, and the
events associated with World War II" (Hall 1989, 363).

who knew how to seize opportunities and use them, and citizens who were adequately protected, patriotic, proud of their State, epitomes of manly, pagan virtues.

But Machiavelli also sets side by side this the notion of Christian virtues—humility, acceptance of suffering, unwordliness, the hope of salvation in an afterlife—and he remarks that if, as he plainly himself favours, a State of a Roman type is to be established, these qualities will not promote it: those who live by the precepts of Christian morality are bound to be trampled on by the ruthless pursuit of power on the part of the men who alone can recreate and dominate the republic which he wants to see. He does not condemn Christian virtues. He merely points out that the two are incompatible, and he does not recognize an overarching criterion whereby we are enabled to decide the right life for men. (1997, 6, 7)

Berlin refuses to see this as relativism: "It is what I would describe as pluralism—that is, the conception that there are many different ends men may seek and still be fully rational, fully men, capable of understanding each other and sympathising and deriving light from each other, as we derive it from reading Plato or the novels of medieval Japan—worlds, outlooks very remote from our own" (ibid., 9).

Furthermore, even within a single settled cultural pattern values have to be—and are—weighed against each other. Berlin illustrates this with the tension between equality and liberty. "Equality may demand the restraint of the liberty of those who wish to dominate; liberty—without some modicum of which there is no choice and therefore no possibility of remaining human as we understand the word—may have to be curtailed to make room for social welfare, to feed the hungry, to clothe the naked, to shelter the homeless, to leave room for the liberty of others, to allow justice and fairness to be exercised. . . . These collisions of values are of the essence of what they are and of what we are. . . . We are doomed to choose, and every choice may entail an irreparable loss" (ibid., 10–11).

Even though the philosopher's language describes this choice as if it were an individual option, the choices made are stabilized and underwritten by groups, organizations, and institutions. If they are fully embedded in the routines and codes of everyday life, the quality of choice tends to disappear, and value patterns present themselves as self-evident.

Values often stand in tension with prevailing practices. This engenders complicated mediating mechanisms. While full of contradictions, these mechanisms are familiar and routinely accepted. Values are often treated "just as ideals." They are then typically couched on a level of generality that leaves the contrary practices in effect uncriticized. Such ritual, symbolic affirmation implicitly condones practices contravening the stated values; but it is more than sheer hypocrisy. We must recognize that it has multiple consequences. It does conceal the discrepancy of practices and ideals, and it weakens the translation of values into norms, critique, and sanctions; but it also maintains and preserves the values in question. To put it paradoxically: hypocrisy preserves values as it undercuts them. It gives them autonomy and the capacity to transcend the social realities that constitute their grounding, and at the same time it diminishes their causative power.

These observations can be generalized to other cultural patterns, yielding a last orienting rule of thumb: *Cultural patterns can be associated with complex mechanisms of articulation and disarticulation, which at once maintain their integrity, grant them a certain autonomy, and limit their influence.*

CONCLUSION

The results of this discussion of cultural explanation can be stated briefly. Cultural patterns—the collective creations arising from the subjective dimension of action—are of great causal consequence. The emerging theoretical approaches for understanding the role of knowledge and ignorance, preference structures, normative orientations, and emotions offer fundamental elements of a theory of cultural explanation. To this is added one central claim: cultural patterns become effective to the extent that they are grounded in groups, organizations, and institutions and in the routines and codes of everyday life. This principle cautions that the grounding of cultural patterns may be varied and fragmented, but it does not exclude the possibility of broad, comprehensive cultural formations.

I have also claimed that—serendipitously—the same principle eases the inherent difficulties of identifying and describing cultural patterns. It makes the task of understanding and interpretation far more manageable because it points the investigation to specific social carriers and their internal discourse about beliefs, preferences, and normative orientations, as well as about their relations to other collective actors.

Chapter XVI

CONCLUSION: USABLE THEORY?

This volume is built on a few basic premises. A first set concerns the state of social and political theory. The social sciences are not rich in full-scale empirical theories—or even tested complex hypotheses—that are ready to be taken off the shelf and put to satisfactory use in explanation or prediction. We do, however, have a significant and growing stock of focused theory frames, which offer conceptualizations of problems as well as reasoned identifications of the factors likely to be of causal relevance. In contrast to fully developed theories, these frames do not contain ordered sets of empirical hypotheses capable of explanation or prediction; nor do they allow the derivation of such hypotheses. But they can guide the creation of theoretical hypotheses in the course of social and political research, propositions that are suitable for making sense of the empirical evidence. Focused theory frames are the most important of the analytic tools discussed in this volume.

The second set of premises helped shape the substance of the book. I opted for action theory as a framework for the ordering and integration of the analytic tools considered. This was a pragmatic choice. It was a tentative, suspendable, and reversible option, certainly not a commitment to the ontological presuppositions of different metatheories and even less an expression of allegiance to the ideological tenets often associated with them. However, I chose to take a stab at recovering action theory before adopting it as an integrative baseline for the discussion of varied analytic tools.

Action theory, I argue, has to be "recovered" in three ways. It has to be freed from the abstract complexities that engulfed it in Parsons's work. It has to be enriched through recognition of the importance of the "internal" dimensions of action—the importance of different degrees of knowledge and ignorance, of variations in preferences, of contrasts in normative orientations, and of the role of emotions. This recognition could build on the models of action developed by Weber, Mead, and Parsons, as well as on more recent sophisticated versions of rational choice theory.[1] Finally,

---

[1] Consider this judgment of Douglass North (1990, 111): "There is nothing the matter with the rational actor paradigm that could not be cured by a healthy awareness of the complexity of human motivation and the problems that arise from information processing. Social scientists would then understand not only why institutions exist, but also how they influence outcomes" (cited by Moe 2005, 223).

action theory has to be oriented toward causal arguments. It has to be saved from the radical skepticism about explanatory theory that for many follows from the complexities of the subjective space of action, a skepticism that seems further confirmed by the sparse theoretical accomplishments of political science and sociology.

ON THE DIFFICULTIES AND POSSIBILITIES OF THEORETICAL ADVANCE

Why are theoretical propositions, capable of explanation, difficult to come by in the social sciences? The outlines of an answer are well known. Experimental isolation of causal effects is rarely feasible. At the same time, human motivation and behavior seem shaped by an endless number of factors, some blocking or counterbalancing others, some possibly substituting for each other as they bring about similar effects.

The internal dimensions of action induce skepticism above all because this subjective space is not easily understood with any certainty. Even introspection has to deal with ambivalence, confusion, and obfuscation.[2] Moreover, the subjective side of action requires in any case interpretation as well as rendition into the analysts' language; and much can get lost in such translations. Paradoxically, skepticism about delving into the subjective space of action also arises precisely because so many of its elusive features seem to have great causative power—think of various forms of ignorance, the fear or the readiness to break norms others respect, or acting in heated emotion.

In addition, "the facts of the situation" often become relevant only as they are filtered through subjective understandings. That means that the same "objective" givens are in their effects dependent on the understanding, desires, and normative views that people in varied positions bring to them. This can limit subtly—yet in its effects drastically—the conditions under which a given hypothesis holds, under which for instance we can claim that personal loyalties and aversions can be controlled in an organization by bureaucratic rules and sanctions. That is obvious if a hypothesis extends across very different historical and cultural contexts; but similar differences within our own world may have the same effect, constraining the validity of our theoretical propositions or leaving their scope uncertain.

---

[2] Jim Mahoney related this point—familiar since the French moralists, Nietzsche, and Freud—to the facts of biological evolution: "Human consciousness only dimly perceives the sources of action. Our minds evolved not to understand why we act the way we do. Rather, the stories our consciousness tells us about why we act in certain ways may have very little to do with the real reasons why we act in certain ways" (personal communication).

The complexity and variability of the subjective dimensions of action are a major challenge to theoretical explanation and prediction. Yet their variability is, as we have seen, reduced by the fact that this internal space of action is to some extent molded by broader social conditions. This makes cognition, preferences, normative orientations, emotions, and their effects more predictable. And so do the relatively stable social structures, small and large, into which cognition, norms, and preferences congeal as the result of sustained interaction and symbolic mediation.

Yet a similar variability reappears, if to a lesser extent, on the levels of meso- and macrostructures and -processes. If, for instance, close-knit groups with their power both to constrain and to enable are significant causal agents, it is clear that their form and the specific mechanisms they activate vary considerably in detail. The same is true of states, to add an example of an even more complex composite causal agent. Causal mechanisms grounded in groups or states take on a great variety of forms, and they vary in the conditions that activate them as well as in the outcomes they create. That means that in exploring specific causal outcomes, we have to pay close attention to the exact features of the face-to-face groups and the states in question as well as to the contexts in which they operate. And for the same reason we have to take care not to extend the scope conditions of our hypotheses loosely.

It is this individual and social variability and the different ways in which such variation is constrained that explain why focused theory frames are as helpful as they are. Focused theory frames combine clearly formulated research problems with arguments about which broad factors are likely to be causally relevant and which kinds of causal processes may account for expected outcomes. As these theoretical ideas are not sufficiently specific to predict outcomes or to explain results empirically identified, theory frames fall short of the explanatory and predictive power expected of ideal theories. Yet they can advance further hypothesis development. Their grounding in comparable past research and its interpretation not only may suggest explanatory ideas; it also can increase our confidence that a causal interpretation of numerical associations or historical sequences makes sense and does not mistakenly seize on spurious correlations and strings of unrelated events.

This leads to a second conclusion: we can often come to more specific explanations if we are ready to develop new, sufficiently specific explanatory hypotheses in the course of empirical research. It is particularly to that undertaking that this volume offers analytic tools. For instance, workers' groups may resist or be quite willing to cooperate with management. Past theory frames lead us to expect that the groups' effect on cooperation will be the stronger, the more cohesive a group. Yet the very direction of this group effect is likely to depend on such conditions as the

overall relations of trust and mistrust between management and employees, on the particular relations between workers and lower management,
or on job security and the role of competition among group members.

What can such theory work in the course of local research rely on?
There is likely to be the initial theory frame, built on a review of relevant
past research and theory. The causal factors it points to can guide research
but do not yield specific predictions. If it offers causal mechanism hypotheses, these may derive from similar research projects; but they gain special
power if they have been used in explanations of a variety of substantively
different empirical patterns. Small group research, to keep with the example chosen, has yielded a number of causal mechanism ideas regarding
the constraining and enabling of members in a large variety of settings.
The role of other factors, potentially significant in the research site at
hand, must be assessed with multiple observations in the particular setting
and, if possible, in other, comparable sites as well. That may include assessments of the relative strengths of factors working in opposite directions, such as the effects of competition among workers in an environment
of high unemployment vs. the strength of group coherence. In the famous
Hawthorne experiments, the *combination* of these two mechanisms may
have led to strong, group-enforced output restrictions (Roethlisberger
and Dickson 1939).

The bottom line of this brief restatement of the difficulties and the prospects of social and political theory development is clear and fairly simple:
causal explanation, based on general (though not unbounded!) theoretical
statements, is a difficult but not an unattainable goal. It is critically facili-
tated by the continuous improvement of focused theory frames, and by
the willingness and ability of researchers to engage in theory building "on
the ground," in the course of empirical research.

ANALYTIC ROUTINES AND PITFALLS

If single-minded behaviorism, which shut out any consideration of subjective reasoning and motivation, has failed, and if crude attributions of
insight and motives across all areas of social life are clearly inadequate,
exploring the subjective dimension of action seems a promising strategy.
The quartet of chapters discussing this internal space of action made it
clear that the complexities of knowledge and ignorance, of normative
orientations, of variations in preferences, and of emotional response do
not preclude causal analysis. Not only are their results helpful in interpreting empirical findings; they yield hypotheses about the causal relevance
of cognition, preferences, norms, and emotions, both in their own right

and as constitutive elements of composite—"emergent"—causal agents that function on the meso- and macrolevels of social life.

Some of the arguments in these chapters, as well as in those following them, point to what might be called "theoretical routines." Norms and their clustering in roles and role sequences belong here, as well as class, status, and power as dimensions of social inequality, different types of organizations, and social institutions. These constitute the stock of ideas commonly used in social and political analysis, though—perhaps paradoxically—for that very reason they are often given divergent definitions and therefore may require extended conceptual analysis. Other discussions—of varying preferences, of emotions, of attachments and identities, as well as of aggregation—are less well established in social and political discourse.

Emotions and social attachments—attachments to particular persons or, symbolically mediated, to social identities—emerged at several points as critical linkage elements, binding together cognition with evaluations and desires. They also fuse them into combined causal mechanisms (think of hostile stereotypes or the readiness for the ultimate sacrifice), and they play a critical role in constituting more complex social structures such as groups or nations and their leadership.

My discussion of action is structured by the rational actor model and its limitations. The chapters on knowledge, norms, preferences, and emotions recover action theory and complement that model. There is no parsimonious macromodel that could similarly serve as a point of departure, framing qualifications and extensions, as the rationalist model did for elementary action and interaction. Older conceptions—for instance, models of societies that are functionally and structurally integrated around stable and universal functional prerequisites of social life—are too far removed from the realities at least of complex modern social formations (see chapter 2).

However, a number of interrelated guiding ideas proved to be of pervasive importance in meso- and macroanalysis. Institutions are acknowledged as critical across a wide range of theoretical positions. Power in all its different manifestations is an important aspect of institutions and, more generally, must be considered in any analysis of structural innovation, stability, and transformation. Particular attention is due to one-sided power balances and to the use and control of violence and coercion. The latter gives one set of institutions—those structuring states and state-society relations—a central place in meso- and macroanalysis. Our exploration of the causal impact of cultural patterns returned to the subjective space of action, looking at it now from the macro–point of view. Culture is considered here as the "collective structuring of the internal dynamics of action." Yet the different elements of culture—diverse bodies of belief, norms, preference structures, and templates of emotion—acquire causal power only if they are grounded in groups, organizations, and institutions or in the diverse routines and codes of communication of everyday life. Finally, we learned that structural and cultural analysis must be sensitive to time- and sequence-bound causal effects. This has secured historical institutionalism a central role in macrosociology, comparative politics, and international relations.

As the chapters moved beyond the microlevel of analysis, a number of more specific useful ideas came into view that cut across different areas of inquiry. To single out a first, the interrelations between social patterns have critical implications for mutual reinforcement as well as for undercutting stability and inducing change. This was clear when we considered the fact that norms are often part of normative clusters, and it was also important for an understanding of institutional persistence and change. In chapter 8, we encountered the extravagant idea of a "calendar model of social stability" that focused on the sheer fact of interrelated schedules, independent of the weight of diverse material and immaterial interests involved.

Another such insight of some consequence is that the causal relations between the micro- and macrolevels of social life exhibit a rough asymmetry. Encompassing social conditions are in many ways causally relevant for the lives of individuals and small groups, while they themselves remain often beyond the reach of smaller social units. This must not be conceived as an overpowering impact of macrocontexts; but it has, as we have seen, the interesting correlate that macro- as well as mesopatterns may be quite stable while great variability prevails at the microlevels. This has important implications for research design.

It is perhaps useful to recall also some comments that point specifically to analytic pitfalls. Again, some are well understood and often rehearsed in social and political discourse. A first case in point is the fallacy of taking functionalist arguments as substitutes for causal hypotheses without pointing to any "feedback" mechanisms that link the "steady state" outcomes to possible causal conditions (as the selective chances of procreation in a given environment do in the Darwinian theory of evolution). Another example is the unqualified insistence of some on "essentialist" concepts, concepts that seek to describe the true and full nature of a phenomenon without regard to its features that are distinctively relevant in a given set of hypotheses.

One of the most common analytic pitfalls—if also one of the most trivially wrongheaded—is the idea that one can get important insights into the character of a collectivity, large or small, by just summing the characteristics, views, and attitudes of its individual members, or, inversely, that one learns about most individual members by inferring their characteristics from the actions of the collectivity. For many issues, this procedure simply ignores the better part of the social and political analysis of collectivities. At the same time, I contrasted this fallacy of simplistic aggregation by an observer with institutionally grounded aggregations (such as the aggregation of many expressions of preference through the market mechanism or the political results of voting outcomes) that play a critical role in the life of large collectivities.

Finally, a few comments are due on the desirable form of analytic achievements. While I am not at all prepared to give up on the goals of integrated empirical theories capable of explanation and prediction (though perhaps in limited and partial form only), I believe that the better part of the analytic accomplishments of sociology and political science consists of focused theory frames. Though these frames fall short in explanatory and predictive power, they share a number of important features (see chapter 1):

- building on past research, they identify intriguing and important research problems as well as major factors of causal relevance;
- they often come in interrelated clusters illuminating common concerns;
- they can guide further theory development in the course of empirical research, and they are judged by how useful they are in such theory-building endeavors;
- in particular, they offer relevant context for hypothesis development;
- they provide an analytic background guiding the interpretation of research findings;
- they indicate directions for plausible theoretical generalization from empirical findings; and
- they are open to revision in light of research results.

As they focus on causally relevant factors for a well-defined problem, theory frames are good places to assemble causal mechanism hypotheses. Ultimately there is no satisfactory explanation unless we can offer causal mechanisms that account for an outcome.

Causal mechanisms come in quite different forms, with some arising from interpretation of frequency correlations, others emerging from the study of diverse, qualitatively identified event sequences that suggest causation. Causal mechanism hypotheses may focus on large or minute consequences and are often more or less isolated from each other. Often they will explain only one aspect of an outcome and remain in this sense partial. Thus strong group support may explain why people hold on to unpopular convictions; but it may not explain the substance of those convictions. Nevertheless, the systematic pursuit of causal mechanisms holds great promise, not least for a closer integration between empirical research and theoretical analysis.

Even if we look toward focused theory frames and causal mechanisms as the more accomplished and desirable analytic tools, it is quite important that we not denigrate lesser achievements. Thus many of us are familiar with more or less improvised lists of factors that seem causally relevant for outcomes of interest. Such preliminary estimates are, of course, the raw material out of which—after the inspection of diverse evidence about possible causal sequences and frequency associations—causal mechanisms and well-reasoned theory frames are formulated.

Another important analytic achievement consists of the identification of common or even universal problems that find different solutions in different social contexts. This was a central objective of the comparative political sociology of Reinhard Bendix (1964, 1978). We encountered similar issues when discussing the social control of expertise in different societal contexts (see chapter 3). Others have made this a central objective in comparative research on education (Schriewer 1999).

Ideally, the problems identified in such research turn out to be "generative problems," suggesting further and further questions as contrasting solutions are being pursued in different contexts. The fundamental problem of the social control of expertise is such a generative problem (see chapter 3). It derives from the asymmetry of knowledge between professionals and their clients in conjunction with the fact that their relation involves matters of great interest to the clients as well as to the wider community. But the control of expertise will take very different forms in different professions. The initial problem formulation suggests that it is likely to vary with the composition of their clientele, its knowledge and power resources, with the moral relevance the community ascribes to a profession's work, with the predictability of the results of experts' efforts, and even with the availability of empirical evidence about the success or failure of their work and advice. These and similar differences make different modes of control more or less effective—control by the market, control by state regulation and supervision, collective self-control by a profession's organization, and control of employed experts by other employed experts. A generative problem of this kind leaves us with different sequences of questions, each of which illuminates a variant of the original issue, using a set of interrelated critical variables.

A last example from a virtually inexhaustible list of "minor" analytic accomplishments is the identification of conceptual equivalences across different social and cultural contexts. It involves the careful translation of indigenous descriptions of various practices—for instance, of varieties of legal or medical work—into a common conceptual language. This achievement requires painstaking comparative research. It obviously links up with the need for distinctive concept formation suitable for specific research questions and preliminary hypotheses. Searching for conceptual equivalences may also lead back to the detection of widespread problems and contrasting responses to them, as well as to the identification of factors of causal relevance in focused theory frames. But the construction of conceptual equivalences is a worthwhile effort in itself. Leaving these questions unresolved constitutes one reason why detailed comparison across countries with different institutions is so difficult. It may also explain why sociological analysis too often either remains confined to one's own country or resorts to a more abstract discussion of societies in general.

PRAGMATIC RULES OF THUMB

Throughout this volume, I have offered some pragmatic suggestions for theory construction, complementing the reflections on useful analytic elements of theory, whether they are routine or not, helpful tools, or warnings about pitfalls. I begin this brief review with the need to unlock the implicit theoretical knowledge without which we would not be able to conduct our lives as well as we do. All intelligent actors in social life are in effect social theorists with a great deal of analytic knowledge. This, on the one hand, complicates the task of theoretical generalization because all social behavior is knowledge-dependent and thus variable across social positions and historical contexts. But it also means that within a given sociocultural context and knowledge horizon people know a great deal about how social life works. This knowledge typically remains implicit, as illustrated by the fact that we use the grammar of our language correctly even if we are unable to write down its rules; but it can often be made available.[3]

A first and fairly obvious tack of making implicit knowledge explicit is to focus on puzzles in social patterns or event sequences with which one is thoroughly familiar. A number of possible explanations will, in the light of that familiarity, be quickly disposed of as inadequate. Others can be weighed and assessed if things are explored only a little further. Focusing

---

[3] Most teaching of theory in the social sciences is not particularly helpful in unlocking this implicit knowledge. Oriented toward efficient instruction, it offers capsules of past theories in a well-ordered scholastic mode, in effect separating everyday life experience from thinking about social and political theory. Yet the best way to activate the implicit knowledge is regular attempts to solve puzzles derived from the students' social environment. In this volume I have resorted to another device—avoiding too conventional an arrangement of topics and seeking out unexpected and sometimes perhaps startling connections between themes. A less predictable assembly of ideas may be more effective in jogging the reader's memory and imagination.

on explanatory ideas that transcend the immediate case may yield initial ideas about the extension or limitations of the scope of their applicability. It may also generate hypothetical ideas of what in other circumstances can lead to similar outcomes, and what factors might counterbalance causal mechanisms that seem important in the situation at hand. A skeleton of theoretical ideas, then, will emerge from reflection on patterns that are well-known if we merely focus away from descriptive detail and toward analytic generalization. This is, of course, an exact parallel to what the textbooks declare to be the proper function of case studies—the development of hypotheses.

As in case studies, much may be gained through a move from one well-known pattern or event sequence to another; for it is only when we go beyond a single case that we can observe the effects of factors whose presence or absence is invariant within the first case. The rich recent literature on case studies may be helpful in prompting the right moves in such preliminary and tentative assessments of causal factors involved in well-understood patterns (Brady and Collier 2004; George and Bennett 2005; Gerring 2007).

A similar tack involves well-understood patterns that are familiar not from one's own experience but from the literature. Several of Max Weber's ideal types can serve as examples. Many of these may, as noted earlier, be read as embryonic theories—for instance, the pure type of bureaucracy is claimed to be the most effective tool for large-scale administrative tasks, or formally rational law is considered most suitable for, and supportive of, early commercial capitalism. Here the task is to specify the detailed hypotheses, which are often left implicit—about what helps increase productivity, makes corporate action possible, ensures long-term predictability, and the like. The large later literature on formal organizations or the more compact body of work on Weber's views on law and capitalism (e.g., Rheinstein 1954; Trubek 1972; Ewing 1987) can greatly help in improving the results of such theory explication; but the main point is the learning and fun involved in doing it oneself.

A greater challenge to the theorist's inventiveness is posed by contradictions between underspecified causal mechanisms. I have commented on several trivially contradictory ideas, predicting in one case that people would decline to participate in a common cause because so many do so already, or because very few others are as yet involved (see chapter 1). In another context I have sought to resolve the apparent contradiction between the sour-grapes metaphor for giving up on an ambition because success turns out to be too difficult and the opposite idea that people may insist on persevering with a goal precisely because it is hard to satisfy (see chapter 5). As many causal mechanism hypotheses have their origins in commonplace views, such contradictions are not at all infrequent; but these ideas need some reconciliation—most typically with specifications that make a difference—before they can even tentatively be deployed as causal mechanism hypotheses.

Inspiration for new ideas has many different sources.[4] One of the most important sources for new ideas is building on analogies. The long-established analogy between social formations and organic bodies has left analogical thinking with a bad reputation. This is partly due to the fact that such analogies were pushed to literalist extremes, as in inquiries about which social phenomenon corresponds to brain or stomach rather than whether both organic bodies and social formations exhibit significant equilibrium tendencies. More important, both opponents and advocates of arguments by analogy have often failed to distinguish between the invention of ideas and their testing. When used by many, analogical arguments were often wrongly taken as proven. Yet if we separate the contexts of invention and of validation, judicious use of analogy can be very helpful in theory development.

In using analogies we must keep an eye on critical differences as well as similarities. Thus social ranking in face-to-face groups highlights a number of features of more inclusive systems of inequality; but it misleads profoundly if we do not remain aware that what is at stake in many small groups are just differences in liking and appreciation rather than inequality in the necessities of life and long-term life chances.

The utility of analogical thinking derives in large part from a move that has even wider applicability—the attempt to see a given set of issues in a new light by linking it to phenomena not routinely associated with them. Thus one can break out of the constraints of commonplace ideas about family life by seeing families in the same frame as the dynamics of ephemeral student discussion groups, or by relating decision making about having children to the broad economic problems of choice under constraints of scarcity.

When we explore a new set of issues, it is often useful to have devices for ordering ideas. Resorting to a simple two-by-two classification of conditions or outcomes is so common that some wits have claimed that social scientists respond to any serious problem by making the sign of the cross. Yet while the utility of even the most straightforward ordering of ideas is not to be dismissed, one may reap great insights by paying special atten-

---

[4] Two recent publications give suggestions for stimulation and discovery of ideas: Abbott (2004) and Snyder (2007). Abbott offers a whole book on "heuristics," going back in part to older traditions of rhetoric. One great suggestion is to review the tensions and controversies between major metatheories and fundamental methodological positions as a source of ideas. Snyder introduces an intriguing set of interviews with major authors in comparative politics with an essay of reflections on what made their work vibrant and successful, and what might help students in the same endeavor.

tion when a master deviates from such simple conceptualizations of a problem. Which intuitions (or explicit reasonings) stand, for instance, behind Weber's threefold typology of authority based on rational-legal, charismatic, and traditional legitimation? If we cross-categorize the complex defining features of these three types, how many cells would define the underlying "property space" (Barton 1955)? Why are some category cells neglected or considered empty? By answering these questions we may come either to find fault with Weber's categorization or to uncover powerful intuitions.

Weber presents this same threefold typology with a large claim for its utility as a theory frame. The theoretical orientations it implies are to open a more powerful understanding of systems of rule than the ancient typology of the one, the few, and the many as rulers. Weber makes it clear that the three pure types involve more than contrasting versions of sheer legitimation; they also include the distinctive organizational machineries that are associated with each pattern of legitimating ideas. Again, by reconstructing the reasoning behind the overall claim, we can learn a great deal about one of the most influential theory frames of modern social science.

Most attempts to create an effective theory frame will not have the large sweep of Weber's reorientation of the study of systems of rule. Most are based on a careful review of the recently accumulated research experience. Our own efforts will gain if we both understand the purpose of routine reviews of the literature introducing most research reports and identify the rationales of agenda-transforming theory frames.

When we turn to lesser forms of analytic accomplishments than theories and theory frames, the distinction between elements of theory building and pragmatic advice for theory construction becomes less and less clear. Preliminary and intuitively plausible lists of causally relevant factors are indeed a humble form of theoretical accomplishment. Yet they are the raw material for developing causal mechanism hypotheses as well as orienting theory frames, though they have to be subjected to searching examination in diverse attempts at explanation of empirical findings.

We have repeatedly seen that a good understanding of different types of concepts—distinguishing relational from classificatory, operational from nominal, and distinctively identifying from essentialist concepts—is of critical help in generating hypotheses. Thus we have seen that unrecognized tautologies and wasted opportunities for formulating and exploring substantive hypotheses can result from a failure to differentiate sharply between concepts defining causal conditions and those defining outcomes. (An illustration used was overlapping definitions of civil societies and democratization; see chapter 1.) Of special importance is the insight that adjustments of hypotheses almost invariably require modifications of the concepts used. This is at odds with the widely held notion that conceptual clarity requires conceptual stability. At the level of orienting theory frames, this inescapable interrelation between conceptual change and innovative hypothesis formation entails an even more irritating paradox. It is precisely in the most important areas of inquiry, for instance in arguments about institutions and institutionalization, that we find a great variety of central concepts and the most intense contests about promising conceptualizations, an inevitable condition that strikes many as a simple case of conceptual confusion.

The quality of focused theory frames depends critically on the judicious choice of the central concepts. Concepts that articulate well with the envisioned causal and structural hypotheses are the secret of success of the best theory frames. Max Weber's triad of rational-legal, charismatic, and traditional systems of domination illustrates this very well.

Two final pragmatic rules of thumb for theory construction derive from the particular difficulties of identifying theoretically useful empirical regularities at the microlevel of individual action. It is a fundamental, yet not often recognized insight that the emergence of social structures large and small and their "feedback" effects constrain the variability of individual insight and motivation. This leads to two suggestions: First, structuralist approaches may have a chance to bypass some of the complexities of the subjective space of action. And second, in the search for explanations it may be useful to pay special attention to mesolevel factors.

Structuralist approaches can gain an advantage in two ways (see chapter 8). Some theories, such as the late Peter Blau's work as well as contemporary network theory, leave aside subjective consciousness, confine themselves to structural regularities such as the heterogeneity of membership in a social formation, and relate them to, say, intermarriage rates. This is a limited advantage, but one that does yield interesting results. The second form of the structuralist strategy just focuses on the ways in which more inclusive social structures shape individual attitudes and actions.[5]

---

[5] Beyond that, it is often possible to come to conclusions at the meso- and macrolevel from microlevel assumptions that are roughly right, rather than right in all particulars. Often the behavior of a simple majority or even a significant minority of individual actors is sufficient to permit predictions about social movements or other causal factors involved in revolutions (Skocpol 1979; Goldstone 2003).

Similar constellations offer a remedy for a drawback of probabilistic hypotheses—that they normally cannot predict single or a small number of cases. This is the case if causal conditions and outcomes occur at the same level of analysis. However, if they are located at different levels—if we consider, for instance, a certain degree of popular support or opposition as a partial positive or negative causal condition for a system of rule or a cluster of policies (see, e.g., Brooks and Manza 2007)—this handicap of probabilistic hypotheses vanishes.

The second structuralist route to theory formation brings us to the pragmatic rule of thumb emphasizing the special causal significance of mesolevel social structures and developments (chapters 14 and 15). These are constrained and shaped by more encompassing social phenomena over which they typically have little influence, and they are at the same time causally relevant for microphenomena, which on their part can rarely shape such mesopatterns as formal organizations, associations, or political parties. The mesolevel of social life, then, stands in a doubly asymmetrical causal relation to the macro- and microlevels. This gives it a critical place in many attempts at causal explanation. If a study is confined to a given country or to countries that share important similarities relevant for the investigation, mesolevel factors acquire great relevance because macrofactors are implicitly held constant. Moreover, mesofactors such as parties, unions, and other interest organizations may be decisive even in macrocomparative research if the macrodifferences across countries that were considered prove to make little difference for the issues at hand.

A FINAL NOTE

I have sought to focus my discussion on a variety of analytic tools as well as on a number of pragmatic suggestions. There is a large repertoire of analytic tools that can be used independent of diverse philosophical and metatheoretical positions one may adopt. Most of the analytic tools discussed are relatively neutral vis-à-vis different grand theory frames, such as those focused on power and conflict, on values and legitimation, on purposive rationality, or on cultural templates, and associated with such names as Bates, Bourdieu, Foucault, Giddens, Gramsci, Parsons, or Weingast.

The starting point of my deliberation was the disappointing achievements of empirical social and political theory when measured against the ambitions of a social science modeled after the natural sciences. If there is one point in the ideal of a unity of all science I prefer to hold on to, it is that the fundamentals of valid explanation and conditional prediction are the same across all fields of inquiry. This applies with particular force also to the differences in methodological approach in areas of social science that allow greater or lesser use of quantification than others. Yet while the fundamental standards of validity are the same, it is hard to claim that—with the possible exception of economics—specific areas and modes of social inquiry show significantly greater theoretical achievement than others. If this estimate is roughly correct, one cannot easily point to strategies that promise greater theoretical advance than others.

What, then, emerges from our considerations as reasonable prospects of theoretical advance in the social sciences? The future of empirical social and political theory does not look dismal, even if there is no single grand remedy for the very real difficulties. For the foreseeable future, theory frames with increasing, though still limited theoretical power will probably be the major carriers of advance.

Over time, the interaction among theoretical orientations, empirical evidence, and theory work in the course of empirical research not only can yield plausible and even sturdy local results; but it is also likely to contribute to theoretical generalizations, be that in the form of richer theory frames, by way of specific tested theoretical propositions (including prominently causal mechanism hypotheses), or even in some cases resulting in integrated sets of theorems deserving the label "theory" without qualification. This differs from the old (and false) hope that an accumulation of empirical findings will eventually amount to theoretical knowledge. There are too many directions of possible generalization for that hope to be reasonable. But the guidance of revisable focused theory frames makes reasonable "analytic induction" possible.

REFERENCES

Abbott, Andrew. 2004. *Methods of Discovery: Heuristics for the Social Sciences.* New York: Norton.

Adams, Julia, Elizabeth S. Clemens, and Ann Shola Orloff, eds. 2005. *Remaking Modernity: Politics, History, and Sociology.* Durham, NC: Duke University Press.

Alchian, Armen A., and Harold Demsetz. 1972. "Production, Information Costs, and Economic Organization." *American Economic Review* 62(5):77–95.

Alexander, Gerard. 2002. *The Sources of Democratic Consolidation.* Ithaca, NY: Cornell University Press.

Alexander, Jeffrey C. 1990. "Analytic Debates: Understanding the Relative Autonomy of Culture." In *Culture and Society: Contemporary Debates*, edited by Jeffrey C. Alexander and Steven Seidman, 1–27. Cambridge: Cambridge University Press 1990.

———. 2006. *The Civil Sphere.* New York: Oxford University Press.

Alloy, Lauren, and Lyn Abramson. 1988. "Judgment of Contingency in Depressed and Nondepresssed Students: Sadder but Wiser?" *Journal of Experimental Psychology: General* 108:441–85.

Almond, Gabriel A., and Sidney Verba. 1963. *The Civic Culture: Political Attitudes and Democracy in Five Nations.* Princeton, NJ: Princeton University Press.

———. 1989. *Civic Culture Revisited.* Newbury, CA: Sage.

Alter, Robert. 2004. *Five Books of Moses: A Translation and Commentary.* New York: Norton.

Amsden, Alice. 1989. *Asia's Next Giant: South Korea and Late Industrialization.* New York: Oxford University Press.

———. 2001. *The Rise of "the Rest": Challenges to the West from Late-Industrializing Economies.* New York: Oxford University Press.

Anderson, Benedict. 1983. *Imagined Communities: Reflections on the Origin and Spread of Nationalism.* London: Verso.

Archer, Margaret, Roy Bhaskar, Andrew Collier, Tony Lawson, and Alan Norrie, eds. 1998. *Critical Realism: Essential Readings.* London: Routledge.

Arendt, Hannah, 1963. *Eichmann in Jerusalem: A Report on the Banality of Evil.* New York: Viking Press.

———. 1967. "Truth and Politics." In *Philosophy, Politics and Society*, edited by P. Laslett and W. G. Runciman. 3rd ser. Oxford: Blackwell.

Arensberg, Conrad M., and D. Macgregor. 1942. "Determination of Morale in an Industrial Company." *Applied Anthropology* 1:12–34.

Arthur, W. Brian. 1989. "Competing Technologies and Lock-In by Historical Events." *Economic Journal* 99:116–31.

Asch, Solomon E. 1952. *Social Psychology.* New York: Prentice-Hall.

Axelrod, Robert. 1984. *The Evolution of Cooperation.* New York: Basic Books.

Bacon, Francis. 1620. *Novum Organon.*

Barbalet, J. M. 1998. *Emotion, Social Theory, and Social Structure: A Macro-sociological Approach.* Cambridge: Cambridge University Press.

Barkey, Karen. 2008. *Empire of Difference: The Ottomans in Comparative Perspective.* New York: Cambridge University Press.

Barnard, Chester I. 1938. *The Functions of the Executive.* Cambridge: Harvard University Press.

Barth, Frederik. 1969. *Ethnic Groups and Boundaries: The Social Organization of Cultural Difference.* London: George Allen and Unwin.

Barton, Alan H. 1955. "The Concept of Property Space in Social Research." In *The Language of Social Research*, edited by Paul F. Lazarsfeld and Morris Rosenberg, 40–57. Glencoe IL: Free Press.

Bates, Robert H., Avner Greif, Margaret Levi, Jean-Laurent Rosenthal, and Barry Weingast. 1998. *Analytic Narratives.* Princeton, NJ: Princeton University Press.

Baum, Rainer C. 1981. *The Holocaust and the German Elite: Genocide and National Suicide in Germany 1871–1945.* Totowa, NJ: Rowman and Littlefield; London: Croom and Helm.

Becker, Gary S. 1986. First published in 1976. "The Economic Approach to Human Behavior." In *Rational Choice*, edited by Jon Elster. New York: New York University Press.

Bell, David A. 2007. *The First Total War: Napoleon's Europe and the Birth of Warfare As We Know It.* New York: Houghton Mifflin.

Bellah, Robert N. 2005. "McCarthyism at Harvard." *New York Review of Books* 52(2):42–43.

Ben-David, Joseph. 1971. *The Scientist's Role in Society: A Comparative Study.* Englewood Cliffs, NJ: Prentice-Hall.

Bendix, Reinhard. 1964. *Nation-Building and Citizenship: Studies of Our Changing Social Order.* New York: Wiley.

———. 1978. *Kings or People: Power and the Mandate to Rule.* Berkeley and Los Angeles: University of California Press.

Bendix, Reinhard, and Bennett Berger. 1959. "Images of Society and Problems of Concept Formation in Sociology." In *Symposium on Sociological Theory*, edited by L. Gross. Evanston, IL: Row, Petersen.

Bendix, Reinhard, and Seymour M. Lipset.1966. First published in 1953. *Class, Status, and Power: Social Stratification in Comparative Perspective.* New York: Free Press.

Ben-Ner, Avner, and Louis Putterman, eds. 1998. *Economics, Values, and Organizations.* Cambridge: Cambridge University Press.

Berger, Peter, and Thomas Luckmann. 1967. *The Social Construction of Reality.* New York: Doubleday.

Berkowitz, Leonard. 2000. *Causes and Consequences of Feelings.* Cambridge: Cambridge University Press.

Berlin, Isaiah. 1997. "The Pursuit of the Ideal." In I. Berlin, *The Proper Study of Mankind: An Anthology of Essays*, 1–16 New York: Farrar, Straus and Giroux.

Berman, Harold J. 1983. *Law and Revolution: The Formation of the Western Legal Tradition.* Cambridge: Harvard University Press.

Biersteker, Thomas J., and Cynthia Weber, eds. 1996. *State Sovereignty as Social Construct*. New York: Cambridge University Press.

Black, Donald. 1976. *The Behavior of Law*. New York: Academic Press.

Blake, Judith, and Kingsley Davis. 1964. "Norms, Values, and Sanctions." In *Handbook of Modern Sociology*, edited by Robert E. L. Faris, 456–84. Chicago: Rand McNally & Company.

Blau, Peter M. 1970. "A Formal Theory of Differentiation in Organizations." *American Sociological Review* 35:201–18.

———. 1977. *Inequality and Heterogeneity: A Primitive Theory of Social Structure*. New York: Free Press.

Bott, Elizabeth. 1957. *Family and Social Network: Roles, Norms and External Relationships in Urban Families*. New York: Free Press.

Boudon, Raymond, and François Bourricaud. 1989. "Social Stratification." In *A Critical Dictionary of Sociology*, edited by R. Boudon and F. Bourricaud, selected and translated by Peter Hamilton. Chicago: University of Chicago Press.

Bourdieu, Pierre. 1977. *Outline of a Theory of Practice*. Cambridge: Cambridge University Press.

———. 1984. *Distinction: A Social Critique of the Judgment of Taste*. Cambridge: Harvard University Press.

———. 1990. *The Logic of Practice*. Stanford, CA: Stanford University Press.

———. 1998. *Practical Reason: On the Theory of Action*. Stanford, CA: Stanford University Press.

———. 1999. "Rethinking the State: Genesis and Structure of the Bureaucratic Field." In *State/Culture: State Formation after the Cultural Turn*, edited by George Steinmetz. Ithaca, NY: Cornell University Press.

Bowles, Samuel. 1998. "Endogenous Preferences: The Cultural Consequences of Markets and Other Institutions." *Journal of Economic Literature* 36 (March): 75–111.

Bowles, Samuel, and Herbert Gintis. 1993. "The Revenge of Homo Economicus: Contested Exchange and the Revival of Political Economy." *Journal of Economic Perspectives* 7(1):83–102.

Boyd, Robert, and Peter Richerson. 1985. *Culture and the Evolutionary Process*. Chicago: University of Chicago Press.

Brady, Henry E., and David Collier, eds. 2004. *Rethinking Social Inquiry: Diverse Tools, Shared Standards*. Boulder, CO: Rowman & Littlefield.

Braumoeller, Bear F., and Gary Goertz. 2000. "The Methodology of Necessary Conditions." *American Journal of Political Science* 44:844–58.

Brooks, Clem, and Jeff Manza. 2007. *Why Welfare States Persist: The Importance of Public Opinion in Democracies*. Chicago: University of Chicago Press.

Brown, Richard Harvey. 1987. *Society as Text: Essays on Reason, Ethics, and Reality*. Chicago: University of Chicago Press.

———. 1994. "Rhetoric, Textuality, and the Postmodern Turn in Sociological Theory." In *The Postmodern Turn: New Perspectives on Social Theory*, edited by Steven Seidman, 229–41. Cambridge: Cambridge University Press.

Brubaker, Rogers. 1992. *Citizenship and Nationhood in France and Germany*. Cambridge: Harvard University Press.

Brubaker, Rogers. 1996. *Nationalism Reframed: Nationhood and the National Question in the New Europe.* Cambridge: Cambridge University Press.

———. 2002. "Ethnicity without Groups." *Archives Européennes de Sociologie* 43:163–89.

Brubaker, Rogers, and Frederick Cooper. 2000. "Beyond 'Identity.'" *Theory and Society* 29:1–47.

Brubaker, Rogers, Mara Loveman, and Peter Stamatov. 2004. "Ethnicity as Cognition." *Theory and Society* 33:31–64.

Caldwell, John C. 2006. *Demographic Transition Theory.* Dordrecht, Netherlands: Springer.

Campbell, Donald T. 1975. "'Degrees of Freedom' and the Case Study." *Comparative Political Studies* 8:178–93.

Cantril, Hadley. 1965. *Patterns of Human Concerns.* New Brunswick, NJ: Rutgers University Press.

Cardoso, Fernando Henrique, and Enzo Faletto. 1979. *Dependency and Development in Latin America.* Berkeley and Los Angeles: California University Press.

Castells, Manuel. 1997. *The Power of Identity.* Malden, MA: Blackwell.

Centeno, Miguel Angel. 2002. *Blood and Debt: War and the Nation-State in Latin America.* University Park: Pennsylvania State University Press.

Chambliss, William J. 1966. "The Deterrent Influence of Punishment." *Crime and Punishment* 12:70–75.

———. 1967. "Types of Deviance and the Effectiveness of Legal Sanctions." *Wisconsin Law Review* 1967:703–19.

Chorev, Nitsan. 2007. *Remaking U.S. Trade Policy: From Protectionism to Globalization.* Ithaca, NY: Cornell University Press.

Coale, Ansley J., and Susan C. Watkins, eds. 1986. *The Decline of Fertility in Europe.* Princeton, NJ: Princeton University Press.

Coase, Ronald H. 1937. "The Nature of the Firm." *Economica* 4:386–405.

Coch L., and J.R.P. French, Jr. 1948. "Overcoming Resistance to Change." *Human Relations* 1:512–32.

Coleman, James S. 1961. *The Adolescent Society.* New York: Free Press of Glencoe.

———. 1990. *Foundations of Social Theory.* Cambridge: Harvard University Press.

Collier, Ruth Berins, and David Collier. 1991. *Shaping the Political Arena: Critical Junctures, the Labor Movement, and Regime Dynamics in Latin America.* Princeton, NJ: Princeton University Press.

Collins, Randall. 1981. "On the Micro-Foundations of Macro-Sociology." *American Journal of Sociology* 86:984–1014.

———. 1988. *Theoretical Sociology.* San Diego, CA: Harcourt Brace Jovanovich.

———. 1990. "Stratification, Emotional Energy, and the Transient Emotions." In *Research Agendas in the Sociology of Emotions*, edited by Th. D. Kermper, 27–75. Albany: State University of New York Press.

———. 2004. *Interaction Ritual Chains.* Princeton, NJ: Princeton University Press.

Commons, John R. 1931. "Institutional Economics." *American Economic Review* 21(4):648–57.

Converse, Philip E. 1964. "The Nature of Belief Systems in Mass Publics." In *Ideology and Discontent*, edited by D. E. Apter, 206–61. New York: Free Press.

Coser, Lewis A. 1956. *The Functions of Social Conflict*. Glencoe, IL.: Free Press.

Cutright, Phillips. 1963. "National Political Development: Measurement and Analysis." *American Sociological Review* 28 (April).

Cyert, Richard M., and James G. March. 1963. *A Behavioral Theory of the Firm*. Englewood Cliffs, NJ: Prentice-Hall.

Dahrendorf, Ralf. 1959. *Class and Class Conflict in Industrial Society*. Stanford, CA: Stanford University Press.

Damasio, Antonio. 1994. *Descartes' Error*. New York: Putnam.

———. 2003. *Looking for Spinoza: Joy, Sorrow, and the Feeling Mind*. Orlando, FL: Harcourt Books.

De Quervais, D., U. Fischbacher, V. Treyer, M. Schellhammer, U. Schnyder, A. Buck, and E. Fehr. 2004. "The Neural Basis of Altruistic Punishment." *Science* 305:1254–58.

Derrida, Jacques. 1981. *Positions*. Chicago: University of Chicago Press.

De Schweinitz, Karl. 1964. *Industrialization and Democracy: Economic Necessities and Political Possibilities*. New York: Free Press.

Dion, Douglas. 1998. "Evidence and Inference in Comparative Case Study." *Comparative Politics* 30:127–46.

Dirks, Nicholas B. 2001. *Castes of Mind: Colonialism and the Making of Modern India*. Princeton, NJ: Princeton University Press.

Dror, Yeheskel. 1959. "Law and Social Change." *Tulane Law Review* 33:749–801.

Durkheim, Emile. 1950. First published in 1895. *The Rules of Sociological Method*. New York: Free Press.

———. 1951. First published in 1897. *Suicide*. New York: Free Press.

———. 1954. First published in 1912. *The Elementary Forms of Religious Life*. New York: Free Press.

———. 1961. First published in 1903. *Moral Education*. New York: Free Press.

———. 1964. First published in 1893. *The Division of Labor in Society*. New York: Free Press.

Durkheim, Emile, and Marcel Mauss. 1903. "De quelques formes primitives de classification." *Année Sociologique* 6:1–72.

Easterlin, Richard A. 1974. "Does Economic Growth Improve the Human Lot? Some Empirical Evidence." In *Nations and Households in Economic Growth: Essays in Honor of Moses Abramovitz*, edited by P. A. David and M. W. Reder, 89–125. New York: Academic Press.

Eckstein, Harry. 1975. "Case Studies and Theory in Political Science." In *Handbook of Political Science*, vol. 7, edited by Fred Greenstein and Nelson W. Polsby, 79–138. Reading, MA: Addison-Wesley.

Eisenstadt, S. N. 1963. *The Political System of Empires*. New York: Free Press.

———. 1964. "Institutionalization and Change." *American Sociological Review* 29:235–67.

———. 1998. "The Construction of Collective Identities in Latin America: Beyond the European Nation State Model." In *Constructing Collective Identities and Shaping Public Spheres: Latin American Paths*, edited by Luis Roniger and M. Snaijder. Brighton: Sussex Academic Press.

——. 2003. *Comparative Civilizations and Multiple Modernities.* 2 vols. Leiden: Brill.

Elster, Jon. 1982. "Marxism, Functionalism, and Game Theory." *Theory and Society* 11:453–82.

——. 1983. "Sour Grapes." In J. Elster, *Sour Grapes: Studies in the Subversion of Rationality*, 109–140. Cambridge: Cambridge University Press.

——. 1989a. *Nuts and Bolts for the Social Sciences.* Cambridge: Cambridge University Press.

——. 1989b. *The Cement of Society.* Cambridge: Cambridge University Press.

——. 1998. "A Plea for Mechanisms." In *Social Mechanisms: An Analytical Approach to Social Theory*, edited by Peter Hedström and Richard Swedberg, 45–73. Cambridge: Cambridge University Press.

——. 1999. *Alchemies of the Mind: Rationality and the Emotions.* Cambridge: Cambridge University Press.

——, ed. 1986. *Rational Choice.* New York: New York University Press.

Evans, Peter B. 1979. *Dependent Development: The Alliance of Multinational, State, and Local Capital in Brazil.* Princeton, NJ: Princeton University Press.

——. 1995. *Embedded Autonomy: States and Industrial Transformation.* Princeton, NJ: Princeton University Press.

——. 2005. "Harnessing the State: Rebalancing Mechanisms for Monitoring and Motivation." In *States and Development: Historical Antecedents of Stagnation and Advance*, edited by Matthew Lange and Dietrich Rueschemeyer, 26–47. New York: Palgrave Macmillan.

Evans, Peter B., and James Rauch. 1999. "Bureaucracy and Growth: A Cross-National Analysis of the Effects of Weberian State Structures on Economic Growth." *American Sociological Review* 64:748–65.

Evans, Peter B., Dietrich Rueschemeyer, and Theda Skocpol, eds. 1985. *Bringing the State Back In.* Cambridge: Cambridge University Press.

Evans, Peter B., and John D. Stephens. 1988. "Development and the World Economy." In *Handbook of Sociology*, edited by N. Smelser. Newbury Park, CA: Sage.

Ewing, Sally. 1987. "Formal Justice and the Spirit of Capitalism: Max Weber's Sociology of Law." *Law and Society Review* 21(3):487–512.

Fehr, Ernst, and U. Fischbacher. 2002. "Crime in the Lab: Detecting Social Interaction." *European Economic Review* 46:858–69.

——. 2004. "Social Norms and Human Cooperation." *Trends in Cognitive Science* 8:185–90.

Fehr, Ernst, and Simon Gächter. 2002. "Altruistic Punishment in Humans." *Nature* 415:137–40.

Festinger, Leon. 1950. "Informal Social Communication." *Psychological Review* 57:271–82.

——. 1954. "A Theory of Social Comparison Processes." *Human Relations* 7:117–40.

Finer, S. E. 1966. "Introduction." In *Vilfredo Pareto: Sociological Writings*, 1–91. New York: Praeger.

Firth, Raymond. 1936. *We, the Tikopia: A Sociological Study of Kinship in Primitive Polynesia.* New York: American Book Co.

Freidson, Eliot. 1970. *Profession of Medicine: A Study of the Sociology of Applied Knowledge.* New York: Dodd, Mead & Co.

———. 1988. *Professional Powers: A Study of the Institutionalization of Formal Knowledge.* Chicago: University of Chicago Press.

Friedan, Betty. 1963. *The Feminine Mystique.* New York: Norton.

Friedman, Lawrence M., and Stewart Macaulay. 1969, 1977. *Law and the Behavioral Sciences.* 1st and 2nd eds. Indianapolis: Bobbs-Merrill.

Fuchs, Stephan. 2001. *Against Essentialism.* Cambridge: Harvard University Press.

Galbraith, John Kenneth. 1998. First published in 1958. *The Affluent Society.* Boston: Houghton Mifflin.

Gallie, W. B. 1955–56. "Essentially Contested Concepts." *Proceedings of the Aristotelian Society* 56:167–98.

Garrett, Geoffrey. 2001. "Globalization and Government Spending around the World." *Studies in Comparative International Development* 35(4):3–29.

Geertz, Clifford. 1973. *The Interpretation of Cultures.* New York: Basic Books.

———. 1983. *Local Knowledge.* New York: Basic Books.

———, ed. 1963. *Old Societies and New States: The Quest for Modernity in Asia and Africa.* New York: Free Press.

Geiger, Theodor. 1932. *Die soziale Schichtung des deutschen Volkes.* Stuttgart.

———. 1964. First published in 1947. *Vorstudien zu einer Soziologie des Rechts.* Neuwied: Luchterhand.

Gellner, Ernest. 1983. *Nations and Nationalism.* London: Oxford University Press.

George, Alexander L., and Andrew Bennett. 2005. *Case Studies and Theory Development in the Social Sciences.* Cambridge: MIT Press.

Gerring, John. 2007. *Case Study Research: Principles and Practice.* New York: Cambridge University Press.

Giddens, Anthony. 1973. *The Class Structure of Advanced Societies.* New York: Harper and Row.

———. 1979. *Central Problems in Social Theory: Action, Structure, and Contradiction in Social Analysis.* London: Macmillan.

———. 1984. *The Constitution of Society: An Outline of the Theory of Structuration.* Cambridge: Polity Press.

———. 1987. *The Nation-State and Violence.* Berkeley and Los Angeles: University of California Press.

———. 1991. *Modernity and Self-identity: Self and Society in the Late Modern Age.* Cambridge: Polity.

Glatzer, Miguel, and Dietrich Rueschemeyer. 2005. "Conclusion: Politics Matters." In *Globalization and the Future of Welfare States,* edited by M. Glatzer and D. Rueschemeyer, 203–25. Pittsburgh, PA: Pittsburgh University Press.

Goblot, Edmond. 1967. First published in 1925. *La Barrière et le Niveau. Etude Sociologique sur la Bourgeoisie Française.* Paris: Presses Universitaires de France.

Goertz, Gary. 2006. *Social Science Concepts: A User's Guide*. Princeton, NJ: Princeton University Press.

Goertz, Gary, and James Mahoney. 2005. "Two-Level Theories and Fuzzy-Set Analysis." *Sociological Methods and Research* 33(4):497–538.

Goffman, Erving. 1967. *Interaction Ritual*. New York: Doubleday.

Goldstone, Jack A. 2003. "Comparative Historical Research and Knowledge Accumulation in the Study of Revolutions." In *Comparative Historical Analysis in the Social Sciences*, edited by James Mahoney and Dietrich Rueschemeyer, 41–90. New York: Cambridge University Press.

Goldthorpe, John H. 1997. "Current Issues in Macrosociology: A Debate on Methodological Issues." *Comparative Social Research* 16:1–26.

Goodin, Robert E., ed. 1996. *The Theory of Institutional Design*. Cambridge: Cambridge University Press.

Goodwin, Jeff, and James M. Jasper, eds.. 2004. *Rethinking Social Movements: Structure, Meaning, and Emotion*. Lanham, MD: Rowman & Littlefield.

Gorski, Philip S. 2004. "The Poverty of Deductivism: A Constructive Realist Model of Sociological Explanation." *Sociological Methodology* 34:1–33.

———. 2007. "Social 'Mechanisms' and Comparative Historical Sociology: A Critical Realist Proposal." Unpublished manuscript.

Gould, Roger V. 1991. "Multiple Networks and Mobilization in the Paris Commune, 1871." *American Sociological Review* 56:216–29.

———. 2003. "Uses of Network Tools in Comparative Historical Research." In *Comparative Historical Analysis in the Social Sciences*, edited by James Mahoney and Dietrich Rueschemeyer, 241–69. New York: Cambridge University Press.

Gramsci, Antonio. 1975. Written 1928–37. *Prison Notebooks*. New York: Columbia University Press.

Granovetter, Mark. 1985. "Economic Action and Social Structure: The Problem of Embeddedness." *American Journal of Sociology* 91:481–510.

Greenfeld, Liah. 1992. *Nationalism: Five Roads to Modernity*. Cambridge: Harvard University Press.

Gutierrez, Natividad. 1999. *Nationalist Myths and Ethnic Identities: Indigenous Intellectuals and the Mexican State*. Lincoln: University of Nebraska Press.

Habermas, Jürgen. 1984. *The Theory of Communicative Action*. 2 vols. Boston: Beacon Press.

Haggard, Stephan, and Robert R. Kaufman. 2008. *Development, Democracy, and Welfare States: Latin America, East Asia, and Eastern Europe*. Princeton, NJ: Princeton University Press.

Hall, Peter A. 2003. "Aligning Ontology and Methodology in Comparative Research." In *Comparative Historical Analysis in the Social Sciences*, edited by James Mahoney and Dietrich Rueschemeyer, 373–404. New York: Cambridge University Press.

———, ed. 1989. *The Political Power of Economic Ideas: Keynesianism across Nations*. Princeton, NJ: Princeton University Press.

Hall, Peter A., and David Soskice, eds. 2001. *Varieties of Capitalism: The Institutional Foundations of Comparative Advantage*. Oxford: Oxford University Press.

Hall, Peter A., and Rosemary C. R. Taylor. 1996. "Political Science and the Three New Institutionalisms." *Political Studies* 44:936–57.

Hannerz, Ulf. 1969. *Soulside: Inquiries into Ghetto Culture and Community.* New York: Columbia University Press.

Hardin, Garret. 1968. "The Tragedy of the Commons." *Science* 162(3859): 1243–48.

Hardin, Russell. 1982. *Collective Action.* Baltimore, MD: Johns Hopkins University Press.

Harrington, Brooke, and Gary Alan Fine. 2000. "Opening the Black Box: Small Groups and Twenty-First Century Sociology." *Social Psychology Quarterly* 63: 312–23.

Hatch, D. L. 1948. "Changes in the Structure and Function of a Rural New England Community since 1900." Ph.D. diss., Harvard University.

Hayek, Friedrich A. von. 1939. *Freedom and the Economic System.* Public Policy Pamphlet No. 29. Chicago: University of Chicago Press.

———. 1945. "The Use of Knowledge in Society." *American Economic Review* 35:519–30.

Hechter, Michael, and Elizabeth Borland. 2001. "National Self-Determination: The Emergence of an International Norm." In *Social Norms,* edited by Michael Hechter and Karl-Dieter Opp, 186–233. New York: Russell Sage Foundation.

Hechter, Michael, and Karl-Dieter Opp, eds. 2001. *Social Norms.* New York: Russell Sage Foundation.

Hechter, Michael, and Christine Horne, eds. 2003. *Theories of Social Order: A Reader.* Stanford, CA: Stanford University Press.

Heckathorn, D. D. 1989. "Collective Action and the Second-Order Free-Rider Problem." *Rationality and Society* 1:78–100.

Hedström, Peter. 2005. *Dissecting the Social: On the Principles of Analytical Sociology.* Cambridge: Cambridge University Press.

Hedström, Peter, and Richard Swedberg. 1998. *Social Mechanisms: An Analytical Approach to Social Theory.* Cambridge: Cambridge University Press.

Hirschman, Albert O. 1977. *The Passions and the Interests: Political Arguments against Capitalism before Its Triumph.* Princeton, NJ: Princeton University Press.

———. 1982. *Shifting Involvements: Private Interest and Public Action.* Princeton, NJ: Princeton University Press.

Hirschman, Charles. 1994. "Why Fertility Changes." *Annual Review of Sociology* 20:203–33.

Hobsbawn, Eric J. 1990. *Nations and Nationalism since 1780: Programme, Myth, Reality.* Cambridge: Cambridge University Press.

Hochschild, Arlie Russell. 1983. *The Managed Heart: Commercialization of Human Feeling.* Berkeley and Los Angeles: University of California Press.

Hoebel, E. Adamson. 1940. *The Political Organization and Law-Ways of the Comanche Indians.* Memoirs of the American Anthropological Association, no. 54. Menasha, WI: American Anthropological Association.

Hofstätter, Peter R. 1957. *Gruppendynamik: Kritik der Massenpsychologie.* Hamburg: Rowohlt's Deutsche Enzyklopädie.

Homans, George C. 1950. *The Human Group.* New York: Harcourt.

Horkheimer, Max, and Theodore W. Adorno. 1972. First published in 1944. *Dialectic of the Enlightenment.* New York: Seabury Press.

Horne, Thomas A. 1978. *The Social Thought of Bernard Mandeville: Virtue and Commerce in Early Seventeenth Century England.* New York: Columbia University Press.

Horwitz, Morton J. 1977. *The Transformation of American Law, 1780–1860.* Cambridge: Harvard University Press.

———. 1992. *The Transformation of American Law, 1870–1960.* Oxford: Oxford University Press.

Huber, Evelyne, and John D. Stephens. 2001. *Development and Crisis of the Welfare State: Parties and Policies in Global Markets.* Chicago: University of Chicago Press.

Huizinga, Johan. 1970. First published in 1944. *Homo Ludens: A Study of the Play Element in Culture.* New York: Harper & Row.

Hume, David. 1985. Pt. 1 first published in 1742. *Essays, Moral, Political, and Literary.* Indianapolis IN: Liberty Classics.

Inglehart, Ronald. 1997. *Modernization and Postmodernization: Cultural, Economic and Political Change in 43 Societies.* Princeton, NJ: Princeton University Press.

Inkeles, Alex, and David H. Smith. 1974. *Becoming Modern: Individual Change in Six Developing Countries.* Cambridge: Harvard University Press.

Ireland, Patrick. 1994. *The Policy Challenge of Ethnic Diversity: Immigrant Politics in France and Switzerland.* Cambridge: Harvard University Press.

Isaacson, Walter. 2007. *Einstein: His Life and Universe.* New York: Simon & Schuster.

Isen, Alice M. 1993. "Positive Affect and Decision Making." In *Handbook of Emotions,* edited by M. Lewis and J. M. Haviland, 261–77. New York: Guilford Press.

Islamoglu, Huri, and Peter C. Perdue. 2001. "Introduction." Special issue on Shared Histories of Modernity in China and the Ottoman Empire. *Journal of Early Modern History* 5:4.

James, Harold. 1989. "What is Keynesian about Deficit Financing? The Case of Interwar Germany." In *The Political Power of Economic Ideas: Keynesianism across Nations,* edited by Peter A. Hall, 231–62. Princeton, NJ: Princeton University Press.

Jansen, Robert. 2007. "Resurrection and Reappropriation: Political Uses of Historical Figures in Comparative Perspective." *American Journal of Sociology* 112:953–1007.

Jasso, Guillermina. 2004. "The Tripartite Structure of Social Science Analysis." *Sociological Theory* 22(3):401–31.

Jenkins, Richard. 1997. *Rethinking Ethnicity: Arguments and Explorations.* Thousand Oaks, CA: Sage.

Kalberg, Stephen. 1994. *Max Weber's Comparative Historical Sociology.* Chicago: University of Chicago Press.

Kastoryano, Riva. 2002. *Negotiating Identities: States and Immigrants in France and Germany.* Princeton, NJ: Princeton University Press.

Katz, Elihu, and Paul F. Lazarsfeld. 1955. *Personal Influence: The Part Played by People in the Flow of Mass Communication*. New York: Free Press of Glencoe.

Katznelson, Ira. 1981. *City Trenches: Urban Politics and the Patterning of Social Class in the United States*. New York: Pantheon.

———. 1986. "Working-Class Formation: Constructing Cases and Comparisons." In *Working-Class Formation: Nineteenth-Century Patterns in Western Europe and the United States*, edited by Ira Katznelson and Aristide R. Zolberg, 3–41. Princeton, NJ: Princeton University Press.

Katznelson, Ira, and Barry R. Weingast, eds. 2005. *Preferences and Situations: Points of Intersection between Historical and Rational Choice Institutionalism*. New York: Russell Sage Foundation.

Kelley, Harold H., and John W. Thibaut. 1954. "Experimental Studies of Group Problem Solving and Process." In *Handbook of Social Psychology*, edited by Gardner Lindzey, 735–85. Cambridge, MA: Addison Wesley.

Kemper, Theodore D. 1978. *A Social Interactionist Theory of Emotions*. New York: Wiley.

———. 1984. "Power, Status, and Emotions: A Sociological Contribution to a Psychophysiological Domain." In *Approaches to Emotions*, edited by K. Scherer and P. Ekman, 369–83. Hillsdale, NJ: Lawrence Erlbaum.

Kertzer, David. 1988. *Ritual, Politics, and Power*. New Haven, CT: Yale University Press.

Kertzer, David, and Dominique Arel. 2002. "Censuses, Identity Formation, and the Struggle for Political Power." In *Census and Identity: The Politics of Race, Ethnicity, and Language in National Censuses*, edited by David Kertzer and Dominique Arel, 1–38. New York: Cambridge University Press.

Keynes, John Maynard. 1936. *The General Theory of Employment, Interest and Money*. London: Macmillan.

King, Gary, Robert O. Keohane, and Sidney Verba. 1994. *Designing Social Inquiry. Scientific Inference in Qualitative Research*. Princeton, NJ: Princeton University Press.

Kitschelt, Herbert, Peter Lange, Gary Marks, and John D. Stephens, eds. 1999. *Continuity and Change in Contemporary Capitalism*. Cambridge: Cambridge University Press.

Knight, Jack. 1992. *Institutions and Social Conflict*. New York: Cambridge University Press.

Kohli, Atul. 2004. *State-Directed Development: Political Power and Industrialization in the Global Periphery*. New York: Cambridge University Press.

Kohn, Melvin L. 1969. *Class and Conformity: A Study in Values*. Homewood, IL: Dorsey Press.

Kohn, Melvin L., and Carmi Schooler. 1983. *Work and Personality: An Inquiry into the Impact of Social Stratification*. Norwood, NJ: Ablex Pub. Corp.

Kohn, Melvin L., et al. 1990. "Position in the Class Structure and Psychological Functioning in the United States, Japan, and Poland." *American Journal of Sociology* 95(4):964–1008.

Korpi. Walter. 1983. *The Democratic Class Struggle*. London: Routledge and Kegan Paul.

Krasner, Stephen D. 1978. *Defending the National Interest: Raw Materials Investments and U.S. Foreign Policy*. Princeton, NJ: Princeton University Press.

Krasner, Stephen D. 1984. "Approaches to the State: Alternative Conceptions and Historical Dynamics." *Comparative Politics* 16:223–46.

Kreps, David M. 1990. "Corporate Culture and Economic Theory." In *Perspectives in Positive Political Economy*, edited by J. Alt and K. Shepsle. 90–142. New York: Cambridge University Press.

Krugman, Paul. 1991. "History and Industry Location: The Case of the Manufacturing Belt." *American Economic Review* 81(2):80–83.

Kuznets, Simon. 1955. "Economic Growth and Income Inequality." *American Economic Review* 45:1–28.

Lange, Matthew. 2005." The Rule of Law and Development: A Weberian Framework of States and State-Society Relations." In *States and Development: Historical Antecedents of Stagnation and Advance*, edited by M. Lange and D. Rueschemeyer, 48–65. New York: Palgrave Macmillan.

Lange, Matthew, and Dietrich Rueschemeyer. 2005. "States and Development: What Insights Did We Gain?" In *States and Development: Historical Antecedents of Stagnation and Advance*, edited by M. Lange and D. Rueschemeyer, 239–58. New York: Palgrave Macmillan.

Lasswell, Harold D. 1936. *Politics: Who Gets What, When and How?* New York: McGraw Hill.

Laumann, Edward O., et al. 1994. *The Social Organization of Sexuality: Sexual Practices in the United States*. Chicago: University of Chicago Press.

Le Bon, Gustave. 2002. First published in 1895. *The Crowd: A Study of the Popular Mind*. Mineola, NY: Dover Publications.

Lenski, Gerhard E. 1966. *Power and Privilege: A Theory of Social Stratification*. New York: McGraw-Hill.

Levi, Margaret. 2005. "Inducing Inferences within Organizations: The Case of Unions." In *Preferences and Situations: Points of Intersection between Historical and Rational Choice Institutionalism*, edited by Ira Katznelson and Barry R. Weingast, 219–46. New York: Russell Sage Foundation.

Levy, Marion J., Jr. 1966. *Modernization and the Structure of Societies*. Princeton, NJ: Princeton University Press.

Lewin, Kurt. 1947. "Group Decision and Social Change." In *Readings in Social Psychology*, edited by Th. H. Newcomb and E. L. Hartley, 330–44. New York: Henry Holt.

Lewin, Kurt, R. Lippitt, and R. White. 1939. "Patterns of Aggressive Behavior in Experimentally Created 'Social Climates.'" *Journal of Social Psychology* 10:271–99.

Lewis, David. 1986. *Philosophical Papers*. Vol. 2. Oxford: Oxford University Press.

Lewis-Beck, Michael, Alan Bryman, and Ti Futing Liao, eds. 2003. *Encyclopedia of Social Science Research*. 3 vols. Newbury Park, CA: Sage.

Lichbach, Mark Irving. 1995. *The Rebel's Dilemma*. Ann Arbor: University of Michigan Press.

———. 1996. *The Cooperator's Dilemma*. Ann Arbor: University of Michigan Press.

Lipset, Seymour M. 1959. "Some Social Requisites of Democracy: Economic Development and Political Legitimacy." *American Political Science Review* 53:69–105. Reprinted in Lipset 1963.

———. 1963. *Political Man: The Social Bases of Politics*. Garden City, NY: Doubleday Anchor Books.

Lipset, Seymour M., Martin Trow, and James Coleman. 1956. *Union Democracy: What Makes Democracy Work in Unions and Other Organizations?* Glencoe, IL: Free Press.

Loveman, Mara. 2005. "The Modern State and the Primitive Accumulation of Symbolic Power." *American Journal of Sociology* 110:1651–83.

Lukes, Steven. 1967. "Alienation and Anomie." In *Philosophy, Politics and Society*, 3rd ser., edited by Peter Laslett and W. G. Runciman, 134–56. Oxford: Blackwell's.

———. 1974. *Power: A Radical View*. London: Macmillan.

Machiavelli, Niccolò. 1996. First published in 1531. *Discourses on Livy*. Translated by H. C. Mansfield and N. Tarcov. Chicago: University of Chicago Press.

Mahoney, James. 1999. "Nominal, Ordinal, and Narrative Appraisal in Macrocausal Analysis." *American Journal of Sociology* 104:1154–96.

———. 2000. "Path Dependence in Historical Sociology." *Theory and Society* 29:507–48.

———. 2001a. *The Legacies of Liberalism: Path Dependence and Political Regimes in Central America*. Baltimore, MD: Johns Hopkins University Press.

———. 2001(b). "Beyond Correlational Analysis: Recent Innovations in Theory and Method." *Sociological Forum* 16(3):575–93.

———. 2003. "Strategies of Causal Assessment in Comparative Historical Analysis." In *Comparative Historical Analysis in the Social Sciences*, edited by James Mahoney and Dietrich Rueschemeyer, 337–72. New York: Cambridge University Press.

———. 2004. "Revisiting General Theory in Historical Sociology." *Social Forces* 83(2):459–89.

———. 2005. "Combining Institutionalisms: Liberal Choices and Political Trajectories in Central America." In *Preferences and Situations: Points of Intersection between Historical and Rational Choice Institutionalism*, edited by Ira Katznelson and Barry Weingast, 331–33. New York: Russell Sage Foundation.

———. 2008. "Toward a Unified Theory of Causation." *Comparative Political Studies* 41(4/5):412–36.

———. Forthcoming. "Colonialism and Development: Spanish America in Comparative Perspective." Unpublished manuscript, Northwestern University.

Mahoney, James, and Gary Goertz. 2004. "The Possibility Principle: Choosing Negative Cases in Comparative Research. *American Political Science Review* 98(4):653–69.

Mahoney, James, Erin Kimball, and Kendra L. Koivu. 2009. "The Logic of Historical Explanation in the Social Sciences." *Comparative Political Studies* 42:114–46.

Mahoney, James, and Dietrich Rueschemeyer. 2003. *Comparative Historical Analysis in the Social Sciences*. Cambridge: Cambridge University Press.

Mahoney, James, and Daniel Schensul. 2006. "Historical Context and Path Dependence." In *The Oxford Handbook of Contextual Political Analysis*, edited by Robert Goodin and Charles Tilly, 454–71. Oxford: Oxford University Press.

Malinowski, Bronislaw. 1948. *Magic, Science, and Religion*. Glencoe, IL: Free Press.

Mallon, Florencia. 1995. *Peasant and Nation: The Making of Postcolonial Mexico and Peru*. Berkeley and Los Angeles: University of California Press.

Mandeville, Bernard de. 1988. First published in 1714. *The Fable of the Bees or Private Vices, Publick Benefits*. Indianapolis: Liberty Fund.

Mann, Michael. 1984. "The Autonomous Power of the States: Its Origins, Mechanisms, and Results." *European Journal of Sociology* 25:185–213.

———. 1986. *The Sources of Social Power*. Vol. 1. *A History of Power from the Beginning to AD 1760*. Cambridge: Cambridge University Press.

———. 1988. *States, War, and Capitalism: Studies in Political Sociology*. New York: Blackwell.

———. 1993. *The Sources of Social Power*. Vol. 2. *The Rise of Classes and Nation States, 1760–1914*. Cambridge: Cambridge University Press.

Mannheim, Karl. 1936. *Ideology and Utopia*. New York: Harcourt.

———. 1940. *Man and Society in an Age of Reconstruction*. New York: Harcourt, Brace & Co.

———. 1952. First published in 1928. "The Problem of Generations." In Karl Mannheim, *Essays on the Sociology of Knowledge*, 276–322. New York: Oxford University Press.

March, James G., and Johan P. Olsen. 1975. *Ambiguity and Choice in Organizations*. Bergen, Norway: Universitetsforlaget.

———. 1984. "The New Institutionalism: Organizational Factors in Political Life." *American Political Science Review* 78(3):734–49.

Marx, Anthony W. 1998. *Making Race and Nation: A Comparison of the United States, South Africa, and Brazil*. Cambridge: Cambridge University Press.

Massell, Gregory J. 1974. *The Surrogate Proletariat: Moslem Women and Revolutionary Strategies in Soviet Central Asia, 1919–1929*. Princeton, NJ: Princeton University Press.

McAdam, Douglas, John D. McCarthy, and Mayer N. Zald. 1988. "Social Movements." In *Handbook of Sociology*, edited by Neil J. Smelser, 695–737. Newbury Park, CA: Sage Publications.

McAdam, Douglas, Sidney Tarrow, and Charles Tilly. 1997. "Toward an Integrated Perspective on Social Movements and Revolution." In *Comparative Politics: Rationality, Culture, and Structure*, edited by Mark Irving Lichbach and Alan S. Zuckerman, 142–73. New York: Cambridge University Press.

———. 2001. *Dynamics of Contention*. Cambridge: Cambridge University Press.

Mead, George Herbert. 1934. *Mind, Self and Society*. Chicago: University of Chicago Press.

Merton, Robert K. 1945. "Sociological Theory." *American Journal of Sociology* 50:462–73.

———. 1948. "Discussion" (of T. Parsons, "The Position of Sociological Theory"). *American Sociological Review* 13:164–68.

———. 1968a. "On Sociological Theories of the Middle Range." In R. K. Merton, *Social Theory and Social Structure*, 39–72. Enlarged ed. New York: Free Press.

———. 1968b. "The Bearing of Sociological Theory on Empirical Research." In R. K. Merton, *Social Theory and Social Structure*, 139–55. Enlarged ed. New York: Free Press.

———. 1968c. First version written in 1948. "Manifest and Latent Functions." In R. K. Merton, *Social Theory and Social Structure*, 73–138. Enlarged ed. New York: Free Press.

———. 1968d. First published in 1941. "Karl Mannheim and the Sociology of Knowledge." In R. K. Merton, *Social Theory and Social Structure*, 534–62. Enlarged ed. New York: Free Press.

———. 1968e. First published in 1945. "The Sociology of Knowledge." In R. K. Merton, *Social Theory and Social Structure*, 510–42. Enlarged ed. New York: Free Press.

———. 1968f. First published in 1936. "Puritanism, Piety and Science." In R. K. Merton, *Social Theory and Social Structure*, 628–60. Enlarged ed. New York: Free Press.

———. 1968g. First published in 1938. "Science and the Social Order." In R. K. Merton, *Social Theory and Social Structure*, 591–603. Enlarged ed. New York: Free Press.

———. 1968h. "Continuities in the Theory of Social Structure and Anomie." In R. K. Merton, *Social Theory and Social Structure*, 215–48. Enlarged ed. New York: Free Press.

———. 1968i. "Continuities in the Theory of Reference Groups and Social Structure." In R. K. Merton, *Social Theory and Social Structure*, 335–440. Enlarged ed. New York: Free Press.

———. 1973. *The Sociology of Science: Theoretical and Empirical Investigations*. Chicago: University of Chicago Press.

Merton, Robert K., and Alice S. Rossi. 1968. First published in 1950. "Contributions to the Theory of Reference Group Behavior." In R. K. Merton, *Social Theory and Social Structure*, 279–334. Enlarged ed. New York: Free Press.

Meyer, John. 2000. "Globalization: Sources and Effects on National States and Societies." *International Sociology* 15(2):233–48.

Meyer, John, John Boli, George Thomas, and Francisco Ramirez. 1997. "World Society and the Nation-State." *American Journal of Sociology* 103(1):144–81.

Michels, Robert. 1949. First German publication in 1911. *Political Parties: A Sociological Study of the Oligarchical Tendencies of Modern Democracy*. Glencoe, IL: Free Press.

Migdal, Joel S. 1988. *Strong Societies and Weak States: State-Society Relations and State Capabilities in the Third World*. Princeton, NJ: Princeton University Press.

Mills, C. Wright. 1951. *White Collar*. New York: Oxford University Press.

———. 2000. First published in 1959. *The Sociological Imagination*. New York: Oxford University Press.

Moe, Terry M. 1979. "On the Scientific Status of Rational Models." *American Journal of Political Science* 23(1):215–43.

Moe, Terry M. 1984. "The New Economics of Organization." *American Journal of Political Science* 28(4):739–77.

———. 1995. "The Politics of Structural Choice: Toward a Theory of Public Bureaucracy." In *Organization Theory: From Chester Barnard to the Present and Beyond*, edited by O. E. Williamson, 116–53. New York: Oxford University Press.

———. 2005. "Power and Political Institutions." *Perspectives on Politics* 3(2):215–33.

Moore, Barrington. 1966. *The Social Origins of Dictatorship and Democracy.* Boston: Beacon Press.

———. 2006. "Barrington Moore, Jr.: The Critical Spirit and Comparative Historical Research." Interview with Barrington Moore, Jr., conducted and edited by Richard Snyder. In *Passion, Craft, and Method in Comparative Politics*, edited by Gerardo L. Munck and Richard Snyder, 86–112. Baltimore, MD: Johns Hopkins University Press.

Munck, Gerardo L., and Richard Snyder, eds. 2006. *Passion, Craft, and Method in Comparative Politics.* Baltimore, MD: Johns Hopkins University Press.

Nolan, Patrick, and Gerhard Lenski. 2006. *Human Societies: An Introduction to Macrosociology.* Boulder, CO: Paradigm Publishers.

North, Douglass C. 1990. *Institutions, Institutional Change, and Economic Performance.* Cambridge: Cambridge University Press.

Nozick, Robert. 1974. *Anarchy, State, and Utopia.* New York: Basic Books.

Ober, Josiah. 2008. *Democracy and Knowledge: Innovation and Learning in Classical Athens.* Princeton, NJ: Princeton University Press.

O'Donnell, Guillermo. 1973. *Modernization and Bureaucratic Authoritarianism.* Berkeley, CA: Institute of International Studies.

Olson, Mancur. 1965. *The Logic of Collective Action: Public Goods and the Theory of Groups.* Cambridge: Harvard University Press.

Opp, Karl-Dieter. 1973. *Soziologie im Recht.* Reinbek: Rowohlt.

———. 2001. "Norms." In *International Encyclopedia of the Social and Behavioral Sciences*, edited by Neil J. Smelser and Paul B. Baltes, 10714–20. Amsterdam: Elsevier.

Orloff, Ann. 1996. "Gender in the Welfare State." *Annual Review of Sociology* 22:51–78.

Ortega y Gasset, José. 1993. First published in 1930. *The Revolt of the Masses.* New York: Norton.

Parsons, Talcott. 1937. *The Structure of Social Action.* New York: McGraw-Hill.

———. 1940. "The Motivation of Economic Activities." *Canadian Journal of Economics and Political Science* 6:187–203. Reprinted in Talcott Parsons, *Essays in Sociological Theory*, rev. ed. Glencoe, IL: Free Press, 1954.

———. 1945. "The Present Position and Prospects of Systematic Theory in Sociology." In *Twentieth Century Sociology: A Symposium*, edited by Georges Gurvitch and Wilbert E. Moore. New York: Philosophical Library. Reprinted in Talcott Parsons, *Essays in Sociological Theory*, rev. ed. Glencoe, IL: Free Press 1954, 212–37.

———. 1947. "Introduction." In Max Weber, *The Theory of Social and Economic Organization*, edited by T. Parsons, 1–86. Oxford: Oxford University Press.

———. 1948. "The Position of Sociological Theory." *American Sociological Review* 13:156–64.

———. 1949. "Social Classes and Class Conflict in the Light of Recent Sociological Theory." *American Economic Review*, Papers and Proceedings, 39:16–26. Reprinted in Talcott Parsons, *Essays in Sociological Theory*, rev. ed. Glencoe, IL: Free Press 1954, 323–35.

———. 1950. "The Prospects of Sociological Theory." *American Sociological Review* 15:3–16. Reprinted in Talcott Parsons, *Essays in Sociological Theory*, rev. ed. Glencoe, IL: Free Press 1954, 348–69.

———. 1951. *The Social System*. Glencoe, IL: Free Press.

———. 1967. "An Approach to the Sociology of Knowledge." In T. Parsons, *Sociological Theory and Modern Society*, 139–65. New York: Free Press.

Phillipson, Michael. 1971. "The Paradox of Social Control and the Normality of Crime." In M. Phillipson, *Sociological Aspects of Crime and Delinquency*, chap. 3. London: Routledge and Kegan Paul.

Pierson, Paul. 2000. "Increasing Returns, Path Dependence, and the Study of Politics." *American Political Science Review* 94:251–68.

———. 2001. "The Prospects of Democratic Control in an Age of Big Government." In *Politics at the Turn of the Century*, edited by A. M. Meltzer, J. Weinberger, and M. R. Zinman, 140–61. Lanham, MD: Rowman & Littlefield.

———. 2004. *Politics in Time: History, Institutions, and Social Analysis*. Princeton, NJ: Princeton University Press.

Pitts, Jesse R. 1990. First published in 1964. "French Catholicism and Secular Grace." In *Culture and Society: Contemporary Debates*, edited by Jeffrey C. Alexander and Steven. Seidman, 134–43. Cambridge: Cambridge University Press.

Polanyi, Karl. 1957. First published in 1944. *The Great Transformation*. Boston: Beacon Press.

Portes, Alejandro. 1995. "Economic Sociology and the Sociology of Immigration: A Conceptual Overview." In *The Economic Sociology of Immigration: Essays on Networks, Ethnicity, and Entrepreneurship*, edited by Alejandro Portes, 1–141. New York: Russell Sage Foundation.

Posner, Richard A., and Eric B. Rasmussen. 1999. "Creating and Enforcing Norms, with Special Reference to Sanctions." *International Review of Law and Economics* 19(3):369–82.

Powell, Walter W., and Paul J. DiMaggio, eds. 1991. *The New Institutionalism in Organizational Analysis*. Chicago: University of Chicago Press.

Putterman, Louis, and Randall S. Kroszner, eds. 1996. *The Economic Nature of the Firm: A Reader*. 2nd ed. New York: Cambridge University Press.

Ragin, Charles C. 1987. *The Comparative Method: Moving beyond Qualitative and Quantitative Strategies*. Berkeley and Los Angeles: University of California Press.

———. 2000. *Fuzzy-Set Social Science*. Chicago: University of Chicago Press.

Rawls, John. 1971. *A Theory of Justice*. Cambridge: Harvard University Press.

Reddy, William M. 2001. *The Navigation of Feeling: A Framework for the History of Emotions*. Cambridge: Cambridge University Press.

Reeves, Madeleine. 2008. "Clean Fake: Ambiguous Documents, Registration Regimes and Everyday 'Illegality' in Migrant Moscow." Paper presented during the SSRC Workshop on New Eurasian Lives and Livelihoods, International Conference on Inter-Asian Connections, Dubai, UAE, February 21–24.

Rheinstein, Max, ed. 1954. *Max Weber on Law in Economy and Society*. Cambridge: Harvard University Press.

Richerson, Peter J., and Robert Boyd. 2005. *Not by Genes Alone: How Culture Transformed Human Evolution*. Chicago: University of Chicago Press.

Riecken, Henry W., and George C. Homans. 1954. "Psychological Aspects of Social Structure." In *Handbook of Social Psychology*, edited by Gardner Lindzey, 2:786–829. Cambridge, MA: Addison-Wesley.

Rodrik, Dani. 1998. "Why Do More Open Economies Have Bigger Government?" *Journal of Political Economy* 106:997–1032.

Roemer, John. 1982. *A General Theory of Exploitation and Class*. Cambridge: Harvard University Press.

Roethlisberger, Fritz Jules, and William John Dickson. 1939. *Management and the Worker*. Cambridge: Harvard University Press.

Rohlinger, Deana A. 2007. "American Media and Deliberative Democratic Processes." *Sociological Theory* 25 (2):122–48.

Rothstein, Bo. 1998. *Just Institutions Matter: The Moral and Political Logic of the Universal Welfare State*. Cambridge: Cambridge University Press.

Rueschemeyer, Dietrich. 1958a. *Probleme der Wissenssoziologie*. Doctoral dissertation, University of Cologne, printed for library distribution.

———. 1958b. "Mentalität und Ideologie." In *Soziologie—Das Fischerlexikon*, edited by René König. Frankfurt a.M.: Fischer.

———. 1973. *Lawyers and Their Society: A Comparative Study of the Legal Profession in Germany and the United States*. Cambridge: Harvard University Press.

———. 1976. "Ideology and Modernization." In: *Explorations in General Theory in the Social Sciences: Essays in Honor of Talcott Parsons*, edited by J. J. Loubser, R. C. Baum, A. Effrat, and V. M. Lidz, 736–55. New York: Free Press.

———. 1986. *Power and the Division of Labour*. Cambridge: Polity Press; Stanford, CA: Stanford University Press.

———. 1991. "Different Methods—Contradictory Results? Research on Development and Democracy." *International Journal of Comparative Sociology* 32(1/2):9–38.

———. 2003. "Can One or a Few Cases Yield Theoretical Gains?" In *Comparative Historical Analysis in the Social Sciences*, edited by J. Mahoney and D. Rueschemeyer, 305–36. Cambridge: Cambridge University Press.

———. 2006. "Why and How Ideas Matter." In *Oxford Handbook of Contextual Political Analysis*, edited by Robert E. Goodin and Charles Tilly, 227–52. Oxford: Oxford University Press.

Rueschemeyer, Dietrich, and Marilyn Rueschemeyer. 1990. "Progress in the Distribution of Power: Gender Relations and Women's Movements as a Source of Change." In *Rethinking Progress: Movements, Forces, and Ideas at the End of the 20th Century*, edited by J. C. Alexander and P. Sztompka, 106–22. Boston: Unwin Hyman.

Rueschemeyer, Dietrich, Marilyn Rueschemeyer, and Björn Wittrock. 1998. "Conclusion: Contrasting Patterns of Participation and Democracy." In *Participation and Democracy East and West: Comparisons and Interpretations*, edited by D. Rueschemeyer, M. Rueschemeyer, and B. Wittrock, 266–84. Armonk, NY: M. E. Sharpe.

Rueschemeyer, Dietrich, Evelyne H. Stephens, and John D. Stephens. 1992. *Capitalist Development and Democracy*. Cambridge: Polity Press; Chicago: University of Chicago Press.

Rueschemeyer, Dietrich, and John D. Stephens. 1997. "Comparing Historical Sequences: A Powerful Tool for Causal Analysis." *Comparative Social Research* 16:55–72.

Rueschemeyer, Marilyn. 1982. "The Work Collective: Response and Adaptation in the Structure of Work in the German Democratic Republic." *Dialectical Anthropology*, 155–63.

———. 1982–83. "Integrating Work and Personal Life: An Analysis of Three Work Collectives in the German Democratic Republic." *GDR Monitor*, Winter, 27–47.

Rueschemeyer, Marilyn, and Bradley Scharf. 1986. "Labor Unions in the German Democratic Republic." In *Trade Unions in Communist States*, edited by Alex Pravda and Blair Ruble, 53–84. London: Allen & Unwin.

Samuelson, Paul. 1938. "A Note on the Pure Theory of Consumer's Behaviour." *Economica 5*.

Sanday, Peggy Reeves. 1981. *Female Power and Male Dominance: On the Origins of Sexual Inequality*. Cambridge: Cambridge University Press.

Sawyer, R. Keith. 2001. "Emergence in Society: Contemporary Philosophy of Mind and Some Implications for Sociological Theory." *American Journal of Sociology* 107(3):551–85.

Scheff, Thomas J. 1990. *Microsociology: Discourse, Emotion, and Social Structure*. Boulder, CO: Westview.

———. 1997. *Emotions, the Social Bond, and Human Reality*. New York: Cambridge University Press.

Scheler, Max. 1980. First published in 1926. *Problems of a Sociology of Knowledge*. London: Routledge & Kegan Paul.

Schriewer, Jürgen. 1999. "Vergleich und Erklärung zwischen Kausalität und Komplexität." In *Diskurse und Entwicklungspfade: Der Gesellschaftsvergleich in den Geschichts- und Sozialwissenschaften*, edited by Hartmut Kaelble and Jürgen Schriewer, 53–102. Frankfurt: Campus.

Schumpeter, Joseph A. 1947. *Capitalism, Socialism and Democracy*. New York: Harper and Brothers.

Schwartz, Richard D., and Sonya Orleans. 1967. "On Legal Sanctions." *University of Chicago Law Review* 34:274–300.

Scott, James C. 1998. *Seeing Like a State: How Certain Schemes to Improve the Human Condition Have Failed*. New Haven, CT: Yale University Press.

Scott, W. Richard. 1995. "Symbols and Organizations: From Barnard to the Institutionalists." In *Organization Theory: From Barnard to the Present and Beyond*, edited by O. E. Williamson, 38–55. New York: Oxford University Press.

Seidman, Steven. 1994. "The End of Sociological Theory." In *The Postmodern Turn: New Perspectives on Social Theory*, edited by Steven Seidman, 119–39. Cambridge: Cambridge University Press.

Sen, Amartya. 1973. "Behaviour and the Concept of Preference." *Economica* 40:241–59. Reprinted in Elster 1986.

———. 1999. *Development as Freedom*. New York: Knopf.

———. 2004. "How Does Culture Matter?" In *Culture and Public Action*, edited by Vijayendra Rao and Michael Walton, 37–58. Stanford, CA: Stanford University Press.

Sewell, William H. Jr. 2005. "Refiguring the 'Social' in Social Science: An Interpretivist Manifesto." In W. H. Sewell Jr., *Logics of History: Social Theory and Social Transformation*, 318–72. Chicago: University of Chicago Press.

Sherif, Muzafer. 1935. "A Study of Some Social Factors in Perception." *Archives ofPsychology* 27(187):23–46.

Shils, Edward A. 1950. "Primary Groups in the American Army." In *Continuities in Research Method: Studies in the Scope and Method of "The American Soldier"*, edited by: R. K. Merton and P. F. Lazarsfeld, 16–39. Glencoe, IL: Free Press.

———. 1968. "Charisma." *International Encyclopedia of the Social Sciences*, 2:386–90. New York: Macmillan.

Shils, Edward A., and Maurice Janowitz. 1948. "Cohesion and Disintegration of the Wehrmacht in World War II." *Public Opinion Quarterly* 12:280–315.

Simmel, Georg. 1950. *The Sociology of Georg Simmel*. Edited by Kurt Wolff. Glencoe, IL: Free Press.

———. 1955. First published in 1908. *Conflict: The Web of Group Affiliations*. Glencoe IL: Free Press.

Simon, Herbert A. 1952. "A Formal Theory of Interaction in Social Groups." *American Sociological Review* 17:202–11.

———. 1955. "A Behavioral Model of Rational Choice." *Quarterly Journal of Economics* 69: 99–118.

———. 1957. *Administrative Behavior*. New York: Macmillan.

Skocpol, Theda. 1973. "A Critical Review of Barrington Moore's *Social Origins of Dictatorship and Democracy*." *Politics and Society* 4(1):1–34.

———. 1979. *States and Social Revolutions: A Comparative Analysis of France, Russia, and China*. Cambridge: Cambridge University Press.

———. 1985. "Bringing the State Back In: Strategies of Analysis in Current Research." In *Bringing the State Back In*, edited by Peter B. Evans, Dietrich Rueschemeyer, and Theda Skocpol, 3–37. Cambridge: Cambridge University Press.

Smith, Adam. 1937. First published in 1776. *An Inquiry into the Nature and Causes of the Wealth of Nations*. Cannan edition. New York: Random House Modern Library.

Smith, Anthony. 1986. *The Ethnic Origins of Nations*. Oxford: Blackwell.

———. 1991. *National Identity*. Reno: University of Nevada Press.

Sniderman, Paul, Henry Brody, and Philip Tetlock. 1991. *Reasoning and Choice: Explorations in Political Psychology*. New York: Cambridge University Press.

Snyder, Richard. 2007. "The Human Dimension of Comparative Research." In *Passion, Craft, and Method in Comparative Politics*, edited by Gerardo L. Munck and Richard Snyder, 1–31. Baltimore, MD: Johns Hopkins University Press.

Soifer, Hillel, and Matthias vom Hau, eds. 2008. *Revisiting State Infrastructural Power*. Special issue of *Studies in Comparative International Development* 43 (3–4).

Somers, Margaret. 1994. "The Narrative Constitution of Identity: A Relational and Network Approach." *Theory and Society* 23:605–49.

Sørensen, Aage B. 1998. "Theoretical Mechanisms and the Empirical Study of Social Processes." In *Social Mechanisms: An Analytical Approach to Social Theory*, edited by Peter Hedström and Richard Swedberg, 238–66. Cambridge: Cambridge University Press.

Sørensen, Aage B., Erik O. Wright, John H. Goldthorpe, Dietrich Rueschemeyer, and James Mahoney. 2000. "Symposium on Class Analysis." *American Journal of Sociology* 105 (6) (May): 1523–91.

Sorokin, Pitirim A. 1956. *Fads and Foibles in Modern Sociology and Related Sciences*. Chicago: Regnery.

Starobinski, Jean. 2002. "Rousseau and Revolution." *New York Review of Books*, April 25, 55–60.

Steinmo, Sven, Kathleen Thelen, and Frank Longstreth, eds. 1992. *Historical Institutionalism in Comparative Politics*. Cambridge: Cambridge University Press.

Stephens, John D. 1979a. "Class Formation and Class Consciousness: A Theoretical and Empirical Analysis with Reference to Sweden and Britain." *British Journal of Sociology*, Special Issue: *Current Research on Stratification*, 30(4):389–414.

———. 1979b. *The Transition from Capitalism to Socialism*. London: Macmillan.

Stinchcombe, Arthur L. 1968. *Constructing Social Theories*. New York: Harcourt, Brace & World.

———. 1990. *Information and Organizations*. Berkeley and Los Angeles: University of California Press.

———. 1991. "The Conditions of Fruitfulness of Theorizing about Mechanisms in Social Science." *Philosophy of Social Science* 21:367–87.

———. 1997. "On the Virtues of the Old Institutionalism." *Annual Review of Sociology* 23:1–18.

———. 1998. "Monopolistic Competition, as a Mechanism: Corporations, Universities, and Nation-States in Competitive Fields." In *Social Mechanisms: An Analytical Approach to Social Theory*, edited by Peter Hedström and Richard Swedberg, 267–305. Cambridge: Cambridge University Press.

Strayer, Joseph R. 1970. *On the Medieval Origins of the Modern State*. Princeton, NJ: Princeton University Press.

Sugden, Robert. 1986. *The Economics of Rights, Co-operation, and Welfare*. Oxford: Basil Blackwell.

Sugden, Robert. 1989. "Spontaneous Order." *Journal of Economic Perspectives* 3(4):85–97.

Surowiecki, James. 2004. *The Wisdom of Crowds: Why the Many Are Smarter Than the Few and How Collective Wisdom Shapes Business, Economies, Societies, and Nations.* New York: Doubleday.

Swers, Michele L. 2002. *The Difference Women Make.* Chicago: University of Chicago Press.

Swidler, Ann. 1986. "Culture in Action: Symbols and Strategies." *American Sociological Review* 51:273–86.

Sykes, Gresham M., and David Matza. 1957. "Techniques of Neutralization: A Theory of Delinquency." *American Sociological Review* 22:664–70.

Tarrow, Sidney. 1994. *Power in Movement.* New York: Cambridge University Press.

Taylor, Michael. 1987. *The Possibility of Cooperation.* Cambridge: Cambridge University Press.

Thelen, Kathleen. 1999. "Historical Institutionalism and Comparative Politics." *Annual Review of Political Science* 2:369–404.

———. 2003. "How Institutions Evolve: Insights from Comparative Historical Analysis." In *Comparative Historical Analysis in the Social Sciences*, edited by James Mahoney and Dietrich Rueschemeyer, 208–40. New York: Cambridge University Press.

———. 2004. *How Institutions Evolve: The Political Economy of Skills in Germany, Britain, the United States, and Japan.* New York: Cambridge University Press.

Thomas, William I., and Dorothy Swaine Thomas. 1928. *The Child in America.* New York: Alfred A. Knopf.

Thompson, E. P. 1963. *The Making of the English Working Class.* London: Gollancz.

Thornton, Arland. 2005. *Reading History Sideways: The Fallacy and Enduring Impact of the Developmental Paradigm on Family Life.* Chicago: University of Chicago Press.

Tilly, Charles. 1978. *From Mobilization to Revolution.* Reading, MA: Addison-Wesley.

———. 1985. "War Making and State Making as Organized Crime." In *Bringing the State Back In*, edited by Peter Evans, Dietrich Rueschemeyer, and Theda Skocpol, 169–91. New York: Cambridge University Press,

———. 1995. "To Explain Political Processes." *American Journal of Sociology* 100(6):1594–1610.

———. 1996. "Citizenship, Identity and Social History." In *Citizenship, Identity, and Social History*, edited by Charles Tilly, 1–17. Cambridge: Cambridge University Press.

———. 1997. "Means and Ends of Comparison in Macrosociology." *Comparative Social Research* 16:43–53.

———. 1998. *Durable Inequality.* Berkeley and Los Angeles: University of California Press.

———. 2006. "Why and How History Matters." In *Oxford Handbook of Contextual Political Analysis*, edited by Robert E. Goodin and Charles Tilly, 417–37. Oxford: Oxford University Press.

Torpey, John C. 2000. *The Invention of the Passport: Surveillance, Citizenship, and the State.* New York: Cambridge University Press.

Treiman, Donald J. 1977. *Occupational Prestige in Comparative Perspective.* New York: Academic Press.

Trubek, David M. 1972. "Max Weber on Law and the Rise of Capitalism." *Wisconsin Law Review,* 720–53.

Turner, Jonathan H. 2000. *On the Origins of Human Emotions: A Sociological Inquiry into the Evolution of Human Affect.* Stanford, CA: Stanford University Press.

———. 2002. *Face to Face: Toward a Theory of Interpersonal Behavior.* Stanford, CA: Stanford University Press.

Turner, Jonathan H., and Jan E. Stets. 2005. *The Sociology of Emotions.* New York: Cambridge University Press.

Varshney, Ashutosh. 2001. "Ethnic Conflict and Civil Society: India and Beyond." *World Politics,* April, 362–98.

———. 2002. *Ethnic Conflict and Civic Life: Hindus and Moslems in India.* New Haven, CT: Yale University Press.

vom Hau, Matthias. 2008a. "State Infrastructural Power and Nationalism: Comparative Lessons from Mexico and Argentina." *Studies in Comparative International Development* 43(3–4):334–54.

———. 2008b. "Liberal and Popular Conceptions of Nationhood in Mexico, Argentina, and Peru: Towards an Alternative Typology of Nationalism." Unpublished manuscript.

Wade, Robert. 1990. *Governing the Market: Economic Theory and the Role of Government in Taiwan's Industrialization.* Princeton, NJ: Princeton University Press.

Wallerstein, Immanuel. 1974. *The Modern World System.* Vol. 1. *Capitalist Agriculture and the Origins of the European World-Economy in the Sixteenth Century.* New York: Academic Press.

———. 1980. *The Modern World System.* Vol. 2. *Mercantilism and the Consolidation of the European Work Economy.* New York: Academic Press.

———. 1989. *The Modern World System.* Vol. 3. *The Second Era of Great Expansion of the Capitalist World Economy, 1730–1840s.* New York: Academic Press.

Weber, Eugen. 1976. *Peasants into Frenchmen: The Modernization of Rural France, 1870–1914.* Stanford, CA: Stanford University Press.

Weber, Max. 1906. "Zur Lage der bürgerlichen Demokratie in Russland." *Archiv für Sozialwissenschaft und Sozialpolitik,* n.s., 22.

———. 1946. First published in 1919. "Politics as a Vocation." In *From Max Weber: Essays in Sociology,* edited by Hans H. Gerth and C. Wright Mills, 77–128. New York: Oxford University Press.

———. 1958. First published in 1915. "The Social Psychology of the World Religions." In *From Max Weber: Essays in Sociology,* edited by Hans H. Gerth and C. Wright Mills, 267–301. New York: Oxford University Press.

———. 1978. First published in 1922. *Economy and Society.* 2 vols. Berkeley and Los Angeles: University of California Press.

Weingast, Barry R. 2005. "Persuasion, Preference, Change, and Critical Junctures: The Microfoundations of a Macroscopic Concept." In *Preferences and*

Situations: Points of Intersection between Historical and Rational Choice Institutionalism, edited by Ira Katznelson and Barry R. Weingast, 129–60. New York: Russell Sage Foundation.

Wellman, Barry, and S. D. Berkowitz, eds. 1988. *Social Structures: A Network Approach*. New York: Cambridge University Press.

Wendt, Alexander. 1999. *Social Theory of International Relations*. New York: Cambridge University Press.

Wharton, Amy S. 1993. "The Affective Consequences of Service Work." *Work and Occupations* 20(2):25–32.

Whyte, William F. 1943. *Street Corner Society*. Chicago: University of Chicago Press.

Wikan, Unni, 1989. "Managing the Heart to Brighten Face and Soul: Emotions in Balinese Morality and Health Care." *American Ethnologist* 16: 294–312.

———. 1990. *Managing Turbulent Hearts: A Balinese Formula for Living*. Chicago: University of Chicago Press.

Williamson, Oliver E. 1985. *The Economic Institutions of Capitalism: Firms, Markets, and Relational Contracting*. New York: Free Press.

———, ed. 1995. *Organization Theory: From Chester Barnard to the Present and Beyond*. New York: Oxford University Press.

Wimmer, Andreas. 2002. *Nationalist Exclusion and Ethnic Conflict: Shadows of Modernity*. New York: Cambridge University Press.

———. 2008. "The Making and Unmaking of Ethnic Boundaries: A Multilevel Process Theory." *American Journal of Sociology* 113:970–1022.

Winant, Howard. 2001. *The Whole World Is a Ghetto*. New York: Basic Books.

Winch, Peter. 1958. *The Idea of a Social Science and Its Relation to Philosophy*. London: Routledge and Kegan Paul.

Wolff, Kurt H., ed. 1971. *From Karl Mannheim*. Oxford: Oxford University Press.

World Bank. 1997. *The State in a Changing World: World Development Report 1997*. New York: Oxford University Press.

Wright, Erik Olin. 1985. *Classes*. London: Verso.

———, ed. 2005. *Approaches to Class Analysis*. New York: Cambridge University Press.

Wrong, Dennis H. 1961. "The Oversocialized Conception of Man in Modern Sociology." *American Journal of Sociology* 26:183–93.

Yashar, Deborah. 2005. *Contesting Citizenship in Latin America: The Rise of Indigenous Movements and the Postliberal Challenge*. New York: Cambridge University Press.

Zaller, John R. 1992. *The Nature and Origins of Mass Opinion*. Cambridge: Cambridge University Press.

Znaniecki, Florian. 1934. *The Method of Sociology*. New York: Farrar & Rinehart.

Zolberg, Aristide R. 1986. "How Many Exceptionalisms?" In *Working-Class Formation: Nineteenth-Century Patterns in Western Europe and the United States*, edited by Ira Katznelson and Aristide R. Zolberg, 397–455. Princeton, NJ: Princeton University Press.

INDEX

Items of special importance for this book's argument have been italicized.

Abbott, A., on heuristics and inspiration, 296n

action, social: analytic components of, 25, chs. 3, 4, 5, and 6, 135; embedded in social relations and institutions, 8–9, 29; expressive type of, 7, 8–9, 71, 71n, 73; innate basis of, 29–30, 90–1, 104–5, 247; instrumental type of, 7, 8–9, 71, 71n; integration of, 205–6; model of, 28–9. See also *action theory; constitutive elements; internal dimensions of action; micro-macro relations among social phenomena*

action theory: as framework, 28–9, 38–9; questions about, 32–7; recovery of, 31, 88, 286–7; voluntarism of, challenged, 34

Adorno, T. W., on *Dialectic of Enlightenment,* 104

aggregation, ch. 9; fallacy of simplistic, 152, 153–5; and institutions, 152–3, 155–7; of knowledge, 164; socially grounded, 152–3, 155–7

Alexander, J. C., on historicity of cultural patterns, 265; on societal community as source of integration and exclusion, 275

analogies, 296; from face-to-face groups to larger structures, 133–4, 296; as inspiration vs. persuasion, 296

analytic pitfalls, 291–2; essentialist concepts as, 19; naive functionalism as, 36–7; simplistic aggregation as, 152, 153–5; unrecognized tautologies as, 19–20, 297

analytic tools, 1; neutral as to grand theories, 3, 299; varieties of, 6–10, 25. See also *concepts; hypotheses, theoretical; mechanisms, causal; metatheories;* theory; theory frames, focused

Anderson, B., on imagined communities, 110, 229, 232

Arendt, H., on truth and interests, 45

associations, purposive: bridging cleavages, 114, 252n; as channel of influence, 98–

9, 179–80, 202, 276; and civil society, 201; control by, 60–1; 293; democracy/oligarchy in, 180–1; formation of, 174–5; goals of, 177, 179–81; and indirect power, 186, 188, 190, 191, 192, 196–7, 256; and institutions, 204, 215 satisfaction of members in, 174–5

attachments: and beliefs, 53–4, 58; and collective action, 174, 181, 232; as constitutive and linkage elements, 110, 147, 242, 290; and emotions, 32, 112–3, 116, 143; and norms, 67–8, 81, 84, 85; and preferences/interests, 91, 94, 97; and social identities, 228, 231, 238; and values, 68. See also *identities, social; internal dimensions of action*

authority. See legitimation of rule; rule: systems of

Axelrod, R., on evolution of cooperation, 170

Bacon, F., on distortions built into modes of communication, 43n

Barton, A. H., on conceptual property space, 296–7

Becker, G. S., on invariant preferences, 87n behaviorism, 289

Bendix, R., on balancing conceptual orientations, 28n

Ben-Ner, A., on motivation of economic activities, 88

Berger, P., on balancing conceptual orientations, 28n; on opaqueness of inherited orientations, 43

Berkowitz, L., on emotions and cognition, 114–5

Berlin, I., on irreconcilable human values, 211, 283–4

Black, D., on law and inequality, 7–8

black box in correlational analysis, 21, 24

Blau, P., on structuralist approach, 140, 296

Bott, E., on network effects on beliefs, 55

Bourdieu, P.: on habitus, 47; on unreflected routine action, 34

Boyd, R.: on cooperation in large groups, 90–1; on culture and evolution, 104; on small groups, 90–1

Brubaker, R., on reification of social identities, 230

bureaucracy, 18–9, 35n, 197–9, 295; as domination through knowledge, 58; and emotions, 118; motivations for compliance in, 7, 75–6, 199. *See also* legitimation of rule; *organizations, formal*; rule, systems of

Cardozo, B. N., innovating on liability, 82–3

causality, 20–1; and causal overdetermination, 37, 146, 219; doubts about, 32–3, 138n historicist forms of, 149–50; necessary/sufficient conditions of, 10n, 14, 37, 148–9, 261–2, 270n4. See also *explanation*; *mechanisms, causal*; prediction; theory frames: focused; theory, full-fledged

causal relevance: vs. constitutive relevance, 52n; of culture, 265–7, 270, 280–5; identified by theory frames, 1, 286, 292; of internal dimensions of action, 135, 136, 289–90

change: and class, 174–5, 249, 253n; democratization as, 13, 14, 16, 22–3; and dualism in classic sociology, 186–9; in family patterns, 126, 130, 189–92, 192–6; in gender relations, 7, 192–6; generational, 57; and history, 147–51; and ideology, 48; and innate dispositions, 104, 247; institutionalization of, 57, 58–62; and institutions, 215–6, 219–26; interdependence of processes of, 35–6; and law, 82–3, 83n, 162–3, 188, 221; long-term, 187–9, 216n4, 246–7, 249, 254n; and market exchange, 105, 161; and modernization theory, 187; in norms, 68, 82–5; obstacles to, 7, 71–2, 143; and overdetermination, 37; pace of, 201, 266–7, 280; in power-cooperation nexus, 189–202; in preferences, 92–3, 95–8, 99–104; planned, 7, 129, 220–2; in race relations, 7; and revolution, 16, 23–4; and risk/uncertainty, 41–3; and tradition, 42–3. See also *clusters*; modernity; *stability, social*

charisma and its routinization, 76, 94, 120, 171, 235, 268

Chorev, N., on designed institutional change, 210–1

civil society, 201; balancing state power, 188; and democracy, 20, 202; and face-to-face groups, 132; and infrastructural power, 186n; and national identities, 240; and subordinate class interests, 202. See also *associations, purposive*; *collective action*; democracy

class: and closure of status groups, 251–2; conceptualization of, 20, 249–53; and democracy, 13–4, 16, 22–3; and exploitation, 249–50, 252–3; formation of, 174–5, 252; and multiple identities, 241; and preferences, 89. *See also* inequality: in social status; status and status groups; stratification

clusters, 291; "calendar model of social stability," 291; of institutions, 213; of norms, 66–9, 77n, 84, 136, 147; of preferences, 93–5; of theory frames, 15. *See also* change; *interdependence*; *stability, social*

Coase, R. H., on economic firms, 199

coercion, 146; and collective action, 168–70, 176–8; and collective memory, 275; and cooperation, 177, 256; and cultural influence, 275; and elections, 163, 166; and law, 19; as power resource, 185, 290–1; and social stabilization, 146; and states, 254; and values, 178. *See also* legitimation of rule; rule, systems of

Coleman, J. S., on collective right to social control, 178n; on conjoint and disjoint norms, 78n12; on democracy and oligarchy, 180; on formal organizations, 199

collective action, 27, 98–9, 154, ch. 10; and coercion, 168–70, 176–8; and collective goods, 168–70, 179, 181–2; and direct appeal of collective goods, 170, 172, 179; and emotions, 176; and ethnicity, 175, 176, 236, 274; futility of, 169, 173; and ideology, 170, 171, 175, 176; individual incentives for, 168, 176; inherent ambiguity of, 179–81; and leadership, 171, 175; and multitask organizations, 178; the problem of, 168–70, 181–2; in revolution, 13; and small groups, 168–9, 173, 175; and social identities, 240, 241;

theory frame of, 2, 181–2; and values/
norms, 171–2, 173–4, 176. See also *cooperation*; *latent groups*; movements
Collins, R., on natural rituals, 112–3
common good: as inherently contested,
80–1, 89, 201, 255
common sense: and action theory frame,
38; and cultural explanations, 282–4; as
distorting influence, 38; and implicit theory, 38; and methodological individualism, 39; and political/social theory, 6;
versions of functionalism as, 36
concepts: cross-cultural equivalence of,
293–4; defining culture, 265–7; defining
identities, 229–31, 242; defining institutions, 210–2; defining power, 184–6
essentialist vs. distinctive, 19, 184n, 230;
essentially contested, 81, 101n10; and
hypothesis development, 19–20, 171–2;
metric for, 8; multidimensional, 8; multiple, 297–8; operational, 20; property
space of, 296–7; relational vs. classificatory, 19; and theory frames, 298. See
also *hypotheses, theoretical*; ideal type;
theory frames, focused
conflict: over collective goods, 179; within
communal relations, 54; and conditions
of collective action, 175; and cross-cutting loyalties, 241; and culture, 279,
283–4
ethnic, 114; and institutions, 204, 216–7;
in international relations, 259; metatheory of, 2–3, 11; over norms, 83; and
social identities, 231, 241. See also ingroup-outgroup dynamic
constitutive elements: of action, 50–1, 135;
attachments as, 290; and causal effects,
35, 52n; of emergent patterns, 35, 128,
289–90; emotions as, 122, 218, 290; internal dimensions of action as, 31, 35,
51–2, 123, 128, 136, 142–3, 266; knowledge as, 49, 51–2, 54, 62, 142, 217,
231; norms as, 64–5, 68, 218; preferences as, 218; of social structuration, 31,
49, 50–1. See also *emergent phenomena*;
internal dimensions of action
control, social: collective right to, 178n; of
emotions, 116–9; of expertise, 60–1,
293; and family, 190; of knowledge, 44,
56–8; of preferences, 92–3; in small
groups, 1, 8, 125

Converse, P., on inconsistent beliefs in
mass publics, 46
cooperation: and coercion, 177, 256; and
co-optation, 180; and division of labor,
183–4; enabled by institutions, 216–7;
evolution of, 170; and free-riding, 66,
169, 170; innate base of, 90, 91; motivation for, 17, 119–20; and norms, 66, 77;
and power, 183–4, ch. 11; and sense of
futility, 57, 169, 171, 173; and small
groups, 105, 168–9, ch. 7; spontaneous,
58, 71; and states, 179, 255–6. See also
collective action; cooperation, modes of
cooperation, modes of: in associations,
191–2, 196–7; in family and kin relations, 189–91; in formal organizations,
191–2, 196–201; in informal groups,
ch. 7, 259; in market exchange, 157–63,
196–7; secured by states, 189–93, 196–
202, 255–6. *See also* power-cooperation
nexus
coordination: in bureaucracy, 19, 197–8;
change in prevailing forms of, 186–9;
and family, 189–92; and business firms,
199–202; and institutions, 215, 216; and
markets, 159–63; and power, 183–4,
186, 189–93, 196–202, 255–6. See also
collective action; *cooperation*; cooperation, modes of
Coser, L. A., on cross-cutting loyalties, 241
critical junctures, 207, 222–3. *See also*
change; *institutions*
cultural turn: and internal dimensions of action, 32–3, 137–8
culture, 31; causal relevance of, 265–7,
280–5; as collective structuring of the internal dimensions of action, 265–6, 290–
1; concept of, 265–6; and conflict, 279,
283–4; contention about explanations
by, 267–70; and emotions, 109; and ethnicity, 278–9; grounding of in social
structures, 290–1; heterogeneity of in
large traditions, 279; historicity of, 265–
6, 269–70; not identical with ethnonational culture, 278–9; methodological
gains in study of, 278; mistaken common sense about, 278–80, 282–5; and
rapid change, 280; reception of, within
and across status groups, 272–6; role of
in revolutions, 16; structural grounding
of, 270–2, 276–80; transmission of,

culture (*cont'd*)
272–6. See also *explanation*; *institutions*; *macropatterns*
Cutright, P., on causes of democracy, 22
cycles, vicious and virtuous, 145

Dahrendorf, R., on class mobilization, 174–5
Damasio, A.: on emotions, body, and mind, 108–9; on emotions and cognition, 115; on emotions and decisions, 111
democracy, 13, 14–5, 16, 22–3, 245; and civil society, 20, 202; vs. formally rational law, 256; and "fundamental democratization," 188; and market economies, 258n; vs. oligarchy, 179–80; and states, 256–7; and virtue, 166n. See also civil society; voting
dependency theory, 259
De Schweinitz, K., on causes of democracy, 22
dialectic, 27, 226
Dickson, W. J., on groups in workplace, 289
Dror, Y., on effectiveness of law, 7, 71
dualisms of classic macrosociology, 186–9
Durkheim, E.: on functionalism, 35; on individuation, 1; on internal dimensions of action, 28; on macroeffects on action, 34; on noncontractual bases of contract, 197, 219; on normality of crime, 70; on ritual and solidarity, 112; on sanctions restoring moral balance, 72; on social forms shaping category frames, 47; on suicides in booms and busts, 100–1

efficiency: in bureaucracy 19, 198; and communication in groups, 128; as conceptualized by Pareto, 80; and despotic power, 202; and interests, 201, 221; and market exchange, 157–63; and indirect power, 196–202; and problems of conceptualization, 201, 208, 225; and rational choice theory, 224; secular increase of, 201. See also *common good*
Elster, J.: on adaptive preference formation, 101; on *amour-propre*, 112; on causal mechanisms, 24; on cooperation, 9; on emotions and cognition, 114, 115, 116; on Marxian functionalism, 35; on

pervasiveness of emotions, 107; on rational choice vs. norm theory, 65
emergent phenomena, 35, 289–90; and internal dimensions of action, 49, 142; small groups as, 128, 129, 134, 135, 139; and reductionism 34, 34n, 136; states as, 139. See also *constitutive elements*; mechanisms, causal; *micro-macro relations among social phenomena*; *reductionism*; *structuration, social*
emotions, 29–32, ch. 6; in classic sociology, 107; and cognition, 114–6; and collective action, 176; conceptualization of, 108–10; as constitutive elements, 122; and culture, 109; in groups, 130; and guilt/shame, 117–8; and ingroup-outgroup relations, 113–4, 116; institutionally shaped, 218; intensity of, 110; integrating internal dimensions of action, 109–10; as linkage elements, 108–10, 290; and preferences, 111–14; and ritual, 112–3, 118–9; shaping structures and processes, 119–21; social control of, 116–9; social effects of, 119–21; socially influenced, 116–9. See also *internal dimensions of action*
equilibrium, 35, 37, 38; and organic analogies, 296; as conceptualized by Nash, 218; in groups, 133; in macroeconomics, 205; punctuated, 222. See also *functionalism*; *interdependence*
ethics: of responsibility vs. of conscience, 40n; and market exchange, 88, 95
ethnicity: and class formation, 252; and collective action, 175, 176, 236, 274; and conflict, 114, 241, 252n; and culture, 278–9; essentialist conceptions of, 230; and social identities, 91, 144, 230, 233, 235; as imagined communities, 229; and institutions, 216n4; shaping internal dimensions of action, 99, 113, 144; and multiple identities, 231; and social integration, 275, 277; and states, 235–6, 237, 274n7. See also *identities, social*; *latent groups*
Evans, P. B.: on economic effects of "Weberian" state organizations, 199n; on "taming" states, 256
expertise, control of, 60–1, 293
explanation, 32–3; alternative explanations (of democracy), 22–3; and causal mecha-

nisms, 22, 52n, 292; challenged by variability of patterns and processes, 6, 138, 288; and correlation, 21–2; in the course of research, 18, 39, 106, 140, 288–9; by cultural factors, ch. 15; deficit of in theory frames, 1, 13, 286; and historicity, 149–50, 260–1, 265–6, 269–70, 270n4; and mesolevel factors, 245, 276, 298, 299; and "other things being equal," 12; "paradigmatic" version of, 32; partial, 8, 10–1, 50, 100, 149, 292, 293; possibility of, 289, 292; vs. prediction, 139; premature sense of, 12; and reductionism, 23–4, 34n; and scope conditions, 18, 30n, 136, 140, 270; skepticism about, 6, 33, 137–8, 138n, 286–7; structuralist approaches to, 140–1, 298–9; and theory construction, 7–8. See also *causality*; *feedback mechanisms*; *hypotheses, theoretical*; mechanisms, causal; prediction; theory; theory frames, focused; theory, full-fledged

exploitation: and inequality, 249–50, 252–3; and norms, 78–9; and feudal rule, 141, 198

extrapolation of trends, 5

fallacies. See *analytic pitfalls*
family: changes in, 126, 130, 189–92, 192–6; and contrast to other modes of coordination, 191–2; as mode of cooperation, 189–91; as multipurpose organization, 188, 190–1. *See also* gender relations; power-cooperation nexus

feedback mechanisms, 36–7, 38–9n10, 40, 49, 292, 298

fertility: decline of and theory of action, 94n; and education, 21–22; and grounded aggregation, 163–6; and preferences, 94; and rational choice theory, 30n, 156n

Festinger, L., on "social reality," 46
fields of action: economic activities as, 157–63; and institutions, 153, 156–7, 211, 217–9

Friedan, B., on functionalist views of the family, 130n

Fuchs, S.: on common sense, 38n; on macroeffects on action, 34

functionalism, 8, 10–1, 35–7, 290; "actor-centered," 221–2, 225; fallacy of

naive, 36–7, 126; in Marxian analysis, 35; and policy studies, 36; reservations of proponents about, 37n10. See also *macropatterns*

Galbraith, J. K., on public/ private affluence, 103

Gallie, W. B., on essentially contested concepts, 81, 101n10, 255

game theory: and the collective action problem, 169–70; as theory frames, 2, 27, 31n. See also *rational action theory*

Geertz, C.: on "contextual relativism," 275; on ideologies, 48

Geiger, Th., on mentalities, 47

gender relations: change in, 7, 71, 192–6; and civilizational differences, 281; and consent of the disadvantaged, 78–9, 273n; and double morality, 85; and emancipation of women, 192–6, 224; and fertility, 22, 165; inequality in, 224–5, 252; and power balance, 195–6, 225; and transnational culture, 224; and vested interests, 195. See also *family*; power-cooperation nexus

Giddens, A., on unreflected routine action, 34

Goertz, G., on Skocpol's analysis of revolution, 14n

Goldstone, J. A., on micro-macro relations, 298n

Goode, W. J., on concepts and hypothesis development, 20

Goodwin, J., on conditions of movements, 1–2, 175

Gould, R., on network theory, 140

Gramsci, A., on cultural hegemony and counterhegemony, 44, 275

Grossman, H., on rational action theory and aggregation, 156n

groups, face-to-face, ch. 7; in broader contexts, 131–2; as causal mechanisms, 35, 124, 139, 288, 289; and collective action, 173, 175; communication in, 127–8; definition of, 124; family as, 126, 130; full-fledged theory of, 1, 8, 123, 124–8, 133; internal dimensions of action as constitutive of, 123, 128–30, 133; leadership in, 126; norms in, 125–6, 127, 129; social control in, 125; and

groups, face-to-face (cont'd)
　socialization, 131; stratification in, 126,
　133; in war, 131
guilt, 72–3, 117–8

Habermas, J., on uncoerced communica-
　tion, 80
Hall, P. A., on current institutionalisms,
　206
Hayek, F. von, on local knowledge, 59
Hechter, M.: on norms of cooperation in ra-
　tional choice theory, 80; on norms stabi-
　lizing advantage, 79; on problem of
　order, 50
Hegel, G.W.F., on dialectic, 27
hegemony, cultural: 44–5, 59–60, 275–6.
　See also conflict; *culture*
Hirschman, A. O., on collective action, 170
history matters, 47–51; in culture, 265–6,
　269–70; in explanation, 149–50, 265–6,
　269–70, 270n4; in ideas about reality,
　43; and social identities, 233
Hobbes, Th.: on ideas and interests, 45; on
　the problem of order, 50
Hoebel, E. A., on "champions at law,"
　77n10
Homans, G. C., on groups, 8, ch. 7
Horkheimer, M., on *Dialectic of Enlighten-
　ment*, 104
Horne, C., on the problem of order
Horwitz, M. J.: on rationales for legal cor-
　porate entities, 217; on transformation
　of law, 83n, 162–3
Huber, E., on power and welfare state,
　202. *See also* Stephens, E. Huber
Huizinga, J., on play, 63n, 113n.5
Hume, D., on causation, 21
hypotheses, theoretical: development of,
　17–20, 25, 39, 138–41, 288–9, 294–9;
　domain and scope conditions of, 16, 17,
　18, 136, 139, 140, 270, 288; elaboration
　of, 17, 18, 101n12, 119–20, 295–6; and
　embryonic theory, 19; generality of,
　139n; probabilistic, 298n; and reconcep-
　tualization, 19–20; and scope condi-
　tions, 136, 139, 140, 288; underspeci-
　fied, 17, 101, 295–8. See also *concepts*;
　mechanisms, causal; theory frames, fo-
　cused; theory, full-fledged
hypotheses, theoretical, examples of: on
　adaptive preference change, 101n12; on
　bureaucracy, 18, 58, 197–9, 295; on co-

operation, 17, 119–20, 295; on effective-
　ness of law, 7–10; on law and inequality,
　7–10; on small groups at work, 288–9

ideal type: as embryonic theory, 19–20,
　197–9, 295; and "property space," 296–
　7; as relational concept, 18–9
identities, social, 228–31; acceptance/rejec-
　tion of, 238–40; and attachments, 231;
　causal conditions of, 232–3; and cogni-
　tive maps, 230, 233, 242; and collective
　action, 240, 241; and conflict, 231, 241;
　and discrimination/recognition, 233–4,
　236; effects of, 240–1; ethnic, 91, 144,
　230, 233, 235; historicity of, 233; as
　imagined communities, 229; and in-
　group-outgroup dynamic, 241; and inter-
　nal dimensions of action, 230–1, 233,
　242; and leaders, 234–5; multiple, 231;
　national, 235, 237–8; "primordial,"
　232; vs. social categories, 230; and
　states, 235–8; and symbolic mediation,
　232. See also *attachments*
ideology: and collective action, 170, 171,
　176; contrasting conceptions of, 48; as
　fusion of beliefs, values, and emotion,
　53; and metatheory, 3, 28–9
induction: analytic version of, 16, 292,
　300; problem of, 15–6, 300
inequality: and class analysis, 249–53; in-
　herent in social formations, 152, 183–4;
　and institutions, 215, 216–7, 219, 224–
　5; and law, 7–8, 200, 217; material, 4;
　and modes of cooperation, 201; and
　norms, 78–9, 80–1, 84, 145–6; and over-
　determination, 219; in social status,
　251–2. *See also* class; *power*; status and
　status groups; stratification
Inglehart, R., on culture and preferences,
　89, 102
ingroup-outgroup dynamic, 53–4; and emo-
　tions, 113–4, 116; and social identities,
　241. *See also* conflict
institutionalisms: change in, 205–8; in clas-
　sic economics, 205; historical version of,
　206–7, 224; limited convergence of,
　208–10; after the marginalist revolution,
　205n; new economic version of, 207–8,
　224; new sociological version of, 206,
　224, 259; old sociological version,
　205–6. *See also* institutionalization;
　institutions

institutionalization: of change, 57; degree
of, 211; of evasion of norms, 70; extreme model of, 211, 212; of knowledge
creation, 60–1; of preferences, 103. *See
also* institutionalisms; *institutions*

institutions, 204–5, 226–7; and aggregation, 152–3, 155–7; and beliefs, 212,
217–8; breakdown of, 103; change in,
219–26; clusters of, 213; and conflict,
204, 216–7; constraining subjective variability, 139–40, 217–9; and creation of
collective actors, 215–6; and critical junctures, 222–3; demand for, 212–3; design
of, 219–22; and economic activities,
157–63; enabling cooperation vs. creating conflict, 216–7; and ethnicity, 216n4;
as established practices, 211, 218–9; and
fields of action, 153, 156–7, 211, 217–9;
formal vs. informal, 213; inconsistency
among, 214; and inequality, 211, 215,
216–7, 219, 224–5; and internal dimensions of action, 137, 217–9; of knowledge, 58–62; and market exchange, 167–
3; norms as central to, 69, 210–1, 218;
and organizational forms, 215; outcomes of, 215–9; planned, 220–2; and
power, 211, 224–6; and preferences,
218; and social change, 215–6; and socially grounded aggregation, 153, 155;
and social stability, 146; supports for,
211; and values, 212. *See also macropatterns; micro-macro relations among social phenomena; power; stability, social;*
variability of patterns and processes

interdependence, 35–7, 38, 291; of causal
relations, 35–7, 133, 273; of internal dimensions of action, 49; of knowledge
and attachments, 53–4; knowledge
model of, 48–50, 62–3; of knowledge
and preferences/interests, 51–2, 54; of
knowledge and values, 52–3; small
group model of, 124–30. *See also clusters; functionalism;* systems theories

interests: and attachments, 97; belief in harmony of, 54; class, 28, 254, 277; and
cognition, 40–1, 44, 51–2; collective,
98–9, 179–81; and democracy, 22–3,
209; and efficiency, 201; and gender relations, 195; and ideology, 48; and institutions, 204, 207, 213, 215–6; life, 133,
194, 238, 242; material, 8, 35n, 67, 75–
6, 267; and norms, 65, 78–9; "objec-

tive," 44n; in organizations, 199, 201;
shared, 17, 80–1, ch. 10, 255; subordinate, 201–2, 225–6. *See also common
good;* conflict; *preferences*

internal dimensions of action, 29–32, 135–
8; causal relevance, 135, 136, 289–90;
as constitutive elements of meso- and
macrophenomena, 31, 35, 51–2, 123,
128, 136, 142–3, 265–6; as constitutive
of groups, 123, 128–30, 133; and culture, 265–6; and ethnicity, 99, 113, 144;
integrating effect of emotions among,
109–110; interdependence among themselves, 49; interdependence with meso-
and macrophenomena, 49; and linguistic
and cultural turns, 32–3; shaped by macrophenomena, 39, 135, 139; and social
identities, 230–1, 242. *See also emotions; knowledge; norms; preferences;*
variability of patterns and processes

internalization: of norms and values, 67,
72, 92, 117–8. *See also internal dimensions of action;* socialization

Jasper, J. M., on conditions of movements,
1–2, 175

Kalberg, S., on Weber's ideal types, 19,
35n, 197

Katz, E., on the two-step flow of communication, 44, 132

knowledge, 29–32, ch. 3; acceptance of,
282; action as dependent on, ch. 3, 294;
asymmetries of, 44, 60–1, 293; as constitutive of social patterns, 49, 51–2, 54,
62, 142, 217–8, 231, 266; different
kinds of, differently embedded, 45–8;
and divergent interests, 44–5; economies
based on, 131, 188, 194, 246; and emotions, 114–6; empirical evidence vs. social influence on, 46; frames of, 40, 41,
44, 46; fusion of valuation and cognition, 47, 52–3; generalization of immediate experience, 47; groups' potential superiority in, 43, 164; implicit forms of,
17–8, 46; information vs. analytic
frames of, 40, 41; and institutionally
shaped beliefs, 212, 217–8; interaction
of elite and popular outlooks, 47; linked
to attachments and aversions, 53–4;
linked to preferences and interests, 40–5,
54, 136; linked to values, 52–3; local

knowledge (*cont'd*)
    knowledge, 58–9; and markets, 160;
    model of doubly engaged ideas, 48–63;
    model of rational search for, 40–5; and
    precedents, 144; risk and probability,
    41–2; realistic, 40–1, 43, 136, 137;
    shaped by two sets of determinants, 49,
    62–3; and small-scale interaction, 128–
    9; social control of, 56–7; and social
    identities, 230, 233, 242; social influ-
    ences on, 54–8, 128–9; as "social real-
    ity," 46; and tradition, 42–3, 144–5;
    and trust, 44; and two-step flow of
    communication, 44; and uncertainty,
    41–3. See also *internal dimensions of
    action*; *rationality*
Kocka, J., on national solidarity, 113n6
Koenig, R., on visibility of social phenom-
    ena, 38
Kohn, M. L., on class and preferences, 89

latent groups: and heterogeneity, 175–6;
    and ideology, 176; leadership in, 171;
    mobilization of, 169, 174, 176. See also
    collective action; movements
law: and capitalism, 162–3, 295; change
    in, 82–3, 83n, 162–3, 188, 221; and co-
    ercion, 19; definition of, 19, 77n10, 268;
    effectiveness of, 7, 10, 70n, 71–2, 225–
    6; and equity, 162; and inequality, 7–8,
    200, 217; interpretation of, 82–3; nonle-
    gal bases of, 190, 197, 200, 219; rule of,
    78, 162–3, 196, 200, 256–7; and social
    stability, 146; universalism in, 78. *See
    also* legitimation of rule; *norms*; *power*;
    rule, systems of; *states*
Lazarsfeld, P., on two-step flow of commu-
    nication, 44, 132
legitimation of rule: and other aspects of
    domination, 20, 297; and motivation
    for compliance, 76; three forms of,
    20, 254n, 297. See also *power*; rule,
    systems of
Levi, M., on inducing preferences in organi-
    zations, 99
Levy, M. J., Jr., on "universal social
    solvent," 192
Lewis, D., on reductionism, 24
Lichtenberg, G. C., on making dispersed
    knowledge accessible, 27
linguistic turn: and internal dimensions of
    action, 32–3, 137–8

Lipset, S. M.: on causes of democracy, 22;
    on democracy and oligarchy, 180
Luckmann, Th., on opaqueness of inher-
    ited orientations, 43
Lukes, S.: on essentially contested con-
    cepts, 81, 101n10; on power, 2, 21

Machiavelli, N., on wisdom of crowds,
    164
macropatterns, chs. 9, 11, 12, and 14;
    conditions of emergence of, 143–8; as
    constituted by internal dimensions of ac-
    tion, 31, 135–8, 142–4; lower variability
    of patterns and processes in, 245, 291;
    and methods of study, 148–51, 260–3;
    and normative questions, 248; no parsi-
    monious model of, 37, 290; pervasive
    features of, 290–1; shaping meso- and
    micropatterns, 34, 39, 139–41, 243–6,
    288, 298; and structuralist approaches,
    140–1, 298–9; systems of, 35–7; varie-
    ties of, 246–8. See also *emergent phe-
    nomena*; *functionalism*; *micro-macro re-
    lations among social phenomena*;
    structuration, social
Madison, J., on weakness of reason when
    alone, 43
magic: and uncertainty, 42
Mahoney, J.: on causal mechanisms, 24;
    on colonialism creating collective identi-
    ties, 216n4; on consciousness about
    motivation, 287n; on path dependence,
    57, 150–1; on Skocpol's analysis of
    revolution, 14n
Malinowski, B., on magic, 42
Mandeville, B. de, on self-interest, 112
Mann, M., on historical anatomy of
    power, 184, 185
Mannheim, K., on generalization from im-
    mediate experience, 47n8
March, J. G., on formal organizations, 200
market exchange, 105, 157–63; ethics of,
    88, 95; and indirect power, 196–201;
    and institutions, 157–63, legal infrastruc-
    ture of, 162–3. See also *law*; *power*; pow-
    er- cooperation nexus; *states*
Marx, K., on class, 2, 20, 250; on dialectic,
    27; on exploitation, 249; functionalist
    ideas of, 35
Massell, G., on change in gender
    relations, 7

Mauss, M., on social forms shaping category frames, 47

McAdam, D.: on causal mechanisms, 24; on conditions of movements, 1–2, 175

McCarthy, J. D., on conditions of movements, 1–2

Mead, G. H., on internal dimensions of action, 28

mechanisms, causal, 11, 20–5, 292–3; assessment of, 21, 22, 261, 289; definition of, 21; different conceptions of, 24–5; and internal dimensions of action, 287; and reduction to individual level, 23–4; as required for explanation, 22, 52n, 292; and theory development, 23; and theory frames, 25, 292; underspecified, 24, 295. See also *causality*; *explanation*; *feedback mechanisms*; hypotheses, theoretical; *overdetermination, causal*; *realist philosophy*; theory frames, focused

mechanisms, causal, examples of: clusters of norms as, 69; culture grounded in social structures as, 290–1; determinants of democracy as, 22–3; education and fertility, 21–2; groups as multiple, 35, 124, 139, 288, 289; hostile stereotypes as, 290; motivation for cooperation as, 9; and causal overdetermination, 37, 146, 219; power as, 21; states as multiple, 35, 139, 288; as supportive of social stability, 143–7

Merton, R. K.: on functionalism, 11, 37n10; on institutionalized evasions of norms, 70; on theoretical strategy, 10–12

mesopatterns: and double asymmetry of causal relations, 244–5, 299; importance of in research design, 245, 276, 298, 299; and methods of study, 244–5, 263n. See also *emergent phenomena*; *explanation*; *micro-macro relations among social phenomena*; *structuration, social*; variability of patterns and processes

metatheories, 2–3; defined, 11; divergent, 67, 286, 296n; ideological components of, 3, 28–9, 286; two social action frameworks as, 28–9, 38–9, 286–7; as useful frameworks, 2, 27, 286. See also theory; theory frames, focused

Michels, R., on oligarchy, 179–80, 183

micro-macro relations among social phenomena, 34–5; causal asymmetry in, 243–5, 291; double causal asymmetry

in, 244–5; micro- shaped by macropatterns, 34, 39, 139–41, 243–6, 288, 298. See also *constitutive elements*; *emergent phenomena*; functionalism; macropatterns; mesopatterns; reductionism, social structuration; variability of patterns and processes

modernity, 186–9; and contrasts in power and cooperation, 189–92, 196–202; and culture, 186; and emancipation of women, 192–6

modernization theory, 187

Moe, T. M.: on rational action models as theory frames, 31n; on rational action models of organizations, 198–9n13

Moore, B.: on dictatorship and democracy, 13, 22; on Homans's *The Human Group,* 123n

movements: conditions of mobilization, 175; and emotions, 119–20; theory frame for, 1–2. See also *collective action*; *latent groups*

network theory; 140, 296. See also *structuralist approaches*

norms, 29–32, ch. 4; and attachments, 67–8; change of, 68, 82–5; clusters of, 66–9, 77n, 84, 136, 291; and cognition, 50–1; and collective action, 171–2, 173–4, 176; as constitutive element of structures, 64–5, 68; effectiveness of, 70–7, 287; and emotions, 108–9, 117; enforcement of, 66, 68; in groups, 1, 6, 10, 125–6, 127, 129; imposition of, 78–9; and inequality, 78–9, 80–1, 84, 145–6; institutionalized evasion of, 70; and institutions, 69, 210–1, 218; internal sanctions, 72–5; internalization of, 67, 74–5, 92, 117–8; motivation for compliance with, 72–7; origins of, 77–82; "oughtness" of, 64, 72, 74; and preferences, 88, 91–3; and roles, 68–9, 290; as spontaneous order, 79, 81; and values, 64, 67–8, 71, 72, 74. See also *institutions*; *internal dimensions of action*; *law*; values

Ober, J., on use of citizens' knowledge in democracy, 164

O'Donnell, G., on causes of democracy, 22

oligarchy: organization and, 179–81; as special case of specialization-inequality

oligarchy (*cont'd*)
   nexus, 197. See also *collective action*;
   democracy; *power*
Olsen, J. P., on formal organizations, 200
Olson, M., on the collective action problem, 2, 27, 168–70, 173, 179, 181–2
Opp, K. D., on instrumentality of norms,
   81
order, social, 50; beliefs as constitutive of,
   51–2, 54, 62; break in European, 186–7;
   and division of labor, 195; and gender inequality, 193; internal dimensions of action as constitutive of, 63; spontaneous
   forms of, 79–81. See also *structuration,
   social*
organizations, formal: cognitive advantages of, 58–60; cohesion in, 19, 198; coordination in, 19, 198; domination in,
   200–1, 203; efficiency in, 19, 198, 201;
   and indirect power, 186, 196–201; as information processing systems, 58, 59n;
   and instrumental action, 7, 71; and institutions, 215; and interests, 199, 201; of
   knowledge, 58–62, and preferences, 98–
   9; rationality in, 58, 197–8, 198n, 200;
   small groups in, 105, 131; and social
   change, 189–92, 196–201. See also bureaucracy; power-cooperation nexus
overdetermination, causal, 37, 146, and
   inequality, 219

Pareto, V., on internal dimensions of action, 28; on rationalizations and stable
   inclinations, 49n
Pareto efficiency, 80
Parsons, T.: on functionalism, 10–1, 36,
   37n10; on ideologies, 48; on internal dimensions of action, 28–9; on instrumental vs. expressive actions, 71n; on the
   problem of order, 50; on tensions in modern societies, 104; on theoretical strategy
   and the beginnings of functionalism,
   10–12
path dependence, 57, 149–51
Pierson, P.: on historical causation, 148; on
   path dependence 57, 150
power, 2, 21; and associations, 196–7; as
   causal mechanism, 21; and coercion,
   185, 290; and cooperation/coordination,
   183–4, 189–93, 196–202, 255–6; conceptualizations of, 184–6; and democracy, 14, 23; historical anatomy of, 184,

185; indirect vs. command, 185, 196–
   201, 255–7; infrastructural, 185n,
   256; and institutions, 211, 224–6; and
   long-term change, 189–202; and markets, 196–201; and organizations, 196–
   201; resources of, 185–6; and states, 14,
   202, 254–9 theory frame of, 2, 4, 14,
   21. *See also* cooperation, modes of; inequality; legitimation of rule; power-cooperation nexus; rule, systems of; *states*;
   stratification
power-cooperation nexus, 183–4; changes
   in, 188–202. See also *associations,
   purposive*; *market exchange*; *organizations, formal*
prediction, 12; based on implicit knowledge, 17–8; deficit of in theory frames, 1,
   13; and extrapolation, 5; vs. forecasting,
   130n; "local," 137; overestimation of
   possibility of, 40; skepticism about,
   286–9; and small group theory, 130–1.
   See also *causality*; *explanation*; *overdetermination, causal*; theory frames, focused;
   theory, full-fledged
preferences, 29–32, ch. 5; and attachments,
   91, 94, 97; change in, 92–3, 95–8, 99–
   104; and class, 89; and collective organization, 98–9; clusters of, 93–5; and cultural variation, 89, 102; and emotions,
   111–4; and fertility change, 94; and formal organizations, 98–9; innate bases of,
   90–1, 104–5; institutionalization of,
   103; and institutions, 218; and interaction, 96–7, 129–30; invariant, 87n; and
   knowledge, 40–5, 54, 136; and norms,
   88, 91–3; other-regarding, 88–9; and
   past choices, 95–6; and perception of
   others, 97–8; process-regarding, 88–9;
   and reference groups, 97–8; and resource constraints, 99–104; revealed, 87;
   self-regarding, 88–9; social control of,
   92–3; and socialization, 92–3; and status, 89, 97–8; structures of, 93–5; and
   sunk costs, 96. See also *interests*; *internal dimensions of action*
probability: characterizing hypotheses,
   298n; and potentially superior judgments of many actors, 164; and risk,
   41–2
problems, common: of control of expertise,
   60–1, 293; with diverse solutions, 293;
   generative types of, 293

professions, 60–1, 293

Putterman, L.: on economic firms, 200; on motivation of economic activities, 104

rational action theory: and aggregation of individual action, 156n; as broad framework, 28–9; and classic sociology, 28; and complementary theory belts, 30–2, chs. 3–6, 135–7; and consensus, 183, 208; core model of, 28; and elementary economics, 28; game theoretical models in, 30, 31n; heuristic value of, 30; and institutions, 207–8, 286, 286n; and internal dimension of action, 29–32, 286n; and knowledge, 40–5; with narrow scope conditions, 30n; vs. norm theory, 65, 65n2, 77, 86; and social structuration, 50–2; as theory frame, 3, 27, 31n, 65, 86; "thick" vs. "thin" versions of, 30, 136, 138, 169, 181, 286. See also *action, social*; *action theory*; *collective action*; *rationality*

rationality: and action theory, 32; and emotions, 107, 111, 115–6; and institutions, 207–8; and play, 63n, 113n5; problematic, assessments of, 171n; and specialization, 58, 197n

Rauch, J., on economic effects of "Weberian" state organization, 199n

Rawls, J., on common good, 80–1

realist philosophy, 20–1, 22

realist theory of international relations, 259

Reddy, W. M., on emotions and culture, 109

reductionism, 23–4, 34n. See also *constitutive elements*; *emergent phenomena*; *micro-macro relations among social phenomena*

reference groups: and preferences, 97–8; as theory frame, 11–2; and status groups, 251

revolution: and collective action, 13; discussion of analysis of, 14n, 16, 24, 260–2, 298n; and historical institutionalism, 206; hypotheses about, 14, 18, 222n9, 257; social, 13–4, 16; theory frame for, 13–4

Richerson, P.: on cooperation in large groups, 90–1; on culture and evolution, 104; on small groups, 105

ritual: and emotions, 112–3, 118–9; natural, 112–3; religious, 112; and solidarity, 112

Roethlisberger, F. J., on groups in workplace, 289

roles, 68–9, 142, 290; and cognition, 51, 62, 266; and division of labor, 183; economic, 158; of gender, 7, 71, 85, 99, 192–6, 216, 224–5, 268; identity, 234–5; individual variation of, 68; in informal groups, 126, 127; instrumental vs. expressive, 69, 71, 72n; monitoring, 77, 77n, 83, 85; socialization as a sequence of, 69, 92–3; specialized, and rational organization, 197–8. See also bureaucracy; *family*; *organizations, formal*

Rousseau, J. J., on theory-shaped questions, 4

routine action, 34, 157, 157n, 266n

Rueschemeyer, D.: on ambiguity of collective action, 179–81; on common good and market exchange, 89; on democracy, 14, 22–3; on gender relations, 196n; on relative timing of state and market expansion, 147–8

Rueschemeyer, M.: on active membership in associations, 181n; on gender relations, 196n

rule, systems of, 20; theory frame for, 20, 254n, 297

Samuelson, P., on revealed preferences, 87

Sawyer, R. K., on emergent patterns and reductionism, 34n

Scheff, T. J., on desire for bonding, 112

Scheler, M., on the priority of social experience and knowledge, 47

Schriewer, J., on common problems, 293

Scott, J. C., on local knowledge, 59

Sen, A., on preferences and actions, 87

Sewell, W., on his "Interpretivist Manifesto," 33n

shame, 72–3, 117–8

Shils, E. A., on charisma, 120n

Simmel, G.: on concentric and divergent social circles shaping ideas, 55; on individuation, 2; on membership size and social formations, 173

Simon, H. A.: on formal organizations, 200; on Homans's *The Human Group*, 125n; on uncertainty and "satisficing," 42

Skocpol, T.: on micro-macro relations, 298n; on a theory frame on revolution, 13–4, 16; on "Tocquevillean" effects of states, 257

Smith, A., on law and inequality, 7–8

Snyder, R., on heuristics and inspiration, 296n

social action framework. See *action theory*

socialization, 69; anticipatory, 12, 97; and cognition, 43; and emotions, 117–8; and gender roles; 195; and identities, 242; and imposed norms, 78; and internalization, 56, 67, 72, 92, 117–8; and isolation, 69; and monitoring roles, 77n, 92; and preferences, 92–3, 97; and small groups, 121, 131. See also internalization; roles

"social reality," 46, 49

sociology of knowledge, 48n, 123n

solidarity: and social identities, 110, 112–4, 228–9; and institutions, 204; national, 113n6; and ritual, 112–3

Sorokin, P., on extrapolation, 5

stability, social: of beliefs, 57; "calendar model" of, 146–7, 291; conditions of, 143–7; greater at macrolevel, 139–41; and institutions, 146; and overdetermination 37, 146, 219. See also change, *clusters*; *interdependence*; *micro-macro relations among social phenomena*; variability of patterns and processes

states: as causal mechanisms, 35, 139, 288; and coercion, 254; and cooperation, 179, 255–6; definition of, 254; and democracy, 256–7; as emergent phenomenon, 139; and ethnicity, 235–6, 237, 274n7; extraction of resources by, 256; and globalization, 258; and indirect power, 189–92, 196–203; and infrastructural power, 185n, 256; and revolution, 13–4, 16; slow development of, 257; and social identities, 235–8; "taming" of, 256–7; a theory frame for, 254–9; transnational contexts of, 258–9; on "Tocquevillean" effects of, 257, and welfare, 14, 202. See also bureaucracy; civil society; democracy; *law*; legitimation of rule; rule, systems of

status and status groups, 120–1, 251–2; bases of, 251; and class formation, 251–2; closure tendencies of, 251–2; and emotions, 121; and norms, 97–8; and social identities, 230; and transmission of cultural patterns, 272–6. See also class; inequality; *power*; stratification

Stephens, E. Huber: on ambiguity of collective action, 179–81; on democracy, 14, 22–3. See also Huber, E.

Stephens, J. D.: on ambiguity of collective action; 179–81; on democracy, 14, 22–3; on welfare states and power, 14, 202

Stinchcombe, A.: on feedback mechanisms in functional analysis, 37–8n10; on grand-theory neutral analytic tools, 3; on historicist explanation, 149–50; on organizations as information processing systems, 59

stratification: alternative approaches to, 249; conceptualization of, 8, 121n; different components of, 121n, 251; historical types of, 251; and institutions, 158–9, 215–7; and law, 7–8, 9, 217; in small groups, 126, 133. See also class; inequality; *power*; status and status groups

structuralist approaches, 140–1, 298–9; and variability at the microlevel, 140, 298. See also *order, social*; *structuration, social*; variability of patterns and processes

structuration, social, 50, 143–8; complex forms of, 50–2; and the internal dimensions of action, 50–1, 63, 142–3; and the problem of order, 50; underpinned by beliefs, 51–2. See also *macropatterns*; *mesopatterns*; *micro-macro relations among social phenomena*; *order, social*; variability of patterns and processes

subjective dimensions of action. See *internal dimensions of action*

Sugden, R., on spontaneous order, 79, 81

Surowiecki, J., on wisdom of crowds, 164

Swidler, A., on culture as tool kit, 266n

symbolic mediation: of attachments, 290; and emergent social structures, 288; of emotions, 290; extending social affiliations, 143, 174, 290; and identities, 232; and social action, 29

systems theories: about groups, 133; and interdependence, 35–6, 133; skepticism about, 36–7, 290–1. See also equilibrium; *functionalism*; *interdependence*; *macropatterns*

Tarrow, S.: on causal mechanisms, 24; on conditions of movements, 1–2, 175

tautology, 19–20, 184n, 297

Taylor, R.C.R., on current institutionalisms, 206
theory: and description, 5–6; development
of, 138–41; different elements of, 1, 6–
10; difficulties of, 6, 7–10, 287–9; embryonic forms of, 19; focused on middle
range, 11–2; implicit knowledge of, 17–
8; normative forms of, 2; recovery of implicit knowledge of, 294–5, roles of, 4–
5; strategy debate on development of,
10–12. See also *explanation*; *hypotheses,
theoretical*; *metatheories*; theory frames,
focused; theory, full-fledged
theory frames, focused, 1–2, 139–40, 288,
292; and analytic induction, 15–6, 292,
300; clusters of, 15; and conceptual
choice, 298; definition of, 1, 13; development in the course of research, 25; features of, 2, 15–7, 292; and hypothesis development, 16–7, 288–9; identifying
causally relevant factors, 1, 6, 25, 286,
292; and scope conditions of hypotheses,
17; and variability of patterns and processes, 16–7, 139–40, 288–9. See also
mechanisms, causal; theory
theory frames, focused, examples of, 1–2;
on class, 20, 249–53; on collective action, 2, 27, ch. 10; on cultural explanation, ch. 15; on democratization, 13, 14–
5; on knowledge, ch. 3; on movements,
1–2; on norms, ch. 4; rational action
models as, 30n, 31n; on reference
groups, 11–12; on social structure and individuation, 1–2; on states, 254–9; on
systems of rule, 20, 254n, 297, 298; on
welfare states, 14, 202
theory, full-fledged: definition of, 1, 6; examples of, 7–8; of groups, 1, 8, 123,
124–8, 133; obstacles to, 6, 7–10, 287–
9; omitted variables in, 10; scarcity of, 1,
6n, 25, 286, 289. See also *explanation*;
hypotheses, theoretical; theory, theory
frames, focused
Thornton, A., on the fallacy of the developmental paradigm, 191n
Tilly, C.: on conditions of movements, 1–2,
175; on durable inequality, 252; on exploitation, 253; on mechanisms, 24
totalitarianism, 202
tradition, 144–5; and expressive action,
71; in family patterns, 127, 190–1; vs.
modernity, 92, 143, 144, 162, 275; and

rationality, 34, 58; and uncertainty, 42–
3, 144–5
Trow, M., on democracy and oligarchy,
180
Turner, J. H., on face-to-face groups, 130

uncertainty: and magic, 42; vs. risk, 41–2;
and "satisficing," 42; and tradition, 42–
3, 144–5; and turning to others, 43

validity, standards of, shared by different
research approaches, 299
values: of the analyst, 37; and attachments,
53–4, 61–2, 67–8; centrality of in Parsons's analyses, 36, 50, 67, 206, 211,
266, 266n; and class, 89; and coercion,
178; and collective action, 171–2, 173–
4, 176; contradictions among, 211, 248,
283–4; and cooperation, 184; dominant,
48, 269; and education, 60; of elites, 47;
and expressive behavior, 71, 74; and gender, 195; and ideology, 48, 53, 146; and
internal dimensions of action, 29–32,
86; and internalization, 65, 67, 93; and
institutions, 210, 212, 267; as "just ideals," 284–5; knowledge, 47, 52–3, 54,
55–6, 59; and legitimation, 76, 84; and
noncontractual bases of contract, 196–7;
and norms, 64, 67–8, 71, 72, 74–5; as
power resource, 185–6; shared, 4, 57,
67, 212, 232, 277, 282; stability of, 84,
285; and systems analysis, 36; ultimate,
118. See also *internal dimensions of
action*; *norms*
variability of patterns and processes, 291;
and causal asymmetry in micro-macro relations, 243–5, 291; and explanation,
138–9, 288; in identity construction,
230; and innate dispositions, 104; and institutions, 204, 217; and internal dimensions of action, 63, 109, 139; less at
meso- and macrolevels, 245, 291; max-
imized at the microlevel, 139, 245, 288;
in power resources, 186; reduced by
macroshaping micropatterns, 139–41,
243–6, 288, 298; and scope conditions
of hypotheses, 140; and structuralist approaches, 140–1; and theory frames,
139–40, 288. See also *constitutive elements*; *emergent phenomena*; *fields of action*; *micro-macro relations among social phenomena*; *stability, social*

Varshney, A.: on associations and communal boundaries, 114; on ethnicity and conflict, 252n
voting, 163–6, 256

war, total, 202
Weber, M.: on bureaucracy, 19, 58, 197–9, 295; on charisma, 120; on class, 20, 250; on communal and associational relations, 187n4, 251; on conflict in communal relations, 54; on democracy, 22; on ethics of responsibility, 40n; on ethics in commerce, 95; on ideal types, 20; on internal dimensions of action, 28–9; on law and capitalism, 295; on micro-macro relations, 35; on motivations for compliance, 35, 75–6; on power and domination, 185; on "meaningful action," 32–3; on religious ideas as "switchmen of history," 271; on systems of rule, 20, 254n, 297
Weingast, B. R., on critical junctures, 222n9
Wendt, A.: on deliberation and collective choice, 43; on the distinction between constitutive and causal relations, 52n; on role of beliefs in the construction of interests, 51–2, 93
Williamson, O. E., on formal organizations, 198–199n13
wisdom of crowds, 164
world systems theory, 259
Wright, E. O., on class analysis, 249
Wrong, D., on "oversocialized conception of man," 65

Zald, M. N., on conditions of movements, 1–2